The Edge of Sentience

The Edge of Sentience

*Risk and Precaution in Humans,
Other Animals, and AI*

JONATHAN BIRCH

OXFORD
UNIVERSITY PRESS

OXFORD
UNIVERSITY PRESS

Great Clarendon Street, Oxford, OX2 6DP,
United Kingdom

Oxford University Press is a department of the University of Oxford.
It furthers the University's objective of excellence in research, scholarship,
and education by publishing worldwide. Oxford is a registered trade mark of
Oxford University Press in the UK and in certain other countries

Published in the United States of America by Oxford University Press
198 Madison Avenue, New York, NY 10016, United States of America

British Library Cataloguing in Publication Data
Data available

Library of Congress Control Number: 2024939109

ISBN 9780192870421

DOI: 10.1093/9780191966729.001.0001

Printed and bound by
CPI Group (UK) Ltd, Croydon, CR0 4YY

Links to third party websites are provided by Oxford in good faith and
for information only. Oxford disclaims any responsibility for the materials
contained in any third party website referenced in this work.

For my parents, Peter and Marie

You see, I know that it's difficult to think well about 'certainty', 'probability', 'perception', etc. But it is, if possible, still more difficult to think, or try to think, really honestly about your life & other peoples lives. And the trouble is that thinking about these things is *not thrilling*, but often downright nasty. And when it's nasty then it's *most* important.

Ludwig Wittgenstein, letter to Norman Malcolm,
16 November 1944

Contents

PART V PREPARING FOR ARTIFICIAL SENTIENCE

List of Illustrations

Summary of the Framework
and Proposals

Precautionary Framework

A *sentient being* (in the sense relevant to the present framework) is a system with the capacity to have valenced experiences, such as experiences of pain and pleasure.

A system *S* is a *sentience candidate* if there is an evidence base that (a) implies a realistic possibility of sentience in *S* that it would be irresponsible to ignore when making policy decisions that will affect *S*, and (b) is rich enough to allow the identification of welfare risks and the design and assessment of precautions.

A system *S* is an *investigation priority* if it falls short of the requirements for sentience candidature, yet (a) further investigation could plausibly lead to the recognition of *S* as a sentience candidate and (b) *S* is affected by human activity in ways that may call for precautions if *S* were a sentience candidate.

Framework Principle 1. *A duty to avoid causing gratuitous suffering.* We ought, at minimum, to avoid causing gratuitous suffering to sentient beings either intentionally or through recklessness/negligence. Suffering is not gratuitous if it occurs in the course of a defensible activity despite proportionate attempts to prevent it. Suffering is gratuitous if the activity is indefensible or the precautions taken fall short of what is proportionate.

Framework Principle 2. *Sentience candidature can warrant precautions.* If *S* is a sentience candidate, then it is reckless/negligent to make decisions that create risks of suffering for *S* without considering the question of what precautions are proportionate to those risks. Reasonable disagreement about proportionality is to be expected, but we ought to reach a policy decision rather than leaving the matter unresolved indefinitely.

Framework Principle 3. *Assessments of proportionality should be informed, democratic, and inclusive.* To reach decisions, we should use informed and inclusive democratic processes. These decisions should be revisited periodically and whenever significant new evidence emerges.

An example of an informed, inclusive, democratic process is a citizens' panel or assembly that assesses the proportionality of possible responses by debating their permissibility-in-principle, adequacy, reasonable necessity, and consistency (the 'PARC' tests).

Proposals about Specific Cases

The following should be read as proposals for discussion and debate. There is a case for regarding the proposed measures as proportionate, so they merit consideration by an informed, inclusive democratic process, but my aim is not to pre-judge the outcome of such a process.

People with Disorders of Consciousness

Proposal 1. *Assume sentient (specific).* Any signs that would be interpreted as signs of pain or distress in a conscious patient should still be so interpreted in a patient with any disorder of consciousness, and pain relief administered. This treatment should not be reserved for a subset of patients, e.g. those diagnosed as minimally conscious.

Proposal 2. *Assume sentient (general).* A patient with a prolonged disorder of consciousness should not be assumed incapable of experience when an important clinical decision is made. All clinical decisions should consider the patient's best interests as comprehensively as possible, working on the precautionary assumption that there is a realistic possibility of valenced experience and a continuing interest in avoiding suffering and in achieving well-being, but without taking this assumption to have implications regarding prognosis.

Proposal 3. *Avoid line-drawing (general).* The diagnostic categories of PVS, MCS−, and MCS+ should be phased out in therapeutic and legal contexts. Clinicians should work with the broader category of 'prolonged disorder of consciousness' (PDOC) and with profiles of individual patients, tailoring care to the patient's individual needs.

Proposal 4. *Avoid line-drawing (specific).* Decisions about withdrawing life-sustaining treatment should be based on comprehensive assessment of the patient's best interests, sensitive to the details of their case, and not on the PVS/MCS distinction.

Proposal 5. *The need for more humane options.* Methods of hastening death other than through withdrawal of clinically assisted nutrition and hydration (CANH) are needed. At minimum, clinicians should not face any risk of punishment for administering large doses of sedatives or analgesics after a decision to withdraw CANH has been made.

Proposal 6. *Waiting for more information.* If a humane method of hastening death becomes available, there will be no strong rationale for withdrawing life-sustaining treatment within days after injury, before the patient's condition has stabilized. Given the great uncertainty about prospects for recovery at this stage, the default approach should be to delay the decision until the patient's condition has stabilized.

Human Fetuses and Embryos

Proposal 7. *Sentience and abortion.* The point at which a human fetus becomes sentient is not the point at which abortion becomes morally impermissible. We should separate these issues. The ethics of abortion depend primarily on questions of personhood and bodily autonomy, not on questions of sentience.

Proposal 8. *Human sentience candidature begins early.* Human fetuses are sentience candidates from the beginning of the second trimester. This line may move as new evidence emerges, but it should always track the earliest scientifically credible, evidence-based estimate.

Proposal 9. *Fetal pain relief (in therapeutic contexts).* Direct fetal anaesthesia and pain relief should be considered whenever therapeutic fetal surgery is performed. The public should be involved in discussions about general norms of medical practice (not specific decisions), and data regarding current practices should be collected and published to allow such discussions.

Proposal 10. *Fetal pain relief (in the context of abortion).* Clinicians need to communicate uncertainty about fetal sentience honestly to patients. In some cases, fetal pain relief may be appropriate. Deliberative processes for setting clinical norms must give appropriate weight to the voices of women.

Proposal 11. *Sentience and the 14-day rule.* If the main goal of setting a legal time limit on human embryo research were that of prohibiting research on human sentience candidates, a significant liberalization of the current 14-day rule would still be proportionate to that goal. However, the issue raises deep value conflicts that have little to do with sentience.

Human Neural Organoids

Proposal 12. *Brainstem rule.* If a neural organoid develops or innervates a functioning brainstem (including the midbrain) that regulates arousal and leads to sleep-wake cycles, then it is a sentience candidate. An artificial functional equivalent of a brainstem would also suffice.

Proposal 13. *Targeted bans.* If organoid research leads to the creation of organoids that are sentience candidates, a moratorium (time-limited ban) or indefinite ban on the creation of this particular type of organoid may be an appropriate response. Bans should avoid indiscriminate targeting of all organoid research.

Proposal 14. *Ethical review.* When a neural organoid is a sentience candidate, research on it, if permitted at all, should be subject to ethical review and harm-benefit analysis, modelled on existing frameworks for regulating research on sentient animals.

Other Animals

Proposal 15. *All adult vertebrates are sentience candidates.* Debates about proportionality are warranted in cases where human activities create risks of suffering to any adult vertebrate animal. Further investigation concerning sentience candidature in vertebrates should focus on juvenile/larval stages.

Proposal 16. *Sentience is neither intelligence nor brain size.* We should be aware of the possibility of decouplings between intelligence, brain size, and sentience in the animal kingdom. Precautions to safeguard animal welfare should be driven by markers of sentience, not by markers of intelligence or by brain size.

Proposal 17. *Sentience is not pain.* Although there are pragmatic reasons for the focus on pain in debates about animal sentience, we must be open to the possibility that the class of sentient animals is bigger than the class of animals that feel pain. Other forms of evidence can make an animal a sentience candidate, such as evidence of sophisticated forms of learning, attention, working memory, and planning.

Proposal 18. *Some invertebrates are sentience candidates.* Coleoid cephalopod molluscs, decapod crustaceans of the suborder Pleocyemata, and insects (all when in the adult stage) are sentience candidates. Debates about proportionality are warranted in cases where human activities create risks of suffering to these animals. Decapod crustaceans of the suborder Dendrobranchiata, insect larvae, spiders, gastropods, and nematode worms are investigation priorities.

Proposal 19. *Codes of good practice and licensing.* There should be a licensing scheme for companies attempting to farm sentience candidates or investigation priorities for which no welfare regulations yet exist (such as insects). Obtaining a license should be dependent on signing up to (and, where necessary, funding research leading to) a code of good practice concerning animal welfare.

Proposal 20. *Octopus farming.* It is very unlikely that octopus farming can meet reasonable expectations regarding welfare and humane slaughter. It would be proportionate to ban octopus farming.

Proposal 21. *Towards humane slaughter.* When an animal is a sentience candidate, it is proportionate to ban slaughter methods that needlessly risk extending and intensifying the suffering associated with dying, such as boiling animals alive without prior stunning.

Artificial Intelligence (AI)

Proposal 22. *Sentience is not intelligence (II).* We should be aware of the possibility of a substantial decoupling between intelligence and sentience in the AI domain. Precautions to manage risks of suffering should be driven by markers of sentience, not markers of intelligence. For example, emulations of animal brains could achieve sentience without necessarily displaying impressive intelligence.

Proposal 23. *The gaming problem.* For any set of criteria for sentience candidature, we need to be aware of the risk of the AI system or its designer learning (implicitly or explicitly) that they are regarded as criteria, leading to gaming of the criteria. We need to discount markers we have reason to think may have been gamed.

Proposal 24. *Deep computational markers.* We can use computational functionalist theories (such as the global workspace theory and the perceptual reality monitoring theory) as sources of markers of sentience. If we find signs that an AI system, even if not deliberately equipped with such features, has implicitly learned ways of recreating them, this should lead us to regard it as a sentience candidate.

Proposal 25. *The run-ahead principle.* At any given time, measures to regulate the development of sentient AI should run ahead of what would be proportionate to the risks posed by current technology, considering also the risks posed by credible future trajectories.

Proposal 26. *Codes of good practice and licensing (II).* There should be a licensing scheme for companies attempting to create artificial sentience candidates, or whose work creates even a small risk of doing so, even if this is not an explicit aim. Obtaining a license should be dependent on signing up to (and, where necessary, funding the creation of) a code of good practice for this type of work that includes norms of transparency.

The Edge of Sentience: Risk and Precaution in Humans, Other Animals, and AI. Jonathan Birch, Oxford University Press.
© Jonathan Birch 2024. DOI: 10.1093/9780191966729.003.0001

1

A Walk along the Edge

We all eventually fall from the edge of sentience. If we are lucky, the transition will be sharp and sudden. If we are not, we may spend years on the brink as more fortunate souls debate whether we are sentient or not. When their judgement is mistaken, the consequences can be terrible.

Consider Kate Bainbridge.[1] At age 26, she contracted encephalomyelitis, inflammation of the brain and spinal cord. For around five months, she was unresponsive but still had sleep-wake cycles, a condition called a prolonged disorder of consciousness. She was given a tracheostomy and a feeding tube, but no one explained this to her, because she was presumed unconscious. Bainbridge came back from the edge. When she regained responsiveness, and (later) the ability to communicate via a keyboard, she was able to report that her clinician's presumption had been false. Her testimony is, in places, harrowing:

> I can't tell you how frightening it was, especially suction through the mouth. I tried to hold my breath to get away from all the pain. They never told me about my tube. I wondered why I did not eat.[2]

Bainbridge's testimony was written to be heard, amplified, repeated. It sends a resounding message: never simply *presume* the absence of sentience in a case where it could realistically be present. And in the face of uncertainty, do not treat a potentially sentient being as if they felt nothing.

This is a book about how our practices and ways of thinking need to change, across many areas, once we face up to this principle.

---

[1] I learned about this case via Syd Johnson's (2022) book on the ethics of managing disorders of consciousness, which relates the case in more detail. The case was originally documented by Wilson and Gracey (2001).

[2] Wilson and Gracey (2001, p. 1089).

1.1 The Unmarked Border

A sentient being has ethically significant experiences. They have a subjective point of view on the world and on their own body.[3] If I throw a ball across a field, there are physical facts about the ball's trajectory as it sails through the air, but there is nothing it feels like from the ball's point of view. The ball feels no joy or pain; it doesn't experience the rush of the air or the colour of the sky. The ball is a blank, as far as subjective experience is concerned. Now imagine a child chasing the ball. There will again be facts about the physical processes at work as the child sprints across the grass. But this time, there will also be something it feels like from the child's point of view. There will be experiences of odour, sound, colour, bodily sensations, positive or negative emotions.

The capacity to have subjective experiences does not imply any level of reflective or rational ability. It does not imply an ability to reflect on one's experiences, or to judge oneself to be having them, or to understand that others also have them. It is simply a matter of *having* experiences. (These ideas are developed further in Chapter 2.)

This idea of a 'subjective point of view' is easiest to grasp in the case of vision. Ernst Mach, in the *Analysis of Sensations*, famously attempted to draw his own visual point of view (Fig. 1.1). But there is far more to human subjective experience than vision. Our subjective point of view includes sounds, odours, tastes, tactile experiences: a rich sensory world. And these sensory experiences of a world outside us are integrated with experiences of a world within: bodily feelings, emotions, conscious thoughts, conscious memories, and imagination. When I talk of a subjective point of view, I mean it in this broad sense.

This subjective point of view can be contrasted with a great mass of brain processing that occurs unconsciously, without surfacing in experience. In humans, this mass includes the early stages of sensory processing, as well as many processes of bodily self-regulation and motor control. I don't feel the registration on my retina of light too dim to perceive consciously. I don't feel the release of hormones from my pituitary gland. I don't feel the micro-adjustments of my muscles as I walk. As I grasp a cup, I don't feel my grip strength altering very slightly from one moment to the next, finely tuned to

---

[3] Here I introduce a convention I will use throughout the book: the use of 'they' rather than 'it' to describe a sentient being.

Fig. 1.1 Drawing from Ernst Mach, *The Analysis of Sensations* (1914).
Public domain.

generate just the right amount of friction. My conscious experiences are, it
seems, the tip of an iceberg of unconscious computation.

Given this, we can always wonder, for any other animal: do they too
have a subjective point of view? Or do they just have the unconscious side
of what I have: the underwater part of the iceberg? As we look across the
animal kingdom, all of us have our own threshold of doubt: the point at
which an animal becomes so evolutionarily distant from humans, and so
dissimilar, that hesitancy to ascribe sentience to it begins to creep in. For a
small minority, even other mammals evoke some doubt, especially once
we look beyond the primates.[4] I must say, however, that I have met very
few people who can sustain a doubt that at least all mammals (like cats,
dogs, and rats) are sentient.

---

[4] See, especially, those who defend higher-order theories that link consciousness to granular prefrontal cortex (e.g. Rolls 2004).

For some, doubt begins when we turn to birds. The mammalian and avian lineages diverged between 170 and 340 million years ago.[5] There are substantial similarities between the brains of mammals and birds but many differences too. When we attribute sentience to birds, we are implicitly recognizing that sentience can be achieved in a brain with a substantially different organization from our own.

For others, doubt creeps in when we look beyond mammals and birds to other vertebrates, such as fishes.[6] Could a fish be a total subjective blank, like a ball or a rock? Could a fish feel no pain—or anything at all—when it is caught? Some have argued that we must take this possibility seriously. In response, some animal welfare scientists, motivated by understandable concern about the welfare of fishes, have called the sceptics 'sentience deniers'.[7] Even though I think there is strong evidence for sentience in fishes, I find the 'sentience denier' label too divisive in an area of genuine uncertainty.

Even those fully convinced that fishes are sentient will have their own threshold of doubt. For some, it is to be found at the point where we turn our attention from vertebrates to invertebrates—from animals with a backbone to those without. When we look at an octopus, snail, bee, crab, or spider, we are looking at a lineage that has been separate from our own for at least 560 million years.[8] We are also considering an animal with a very, very differently organized brain. At this point, I think most—though not all—people start to entertain serious doubts about sentience.

Even those who cannot entertain such doubts about octopuses will tend to find doubt assailing them regarding other invertebrates. Think, for example, of cnidarians like jellyfish, sea anemones, and corals. Think also of very small crustaceans. On the windowsill in my kitchen I have an aquarium of brine shrimp, each a few millimetres in length. They are very commonly used in aquaculture—as live feed for other animals. I look at them and wonder: is there anything it's like to be a brine shrimp? Copepods, another type of tiny crustacean, are famously added to New York's tap water to clear out mosquito larvae.[9]

---

[5] For a wonderful tool for dating divergences, see https://www.timetree.org. The methodology is explained by Kumar et al. (2017).

[6] Throughout the book, I will follow Balcombe's (2016) suggestion to say 'fishes' not 'fish' to help us remember that we are talking about individual animals.

[7] Sneddon et al. (2018).

[8] Divergences this ancient are exceptionally hard to date precisely. On the difficulties, see Peterson et al. (2004).

[9] Townsend (2010).

We should not forget that many invertebrates are microscopic, far smaller than even copepods or brine shrimp. Our environment is full of nematode worms, dust mites, tardigrades, rotifers, and more. Many plankton are zoo-plankton, part of the animal kingdom. If all animals are sentient, then sentience must be achievable on a microscopic scale, and our beds and carpets must be teeming with sentient beings. It is not unreasonable to have doubts about that. It is a realistic possibility that sentience could be present in larger, more complex invertebrates, like octopuses, yet absent in many other invertebrates.

We can talk of an edge of sentience in multiple senses. There is an edge *in the world*: a real boundary to the class of sentient beings. There is also a boundary *in our confidence*, marking the point at which beings become dis-similar enough to ourselves that we start to entertain serious doubts about their sentience. We can hope that the two line up well: that the real boundary is located somewhere in the region where we feel least confident. But we should be aware of the risk that we may have got things very wrong: it could be that our levels of confidence systematically fail to track the real boundary. Different again are *practical* edges of sentience: the boundaries we draw in contexts where we have to make decisions. This book is about all three kinds of edge, but it is the practical edges that will receive most attention.

1.2 Decision Points

Where, then, is the line between sentient and non-sentient beings to be drawn? It is tempting to throw our hands aloft and say 'Maybe we'll never know!'. But practical and legal contexts force a choice.

I had some direct experience of this when I advised the UK government on what is now the Animal Welfare (Sentience) Act 2022, or 'Sentience Act'. The UK had just left the European Union, which includes (in its Lisbon Treaty) a commitment to regard animals as sentient beings. The government declined to import this clause directly into UK law, leading to some bad press. It reacted by promising to introduce new legislation to enshrine respect for ani-mal sentience, and the proposed new law aimed to do that. Moreover, it sought to surpass the Lisbon Treaty by putting all ministers under a statutory duty to consider the animal welfare impacts of their decisions.

The government (more specifically, the Department for Environment, Food, and Rural Affairs, Defra) ran into a thorny problem: *which* animals should be covered by this duty? *All* of them, including copepods, dust mites, tardigrades, microscopic zooplankton? Just mammals? Their first draft covered all vertebrates, leading to understandable criticism from animal welfare organizations, who felt at least some invertebrates—and especially octopuses, crabs, and lobsters—should also be included.

Defra commissioned a team led by me to review the evidence of sentience in two specific invertebrate taxa: the cephalopod molluscs (including octopuses, squid, and cuttlefish) and the decapod crustaceans (including lobsters, crayfish, true crabs, and true shrimps; Fig. 1.2). Defra was clear from the outset that other invertebrate taxa were not on the table for possible inclusion. They wanted an informed opinion about these two. We reviewed over three hundred relevant scientific studies, synthesizing a complicated, gradated, messy evidential picture.[10] We arrived at a clear recommendation: all cephalopod molluscs and decapod crustaceans should be included in the scope of animal welfare laws. To its credit, the government accepted our recommendation and amended its bill. The Sentience Act does encompass all cephalopod molluscs and all decapod crustaceans. It does not extend to brine shrimps or copepods since, like most crustaceans, they are not decapods.

I am pleased we moved past 'Maybe we'll never know!', reviewed all the relevant evidence we could find, and made a sensible practical recommendation on the basis of that evidence. We never achieved—or claimed to have achieved—certainty. Our approach was based on evaluating the evidence and communicating its strength as honestly and transparently as we could. I will reflect more on what I learned from this experience in Chapter 12.

1.3 When to Stop?

In 2022, the journal *Neuron* published an article called '*In vitro* neurons learn and exhibit sentience when embodied in a simulated game-world.'[11] The authors used human stem cells and brain tissue from mouse embryos to grow networks of around 1 million cortical neurons (i.e. cells of a type normally found in the neocortex, the part of the brain traditionally associated with higher-cognitive functions) (Fig. 1.3). The number is comparable to the total number of neurons in the brain of a bee.

They mounted the network on a computer interface called a high-density multi-electrode array, giving it, in effect, control over the paddle in a game of Pong. Just twenty minutes of 'gameplay' was enough to produce a

---

[10] Birch et al. (2021).   [11] Kagan et al. (2022).

Fig. 1.2 Decapod crustaceans. Plate from Ernst Haeckel, *Kunstformen der Natur* (1904). Public domain.

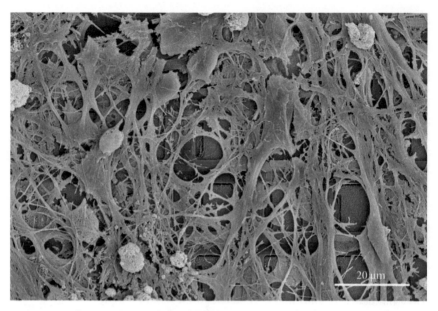

Fig. 1.3 An electron micrograph of DishBrain, a network of cortical neurons mounted on a high-density multi-electrode array. Reproduced from Kagan et al. (2022) under a CC-BY 4.0 licence.

statistically significant improvement in performance, with more hits per minute and longer rallies. The performance was not good in absolute terms, unsurprisingly, but it is remarkable enough that performance measurably *improved*. The system learned. There was no evidence, however, of the learning being retained between sessions. In each session of 'gameplay', the system learned anew.

The researchers' claim about 'sentience' merits scepticism. They defined sentience as 'responsiveness to sensory impressions through adaptive internal processes' and counted electrical stimulation through the array as a sensory impression. This is a definition so minimal that it trivializes the idea of sentience, detaching it entirely from conscious experience and the mind. I see it as a mistake to define sentience in this way. DishBrain is indeed sentient in this minimal sense, but all living cells, including those of brain-dead humans, would also be likely to count as sentient in this sense, and this should give us pause. These issues of definition will be picked up again in the next chapter. For now, I will just say that I think it is important to define sentience in a way that makes the concept apt for its important role in ethics and policy. We should take care not to trivialize it.

This study is a high-profile example of neural organoid research: research on models of human brain functions constructed using human stem cells. This area has tremendous promise, and, in principle at least, it gives scientists ways to model the human brain without experimenting on other animals. Organoid research is steaming ahead with great self-confidence, and even with a sense of humour, as shown by terms such as 'DishBrain'.

I suspect the humour will start to drain away as researchers face up to the gravity of what they are doing. As ethical concerns grow, labels that playfully exaggerate the similarity with human brains will give way to cautious terminology that emphasizes difference. We need to be careful on both sides. We must not overestimate the similarities. But at the same time, we must not rule out the possibility of genuine sentience—ethically significant experience—in constructions made from living human brain tissue.

I have spoken to regulators in this area and found a great deal of worry and perplexity about how to regulate this emerging area of research. The potential scientific and medical benefits are very large. We should not crack down on it heavy-handedly. Yet, intuitively, there is a point at which we should stop doing this kind of research, no matter what the benefits. If we construct sentient beings and force them to live as disembodied brains on which we can experiment freely, we will have crossed an ethical line. The problem is what to do now, when we have not crossed that line but find it hard to see where the line is through the fog of uncertainty.

These questions cannot be fully separated from broader questions about the relation between sentience and human brain development. When a human fetus develops normally, the onset of sentience is no more clearly marked, and no less mysterious, than it is in an organoid. The uncertainty is agonizing, because important clinical decisions hinge on when exactly we start regarding the fetus as a potentially sentient being. As I'll explain in Chapter 10, I do *not* think questions about the permissibility of abortion turn on the issue of sentience, even though they may initially seem to do so. But other very important decisions, such as whether to use anaesthetics during medical procedures on the fetus, do turn on this issue.

1.4 Accidental Golems

Some years ago, my eye was caught by the headline, 'We've put a worm's mind in a Lego robot's body'.[12] The article was about the OpenWorm project, a

---

[12] Fessenden (2014).

long-running attempt to emulate in computer software the entire nervous system of the nematode worm *Caenorhabditis elegans*, an animal with fewer than four hundred neurons (less than one-thousandth the size of DishBrain). Researchers on that project had put their latest emulation in control of a small robot and watched as the robot navigated its environment in something like (but, in truth, not all *that* much like) the way the original worm would. I was struck by a troubling thought: the same uncertainty about sentience that grips us when we think about invertebrates and human fetuses was beginning to resurface in artificial systems. If a worm could be sentient, could a neuron-by-neuron emulation of a worm in a computer also be sentient?

These fears about the emergence of artificial sentience, extremely niche and often dismissed back then, have since become rather more mainstream. I now fear we may achieve artificial sentience long before we realize we have done so. At the same time, we are also facing a different but perhaps even more urgent problem: people rampantly over-attributing sentience to systems that can skilfully mimic the behaviours that make humans think sentience is present.[13] We already see signs of this with current large language models (LLMs). There is already a subculture in which people develop intimate emotional bonds with AI companions—or at least *think* they do. How can we tell skilful mimicry from the real thing?

In late 2022, two colleagues—Patrick Butlin and Rob Long—invited me to join an ambitious project that aimed to devise a list of indicators of sentience in AI.[14] The media coverage of our eventual report was rather generous. *Nature* wrote 'if AI becomes conscious, here's how researchers will know'.[15] In truth, talk of 'knowledge' is inappropriate. As I'll explain in Part V, the difficulties we face in this area are even greater than those we face in the case of other animals. Other animals are not capable of gaming our criteria. They do not have an internet-sized corpus of training data to mine for effective ways of persuading human observers. So, when animals display a pattern of behaviour that is well explained by a feeling (such as pain), the best explanation is usually that they do indeed have that feeling. With AI, by contrast, two explanations compete: maybe the system has feelings, but maybe it is just responding as a human would respond, exploiting its vast reservoir of data on how humans express their feelings.

---

[13] Andrews and Birch (2023).   [14] Butlin et al. (2023).   [15] Lenharo (2023a).

1.5 The Goal: A Precautionary Framework

I could have written an inert discussion of abstract questions, floating past real-world decisions at a great distance. But I did not want to write that book. This book starts with the urgency of real life—matters of life and death that confront us all—and tries to find ways to decide, ways to agree.

The motto of my approach is 'no magic tricks'. We start in a position of horrible, disorienting, apparently inescapable uncertainty about other minds, and then…the uncertainty is still there at the end. Sorry, it is inescapable. Anyone who tells you otherwise is not being honest or has not properly faced up to the problem. I am not in the business of selling magical escape routes from uncertainty. My aim is to construct a framework that allows us to reach collective decisions despite our uncertainty: decisions that command our confidence and reflect our shared values.

At the core of the framework is the thought that we need to find ways to *err on the side of caution* in these cases. The risks of over-attributing and under-attributing sentience are not equal. When we deny the sentience of sentient beings, acting as if they felt nothing, we tend to do them terrible harms. We are often responsible for those harms even though they were unintended, because our actions were negligent or reckless. Think here of Kate Bainbridge. The lack of any intention to cause psychological trauma on the part of her doctors does not mean they acted properly. Meanwhile, when we treat non-sentient beings as if they were sentient, we may still do some harm (if the precautions we take are very costly and time-consuming and distract our attention away from other cases), but the harms are often much less serious and of a different, more controllable kind.

In other contexts (especially in discussions of the environment and public health), this type of idea is sometimes called 'the precautionary principle'. But the logic of my framework is *not* the following: 'the precautionary principle' is the correct general decision rule, so we must apply it to this particular set of decision problems. That is not what I'm saying. The idea is rather that the asymmetry of risk that stares us in the face when we think about cases at the edge of sentience presents us with strong and obvious reasons to start thinking about precautions, independently of whether this is also a good way to approach other policy challenges. The motivation for erring on the side of caution here is 'bottom-up'—it comes from reflecting on the asymmetries of risk that jump out at us in these specific cases—rather than 'top-down', flowing from some high-level commitment to some general truth called 'the precautionary principle'. I doubt there is any such general truth. What I mean will probably become clearer when we reach Chapter 6.

This general idea has been around for a long time in discussions of sentience (the history will be reviewed case by case in later chapters).[16] My framework, however, combines the thought that we need to err on the side of caution with another, equally important thought: it is not enough to simply advise people to 'err on the side of caution' and leave it there. Almost any action at all, from outrageously costly precautions to the tiniest gesture, can be described as 'erring on the side of caution'. We need ways of choosing among possible precautions. As in other areas where precautionary thinking is important, the crucial concept we need is *proportionality*: our precautions should be proportionate to the identified risks.[17]

I do not think proportionality reduces to a cost-benefit calculation. It requires us to resolve deep value conflicts, conflicts that obstruct any attempt to quantify benefits and costs in an uncontroversial common currency. Further down the line (in Chapters 7 and 8), I will give a pragmatic analysis of what it means to be proportionate, emphasizing that proportionate responses need to be permissible-in-principle, adequate, reasonably necessary, and consistent (I call these the 'PARC' tests). I will then turn to the question: what sort of procedures should we use, in a democratic society, to assess proportionality? My proposals will give a key role to citizens' panels or assemblies, which attempt to bring ordinary members of the public into the discussion in an informed way in order to reach recommendations that reflect our shared values.

Because I think these decisions should be made by democratic, inclusive processes—and not by any individual expert—I think my own proposals about specific cases should be read as just that: proposals. They are not supposed to be the final word on any of these issues. I am not auditioning for the role of 'sentience tsar'. It would be a mistake for any government to implement my proposals straight away, without discussion and debate. But I have given a lot of thought to what courses of action are *plausibly* proportionate to the challenges we currently face, and I am publishing my proposals in the hope of provoking debates I see as urgently needed. If I succeed in stimulating discussion, I can dare to hope the discussion may lead, via democratic and inclusive processes, to action.

---

[16] My own first encounter with the idea was in a paper by R. H. Bradshaw (1998).

[17] Colin Klein (2017), in a commentary on my work, urged me to think more about proportionality—and was right.

My framework aspires to generality, but it also tries not to lose sight of the great differences between cases at the edge of sentience. There is a question of taste when humans with brain injuries are discussed in the same book as non-human animals. It raises the question: are you drawing an *equivalence* between the two cases? Are you saying that a brain injury can render a person less than human? That is not what I am saying at all. I think my repeated disavowals of it will make that clear enough. I am not claiming that there is a moral equivalence between these cases, or that our obligations towards an injured person are the same as our obligations towards other animals. Sensitivity to the vast differences between these cases is absolutely crucial.

What these cases do have in common is a resemblance in our *state of uncertainty* when we, as decision-makers, are forced to choose what to do. We must somehow move from horrible, vertiginous uncertainty to action. Our actions will have consequences, those consequences will depend on facts we are not in a position to know, and we may never know what the consequences were, even in hindsight. In all these cases, we feel a general imperative to err on the side of caution but are left wondering what erring on the side of caution requires of us. What precautions must we take and why? Is it possible to go too far in the direction of taking precautions and, if it is, where are the limits?

Once we see that our predicament has this common shape across all cases at the edge of sentience, it raises the hope that there might be versatile, transferrable insights about how to handle that type of predicament: how to move from uncertainty to action, how to adopt an appropriately precautionary attitude. It is in that spirit that I am bringing these cases together in the same book.

Parts I and II of the book will gradually assemble the pieces of an adequate precautionary framework. As I see it, a good framework for designing public policy should ideally be based on what John Rawls called overlapping consensus: principles that all reasonable people, for all their diversity and disagreement, can endorse for the right reasons.[18] But to find principles all reasonable people could get behind, we first need to understand what sentience is and why there is so much disagreement about it in the first place— and which views in that space of disagreement are reasonable and which are not. There is a very wide 'zone of reasonable disagreement', and a good framework for making decisions will respect all the views that lie within that

---

[18] Rawls (1993). Wolff (2020) has emphasized the wide relevance of the 'overlapping consensus' concept to public policy challenges, including challenges concerning non-human animals.

zone, as difficult as that may be. So, the first step towards a good framework is to map out that zone.[19]

In doing this, I will be trying to take a step back from my own personal opinions. Among the reasonable views, there are those I see as more or less likely (and I think my opinions will come across) but access to the zone of reasonable disagreement does not require my stamp of approval. It is fundamentally about whether the view is shaped by, and responds to, evidence and argument.

1.6 A Note on Influences

I imagined, years ago, a book that would begin with a general discussion of precautionary thinking and the science-policy interface and would only then zoom in on the special case of sentience. I came to see that this was the wrong approach. Intellectually wrong, because I think the reasons that drive precautionary thinking about sentience are 'bottom-up' rather than 'top-down' in the sense just explained. But also not true to the trajectory of my own thinking. For me, worrying about sentience has been at the core of this project from the beginning. So, this book maintains a relentless focus on sentience.

An upshot is that there is no natural place for me to acknowledge some of the influences on my approach from the wider philosophical and 'science studies' literature, so I want to do that at the outset. The literature on other precautionary principles is a major influence, especially the work of Daniel Steel, Stephen John, and Andy Stirling.[20] The literature on values in science and inductive risk has also shaped my approach, notably the work of Heather Douglas.[21] So has the literature on the proper relationship between science and policy in a democratic society, in particular the work of Philip Kitcher and Sandra Mitchell.[22] The deliberative democracy literature, and especially

---

[19] Federico Zuolo (2020) has undertaken a related task, mapping out reasonable disagreement in the specific case of the human treatment of other animals. The zone of reasonable disagreement about the edge of sentience is in some dimensions rather wider. It includes, for example, disagreement about substrate neutrality vs sensitivity (§3.5).

[20] Steel (2015); John (2010, 2011, 2019); Stirling (2007, 2016). See also Buchak (2019); Clarke (2005); Dreyer et al. (2008); Driesen (2013); Gardiner (2006); Hartzell-Nichols (2012); Morgan-Knapp (2015); Munthe (2011); Persson (2016); and Steele (2006). I also count as influences those who have criticized 'the precautionary principle' as a general decision rule, such as Carter and Peterson (2015); Sunstein (2005); and Thoma (2022a). Their criticisms dissuaded me from arguing for precautions in a top-down fashion.

[21] Douglas (2009). See also Steele (2012) and the case studies collected in Elliott and Richards (2017).

[22] Mitchell (2009); Kitcher (2001, 2011a, 2011b). See also Barker and Kitcher (2014).

the work of Helene Landemore, Alexander Guerrero, and John Dryzek, has also left a significant mark.[23] And I have been inspired by analyses of very different cases by Anna Alexandrova (on well-being), Richard Bradley and Katie Steele (on climate change), Tim Lewens (on mitochondrial donation), and Anya Plutynski (on cancer screening).[24] I am highlighting these authors here because they have not written directly on the topic of sentience—those who have will be acknowledged in later chapters.

When I first wrote about sentience and the precautionary principle, in 2017, more than twenty commentators kindly offered responses to my arguments.[25] When I wrote another target article (with Andrew Crump, Alexandra Schnell, Charlotte Burn, and Heather Browning) in 2022, this time on sentience in decapod crustaceans, we received thirty commentaries.[26] These critical responses have ended up shaping my thinking in important ways. I am very grateful to the editor of *Animal Sentience*, Stevan Harnad, for facilitating this process, and for his tireless work to encourage everyone to think more carefully about contested cases of sentience.

1.7 Summary of Chapter 1

There is a family of cases at the edge of sentience. In these cases, grave decisions hinge on whether we regard sentience—initially introduced, informally, as 'ethically significant experience'—to be present or absent in a person, animal, or other cognitive system. The family includes people with disorders of consciousness, embryos and fetuses, neural organoids, other animals (especially invertebrates), and AI technologies that reproduce brain functions and/or mimic human behaviour.

---

[23] Dryzek (2010); Guerrero (2014); Landemore (2020).

[24] Alexandrova (2017); Bradley and Steele (2015); Lewens (2018); Plutynski (2012, 2017).

[25] Birch (2017a). The commentaries in the order they appeared: Stauffer (2017); C. Brown (2017); Adamo (2017); Marks (2017); Reber (2017); Mallatt (2017); Rollin (2017); Klein (2017); Mather (2017); Woodruff (2017); Ng (2017); Browning (2017); R. L. Brown (2017); Jones (2017); Leadbeater (2017); Paez (2017); L. Irvine (2017); Carder (2017); Elwood (2017); Seth and Dienes (2017). And my responses in two parts: Birch (2017b, 2018a).

[26] Crump et al. (2022b). The commentaries in the order they appeared: Solms (2022); Reber et al. (2022); Jablonka and Ginsburg (2022); Tye (2022); Ng (2022); C. Brown (2022); Souza Valente (2022); Gorman (2022); E. Irvine (2022); Woodruff (2022); Burrell (2022); Comstock (2022); Walters (2022); Levin (2022); Montemayor (2022); Andrews (2022); Abramson and Calvo (2022); Briffa (2022); Dawkins (2022); Butlin (2022); de Waal (2022); S. Brown (2022); Mallatt and Feinberg (2022); Kakrada and Colombo (2022); Key and D. Brown (2022); Cooper et al. (2022); Gibbons and Chittka (2022); Elwood (2022); Veit (2022); and Montemayor (2023). And our responses: Crump et al. (2022a).

It is worth studying these cases together not because there is a moral equivalence between them but because they present us with similar types of uncertainty. We need frameworks for helping us to manage that uncertainty and reach decisions. This book aims to develop a consistent precautionary framework that enshrines—but also goes beyond—the insight that we must err on the side of caution in these cases, take proportionate steps to manage risk, and avoid reckless or negligent behaviour. Where sentience is in doubt, we should give these systems the benefit of the doubt. What that means in practice will be considered in the rest of the book.

The Edge of Sentience: Risk and Precaution in Humans, Other Animals, and AI. Jonathan Birch, Oxford University Press.
© Jonathan Birch 2024. DOI: 10.1093/9780191966729.003.0002

2

The Concept of Sentience

2.1 Sentience and Consciousness

The issues that matter most at the edge of sentience are scientific, metaphysical, ethical, and political, not semantic. Yet we do need a working definition for the purposes of building up a framework. This chapter puts a definition on the table: sentience as *the capacity for valenced experience*. It then explores the elements of this definition.

The term 'sentience' in English comes from the Latin 'sentire', literally 'to feel'. It is used in different ways in different contexts, with the idea of 'feeling' providing a loose common thread. We saw in Chapter 1 that, sometimes, people use it to mean nothing more than 'responsiveness to sensory stimuli due to adaptive internal processes'. I strongly recommend against using the term in this way, because it creates a large gap with how the term has come to be used in bioethics, animal ethics, animal law, and the science of animal welfare.

More commonly, sentience is taken to imply a capacity for conscious experience. But now we run into another conceptual thicket, because the term 'consciousness' is also used in various ways in different contexts. Herbert Feigl, writing in the middle of the twentieth century, suggested that there are three deeply puzzling features of the mind-body relationship: *sentience, sapience*, and *selfhood*. Unhelpfully, the ordinary term 'consciousness' can gesture towards any of the three, and sometimes to the package of all three together, leading to no end of confusion.[1]

Sentience, our topic, concerns what Feigl called 'raw feels' or qualities. The term 'raw feels' is controversial, for it connotes, I think misleadingly, that sentience is 'unprocessed' rather than a product of complex processing. 'Qualities' is not ideal either, because people sometimes understand it as positing a mysterious, special type of property, distinct from any functional or neurobiological property of the brain (it should not be read as implying this).

[1] Feigl (1958/1967, 1971, 1975).

'Qualia' is even worse in this respect.[2] But Feigl was right to suggest that, when we focus on our immediate, 'raw' experiences of the world and of our own bodies, there is something very puzzling about how these experiences relate to the physical world.

Think of experiencing pain, a quiet or loud noise, the colour of a blue sky or a sunset, the smell of coffee or rotten eggs. As Thomas Nagel put it, there is 'something it's like' to have these experiences.[3] You would not be able to convey what it's like to another human who lacked the relevant sensory ability. Those facts about 'what it's like' seem, at least on the face of it, to be missing from any purely physical description of the brain processes involved. There is a notorious *explanatory gap* between brain processes and the facts about what it's like to have an experience: no amount of information about brain processes seems enough to satisfactorily explain why those processes feel like something from the inside.[4] The problem of explaining how facts about what it's like to be us are related to brain activity is what David Chalmers has called 'the hard problem of consciousness'.[5]

Nagel famously illustrated the point with the example of a bat hunting by echolocation, a sensory ability most humans entirely lack.[6] As a person with no ability to echolocate, I have a strong intuition that I could know everything there is to know about the brain processes going on in the bat as it echolocates and yet still be left wondering: what is it like to echolocate from the point of view of the bat? What is the bat experiencing? This intuitive reaction may ultimately be misleading. Many have resisted the idea that there really are further facts about conscious experience, above and beyond facts about brain processes. We will come back to this debate in Chapter 3. But all can agree the example is a wonderful one for illustrating the puzzle of sentience in Feigl's sense, the sense that generates the explanatory gap and the hard problem. In the 1990s, Ned Block coined the term 'phenomenal consciousness' for this sense of the word 'consciousness'.[7]

---

[2] 'Qualia' sometimes refers to a certain type of theoretical posit in a theory of perception, also called 'mental paint' (Block 1996; Papineau 2021). Meanwhile, some use it to refer to special, non-physical properties posited by dualist theories of consciousness. Carruthers (2000, 2019) uses the term like this, and so declares himself a 'qualia irrealist'. But one could reject both 'mental paint' and dualism and still need a way of talking, in a theoretically non-committal way, about the quality of the experience of seeing a blue sky or a red tomato. 'Qualities' is probably the best we can do for this purpose.

[3] Nagel (1974).   [4] Levine (1983).   [5] Chalmers (1995).

[6] I say 'most' because some blind people navigate the world using sonar and may have some insight into what it's like to echolocate, as Nagel (1974, p. 442 n. 8) observed.

[7] Block (1995).

What are the other puzzling features of the mind-body relationship? Feigl used 'sapience' as a term for human-level intelligence and reflective thought. Writing in 1958, he could see very clearly the potential for decouplings of sentience and intelligence in future technologies:

> The two concepts are not coextensive. The situation has been further complicated in our age by the construction of 'intelligent' machines. Logical reasoning, mathematical proofs and computations, forecasting, game playing, etc. are all being performed by various and usually highly complex electronic devices.[8]

He went on to add that sentience, by contrast, plausibly 'requires complex organic processes', a view many still hold now,[9] but one that I and many others have come to doubt (see Part V). Intelligence too is a source of philosophical problems, but they are different from the problem of sentience and not our main concern in this book. Later on (in Part IV), I will suggest that sentience and intelligence are *methodologically linked*—because intelligent animals have more ways of displaying their sentience to us—but this does not mean they are the same thing.

Selfhood, the third perplexing feature, refers to our possession of a unified self that persists over time. I have a continuous stream of conscious experiences from when I wake in the morning until I fall asleep at night, and my memory connects these daily streams with each other, and with my dreams[10], to form the experiences of a single self. Moreover, I am aware of all this: I am self-conscious. Here, too, there are associated philosophical puzzles, in this case concerning personal identity and the unity of consciousness at a time and across time, but they too can be distinguished from the puzzle of sentience.[11]

Sentience does not *conceptually* imply sapience or selfhood; it is a distinct concept. Sometimes we end up with distinct concepts for properties that are not, in reality, fully distinct. For various reasons, it could turn out that, in reality, there can be no sentience—no 'raw feels', no qualities—without at least some level of sapience and/or selfhood. But that is not something we can safely assume. It is conceivable that there could be something it's like to be a system that wholly lacks thoughts and a unified, persisting self. Experiences could conceivably occur wholly in the moment, with no associated memory

---

[8] Feigl (1958, p. 412).   [9] See e.g. Godfrey-Smith (2016a); Seth (2021).
[10] On the question of whether (and which) other animals dream, and its relation to questions of consciousness, see Peña-Guzmán (2022).
[11] Bayne (2010) and Schechter (2018) offer outstanding discussions of the problems of selfhood.

or reflection, and they could conceivably be entirely devoid of content. For example, Simona Ginsburg and Eva Jablonka have speculated that the earliest nerve nets may have crackled with a contentless form of raw feeling—a sort of 'white noise', the experiential equivalent of static on a TV screen.[12]

Sentience in this sense of the word—the capacity for phenomenal consciousness, with or without sapience or selfhood—does not imply a capacity for pain or pleasure. A being could be sentient in this sense and yet have experiences that feel neither bad nor good to it. In bioethics, animal ethics, animal law, and animal welfare research, the term 'sentience' has come to be used in a deliberately narrower way. In these areas, it usually refers to the capacity for conscious experiences that *feel bad or feel good to the subject*. White noise alone would not count as sentience, on this definition, unless it also feels good or feels bad to the subject. The property of 'feeling bad or feeling good to the subject' is called valence (or hedonic tone). Sentience, in this narrower sense, specifically concerns conscious experiences with valence, whether positive (feels good) or negative (feels bad), or some combination of the two.

In the rest of this book, I will be using the term 'sentience' in this deliberately narrower sense:

A *sentient being* (in the sense relevant to the present framework) is a system with the capacity to have valenced experiences, such as experiences of pain and pleasure.

'Experience' as used here, implies 'phenomenal consciousness'. The definition has two parts: the 'experience' part and the 'valence' part. Sentience, in our sense, requires both. But it implies neither sapience nor selfhood. Figure 2.1 maps out the relevant conceptual terrain.

With any definition, one can ask, of the terms used in the definition, 'but what does *that* mean?' There comes a point at which this game becomes counterproductive. But I think one round is fair. It is reasonable to ask: what is meant by 'phenomenal consciousness'? What is meant by 'valence'? Say more! And what motivates including both properties in the definition, not just one?

---

[12] Ginsburg and Jablonka (2007).

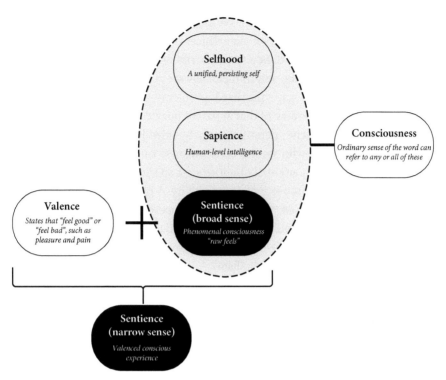

Fig. 2.1 Mapping different senses of 'sentience' and 'consciousness'. Sentience in a broad sense is the capacity for conscious experience, where 'phenomenal consciousness' is the pertinent sense of consciousness. Sentience in a narrower sense adds the further condition that at least some of the conscious experiences must be valenced. In neither sense does sentience imply sapience or selfhood. © Jonathan Birch.

2.2 'Phenomenal Consciousness' as Unstable Common Ground

Fifty years after Nagel's paper, it is still common to define 'phenomenal consciousness' in terms of the phrase 'what it's like'. A state (e.g. the state of a bat echolocating as it swoops down upon its prey) is said to be phenomenally conscious if and only if there is something it's like to be in that state. I cannot believe that Nagel, when using the phrase, ever expected it to end up carrying so much theoretical weight.

'What it's like' is not really a definition at all, as even its proponents often point out. What it does is draw our attention to a central and mysterious aspect of our mental lives, one that seems to elude any attempt at characterization in functional terms. We are supposed to reflect on examples like echolocation and on our own experiences of colour, sound, odour, pain, pleasure, and so on, and the difficulty of describing them to anyone who lacks the relevant sensory abilities, and immediately see at least the appearance of a puzzle—the explanatory gap, the hard problem—and 'phenomenal consciousness' denotes the source of that apparent puzzle.

We can construct a richer definition only by introducing further assumptions that not everyone who studies consciousness can accept. For example, we could add that the experiential qualities are a special type of property, distinct from any physical property of brain activity. A phenomenally conscious state could then be defined as any state that possesses these special non-physical properties. That would give us a substantial definition but clearly not a neutral one: it would be to embrace a controversial dualist metaphysics (see §3.4, for more discussion of dualism).

It is not just dualists who favour building dualistic assumptions into our definitions. Some of their opponents also do this—in order to argue that phenomenal consciousness does not exist at all. Keith Frankish, in a 2016 article, sets up a distinction between two fundamentally different types of property—qualitative and non-qualitative—in order to argue that phenomenal consciousness would, by definition, have to involve properties of the first type, whereas in reality there are no such properties.[13] The strategy of setting up our concepts in a dualistic way in order to then snap back hard, like a coiled spring, on the properties they allegedly denote, is one I find unhelpful. The aim of it seems to be to destroy common ground, when I think we need to cling to whatever common ground we can find.

Other proposals add assumptions in more subtle ways. Eric Schwitzgebel, in a response to Frankish, has proposed that we should define phenomenal consciousness by example.[14] We can list examples of states that clearly have it: dreams, conscious thoughts, conscious mental images, sensory experiences, bodily experiences, experiences of emotion. The concept is nearly always introduced by means of a list like this. When I said 'think of experiencing pain, a quiet or loud noise, the colour of a blue sky or a sunset, the smell of coffee or rotten eggs', I was giving a list of positive examples. Schwitzgebel suggests that there are also clear negative examples, where phenomenal consciousness is absent. Many of your bodily processes operate entirely outside your conscious experience. There is nothing it's like to be generating red

---

[13] Frankish (2016).   [14] Schwitzgebel (2016).

blood cells in your bone marrow, or to be breaking down proteins into amino acids. As mentioned in Chapter 1, the same can be said of many brain processes. Early stages of sensory processing (e.g. processing in the retina and optic tract) and some aspects of low-level motor control (e.g. your tiny adjustments to your grip strength as you grasp a cup, and the computations that produce these adjustments) occur outside conscious experience, as do the processes that occur during dreamless sleep or that prepare you for waking up.

Putting the two lists side by side will not be enough to triangulate a single property, for there will be many properties that differ between them. But to narrow things down, we can say, Schwitzgebel proposes, that 'phenomenal consciousness is the most *folk-psychologically obvious* thing or feature that the positive examples possess and that the negative examples lack'.[15] Yet this assumes that phenomenal consciousness is a posit of folk psychology (i.e. common-sense, everyday psychology) akin to beliefs, desires, thoughts, feelings, emotions, and so on. I doubt this. I think 'phenomenal consciousness' is a term of art, a theoretical concept we acquire through reflection on the mind-body problem and the explanatory gap. Once we see the gap, we see the need for a term that denotes the source of the gap. But the distinctions between sentience, sapience and selfhood, and other related distinctions, take work to get your head around. They are not posits of everyday psychology. My suspicion seems to be borne out by experimental work investigating this issue, which has cast doubt on the idea that non-specialists, prior to any encounter with philosophy, already have a well-formed concept of phenomenal consciousness.[16]

The wider point is that definitions more substantial than 'what it's like' always add contentious assumptions and, consequently, no longer succeed in capturing common ground in the science and philosophy of consciousness. They instead describe common ground for one part of the field, such as the dualist part, the part committed to the 'folk-psychological obviousness' of phenomenal consciousness, and so forth.

What to make of this situation? I think of the 'phenomenal consciousness' concept as unstable common ground. Unstable because no one wants to rest here: everyone wants to pull the science and philosophy of consciousness

---

[15] Schwitzgebel (2016, p. 229, italics added).

[16] Sytsma (2010); Sytsma and Machery (2010); Sytsma and Ozdemir (2019). Sytsma and collaborators take a bold further step: they propose that, since everyday psychology has no concept of phenomenal consciousness, there is no problem of consciousness. This seems to me to exaggerate the relevance of everyday psychology to the mind-body problem.

towards a more mature understanding that will allow a better concept to be constructed. By way of analogy, biology has started with loose notions of 'function', 'adaptation', 'cooperation', and 'altruism' that gesture at real phenomena—and has then tightened up these concepts in the light of evolutionary theory, so that much more precise definitions can be given.[17] We should want consciousness science to eventually do the same to 'phenomenal consciousness'. It is just that, from where we are now, various directions of travel are possible, and the right successor notion will depend on which path is taken (Chapters 3 and 5).

Sometimes we should accept strain on a field's central concept as a marker of the field's immaturity and work to address it over the long term rather than letting the concept (and the field) shatter.[18] We should resist the impulse to say 'a concept this contested can't be used for anything important!'. Attempting to capture what it is that the whole field of consciousness science aims to understand is an important task, and this is what the 'phenomenal consciousness' concept does. We should hold on to it, while at the same time allowing different groups of theorists to develop their own candidates for more theoretically loaded successor notions.

2.3 Affective Space

Let us turn now to the second part of the definition: the valence part. Why 'valence' and not the more familiar 'emotion'? In short, the idea of 'valenced experience' is more general in some respects than 'emotion', and the extra generality is useful. At the same time, it helps us zoom in on the aspect of emotional experience that matters most.

'Emotion' covers a lot, I admit. Happiness, fear, anxiety, joy, boredom, surprise, excitement, comfort, panic, dread, jealousy, guilt, grief...we have many, many concepts for our emotions. I always enjoy discovering words in other languages for emotions that have no English equivalent, such as *hygge* (Danish), the feeling of comfort and cosiness experienced when enjoying food or drink with friends or family, or *koi no yokan* (Japanese), 'the feeling upon first meeting someone that you will inevitably fall in love with them'.[19]

---

[17] Lewens (2007a, 2007b). This is a rare point of contact with the rather more stable conceptual terrain of my previous book, *The Philosophy of Social Evolution* (Birch 2017d, ch. 1).

[18] I have made the same point in relation to the concept of 'animal welfare', which is similarly pulled in different directions by different research programmes (Birch 2022b).

[19] BBC Culture (2018).

Yet we often have feelings that overflow even an expanded emotional vocabulary. In the COVID-19 pandemic, when cases were rising, I found myself experiencing a form of dread associated with the diffuse, spiralling consequences that were looming over all of us, as a collective—I found I had no word for this 'wave dread'. When I attend animal welfare conferences, I often find myself experiencing a feeling that combines horror at the harms humans inflict on animals with admiration for those on the frontline of trying to reduce those harms, plus excitement at the progress they are making—I have no word for this either. One of my favourite feelings of all is that of being absorbed in writing—another feeling with no word of its own.

I can point to these feelings, and describe their typical causes and effects, but I cannot capture them in words. Indeed, when I introspect my own feelings, I seem to find something unclassifiable about as often as I find something I can label. Feelings are akin to fragrances: you can look up what the main 'accords' are supposed to be in a particular perfume, but these attempts at description capture very little of what it actually feels like—they are crude field guides—and so it is with feeling.

If our ordinary concepts do not even allow us to describe our own feelings without missing a lot, we should not expect them to do well at describing the sentience of other beings. We should not flip straight to the other extreme and conclude that terms like 'fear' and 'anger' have no reference at all when applied to other animals. They may well do, but our default stance should be one of humility. We must accept that the feelings of other sentient beings are very likely to overflow any attempt to categorize them with everyday emotion concepts. Because of this, it is helpful to abstract away from our particular emotion concepts (fear, anger, sadness, etc.), and even from the concept of 'emotion' itself, and work instead with more general concepts that are more likely to be applicable to beings very different from ourselves.

But what are these more general concepts? In the mid- to late twentieth century, researchers in social psychology made a sustained effort to map the underlying structure of human emotional language. A landmark in this literature is James A. Russell's 'affective circumplex', which posits that ordinary emotion concepts are picking out arcs on a circle in a two-dimensional space, where the dimensions are valence and arousal (Fig. 2.2).[20] The valence dimension runs from misery to pleasure; the arousal dimension runs from sleepiness to high arousal. Russell proposed this structure as a 'model both

---

[20] J. A. Russell (1980, 2003, 2009). See also Posner et al. (2005, 2009); Yik et al. (2011).

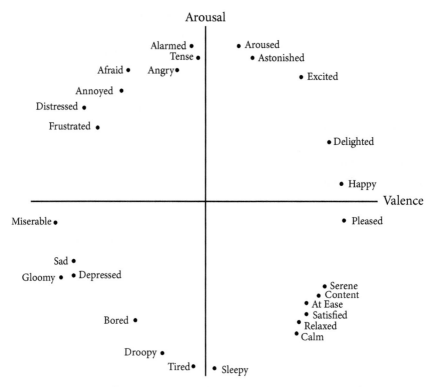

Fig. 2.2 A typical 'affective circumplex', with everyday emotion concepts arranged in a space defined by the axes of valence and arousal. The dimensions do not account for all differences between emotions, but they aim to capture the two main structuring principles. Reproduced from Seo and Huh (2019), CC-BY 4.0 licensed.

for the layman's cognitive structure for affect and for the actual structure of affective experience'.[21]

In Russell's original study, subjects were given twenty-eight common emotion words and asked to group them by similarity in a series of grouping tasks, and the clustering patterns were analysed. The clustering pattern formed a circle in 2D space, aligning well with Russell's proposed structure. For example, the sequence 'alarmed, afraid, tense, distressed, annoyed, frustrated, miserable, sad, depressed, bored, droopy, tired' could be represented as a long arc through the 'negative valence' region of the space, starting at the high-arousal end and finishing at the low-arousal end, with states at the

---

[21]   J. A. Russell (1980, p. 1176).

extremes of the arousal dimension (alarmed, tired) being much less intensely valenced than those in the middle of the arousal dimension (miserable, sad).

Three central components of the affective circumplex model can be distinguished. First, valence and arousal are postulated to be the main dimensions that both organize our thinking about emotional categories and structure our affective experiences. Second, our emotion terms do not just form clusters in valence/arousal space but form a continuous ring around the origin: a circumplex. We have terms that cover, admittedly in a fairly coarse-grained way, all directions out from the origin. Third, there is no strong justification for adding further dimensions to the space.

At the time, this third idea was a controversial one, because many authors had suggested various other candidates for the third main dimension, including 'dominance/submissiveness' and 'attention/rejection'. Russell's conclusion was that adding a third dimension would not help resolve further clusters of emotion categories. Yes, lots of other things matter in *particular cases* (e.g. to the difference between fear and anger, which are similar in valence and arousal), but none of these other factors amounts to a *general structuring principle* for our classification of emotions, orthogonal to valence and arousal.

No consensus around any specific third dimension has since emerged. I should emphasize, though, that it is no part of this model to say that these two dimensions *exhaustively* characterize our experiences of emotion. They do not. The idea is simply that the individuating features that allow us to tease out finer-grained categories (such as anger vs fear) do not amount to general structuring principles.

2.4 Affective Spaces beyond the Human Case

Valence and arousal are likely to be much more widely applicable in the natural world than concepts for particular emotions, such as 'fear' and 'sadness'. They may even be of wider relevance than 'pain', which has traditionally played a dominant role in discussions about the edge of sentience.

Pain is a complex experience with both sensory and affective elements. It is usually triggered by *nociception*: the detection of actual or potential tissue damage by specialized receptors. Accordingly, we usually feel pain 'in' the location on the body at which the nociceptors were triggered. The 'in' here is describing the content of the experience: the pain presents as tied to a specific site on the body, even though the experience is generated by the brain.

Yet there is more to pain than this sensory element. It also feels very bad and is a high-arousal state.[22]

Because of the strong sensory 'injury detection' element of pain, it is usually not described as an emotion, even though it may lead to emotions such as frustration, anguish, or despair.[23] But it clearly has an affective component, and this is one reason why the broader terms 'affect' and 'feeling' are often more useful than the narrower 'emotion'. The affective aspect of pain is very high-arousal and very negatively valenced (feels very bad). Much the same can be said of other deeply unpleasant bodily states, such as hunger, thirst, and breathlessness.[24] They are not purely affective, but they have an affective aspect.

We can try to imagine, though it is not easy, how the sensory and affective aspects of pain might come apart in other animals. In principle, an animal could have a state with similar phenomenal characteristics to pain on the affective side (very high negative valence, high arousal), without much, or even any, associated phenomenal character on the sensory side. We could only describe such a state, imperfectly, as something like a 'feeling of things going very badly, calling for amelioration with high urgency'. In fact, some people describe experiencing a feeling like this during sepsis. Clinicians often struggle to put this feeling into words, sometimes calling it 'the feeling that you're about to die' or 'the feeling of impending doom'. The concept of pain seems inapt in this situation, because the location-specific sensory aspect is absent, and it may conceivably be a poor description of the feelings of some other animals for the same reason.

For instance, the small amount of evidence that exists concerning nociception in sharks suggests they do have nociceptors in the cranial region, yet lack nociceptors in the rest of the body.[25] It does not follow that sharks feel nothing whatsoever when injured on the body, but it does seem likely that bodily injury does not feel to a shark the way it does to us. Perhaps (speculatively) serious injury feels to the shark like sepsis does to humans: a feeling of everything going very badly wrong at once, not tied to a specific location.

---

[22] Auvray et al. (2010); Shriver (2006, 2018a, 2018b).

[23] The term 'suffering' is sometimes used to describe the pain itself, but is also sometimes reserved for the subsequent emotions (leading to the possibility of pain without suffering). I will use the term deliberately broadly, as a synonym for 'negatively valenced experience'. In this sense, both the pain itself and the emotions it typically induces are forms of suffering.

[24] Derek Denton has suggested that these bodily sensations may be among the most evolutionarily ancient feelings, calling them 'primordial emotions' (Denton 2006; Denton et al. 2009).

[25] Lacap (2022).

At the same time, we should also take seriously the possibility that other animals might have states that blend sensory and affective aspects in ways that are impossible for us, because we lack the relevant senses. For example, many animals, including at least one species of dolphin (the Guiana dolphin, *Sotalia guianensis*), possess electroreceptors that register electric fields.[26] It is likely that, in at least some of these species, this sense will have accompanying conscious experiences, and there may be a distinctive feeling associated with it going wrong. Perhaps, for Guiana dolphins, there is a feeling of 'unpleasant disorientation of one's electroreceptors' that is very different from any human feeling.

In short, we should expect there to be far more affective experiences in Heaven and Earth than are dreamt of in our ordinary emotional vocabulary. Affective space, built from the dimensions of valence and arousal, gives us a way of thinking more expansively about the possibilities.[27]

2.5 Three Views on the Nature of Valence

Russell, in introducing the circumplex model, described valence and arousal as features of the 'actual structure of affective experience'. In other words, they were posited to be, as philosophers like to say, *phenomenological* features. They capture part of what it feels like to experience an emotion or bodily sensation from the point of view of the person who feels it.

Your state of arousal has to do with whether you feel lethargic or energized. We can grasp arousal as a phenomenological feature by contrasting our experiences of alarm, excitement, and astonishment (high arousal) with our experiences of tiredness, boredom, and relaxation (low arousal), reflecting on the key difference in the way the two groups of states feel. Meanwhile, the valence of an experience concerns whether it feels bad or feels good. Think about what states such as frustration, annoyance, anxiety, anger, fear, alarm, depression, sadness, and boredom all have in common: they *feel bad*. Think about what states such as joy, excitement, delight, pleasure, contentment, and serenity all have in common: they *feel good*.

---

[26] Czech-Damal et al. (2011).
[27] The value of 'valence' for conceptualizing variation across animals is also a theme of Birch et al. (2020b). Eliza Bliss-Moreau (2017) has made a similar point from within the theoretical perspective of constructionism about emotions. The affective space does not imply constructionism, or vice versa, even though James A. Russell, Lisa Feldman Barrett, and their collaborators (including Bliss-Moreau) have defended both ideas, often in the same articles and books. See Birch (in press) for a detailed discussion of constructionism.

These are definitions-by-example, and I think it is natural to worry (as with attempts to define phenomenal consciousness by example) that they might fail to pin down a unique property. Deeper accounts of valence and arousal would be preferable, but there is no consensus on the correct accounts. In the case of valence, three credible options currently share the stage. To explain how they differ, let us think about an everyday example: the pleasure of eating food. It feels good to eat the food, but what does this 'feeling good' consist in?

One view is that *feels good* and *feels bad* are immediate hedonic qualities of the experience, 'raw feels'. As you eat the food, your experience has an immediate, positive hedonic quality. This view meshes particularly well with hedonic theories of well-being (such as that of Jeremy Bentham), which cast well-being as a function of the intensity and duration of pleasures and pains.[28] A second view, defended by Peter Carruthers, is that valence is the *non-conceptual representation of value*.[29] As you eat the food, your experience represents it as good for you—as having positive value to you. It does this not using concepts, but in a non-conceptual mode, and the experience is positively valenced in virtue of having this evaluative content. A third view, defended by Colin Klein, Manolo Martinex, Luca Barlassina, and Max Khan Hayward, is that valence is a kind of *imperative content*.[30] As you eat the food, your experience presents an imperative or command—roughly, *get more of this!*, where *this* refers to the experience itself. The experience is said to be positively valenced in virtue of this imperative content. A negatively valenced experience, by contrast, contains a command along the lines of *get less of this!*

Does this three-way disagreement matter for our purposes? Since all three views agree about the existence of valence as a real and general feature of affective experience, none provides a reason to contest my proposed definition of sentience. A serious challenge would come from a view that doubts the existence or pervasiveness of valence (clearly, if valence does not exist at all, or is not a general feature of affect, then it would be a misstep to define sentience in terms of it), but none of the above views lends support to such doubts.

It is worth noting, though, that the accounts differ in their attitude towards the idea of *unconscious* valence. On the hedonic quality account, the idea of unconscious valence makes no sense: when we talk about the valence of an

---

[28] Bentham (1789/1879); Crisp (2021).   [29] Carruthers (2018, 2023).
[30] Barlassina and Hayward (2019); Klein (2015); Martínez and Klein (2016); Martínez (2011, 2015).

experience, we are talking about an essentially conscious property. There could be unconscious properties with similar motivational roles to positive and negative valence, but they would not be the exact same properties. By contrast, on Carruthers's account, unconscious valence does make sense. Non-conceptual representations of value may be either conscious or unconscious. You might unconsciously represent the food as good while consciously disliking it. Indeed, your valenced conscious experiences may be the tip of a large iceberg of unconscious valenced states. The third, imperativist view may fall either way on this question, depending on the precise nature of the imperative (if the content is 'more of *this experience!*', it may be essentially conscious). We will pick this question up again in Chapter 5, when we consider whether there is good evidence for unconscious valence.

2.6 The Ethical Significance of Valence

When we think of bodily sensations such as pain, hunger, thirst, and breathlessness, it is the affective aspect of these bodily sensations, and not the sensory information they contain, that lies at the root of their ethical significance.[31] For example, if an analgesic (painkiller) only takes away information about the location of an injury, without removing the unpleasantness—so that the subject just feels a diffuse feeling of unpleasantness, no longer tied to any specific part of the body, but just as intense as it was before, perhaps akin to the feeling of sepsis—it is not a good analgesic. Yet if a drug removes the unpleasantness without removing the registration of an injury at a specific location, it may still be a very useful analgesic. It targets the aspect of pain that there is an ethical imperative to reduce. This point offers further support for definitions of sentience that go beyond pain and encompass all felt affective states. It is not just that these definitions capture more of what matters—they also capture what matters more precisely in the case of pain itself, by drawing our attention to its affective aspect.

However, the two core dimensions of affect are not equal in their ethical significance: valence is more important than arousal. Imagine a drug that flips the valence of pain without altering the arousal aspect, converting a high-arousal pain state into a high-arousal pleasure state. Contrast this with a drug that alters arousal while leaving valence unchanged: the pain still feels extremely bad, but it no longer rouses a patient from a feeling of drowsy

---

[31] Shriver (2018a).

lethargy. The second drug might form part of a pain-management strategy, alongside other drugs that aim to make the pain feel less bad, but that is probably the best that can be said for the second drug. By contrast, the first drug would be a medical revolution that would transform human lives vastly for the better. There would be a strong ethical imperative to prescribe it, unless there were terrible side effects.

The thought experiment illustrates the point that flipping valence can turn a state of great negative ethical value—a state we have a clear ethical imperative to ameliorate, at least when we can do so very easily and at little cost—into a state that has at least some positive ethical value (even if we think intense pleasures should be enjoyed in moderation). By contrast, flipping arousal from high to low will not flip the ethical value of the state from negative to positive, or vice versa. A highly negatively valenced state is still ethically bad, regardless of how drowsy or energized you feel when in it. Your claim to medical resources to help you alleviate that state is still strong either way. The arousal dimension of affect at most modulates the strength of the claim.

This idea that valence has a strong and special ethical significance can be reached from a variety of ethical starting points. One route runs through classical (hedonic) utilitarianism. For the progenitors of the classical utilitarian view, Jeremy Bentham and John Stuart Mill, the basic ethical imperative is to do the most good. Goodness is understood as happiness, and happiness is understood as a state of pleasure and the absence of pain, where both 'pleasure' and 'pain' are interpreted deliberately broadly, capturing what many would now call positively valenced and negatively valenced affect, respectively.[32] As far as possible, then, one should avoid causing negatively valenced experiences and try to promote positively valenced experiences. In this ethical framework, the valence of an experience is crucially important, for it determines whether that experience contributes positively or negatively to the calculation that determines the right course of action. Arousal may matter too for a classical utilitarian, in so far as it may modulate the experienced duration and/or intensity of hedonic states,[33] but the ethical significance of arousal is much less fundamental than the ethical significance of valence.

---

[32] See Bentham (1789/1879); Mill (1861/1887). More recent works in the utilitarian tradition, such as Singer (1980/2011) and Varner (2012) agree about the special significance of valenced experience.

[33] The modulation effect is complicated and depends on valence. It is not just a matter of high-arousal experiences having a longer perceived duration (Piovesan et al. 2019).

A very different route runs through Christine Korsgaard's neo-Kantian ethics.[34] On this view, we have a fundamental obligation to respect all sentient beings as 'ends-in-themselves' and to avoid using them as 'mere means' to our own ends. Sentient beings are not tools or instruments for our use; they have their own lives to lead, and those lives deserve our respect. The terminology comes from Kant, but the picture is vastly more inclusive of other animals than Kant's own ethics (see §4.2). What is it to respect animals as ends-in-themselves? It is to treat as valuable those ends (goals) that animals themselves value, simply because they value them. And, for Korsgaard, it is through having valenced experiences that animals are able to value and disvalue ends in the sense that matters.

Think of a dog eating a dog treat. There are several different senses in which the dog might be said to 'value' the treat. We might mean that the dog strongly prefers the treats over alternatives, or that the treats can be used as positive reinforcers when training the dog. On Korsgaard's view, the sense of 'valuing' that matters from an ethical point of view is that the dog feels positively valenced experiences when eating the treats. Without valenced experiences, there can be no valuing of ends in the sense that can make moral claims on others.

A third route, very different again from the first two, runs through Martha Nussbaum's capabilities approach to justice.[35] On this picture, the fundamental imperative of justice is to help all beings capable of 'significant striving' to achieve a kind of flourishing appropriate to their form of life, without being 'wrongfully thwarted' by others. But which beings are capable of 'significant striving'? The view initially sounds like it will be radically inclusive of all living things, since one can talk even of plants and bacteria striving, flourishing, and being thwarted. But in fact Nussbaum sees only beings with 'a felt orientation towards what is seen as good and a felt aversion to what is seen as bad'[36] as capable of being treated justly or unjustly. A plant can be thwarted but not wrongfully thwarted, because the frustration of its goal-directed behaviours will not register unpleasantly in its subjective point of view on the world. Here, too, it is valenced experiences that matter.

Three very different ethical theories, then, have converged on the idea that valenced experience is of fundamental ethical importance.[37] Not experience

---

[34] Korsgaard (2018). I have criticized Korsgaard's arguments in a detailed review (Birch 2020b).

[35] Nussbaum (2006, 2023). For critical discussion of Nussbaum's views, see Read and Birch (2023).

[36] Nussbaum (2023, p. 119).

[37] DeGrazia (1996) has also noted the wide convergence on this point from a variety of ethical outlooks.

of any kind at all, since non-valenced experiences do not generate the right sort of ethical claims. And not 'affective' experience either, since, strictly speaking, this term also encompasses states that have neutral valence but positive or negative arousal, which would not be enough.

This still leaves plenty of room for dissent from those who reject all three of the pictures just mentioned (for example, it is clear enough that Kant would have rejected all three pictures). We will turn to the issue of reasonable ethical disagreement later (in Chapter 4), because it implies limits on what can be a matter of robust, society-wide consensus in this area. But for now, my aim is simply to motivate the special focus on valenced experience in our working definition of sentience. The fact that three major ethical theories agree on the special importance of valence is enough to achieve that aim.

In the previous section, I outlined three ways of thinking about the nature of valence; this section has now set out three ways of thinking about why it matters ethically. How do the two trios relate to each other? As far as *logical* compatibility is concerned, I think we can mix and match: any theory of valence can be combined with any theory of why valence matters without generating an obvious contradiction. However, there are ways in which certain theories of valence's nature may complement (in a way that falls short of logical implication) certain theories of its ethical significance. Classical utilitarianism fits very neatly with a picture of valence as hedonic quality. By contrast, the Korsgaard and Nussbaum pictures fit best with a picture of valence that ties it closely to the representation of value. What is special about valence, for both Korsgaard and Nussbaum, is that it involves an animal implicitly valuing some situations and disvaluing others. As Nussbaum puts it, some situations are 'seen as good', while others are 'seen as bad'. An account of valence as the non-conceptual representation of value secures this link very directly, though it could probably be secured less directly by the other accounts.

To sum up the message of the chapter: when we ask (for instance) 'Do octopuses have feelings?' the question is not (or at least should not be) whether they have feelings for which we already have words in English. The question should be whether they have *conscious experiences* and whether those experiences are at least sometimes *valenced*. Defining sentience as the capacity for valenced experience sets us on the right track, asking the right questions.

2.7 Summary of Chapter 2

Sentience has broader and narrower senses. In a broad sense, it refers to any capacity for conscious experience. Conscious experience here refers to 'phenomenal consciousness', the idea that there is 'something it's like' to be you. In a narrower sense, it refers specifically to the capacity to have *valenced* experiences—experiences that *feel bad or feel good to the subject*—such as experiences of pain and pleasure. This narrower sense of the term will be used as a working definition in the rest of the book (replacing the initial characterization of sentience in Chapter 1, where it was introduced as 'ethically significant experience').

A definition of sentience as the capacity for valenced experience can be common ground, despite continuing disagreement about the nature of conscious experience and the nature of valence. We can hope that the rather weak 'something it's like' definition of phenomenal consciousness will eventually be superseded by a more theoretically loaded successor, but this must await much more theoretical consensus than currently exists. There are, at present, many theories of phenomenal consciousness, displaying massive variation, some of which will be discussed in Chapters 3, 5, and 6.

Valence, meanwhile, is one of the two major dimensions, along with arousal, that structure our affective experiences, and the one that matters most from an ethical point of view. Valenced experiences do not have to fall under traditional human categories. There may well be valenced experiences in other beings that our everyday categories (e.g. 'pain', 'fear', 'anger') fail to capture well.

There are three main accounts of the nature of valence (hedonic quality, non-conceptual representation of value, and imperative content), though all agree that valence is a real and general feature of affective experience. Meanwhile, three major ethical theories (classical utilitarianism, Korsgaard's neo-Kantian view, and Nussbaum's capabilities approach) have converged from different directions on the special ethical significance of valence. There are no obvious logical entailments between theories of the nature of valence and theories of its ethical significance, but some packages fit together better than others.

The Edge of Sentience: Risk and Precaution in Humans, Other Animals, and AI. Jonathan Birch, Oxford University Press.
© Jonathan Birch 2024. DOI: 10.1093/9780191966729.003.0003

PART I

THE ZONE OF REASONABLE DISAGREEMENT

3

The Mind-Body Problem

Disagreement about the nature of sentience is not going away any time soon. It is fanciful to think that researchers in the science and philosophy of sentience will soon converge on a single, agreed theory. We will consider the reasons for this over the next three chapters. But from the outset, it's important to see that our predicament is not just one of a little uncertainty here and there on the margins of a theoretical picture we know to be broadly true in outline. The situation is one of *radical uncertainty*, with enormously different alternatives on the table, new scientific theories appearing all the time, many further alternatives presumably yet to be conceived,[1] and a lack of agreed strategies for narrowing down the space of possibilities.

This is a disturbing situation given that all of our cases at the edge of sentience—humans, other animals, AI—are cases where the question of *what to do* depends a great deal on which systems we regard as sentient. These cases can drive us to despair when we realize the full extent of disagreement and the difficulty of resolving it. This book is an attempt to find the antidote to that despair. We are working towards a framework for reaching collective decisions that can command our confidence even though we will continue to disagree.

As I emphasized in Chapter 1, at the core of that framework should be the need to in some sense 'err on the side of caution' in the face of radical uncertainty about sentience. A person can harbour a lot of reasonable doubts about whether or not beings of a certain type are sentient, and yet still sign up to the need for precautions, just in case they are. Think of people, such as Kate Bainbridge, who were wrongly presumed unconscious when they were not. All can agree this should never happen. Well-designed precautions can be common ground. They don't have to be controversial or polarizing. They need not reproduce in the domain of action the deep disagreement that exists at the level of theory. Thinking our way through the details of this line of thought will be the work of the next two parts of the book.

---

[1] On the problem of unconceived alternatives in other areas of science, see Stanford (2006).

3.1 Disagreeing Reasonably about Sentience

A first step is to distinguish between *reasonable* and *unreasonable* disagreement about sentience. Our task will then be to find procedures that help us to manage reasonable disagreement while avoiding unreasonable disagreement. An important idea here is that the existence of serious, persistent disagreement about sentience in science and philosophy does not mean *anything goes*, that all opinions on these issues are equally justified. There is a *zone of reasonable disagreement*, wide yet bounded.

Both people and the positions they hold can be reasonable or unreasonable. A reasonable *person* is one who displays certain characteristic virtues to at least a minimal degree: they care about, and respond to, evidence and reasons; they respect scientific evidence, on the whole, even if they are sceptical of some scientific results; they want to reach agreement with those they disagree with; they are not wantonly reckless in the face of risk; and their values are not completely abhorrent. Meanwhile, a reasonable *position* is one that a reasonable person could hold after consulting all the relevant, currently existing evidence. Reasonable *disagreement* happens when both ingredients are in place: we have a disagreement between reasonable people holding reasonable positions.

I realize this description of 'reasonableness' is a little abstract. I hope the following three caricatures will help bring it to life.

Baseless Recommendations

Imagine someone tells you adamantly that you *must not use antibacterial soap*. To do this causes appalling pain to the bacteria. You must first anaesthetize the bacteria by soaking your hands for five minutes in orange juice. Then you can use the soap.

You would not take this person seriously—*why not?* Not because you have a complete, empirically well-established theory of sentience that decisively rules out, with absolute certainty, sentience in bacteria. No one has this. You cannot simply confront this person with undisputed scientific facts that exclude their view. The real reason is that the person is recommending a course of action without being able to provide any positive justification that flows from a credible, evidence-based theoretical and explanatory framework. They are just making stuff up.

You would ask them: what evidence is there that points credibly to a bacterium ever feeling pain? What evidence is there that points credibly to antibacterial agents, in particular, being experienced as painful? What evidence is there to suggest that orange juice works as an anaesthetic for bacteria? They would either be unable to answer or else they would present you with dubious evidence that did not meet scientific norms, and you would rightly reject that purported evidence.

What would you say next? In your place, I think I would say something like this:

> Sorry, but these are serious matters. You are recommending a change to my way of life. It is *not reasonable* to do that without credible supporting evidence. If evidence were not required, I could equally well tell you to always wear gloves on Tuesdays, because gloves give bacteria intense pleasure, but only on Tuesdays. The game of evidence-free speculation has no rules, no constraints. It can be reasonable to speculate sometimes, in the right time and the right place, but to make a *practical recommendation* on the basis of pure speculation is unreasonable.

If you agree with that general line of thought, you will probably find a lot to agree with in the rest of the book. A recurring theme is that, in the absence of certainty, it is still possible and, moreover, extremely important to base recommendations on evidence that favours the recommended course of action over relevant alternatives.

Dogmatism

In Descartes's time, disciplinary divisions were much less entrenched than they are now. As a 'natural philosopher', Descartes roamed across mathematics, physics, philosophy, and indeed physiology, where he made significant contributions.[2] One of Descartes's motivations for studying neuroanatomy was to find the place where conscious experience slipped inside the workings of the brain. He proposed the pineal gland as the most plausible location (Fig. 3.1).[3] In the human brain, this is a small structure right in the centre.

---

[2] T. H. Huxley (1874) opens the essay in which he introduces the idea of epiphenomenalism with a long tribute to Descartes's contributions to neurophysiology.
[3] See Lokhorst (2021) for a wonderful overview of the history of this theory.

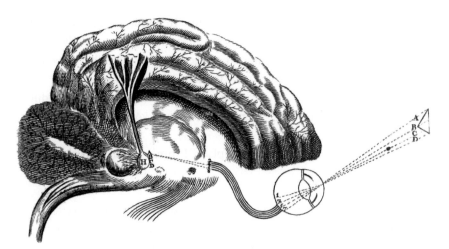

Fig. 3.1 Illustration by Florentio Schuyl from Descartes's *De Homine* (1662), showing the pineal gland (H) and its hypothesized importance to conscious vision. A public domain image from the Wellcome Collection.

Unusually for a brain region, it is unpaired—there is only one—apparently hinting at a unifying or integrative role.

The hypothesis that such a structure might have a special function relating to consciousness was, at the time, a sensible one to put forward, but we now know it to be false. The pineal gland produces melatonin, a hormone important to the regulation of circadian rhythms. It is not part of the neural basis of consciousness or sentience. Damage to the pineal gland can be very disruptive to a person's circadian rhythms, but it does not abolish sentience or even partially impair conscious experience (compare with this, for example, blindsight, which involves damage to the visual cortex and leads to dramatic alterations to conscious experience, discussed in Chapter 5).[4]

Now imagine someone who simply will not accept the modern view of the pineal gland. They think Descartes is the only credible authority on questions of consciousness and insist his theory was correct. There is no need to read this new evidence, they say, because if it disagrees with Descartes it must be wrong. You would not take this person seriously—*why not?* Not because you have a complete, empirically well-established theory of sentience that tells us conclusively where its neural basis is located. No one has this. The problem is not that this person has a controversial view, but that this person is failing to respond to new evidence. To flatly ignore relevant evidence is another way of being unreasonable.

[4] Arendt and Aulinas (2000).

Moral Views beyond the Pale

Here is a third caricature, this time of someone who behaves unreasonably in the ethical rather than the epistemic domain. Imagine someone proposes that we should be trying to *maximize* the suffering of all the animals on the planet. After all, we are the Earth's top species, its ultimate apex predator, and it is only right for an apex predator to aspire to make its victims suffer as much as possible, so as to instil maximum fear.

You would not take this person seriously—*why not?* Not because you know the one true ethical theory and you know it to be incompatible with their view. No one is in that position. The situation is rather this: for all our disagreement about ethical matters, we can all recognize some views as so abhorrent that they do not belong in the space of reasonable ethical disagreement. They belong outside that space, beyond the pale. Debate will be derailed if we give significant airtime to these outlooks. We have no good reason to explore the finer details of such views. We are entitled to reject them without discussion. To make a practical recommendation on the basis of such a view is another way of being unreasonable.

In short, it is not reasonable to base a serious proposal for society-wide action on empirically unconstrained speculation, on dogmatic unresponsiveness to evidence, or on a morally abhorrent background view. However, this still leaves plenty of room for *reasonable* disagreement about what to do regarding cases at the edge of sentience. Indeed, we will never get away from it. This is partly because our evidence is inconclusive, and partly also because there is so much variation in human values. But the zone of reasonable disagreement is not boundless. It is circumscribed by the need for positive evidence in favour of any course of action one recommends, by the need for open-mindedness about following the evidence where it leads, and by the need for values that fall within an acceptable range. Not every possible view about sentience has a place in that zone.

I will use the term 'zone of reasonable disagreement' in a deliberately broad way. The zone includes reasonable *scientific* disagreement about the neural mechanisms linked to sentience in the human brain. As we will see, there are very different views about the neural basis of sentience that all have *some* credible evidence in their favour. None of these views can be dismissed as evidence-free speculation (Chapter 5). The zone also includes reasonable disagreement (part scientific, part metaphysical) about how radically a system can *differ* from a healthy, adult human brain and still support sentience. For example, it includes reasonable disagreement about whether or not sentience depends on the *material substrate* (biological or non-biological) in which the system is realized. The zone also includes reasonable *ethical* disagreement: disagreement about the ethical significance of sentience.

In all cases, the competing views on the table are all 'reasonable' in a specific sense: a proposal for action, based on reasons deriving from within that viewpoint, could not be fairly dismissed as baseless without further argument, in the way that a proposal to ban antibacterial soap, a proposal to disregard animals without pineal glands, or a proposal to maximize animal suffering could be so dismissed. The zone stakes out a space of *reasonable bases for proposed actions* ('bases' is used here as the plural of 'basis'). That is a key step towards constructing a precautionary framework. The next step (to be taken later, in Chapters 6–8) will be to design procedures that help us decide what to do when we find there are multiple proposed actions that all have reasonable bases.

The 'zone' is a spatial metaphor, and I like to visualize the zone of reasonable disagreement in a spatial way. Think of a serious space, a grave space: a parliamentary committee room, a courtroom, an operating theatre. I picture the zone of reasonable disagreement as akin to such a space. Evidence-free speculations may still have their own space elsewhere—the pub or café, or even the seminar room, book group, or lab meeting—but, for the purpose of making important, sober decisions affecting real lives, we need to create a space in which they are left at the door.

That is enough, I hope, to convey the idea of a 'zone of reasonable disagreement' and why it matters, without exaggerating the level of precision with which that zone can be circumscribed. My next task is to give a certain type of map of the zone. It is not a map of the terrain so much as a geological map. I am not trying to give an overview of all the topics on which people currently disagree. My aim is to capture the *sources* of persistent disagreement: sources we should expect to keep throwing up new disagreements, as a volcano expels fresh lava, long after our current disagreements cool and solidify.

This chapter will focus on sources of disagreement that have their origins in the philosophy of mind. The next chapter considers sources of ethical disagreement, considering both secular and religious viewpoints. Chapter 5 turns to arguments of a more scientific nature. The boundary between philosophy and science is not *at all* sharp, and when the topic is sentience the boundary becomes even blurrier than usual. Nonetheless, I think vague distinctions (simply for the purposes of splitting three chapters) can still be drawn.

3.2 Might Conscious Experience Leave No Trace on Behaviour?

When I talk to scientists in unrelated fields about sentience, I often encounter strong expressions of agnosticism. The answers to these questions, some say, are unknowable, beyond the reach of science—one cannot even gather evidence relevant to these questions. I suspect this attitude often flows from a certain type of background philosophical picture. That picture is *epiphenomenalism*, according to which conscious experiences have no physical effects, and so leave no measurable imprint on the physical world. Conscious experience literally *does nothing*, so we cannot study it scientifically.[5] This is a view I reject myself, but I still think it has a place in the zone of reasonable disagreement, provided those who hold it do not dogmatically insist on its correctness.

Let us first try to clarify the idea. The epiphenomenalist picture is *not* one on which experiences accompany brain processes completely at random, senselessly and lawlessly. The epiphenomenalist posits that there are *psychophysical laws* that link particular conscious experiences to particular neural states: the correlations are law-governed, not random. There are regular patterns. So, conscious experiences can be followed very reliably by physical effects, but these effects are caused by the correlated neural state, not by the experience.

Epiphenomenalism was influential in late nineteenth- and early twentieth-century psychology, where it helped to shape the behaviourist tradition. The early behaviourist John B. Watson wrote that 'one can assume either the presence or the absence of consciousness anywhere in the psychological scale without affecting the problems of behavior by one jot or one tittle; and without influencing in any way the mode of experimental attack upon them'.[6] Through behaviourism's long legacy, the picture continues to exert influence, even though very few scientists trained today will hear the term 'epiphenomenalism'. I think it often slips in, namelessly, when people assume that because experience is 'subjective' and 'private',

---

[5] The view in its modern form is usually credited to T. H. Huxley (1874).

[6] Watson (1913, p. 249). Just a few years earlier, Watson (1907) had been happy to talk of conscious mental states having effects that could be measured and detected. What changed? In the 1913 article, Watson describes 'the parallelistic hypothesis' as an obstacle to a functionalist psychology. The parallelist agrees with the epiphenomenalist that conscious experiences have no effects in the physical world, but, unlike a pure epiphenomenalist, allows that they have effects in the mental realm. The two realms proceed in lockstep, exquisitely correlated but never causally influencing each other. It seems Watson's understandable reaction to this idea was: if *that*'s what you mean by 'consciousness', we must purge psychology entirely of this thing called 'consciousness'.

behavioural evidence tells us nothing about it. That could follow only if 'subjective/private' implied 'epiphenomenal'.

The epiphenomenalist picture is one that would, if true, hold bleak consequences for our ability to resolve disputes at the edge of sentience. This is because it is a picture on which there is no *explanatory* connection between consciousness and any physical marker. There may still be markers that reliably *correlate* with consciousness in the case of a healthy adult human, but those markers will not be causally explained by the presence of consciousness.[7] This is bleak because, to make any progress in disputed cases, we need there to be an explanatory connection between consciousness and its markers. This is because we need to use the principle of *inference to the best explanation* (or 'IBE') to infer consciousness from the markers in disputed cases.[8]

To elaborate on this point: if consciousness floats on top of a neural mechanism, so to speak, explaining nothing it does, then IBE will be unable to select between the hypothesis that consciousness is abolished by very small differences in the mechanism (e.g. the differences that exist between humans and chimpanzees) and the hypothesis that consciousness is preserved across those differences. The psychophysical laws connecting inefficacious experiences to brain states could apply only to humans, or only to primates, or only to mammals, and so on, without any consequence for our explanations of any set of physical (e.g. neural, behavioural, cognitive) markers. This leads naturally to the agnosticism espoused by Watson and earlier by T. H. Huxley, whereby, having seen the impossibility of using IBE to settle these questions, we give up on the idea of a science of consciousness.

This explains why I would *like* epiphenomenalism to be false, but the bleakness of a philosophical theory is not a reason to reject it. Luckily, I think we have good reasons for finding epiphenomenalism implausible. William James, in the *The Principles of Psychology* (1890/1918), gave an evolutionary argument for rejecting epiphenomenalism that still stands up well. James appeals to the *adaptive complexity of valenced experience*. James emphasized, in particular, the many grades of intensity that are possible in relation to valenced experiences such as pleasure, comfort, satiety, pain, nausea, thirst, and breathlessness. With occasional exceptions, the valence and intensity of our experiences are strikingly well aligned with the strength of our biological

---

[7] I am setting aside here the possibility that conscious experiences might non-causally explain physical effects.

[8] On IBE, see Lipton (2004). Tye (2016) and Andrews (2020) have also emphasized the key role played by IBE in inferences to animal consciousness.

needs. James writes, against the epiphenomenalist or (in his words) automa-
ton theorist:

> if pleasures and pains have no efficacy, one does not see (without some such
> *a priori* rational harmony as would be scouted by the 'scientific' champions
> of the automaton theory) why the most noxious acts, such as burning, might
> not give thrills of delight, and the most necessary ones, such as breathing,
> cause agony.[9]

The subtle adaptive alignment of our valenced experiences with our biological
needs has the hallmarks of an evolved adaptation. It is scientifically inexplicable
except as the product of gradual shaping by natural selection over evolutionary
time. But to be selected, *it must have effects.*

As James notes, an epiphenomenalist can escape this problem only by positing that the mysterious psychophysical laws that link brain states to conscious experiences—and that are not themselves products of natural
selection—build in a wonderful, fortuitous harmony between experiential
quality and biological need. But then the epiphenomenalist owes us an
explanation for that harmony. Of course, they could reach here for intelligent
design, but that is to abandon any claim to scientific credibility, which is presumably why James puts 'scientific' inside those wry inverted commas.[10]

Where does this leave us? Epiphenomenalism is *not* beyond the pale—it is
a reasonable, coherent picture—but there are good reasons to find it very
unlikely to be true. And so what is unreasonable is to dogmatically insist, in
the manner of Watson, that sentience leaves no imprint on behaviour, as if
this were an obvious truth. Alternative pictures on which sentience *does* make
a difference and *does* leave a detectable signature on cognition and behaviour
are not only possible—they are actually a lot more plausible.

3.3 Is Conscious Experience One Kind or Many?

How, then, might conscious experience influence cognition and behaviour?
In philosophy, three very different ways of securing the causal efficacy of
experience have long shared the stage: materialism, interactionist dualism,
and pan(proto)psychism. Materialism is the majority view, while the other

---

[9] James (1890/1918, pp. 143–144).
[10] For discussion James's objection to epiphenomenalism, see Klein (2019) and Mørch (2017).

two possibilities have the status of radical alternatives. Two related ideas, also radical but not so easy to locate in relation to materialism, are biopsychism and the integrated information theory. I will argue later that all of these radical alternatives have a place in the zone of reasonable disagreement. But first, let us zoom in on the materialist orthodoxy.

A materialist (or physicalist) regards conscious experience as grounded in (and perhaps identical to or constituted by) complex arrangements of physical properties, such as the physical properties of brains. For the materialist, experience may not *seem* physical, but it *is* physical. To the extent that it seems otherwise, this is misleading. This very general commitment leaves room for many varieties of materialism and various ways of carving up the space of materialist theories.[11]

To me, as someone whose concern is with the edge of sentience, the most salient division among materialists is between those who hold that conscious experience is a *single, unified natural kind* and those who see 'conscious experience' and related terms (such as 'phenomenal consciousness', 'qualities', 'raw feels', and 'what it's like to be you') as terms that point indeterminately towards *two or more different kinds* that can come apart, so that we will eventually want to retire this imprecise language in favour of a set of more precise successors.

What are the core commitments of the 'single natural kind' view? In a series of papers, Nicholas Shea and Tim Bayne provide a good account.[12] The idea is not that we can find a precise set of essential properties (or necessary and sufficient conditions) for consciousness, in the way that chemists have uncovered the essential properties of chemical elements. The worlds of biology and psychology tend to be too messy to allow for necessary and sufficient conditions, and we should expect consciousness to be no exception. The thought is rather that phenomenal consciousness will turn out to be a neurobiological/cognitive natural kind that causally explains a large and diverse cluster of other properties and so has an important and distinctive causal role in the overall functioning of the brain.

Most scientific theories currently on the market are instances of this general idea, because they hold that phenomenal consciousness is a distinctive kind of computation: perhaps recurrent processing,[13] global broadcast,[14]

---

[11] See Chalmers (2010, ch. 5), for one influential way of carving up the space.
[12] Shea and Bayne (2010); Shea (2011); Bayne and Shea (2020). See Whiteley (2022) for sympathetic discussion and Phillips (2018) and Taylor (2023) for criticism.
[13] Lamme (2010, 2022).
[14] Baars (1988); Dehaene and Changeux (2011); Mashour et al. (2020).

a special kind of predictive processing,[15] an attention schema,[16] or perceptual reality monitoring.[17] However, the idea of consciousness turning out to be a single natural kind is much more general than any of these specific proposals, which could all be incorrect. The fundamental commitment is simply that consciousness has a causal role in producing a distinctive cluster of correlated markers.[18] These markers (beginning with, but not limited to, verbal reports of experiences) are akin to the symptoms of a disease: they tend to occur together for an underlying reason, such as a single neural mechanism that reliably produces all of them. By studying the cluster of markers and its causes, we will eventually be able to make a theoretical identification: phenomenal consciousness *is* that mechanism responsible for the cluster of markers.

How does this differ from a 'many kinds' view? Daniel Dennett's essay on the 'magic' of consciousness provides an informal statement of such a view. Dennett writes: 'In a proper theory of consciousness, the Emperor is not just deposed, but exposed, shown to be a cunning conspiracy of lesser operatives whose activities jointly account for the "miraculous" powers of the Emperor.'[19] He tells the story of The Tuned Deck, a magic trick that was in fact many different magic tricks, with a new one brought in to throw spectators off the scent each time they seemed close to guessing the secret. 'The trick, in its entirety, is in the name of the trick, "The Tuned Deck", and more specifically, in one word "The"!'[20]

This sketches a picture on which 'consciousness', even when we specify that we mean *phenomenal* consciousness, gestures indeterminately towards a *plurality* of neurobiological/cognitive kinds. As Ian Phillips has noted, Dennett's analogizing of consciousness to 'fame in the brain' suggests a similar picture, since fame is not a phenomenon associated with a single, unified mechanism: there are many routes to fame.[21] Dennett's fondness for magician analogies has led him to embrace the term 'illusionism' for his view,[22]

---

[15] Nave et al. (2022).

[16] Graziano (2013). Graziano's 'attention schema' theory is hard to classify. On the face of it, Graziano identifies conscious content with the content of the attention schema. Yet sometimes he makes comments that sound sceptical of there being such a thing as consciousness as at all, e.g. 'Let me as clear as possible: consciousness doesn't happen. It's a mistaken construct' (Graziano 2016a). See Graziano (2016b) and Kammerer (2018) for discussion of this tension.

[17] Lau (2022).

[18] Here Shea and Bayne are influenced by earlier work on natural kinds from Boyd (1991, 1999) and Millikan (1999), reviewed by Bird and Tobin (2023, §1.2.2).

[19] Dennett (2005, p. 71).

[20] Dennett (2005, p. 73). Thanks to Keith Frankish for drawing my attention to this.

[21] Phillips (2018).   [22] Dennett (2017).

but I do not myself find this an apt name for a view that posits multiple *real* cognitive kinds, all with a genuine but *partial* claim to being the referent of 'phenomenal consciousness'.[23]

Another 'many kinds' view, albeit one that posits only two kinds, has been set out by neuroscientists Stanislas Dehaene, Sid Kouider, and Hakwan Lau. They distinguish the 'selection of information for global broadcasting, thus making it flexibly available for computation and report' from 'the self-monitoring of those computations, leading to a subjective sense of certainty or error'.[24] They label the first kind C1, and the second capacity C2. They argue that the word 'consciousness' conflates C1 and C2. It is fair to surmise they intend this not as a conceptual analysis of the ordinary word 'consciousness' but as an empirical analysis of the cognitive kinds in fact picked out by the concept. While they recognize that some may insist that the word refers to neither of these cognitive kinds, but rather to some third, more mysterious kind, they conclude that 'the empirical evidence is compatible with the possibility that consciousness arises from nothing more than [these] specific computations'.[25]

On a 'many kinds' view, many of the arguments between proponents of different scientific theories of consciousness are misguided. Theorists from different camps should instead recognize that they are studying genuine neurobiological/cognitive kinds that all attract the reference of the word 'consciousness' partially. We are in a situation akin to the following: for years, the residents of a town have been debating 'what it's like around here' but have been unable to agree on what property they are talking about. In the hope of resolving the matter, many residents have developed theories of 'what it's like around here'. All of those theories capture something genuinely in the vicinity of where they were pointing. One person has come up with a theory of the local economy, another has a theory of the local architecture, a third has a theory of local governance structures. But instead of accepting that they have all built useful theories of different properties, all of which have a non-exclusive claim to having captured some element of 'what it's like around here', they instead fight bitterly over which theory truly captures the essence of 'what it's like around here'. Implicitly, they must believe there is a special type of property—the *what-it's-likeness* of a town—that transcends the purely structural and functional properties their theories elucidate. Explicitly, they

---

[23] David Papineau (2002, ch. 7) has defended a similar view, one on which various different cognitive properties and their lower-level neuronal realizers are all equally eligible candidates for the reference of 'phenomenal consciousness'.

[24] Dehaene et al. (2017, p. 489).   [25] Dehaene et al. (2017, p. 492).

dismiss this idea. But if they didn't secretly believe it, why would they still be arguing?

The ability of a 'many kinds' view to defuse heated debates is an attractive feature. Yet, if this view is correct, it leads to a puzzle about the ethical significance of sentience. Sentience is ethically significant; that is why we worry about whether it is present or absent. And phenomenal consciousness is a crucial component of sentience (Chapter 2). So, which of the kinds that partially attract the reference of 'phenomenal consciousness' underlie the ethical significance of sentience and why? For example, if we accept the C1/C2 view, which kind is associated with states that matter ethically: C1 or C2? Is either one of them (i.e. their disjunction) enough to ground moral status? Are both needed (i.e. their conjunction)? These questions are pressing, since these properties are likely to have very different distributions in the natural world. Moreover, in the future, AI may have one but not the other. The option space is larger still if we shift from two kinds to more than two.[26]

Defenders of a 'many kinds' view cannot just ignore these questions, but nor can they easily answer them. There will be a temptation to say: it is surely whichever kind is associated with *feeling*, with *experience*, that inherits the ethical role. But it is part of the 'many kinds' view that there is no further fact about this. If we posited a further fact, the picture would change into a form of dualism, and consciousness would (unambiguously) be the kind associated with feeling and experience. The 'many kinds' picture is not this. It is a picture on which ordinary terms like 'feeling' and 'experience' gesture indeterminately towards two or more kinds. I can see no way to resolve the question of ethical significance in an acceptable way, given these assumptions—a troubling situation.[27]

One radical option for the 'many kinds' materialist is to deny that sentience has ethical significance.[28] That way, the failure of these terms to pick out a unique natural kind would not leave ethical questions with indeterminate answers. We might, for example, pursue a view on which valence is the non-conceptual representation of value (and not essentially conscious) and on which all valenced states matter ethically to the same degree whether conscious or not. Yet if we take that path, we will have to accept that, if AI systems have valenced states, they thereby have morally significant interests on a par with any other bearer of valenced states, even if the states in question are

---

[26] He (2023) has proposed a far more pluralistic view.   [27] Birch (2022a).
[28] An option explored in recent work by Kammerer (2022) and Dung (2022), and supported by Carruthers (2019).

determinately non-conscious. That is an unpalatable implication (see Chapter 4 for further discussion of 'non-sentientist' ethical options and their problems).

3.4 Radical Alternatives

At the start of §3.3 we noted four radical alternatives to materialist orthodoxy: interactionist dualism, pan(proto)psychism, biopsychism, and the integrated information theory.[29] The first two find a place for consciousness in the causal order of the universe (and so differ from epiphenomenalism in this respect) but in a way that does not involve taking consciousness to be essentially physical. The third and fourth, meanwhile, are hard to place in relation to more traditional categories. Let us give these pictures their due. All are sometimes dismissed as examples of exactly the sort of unconstrained speculation that obstructs reasonable disagreement, but this would, I think, be unfair. *Cautiously formulated* versions of these views can be part of the zone of reasonable disagreement.

Interactionist Dualism

An interactionist dualist holds that the ontology of current physics will need substantial augmentation to explain consciousness. Some materialists would agree. But the interactionist adds that physics will need to be augmented with new ontological posits that are distinctive to conscious beings. The idea is that there are as-yet-undiscovered fundamental laws, properties, and maybe even (on the most radical version of the view) particles that are implicated in generating consciousness but absent from ordinary matter.

The need for special ontological posits distinctive to conscious beings is common to all versions of dualism, including epiphenomenalism. The big disagreement with epiphenomenalism is that, for the interactionist, these special properties and/or particles *causally interact* with the ordinary physical properties of our brains, nudging the storm of neural activity one way or another. So, some special causal power distinctive to consciousness must be added to the list of fundamental forces posited by physics. The standard model of contemporary physics says: there is gravity, electromagnetism, the

---

[29] This section draws on Birch (2020d).

weak and strong nuclear forces, and that is all. An interactionist says: there must, in addition, be some currently unknown entry point at the fundamental level of reality for irreducibly mental causation.

The interactionist's task is to find that elusive entry point, the point at which mental causation slips inside the workings of the brain. This has become a very unfashionable project. So unfashionable, in fact, that it is hard to imagine a project of that general shape receiving public funding. For critics, the view deserves its unfashionable status: if there were any fundamental causal powers distinctive to consciousness, we should expect over a century of intensive neuroscientific research to have encountered some glimmer of those powers, but we have not. The whole of contemporary neuroscience is compatible with neurons operating according to standard physical laws.[30] Yet defenders of interactionism can reply that this argument is an 'absence of evidence' argument, where the absence of evidence has resulted from the neglect and marginalization of the relevant questions, not from sustained testing of interactionist hypotheses.

In the late twentieth century, the Nobel laureate John Eccles, an expert on the synapse (the junction at which neurons meet and signal to each other), became convinced that there must be some role for mental causation in how a synapse works. He embarked on an idiosyncratic quest to find the entry point.[31] In a strange but undeniably creative paper, Eccles and collaborator Friedrich Beck set out a hypothesis on which a critical synaptic process, exocytosis, was activated by quantum tunnelling. Mental causation, they hypothesized, is able to nudge the quantum probabilities one way or another by tiny increments.[32]

We can be confident that this particular interactionist hypothesis is false, because it implies a prediction (the probability of exocytosis should be insensitive to temperature) that has been experimentally falsified.[33] But it would be hasty to write off a general type of picture of the mind-body relationship simply because one version of it is false. Moreover, it is surely a positive feature of interactionism that specific versions of it can be tested. Once falsified, interactionist hypotheses have a tendency to look ridiculous because of their inherent boldness—Descartes's pineal gland hypothesis is an early example of this—but it is no virtue when a theory evades falsification by failing to make any bold predictions at all.

---

[30]   Dennett (1991); Papineau (2002, app.).
[31]   Popper and Eccles (1977); Eccles (1989, 1994).   [32]   Beck and Eccles (1992).
[33]   Georgiev and Glazebrook (2014).

Russellian Monism

Dissatisfaction with both materialism and dualism has led to something of a revival, in recent decades, of panpsychist thinking.[34] In its contemporary form ('Russellian monism', after Bertrand Russell)[35] this is not the view that *all* the elements of human consciousness can be found inside fundamental particles. No one is suggesting that quarks consciously reflect or deliberate ('I'm tired of being uranium, fancy trying lead?'). The idea is that the most puzzling elements of conscious experience—the sources of the explanatory gap and hard problem—can be found in a simple form in at least some fundamental particles. What counts as a simple form is then up for debate. The situation is further complicated by 'panprotopsychism', the less radical view that, although even the basic elements of conscious experience are not there in fundamental particles, some important *precursors* to those properties are there, at least partially removing the mystery of why complex, organized assemblies of those particles can generate full-blown consciousness.

Both panpsychism and panprotopsychism face the challenge of explaining how vast multitudes of 'micro-experiences' (or 'micro-proto-experiences') in fundamental particles combine to form the single, unified 'macro-experience' or 'macro-conscious state' of a whole sentient being. In other words, panpsychists need to solve the so-called combination problem.[36] In so far as plausible approaches to this problem give a special role to the integrative properties of the embodied nervous systems of animals, the view can sometimes end up resembling single-kind materialism, at least as far as the distribution of sentience is concerned.

I do not support any version of Russellian monism myself, but I regard the views in this family as having a place in the zone of reasonable disagreement. They can be distinguished from completely unreasonable views that involve ascribing consciousness in something like its evolved, human form to ordinary material objects. The caricature of panpsychism that involves attributing pleasures and pains to rocks really is unreasonable, because it requires us to ignore all the hallmarks of a long evolutionary history in pains and pleasures, a history that links them tightly to the biological needs of living organisms (see James's evolutionary argument against epiphenomenalism, discussed in §3.2). But Russellian monists are not committed to pains in rocks.

---

[34] See the articles collected in Alter and Nagasawa (2015); Brüntrup and Jaskolla (2017); Seager (2019).

[35] Russell (1927/1992).   [36] Chalmers (2017).

Russellian monism, if true, would leave questions about the edge of sentience substantially open—as open as they are on any other philosophical picture. It would not imply, for example, that all animals are sentient, provided sentience is defined as the capacity to form *whole-animal*, *valenced*, *macro*-conscious states. What it takes to form these states would still be an open question, and much the same question that anyone else would ask, but with the term 'macro-conscious' where others would say 'conscious'.

Biopsychism

Many have entertained the idea that sentience might be present in all living things, including unicellular organisms. This idea that life itself suffices for sentience, even in the absence of a nervous system, can be called *biopsychism* (the term may sometimes also be taken to imply that non-living things *cannot* be sentient, but that is not how I am using it here).

It is not clear how to relate such a view to the traditional materialism/dualism/panpsychism axis of disagreement. Because biopsychism is primarily a bold claim about the distribution of sentience in the natural world, I think it is most naturally interpreted as compatible with any of the standard positions on the mind-body problem, none of which is committed to any particular view on the distribution of sentience. A biopsychist could, in principle, be a single-kind materialist who holds that the relevant kind is present in all life, a dualist who holds that psychophysical laws are at work in all life, or a Russellian monist who holds that all life achieves combination. Biopsychism, then, is not a fourth way, but a logically independent claim.

In recent decades, biopsychism has mainly been championed by theorists within the 'autopoiesis' tradition, a body of work that seeks to make sense of the nature of life in terms of 'a self-producing organization that dynamically maintains itself through time and constant material turnover'.[37] Although the connection to sentience strikes many readers (including me) as far from obvious, others see a close relationship. Lynn Margulis and Dorion Sagan, for instance, once claimed:

> Not just animals are conscious, but every organic being, every autopoietic cell is conscious. In the simplest sense, consciousness is an awareness of the

---

[37] Thompson (2022, p. 233). Godfrey-Smith (2016a) has entertained a version of biopsychism (though without endorsing it), leading to criticism from Rosenberg (2018).

outside world. And this world need not be the world outside one's mammalian fur. It may also be a world outside one's cell membrane. Certainly some level of awareness, of responsiveness owing to that awareness, is implied in all autopoietic systems.[38]

As Evan Thompson has stressed, claims such as these often blur a distinction we need to keep sharp: the distinction between mere responsiveness to stimuli, including responsiveness to attractive and aversive stimuli (which I have urged we do *not* call 'sentience') and valenced experience.[39] Undoubtedly all living cells do respond to stimuli, registering some as attractive and others as aversive, and a good theory of the nature of life will explain why. However, it does not follow that all living cells have valenced experiences. The idea of any logical entailment from autopoiesis to valenced experience is incorrect. In Thompson's words, 'if "consciousness" means feeling or sentience of value, then the above passage expresses an intuition or conviction, not an argument'.[40]

The absence of any logical entailments between theories of the nature of life (including the autopoietic theory) and claims about the nature and distribution of sentience does not mean biopsychism is *wrong*, nor does it render it an unreasonable *hypothesis*. On the contrary, it is a reasonable but highly speculative hypothesis. The mistake is to regard it as *more* than just a speculative hypothesis. When proponents of biopsychism claim it to be on a par evidentially with scientific theories of consciousness based on large bodies of empirical evidence—or even claim it to be a certainty—they are making a significant error. We will revisit this point in Part IV, when we will encounter some overconfident statements of biopsychist positions.

The Integrated Information Theory

The integrated information theory of consciousness (IIT) has become one of the most controversial ideas in contemporary consciousness science.[41] Some critics have even gone so far as to call it 'pseudoscience'.[42] It would be fairer, I think, to call it an outlier. Part of what makes it an outlier is that it rests on a

---

[38] Margulis and Sagan (1995, p. 122).   [39] Thompson (2022).
[40] Thompson (2022, p. 241).
[41] This subsection draws on a series of blog posts I wrote for the Brains Blog in 2023. The series also included a reply by Hedda Hassel Mørch (Birch and Mørch 2023).
[42] Lenharo (2023b).

metaphysical background picture very different from the materialist mainstream. As Francis Fallon and James Blackmon have remarked 'though a player in the debate within neuroscience over consciousness...[IIT] requires profound revision, or at the very least reframing, of how we understand the nature of physical reality.'[43]

At first, I saw IIT as complementing Russellian monism by providing a mathematical theory of the conditions in which combination occurs.[44] I now think that was a mistake. I initially underestimated the influence of the idealist tradition in philosophy on IIT. Consider the paper 'Only what exists can cause: an intrinsic view of free will', written by five of IIT's leading lights: Giulio Tononi, the original architect of the theory, plus Larissa Albantakis, Melanie Boly, Chiara Cirelli, and Christof Koch. The paper sets out the ontological commitments of IIT, and the picture it paints is one in which conscious minds are the ontological bedrock from which the rest of reality is constructed. The authors write, for example, that:

> Because I actually exist—as a 'large' intrinsic entity—the neurons of my complex cannot also exist. They cannot exist as constituents of my complex, because what actually exists is not a substrate as such but the substrate unfolded into a Φ-structure expressing its causal powers. And they cannot exist as small intrinsic entities in their own right because, if they specify a large intrinsic entity, they cannot also specify a set of smaller entities. Moreover, because my alternatives, reasons, and decisions exist within my experience—as sub-structures within an intrinsic entity—the neuronal substrates of alternatives, reasons, and decisions cannot also exist.[45]

The message is repeated: my neurons do not truly exist. They exist in a derived, extrinsic sense—as stable appearances that other conscious observers, such as neurosurgeons, can use as handles of control over my experiences—but they do not intrinsically exist. What intrinsically exists is my conscious point of view. Tononi and colleagues explicitly contrast their 'intrinsic powers ontology' with what they call the 'extrinsic substrate+ ontology', a view I would call orthodox metaphysical realism: a view on which fundamental particles are the ontological bedrock, neurons are constituted

---

[43] Fallon and Blackmon (2021).
[44] Hedda Hassel Mørch (2019) has examined the relationship between IIT in Russellian monism in detail. The Orch-OR theory developed by Stuart Hameroff and Roger Penrose also contains strong panpsychist or panprotopsychist elements (Hameroff and Penrose, 2014).
[45] Tononi et al. (2023).

by particles, and conscious experiences are somehow (and this has always been the hard part) produced by or grounded in the activity of neurons.

The closest philosophical precursor to IIT's ontology, in my view, is the idealism of Leibniz. IIT shares with Leibniz a commitment to the idea that what exists (at least, what exists fundamentally) is conscious. But whereas Leibniz's world consisted of conscious 'monads' causally isolated from each other, harmonized by God, IIT posits that conscious beings do causally interact with each other, and indeed this causation is at the heart of the theory. Against this background, the question arises: what is the interface through which one conscious being can interact with another? In IIT's language, what is the 'operational basis' of consciousness? The theory provides an answer: it will be the region of the brain with maximum causal integration, or maximum 'phi' (Φ). This is hypothesized to be a posterior hot zone at the back of the cortex. In short, brains, bodies, and neurons do not exist intrinsically at all, but brain regions of maximal Φ are the way in which conscious beings manifest extrinsically in the experiences of other conscious beings. They are what another conscious being looks like from the outside.

There is a kind of internal elegance, even beauty, to the IIT picture. I can see why it has attracted followers, and indeed why the followers are so ardent. In embracing a form of idealism, it comprehensively rejects the austere materialist outlook of the rest of neuroscience. It avoids any deflation of consciousness to a second-tier ontological status, preserving the intuitively appealing idea that consciousness is real and fundamental. It represents a certain kind of release from an unpleasant set of materialist strictures that seem to downgrade consciousness and its importance. Instead, it is the brain that gets downgraded. Tononi et al. even include illustrations in which a 2D, black-and-white brain dangles off a blossoming, technicolour mind, a mere operational substrate for what truly, intrinsically exists.

At the same time, it is easy to see why IIT has attracted trenchant critics. Some criticize the theory simply for having metaphysical commitments that cannot be tested empirically. I see this as a mistake, since any theory of consciousness must have such commitments (it is just that, when the commitments fall within the window of standard materialism, they are not especially salient). A fairer criticism is that IIT's explanatory credentials are very hard for neutral observers to evaluate, because the theory aims to explain consciousness in a way very unlike the way materialist theories seek to explain it. Indeed, for mainstream cognitive neuroscience, the kind of explanations offered by IIT are hard to recognize as explanations at all. Reading passages like the one I quoted, they are likely to say: 'an "explanation" on which neurons don't intrinsically exist, but exist only in a derived sense, as "operational substrates" for conscious subjects? What sort of explanation is *that*?' IIT may be offering explanations, but they are not the sort of functional-mechanistic-reductive explanations that neuroscience-as-usual recognizes. The charge here should not be 'pseudoscience!' but rather 'science too far away from mainstream neuroscience to be evaluated and tested in a common framework alongside mainstream theories!'.

How should we handle IIT when thinking about practical decisions at the edge of sentience? In consciousness science, researchers outside the IIT fold often distinguish *fundamental IIT* (or *strong IIT*), the full version of the theory including its idiosyncratic metaphysical background picture, from *empirical IIT* (or *weak IIT*), which simply claims that, in the human brain, the neural correlate of conscious experience is the posterior cortical hot zone, and that the high causal integration of this region (as captured in Φ) is what allows it to play this role.[46] Empirical IIT *can* be tested and evaluated alongside other hypotheses about the neural correlates of consciousness (see Chapter 5 for discussion of this type of work). However, it is also a very thin claim, compatible with any metaphysical background picture, and it has no particular implications for the distribution of sentience. The explanatory core of the theory has been taken out. By contrast, fundamental IIT includes elements that are strongly speculative, and therefore has a similar status to biopsychism. Like biopsychism, it can legitimately be offered *as a speculation*. However, it would be a mistake to describe the fundamental version of the theory as empirically supported.

3.5 Are Agency and Embodiment Necessary?

I want to turn now to an axis of disagreement that cross-cuts the divide between materialism and rival big pictures. It concerns whether *agency* and/or *embodiment* are needed for conscious experience.

I find my own thoughts on this fluctuate. When I consider other animals, it seems very plausible that embodiment matters. Yet neural organoids raise the possibility of what Tim Bayne, Anil Seth, and Marcello Massimini have called 'islands of awareness': conscious subjects with neither the ability to perceive the world nor the ability to act in it.[47] Meanwhile, the idea of sentient AI

---

[46] See Michel and Lau (2020); Mediano et al. (2019, 2022). Precise formulations of the distinction vary, and IIT's proponents themselves reject any such distinction.
[47] Bayne et al. (2020).

raises the possibility of dissociations between agency and embodiment. Future AI may have agency without any physical embodiment at all. In some cases, there may be robotic forms of embodiment but no *biological* embodiment (the importance, or not, of biological embodiment will be considered in the next section).

In saying that this debate cross-cuts the traditional debate between materialism and its rivals, I mean that it is possible to mix and match positions. A materialist may think that conscious experience is constituted entirely by brain mechanisms (as seems to be implied by the most popular neurobiological theories of consciousness) or may think the mechanisms loop out into other parts of the nervous system, body, and surrounding world (a view I associate mainly with Susan Hurley, discussed in a moment). A dualist may think the stuff of mind fuses only with neurons, or may think that it pervades the whole body of a conscious being (a view that can be found in the *Bhagavad-gita*, 2.17, and in Descartes's theory of 'animal spirits').[48] A panpsychist, meanwhile, may think a brain in isolation could achieve 'combination' or may think only a whole animal can do so.

Why think agency and/or embodiment might be necessary for experience? The strongest argument I have seen for this idea is in Susan Hurley's *Consciousness in Action* (1998). The starting assumption is that a conscious subject, to be conscious at all, must have a *coherent, unified perspective* on the world and on its own body (think back to Ernst Mach's drawing of his visual perspective in Chapter 1). Hurley then argues that the required unity relies on intentional agency and motor processes. My unified conscious perspective consists of all the content available right now, to me qua agent, for the formation of intentions.[49]

It would be too much of a detour to analyse the argument in detail. It is enough to note that it is inconclusive for a simple reason: the assumption that a conscious subject *must* have a unified conscious perspective to be conscious at all can be contested. We cannot rule out highly fragmentary, disunified forms of consciousness. We find these forms hard to imagine, from our current, highly unified vantage point; but we find any alien form of consciousness hard to imagine (even a bat echolocating), and so our difficulty imagining disunity is not a strong reason to doubt its possibility.

This idea has long been a point of contention in discussions of 'split-brain' cases, where a patient shows characteristic kinds of behavioural disunity after

---

[48] Blum (2019).
[49] The picture is concisely reconstructed by Ward (2016).

the severing of their corpus callosum, a structure linking the two hemispheres of the cerebrum. Due to the wiring of the visual pathways, the left-hand side of the visual field sends information to the right hemisphere and vice versa. In some split-brain patients, information presented to one half of the visual field is unavailable to guide actions controlled by the other. Thomas Nagel and Michael Lockwood took behavioural disunity as a challenge to the assumption that consciousness must always be unified.[50] In later discussions, Hurley and Bayne sought to reconcile the data with the unity of consciousness.[51]

If we grant that some form of embodiment and agency is a necessary condition for conscious experience, the next question is whether *virtual* embodiment and agency, of which a very simple form already exists in 'DishBrain', might be enough. We cannot rule out that it is. Indeed, I am doubtful there is anything real agency and embodment provide that a sufficiently rich virtual environment could not also provide. And so, once again, the zone of reasonable disagreement along this axis is quite wide. Views on which real agency and embodiment are required are reasonable, but so are views on which virtual forms are enough, as are views on which neither is required in any form.

3.6 The Relevant Scale of Functional Organization

Could an AI system achieve sentience? Could a robot? These questions are often said to turn on the 'substrate neutrality' or 'substrate sensitivity' of sentience. In fact, I have come to see this as an oversimplified way of framing the issue. However, I will discuss it in this language first—before explaining why I have come to see this as too simplistic.

According to substrate neutrality, sentience does not depend on the material substrate in which a system is realized, only on the *functional organization* of that substrate. Biology is optional. The functional architecture of the human brain, realized in a different medium, such as a future supercomputer, would still be sufficient for sentience. Substrate sensitivity, by contrast, says the nature of the material substrate does matter.

Framed like this, is there any evidence that could settle the issue? Susan Schneider has made a proposal for how the issue could eventually be resolved.[52] It relies on the conjecture that neural implants will one day be

---

[50] Nagel (1971); Lockwood (1989).
[51] Bayne (2010); Hurley (1998). Schechter (2018) is a good entry point to this debate.
[52] Schneider (2019, 2020).

developed to replace various human cognitive and perceptual functions. This will allow opportunities to test whether there is any associated loss of phenomenology when a function is taken over by an implant. For example, if we replace primary visual cortex with a functionally equivalent implant, does the subject report a total loss of visual phenomenology (similar to blindsight: see §5.2), unaltered visual phenomenology, or something in between: visual phenomenology that is still present but strangely altered? The idea is that, if the replacement robustly leads to loss of phenomenology, no matter how close the functional match gets, then this is evidence that the *substrate itself* is responsible for that loss—substrate sensitivity. Alternatively, if the visual phenomenology is unaltered, that provides evidence for substrate neutrality. An in-between case may suggest an intermediate possibility in which the character of our visual phenomenology is substrate sensitive but its presence or absence is not. Schneider calls this the 'chip test'.[53]

However, the inferences involved strike me as hasty. Loss of phenomenology might also be taken as evidence that we had matched functions at the *wrong level of analysis*. It might point towards the importance of very low-level functions we had neglected to match, such as the computations performed *within* neurons or phase-amplitude couplings between neurons.[54] It could yet be that emulating those low-level functions—in any substrate—would restore phenomenology. Schneider's thought is that if, over the long run, we really do try *everything*—complete matching of functions at *all* levels of analysis right down to the lowest levels—so that nothing except the material substrate is altered, and we *still* find a loss of phenomenology, that would be evidence of substrate sensitivity. I agree, but I am no longer confident the implants now being envisioned are physically possible.

Meanwhile, unaltered phenomenology might be taken as evidence that the neural basis of conscious experience is really somewhere other than where the implant is located. Inferences here are further complicated by the well-known plasticity of the brain. Perhaps the substituted region is *normally* part of the neural basis of consciousness but that basis shifts elsewhere when that region is substituted by an implant. A separate problem with this second inference, emphasized by David Billy Udell and Eric Schwitzgebel, is that

---

[53] The test somewhat resembles Chalmers's (1996, ch. 7) 'fading qualia' thought experiment, except that Schneider is envisaging an actual process of replacement with uncertain outcomes, not a counterfactual, idealized process of neuron-by-neuron replacement. Schneider also proposes a second test that is not a test of substrate neutrality, but looks for signs of consciousness assuming substrate neutrality. This 'artificial consciousness test' will be discussed much later, in §16.2.

[54] On computations within neurons, see Donato et al. (2019). On phase-amplitude coupling, see Munia and Aviyente (2019).

someone sympathetic to substrate sensitivity will doubt the reliability of introspective reports after the insertion of the implant. They will suspect that a loss of phenomenology is slipping under the radar of the subject's introspective mechanisms, which continue to receive the same informational inputs as before, leading to (mistaken) confidence that nothing has changed.[55]

These objections do not just lead me to have doubts about the chip test—they also lead to doubts about the standard way of framing the debate. The brain has functional organization at *many different levels of analysis*, from the high-level connectivity of large brain regions right down to the functioning within individual neurons, with many levels in between. Marr's three levels of analysis—the computational level, the algorithmic level, and the implementation level[56]—are a good starting point, but they subdivide into yet finer levels, and in reality I think that even to talk of 'levels' is to impose a degree of artificial discreteness on continuous variation in the *scale* of functional organization.[57] And to change the substrate (in any physically possible way) *is* to change many functional properties at smaller scales. Various views are then possible about how conscious experience and person-level cognitive processes (such as introspection) relate to these small-scale functions.

It is reasonable to think functional organization at small scales probably matters—and to doubt the idea of AI sentience for this reason.[58] It is important, though, that we do not allow our doubts to become false certainties. When thinking about risk and precaution, it is crucial to also take seriously the opposite view: a view on which only *large-scale* features of the computational architecture—such as the presence or absence of a global workspace or perceptual reality monitoring—need to be recreated in an artificial system for sentience to also be recreated. I will call this view *large-scale computational functionalism*. The tenability of large-scale computational functionalism has wide-ranging implications for the edge of sentience, because it implies a need to take seriously the possibility of sentience in systems that implement a *general type of computation* credibly linked to sentience in humans, even if the precise algorithms and the hardware implementation both differ a great deal.

---

[55] Udell and Schwitzgebel (2021). Chalmers's 'fading qualia' thought experiment faces a related problem. Chalmers says it is implausible to suppose a subject would mistakenly think their phenomenology was unaltered by a partial change of substrate. After all, their brain is functioning just as well as before. But someone sympathetic to substrate sensitivity will not accept that preserving functional organization at the neuronal level suffices for preserving functional organization at the person level. They will suspect the person's capacity for introspection will become unreliable.

[56] Marr (1982).

[57] Potochnik and McGill (2012). Shevlin (2021) has discussed related issues under the heading of 'the specificity problem'.

[58] See Aru et al. (in press); Godfrey-Smith (2016a); Seth (2021) for versions of such views.

3.7 Are There Borderline (Indeterminate) Cases of Sentience?

There is an axis of philosophical disagreement we have not yet considered. This book is called *The Edge of Sentience*, but an edge can be sharp or blurred. Think of transitional processes of various kinds: waking from sleep, emerging from a coma or from general anaesthesia, a fetus developing sentience in the womb, or a lineage evolving sentience over millions of years. In all these cases, we face the question of whether there is a sudden jump from the complete absence of phenomenal consciousness to its presence in at least a minimal form—a 'lights on' moment—or a gradual transition with a region of borderline cases in which there is no determinate fact of the matter about whether phenomenal consciousness is present or absent. On this second view, the metaphor of the light switch is no longer appropriate (not even a dimmer switch, because a dimmer switch still has a sharp transition from off to on). The transition is more like the transition from being non-bald to bald, or young to old, where there is no sharp threshold, no single moment at which the transition happens.[59]

The transitions just listed are very different from each other, and we do not need to take the same view about all of them. For example, one could consistently think that the transition from non-conscious to conscious life over evolutionary time involved borderline cases, while also thinking that transitions in individual humans, such as the transition from dreamless sleep to wakefulness, are sharp, or vice versa. We should, however, feel some pressure to be consistent about processes that *do* resemble each other at the neurophysiological level, such as emerging from general anaesthesia and emerging from a coma.[60]

Let us think for now about the evolutionary transition (while bearing in mind that very similar issues will arise in relation to the other transitions). Here, both views are reasonable, given current evidence. The idea of a sharp boundary may initially sound absurd, because it may sound as though it involves positing a sudden jump from no consciousness at all to consciousness in its rich, complex, human form. That would involve adaptive complexity arising from nowhere, but this is not what anyone is proposing. The idea is rather that there may be a sharp boundary between the absence of consciousness and its presence in an *extremely minimal and simple form*. This is

---

[59] Substantial discussions of this issue include Papineau (1993, ch. 4); Antony (2006, 2008); Birch (2021b); Godfrey-Smith (2020a, 2020b, 2021); Simon (2017); Schwitzgebel (2021); Hall (2022); Tye (2021).

[60] On the similarities, see E. N. Brown et al. (2010).

compatible with positing the gradual evolution of richer, more complex forms, as natural selection shapes the content of experience over time.[61] In other words, a defender of a sharp boundary can still be a gradualist about the evolution of rich, contentful experience. I find it helpful to call the view just described 'shallow gradualism', in contrast to the 'deep gradualism' of those who deny there was even a sharp transition between absence of consciousness and its most minimal form.

What would an 'extremely minimal and simple form' of experience be like? It is something we struggle to imagine, just as we struggle to imagine the experiences of any other animal. As noted in §2.1, Simona Ginsburg and Eva Jablonka have suggested the metaphor of 'white noise'. The idea of content-less, crackling static is still a familiar one, even in the digital age. We can also introspect statistical noise in our own experiences (think of looking around at night, trying to discern objects in the crackling static of your night vision). We can imagine an experiential state that is all noise, no signal. Ginsburg and Jablonka speculate that the first conscious experiences in the earliest nerve nets were something like this. Of course, 'white noise' is an imperfect meta-phor, because white noise has colour and timbre, whereas the state being envisaged is completely contentless. This contentless 'white noise' experience may have come along for free with the electrical activity of the first nervous systems, Ginsburg and Jablonka speculate, perhaps providing the raw mater-ial on which natural selection started working, gradually incorporating more and more content.

When I first thought about this issue, I thought even the idea of a sharp boundary between the absence of phenomenal consciousness and contentless 'white noise' was implicitly dualist and that a materialist should reject it:

> It seems unbelievable, given materialism, that there could be some sharp threshold of entry to the conscious club—parents out, offspring in, a sudden hatching of consciousness into the world—as the complexity of sensori-motor integration and global brain dynamics gradually increases. Such a threshold would seem arbitrary and inexplicable. Some form of dualism would be needed to explain it.[62]

Yet I have come to doubt my own initial reaction. The idea of a 'lights on' moment is certainly a vivid way of introducing the idea of an explanatory gap between the mental and the physical. We picture an animal with no conscious

---

[61] Birch et al. (2020b) outline a picture of this type.   [62] Birch (2021b, p. 121).

experience at all, and then imagine it producing an egg that generates off-spring with crackling white noise—and the explanatory gap hits us in the face with unusual force. What plausible small mutation could possibly produce such an extraordinary change? But this explanatory gap is with us regardless of whether we posit borderline cases. If we posit a region of borderline cases, we will still be able to compare the start point with the end point, and ask: what plausible *series* of small mutations could possibly produce such an extraordinary change? So, the fact that there is a glaring explanatory gap on the sharp boundary view is not a reason to think it implies dualism any more strongly than the deep gradualist alternative.

That said, the sharp boundary view still faces the question: what sort of neurobiological or cognitive property might plausibly have a sharp boundary? Some popular theories of consciousness seem difficult to reconcile with the sharp boundary view if accepted as *complete* theories. The global neuronal workspace (or global workspace) theory is a good example (Fig. 3.2). Interpreted as a theory of phenomenal consciousness, and not just cognitive access, this theory proposes that content becomes phenomenally conscious when it enters a global workspace mechanism that receives and integrates content from a wide range of sensory, evaluative, and memory processes and broadcasts the integrated content back to the input systems and onward to a wide variety of consumer systems, including mechanisms of voluntary report, planning, reasoning, and decision-making.[63] It is part of the theory that, within an individual human, the entry of a particular representation to the workspace is normally a sharp matter: a representation must be all in or all out, not in to some degree. Yet when we think about other animals, we can expect to find a variety of global workspace-like architectures, with variation on both the input side and the output side. The theory is silent on the question of how 'global' the broadcast needs to be to qualify as consciousness-generating, and it seems as though any sharp boundary between 'non-global' and 'global' broadcast would be arbitrary, a point Carruthers has made forcefully.[64]

Other theories, though, seem friendlier to a sharp boundary. For example, Hakwan Lau's 'perceptual reality monitoring' theory proposes that conscious

---

[63] Dehaene and Changeux (2011); Mashour et al. (2020). The basic idea was originally developed by Baars (1988).

[64] Carruthers (2019). For Carruthers, who (in recent work) regards the global neuronal workspace theory as a true and complete theory of consciousness, the result is massive indeterminacy in the distribution of phenomenal consciousness in the natural world. I think this indeterminacy explosion can be resisted (Birch 2020a), but some level of indeterminacy seems likely if the global neuronal workspace theory is true.

Fig. 3.2 The central idea of the global (neuronal) workspace theory of consciousness. Many local processors compete for access to a central workspace that integrates content and broadcasts it back to the input systems and onwards to a range of consumer systems. The theory fits well with a deep gradualist view of the evolution of consciousness, since the architecture of the global workspace is likely to vary in many ways across species, and the theory does not posit any sharp threshold at which the broadcasting is no longer 'global' enough to support consciousness. Drawing by Oryan Zacks (from Zacks and Jablonka (2023), CC-BY 4.0 licensed).

experience is associated with a form of self-monitoring, whereby perceptual representations are tagged as reliable or unreliable guides to the state of the external world right now.[65] Intuitively at least, this process of metacognitive tagging either does or does not occur: as with a checked bag at an airport, a tag is either attached or not attached. In contrast to global broadcasting, the presence/absence of a metacognitive tag is not something that obviously

---

[65] Lau (2022).

comes in degrees or that we should expect to vary by degrees across species. IIT also suggests a sharp boundary (a system is either a local maximum of Φ or it is not), as does Nicholas Humphrey's theory.[66] Humphrey posits a link between conscious experience and a feedback loop linking sensory, evaluative, motor, and self-monitoring brain regions, and argues that the completion of such a feedback loop is a sharp matter: there either is or is not such a loop.

The sharp boundary view, then, is a reasonable one to hold in our current state of uncertainty. But the deep gradualist view is *also* reasonable, and the reasons sometimes given for dismissing it are unconvincing. It has sometimes been said that borderline cases of phenomenal consciousness are inconceivable and therefore impossible.[67] By what standard are they inconceivable? I take the claim to concern what Thomas Nagel has called 'sympathetic imagination': the imaginative mode in which we first-personally project ourselves into another subjective point of view.[68] Critics of the deep gradualist view argue that it is impossible to sympathetically imagine a borderline case that is neither determinately conscious nor determinately non-conscious, and that this imaginative failure counts against the possibility of such a state.

I agree that our attempts to imagine a borderline case sympathetically always fail: they always result in imagining a state that is determinately conscious. When we try to imagine borderline cases, our first thought is to imagine barely perceptible stimuli. But there is, determinately, something it's like to have an auditory experience of a sound so quiet you aren't sure if you heard it at all. There is, determinately, something it's like to have a visual experience of a stimulus that flashes up so briefly you aren't sure whether you saw it or not. So, when we imagine these situations sympathetically, we are imagining determinately conscious states. The stimuli that produce these experiences may constitute borderline cases of *audibility* or *visibility*. However, the experiences are not borderline cases of *phenomenal consciousness*. They are clearly conscious.[69]

However, failures of sympathetic imagination do not imply impossibility. This can be seen by considering Nagel's example of a bat echolocating. When an animal possesses a sensory ability that we lack, the result is a failure of sympathetic imagination: we cannot imagine what it's like to be that animal. But this failure is no reason to think it impossible that other animals have sensory experiences associated with these sensory abilities.

---

[66] Humphrey (2022).   [67] Antony (2006); Simon (2017); Tye (2021).
[68] Nagel (1974).   [69] A point made by Papineau (1993) and Tye (2021).

One response might be to say that failures of sympathetic imagination provide only *defeasible* evidence of impossibility (this appears to be Michael Tye's view).[70] In the case of echolocation, there is a defeater: our imaginative powers depend on our sensory abilities. Yet, as Eric Schwitzgebel has argued, there is a defeater in the case of borderline consciousness too.[71] Sympathetic imagination is an ability that works by producing determinately conscious states. We have substantial control over the content of these states, but their determinately conscious nature is not something we can manipulate at will. We cannot use this ability to imagine anything that is not a determinately conscious state. Given this limitation, the fact that we cannot use sympathetic imagination to conjure up borderline cases is no evidence of their impossibility, any more than our inability to sympathetically imagine a bat echolocating is evidence of its impossibility.

We are not, therefore, in a position to rule out borderline cases of consciousness from the armchair. As with many-kinds materialism, I would *like* deep gradualism to be false, because its consequences for ethics are troubling. Just as many-kinds materialism would seemingly leave many ethical questions with indeterminate answers (because it is indeterminate which of the kinds carries the ethical significance of phenomenal consciousness), deep gradualism would lead to the problems of ethical indeterminacy regarding the borderline region. The problems might be a little easier to handle, especially if the borderline region is small (or if no extant organisms reside in it), but it is a problem nonetheless.

3.8 Summary of Chapter 3

Reasonable disagreement about sentience requires responsiveness to evidence and argument. It excludes baseless recommendations, dogmatic adherence to refuted theories, and morally abhorrent (e.g. sadistic) positions. However, the uncertainty in this area is such that many very different positions can be held by reasonable people who are well versed in the relevant science and philosophy.

This chapter has examined sources of disagreement that have their origins in the philosophy of mind. The focus in this literature has been on the 'phenomenal consciousness' aspect of sentience, not the valence aspect. Epiphenomenalism, the idea that consciousness leaves no causal imprint on

---

[70] Tye (2021).   [71] Schwitzgebel (2021).

the physical world, is a coherent possibility, but one that threatens to leave us unable resolve disputes at the edge of sentience using physical evidence. Luckily, it is empirically implausible, because consciousness bears all the hallmarks of being an evolved adaptation.

There are three main ways to make sense of the idea that consciousness has a place in the causal order of the physical world: materialism, interactionist dualism, and Russellian monism. Materialism covers many different positions on which conscious experience has a physical basis. A significant faultline is between materialists who identify phenomenal consciousness with a single, unified natural kind and those who suspect it gestures indeterminately towards two or more kinds. Interactionist dualism and Russellian monism have the status of radical alternatives, but cautious formulations of these views can be reasonable hypotheses.

Biopsychism can be reasonable too if advanced as a speculative hypothesis, rather than as a claim which receives support from evidence-based accounts of the nature of life. The integrated information theory of consciousness, which in its full form involves a metaphysical background picture with elements of Leibnizian idealism, has a similar status: a reasonable hypothesis to put forward, provided one is prepared to acknowledge its highly speculative nature. In both cases, the key is not to present a speculative metaphysical picture as a claim supported by scientific evidence.

There are several further axes of philosophical disagreement that lead people to disagree about the edge of sentience. One concerns the importance of agency and embodiment, real or virtual. Another concerns the scale of functional organization that matters: can small-scale (e.g. within neuron) functions make a difference to the presence or absence of sentience, or is large-scale functional organization (e.g. possessing a global workspace) all that counts?

A third concerns whether the edge of sentience is sharp or blurred: must there be a sharp transition between the absence of sentience and its presence in its most minimal forms, or can there (as with baldness, tallness, oldness) be borderline cases in which there is no determinate fact of the matter one way or the other? Both positions are reasonable, and the arguments so far given for each position are inconclusive.

The Edge of Sentience: Risk and Precaution in Humans, Other Animals, and AI. Jonathan Birch, Oxford University Press.
© Jonathan Birch 2024. DOI: 10.1093/9780191966729.003.0004

4

Ethics and Religion

Let us shift the focus from the metaphysics of sentience to its ethical significance. Here too, my aim is to map out the zone of reasonable disagreement, not to take sides and dig trenches. Chapter 2 introduced three ethical outlooks on which sentience has great significance: classical utilitarianism, Korgaard's neo-Kantian view, and Nussbaum's expanded capabilities approach. On these views, sentience is *necessary and sufficient* for moral standing, where moral standing (or moral status) implies that a being has interests that matter ethically for their own sake, and not just because they matter to some other being, such as a human owner.

We can call this a *sentientist* view of moral standing.[1] Sentientism, used in this way, is an umbrella term for a range of views that disagree on many things but agree on the special moral importance of sentience. Sentientism, however, does not exhaust the space of reasonable positions regarding the ethical significance of sentience, and it is time to consider the alternatives. One can depart by rejecting the idea that sentience is necessary for moral standing and/or by rejecting the idea that sentience is sufficient.

4.1 Bio- and Ecocentrism

Let us first consider the idea that sentience is unnecessary. There are various ways of developing this idea. One is a view on which *all living things*, sentient or not, but still regarded as individuals, have morally significant interests.[2] Reasonable versions of this view must still, I contend, allow that sentience is a major dividing line, in so far as sentience confers much greater moral significance on an organism's interests and warrants a claim to higher priority.

---

[1] The term 'sentientism' goes back to at least the 1970s, where it was used by critics of Peter Singer and Richard Ryder as a label for their position, and then adopted by Ryder (Woodhouse 2018). Gary Varner (1998, 2012) often used the term as a label for his view. Other sentientists in recent literature include Shepherd (2018); Lee (2019); DeGrazia (2021); and Gilbert and Martin (2022).

[2] Duran (1999); Goodpaster (1978); Kallhoff (2014). The idea that all life has moral standing, whether sentient or not, needs to be distinguished from the view that sentience is present in non-animal life, such as plants or microbes (Reber 2018; Segundo-Ortin and Calvo 2023). This view will receive criticism later.

You can think a non-sentient form of life deserves *some* minimal level of moral consideration and yet still think it appropriate to prioritize the interests of the sentient.

For example, forced to choose between the interests of a sentient dog and those of the non-sentient bacteria that have infected it, we must prioritize the interests of the dog by administering antibiotics. Animal welfare laws rightly force us to prioritize the sentient in such scenarios. They do not leave us with a free choice between the dog and its bacteria. That would be morally beyond the pale.

I suggest, moreover, that the relevant type of priority is *lexical* priority. This means that even the smallest interest of a single sentient being can outweigh even the gravest interests of any number of non-sentient microorganisms. A vet who asks 'How *many* bacteria exactly?' and has some threshold beyond which they would shift to prioritizing the bacteria is acting unethically—and asking one question too many. Rejecting sentience as a strictly necessary condition for moral standing, while accepting it as grounds for lexical priority, is still a view ultimately quite close to sentientism.

When a sentient being is compared with an individual non-sentient organism, the former deserves priority, but what if we instead consider *whole ecosystems*? For 'ecocentrists', the needs of whole ecosystems properly take priority over those of individuals.[3] Yet this view faces the challenge of explaining what counts as a morally significant ecosystem. Its defenders need to explain, in particular, why microbial ecosystems—such as the biofilms on our teeth, or a bacterial infection in a dog—can be legitimately destroyed to promote the interests of a single sentient being. One option would be to appeal to the irreplaceability of the ecosystem, but this leads us to the difficult territory of producing criteria for irreplaceability. A different option for the ecocentrist is to turn back towards sentience: intuitively, the most valuable ecosystems are those that teem with sentient life, not just microbes. This can be a point of agreement with the sentientist, who maintains that the source of an ecosystem's ethical significance is the sentient life it contains. There may still be disagreement regarding how much weight to give to the well-being of sentient animals in relation to other goals, such as preserving biodiversity, but these disagreements can occur against a background of substantial agreement about the relevance of sentience.[4]

---

[3] Callicott (2015); Leopold (1949); Taylor (1981). In a variant on ecocentrism, Palmer (2009) has argued that species are individuals with moral status.

[4] Mikkelson (2018) stresses that the well-being of individual sentient organisms does still matter on the most influential versions of ecocentrism. It is just that other things, such as biodiversity, also matter, so that the value of an ecosystem must be assessed holistically.

4.2 Agency-centric Views

We cannot be sure that insects are sentient (see Chapter 13), but it is harder to doubt that they are *agents* in at least a basic sense: they act in the world, and their actions are guided by internal representations of goals, such as the expected food reward associated with a particular location. Should we take *agency* as a sufficient condition for moral standing by itself, with or without sentience?

Nicolas Delon and colleagues (2020) have proposed a view of this type.[5] The main problem cases for such a view are artificial agents that we usually presume to be non-sentient. Think of a robotic vacuum cleaner steadily exploring a carpet. Perhaps we are hasty to dismiss the idea of sentience in AI (see Chapters 15–17), but for the sake of argument let us assume the vacuum cleaner feels nothing. Its agency alone still gives it moral standing, on the Delon et al. view. We have a moral reason not to wantonly thwart its attempts to achieve its goals.

This leads to a challenge for agency-centric views: how do you see the relationship between the interests of sentient beings and those of non-sentient agents like robotic vacuum cleaners? One answer is that the interests of the sentient take lexical priority over the interests of the merely agential; this brings the view very close to sentientism. But any other answer appears to have repugnant consequences, akin to the vet who prioritizes the bacteria in a dog's wound over the dog. For if we do not grant lexical priority to the interests of sentient beings, there must be some number of robotic vacuum cleaners whose interests, taken together, would outweigh a grave interest of a sentient animal. That position, while I think part of the zone of reasonable disagreement, is not easy to defend.[6]

4.3 Consciousness without Valence

'Sentience' as I use the term has two ingredients: phenomenal consciousness and valence. Are both needed for moral standing? Could it be that a capacity

---

[5] For related ideas, see Kagan (2019) and Wilcox (2020). Wilcox proposes agency as the fundamental criterion for moral status but also suggests it both entails and is entailed by sentience. Sebo (2017) takes 'perceptual agency' to be relevant to moral standing, but only in so far as it implies sentience.

[6] Bradford (2023) has defended a view on which the welfare goods of the conscious have much greater value than those of the non-conscious, but not lexical priority. Yet it seems to me that anything short of lexical priority runs into the 'how many bacteria exactly?' problem.

for phenomenal consciousness *alone* is enough and that a capacity for *valenced* experience is not needed?[7]

At least in principle, there can be phenomenal consciousness without valence: experiences that feel like something but feel neither bad nor good. It is not clear that humans can have such experiences (our overall conscious state arguably always contains an element of mood). But we can conceive of a being that has a subjective point of view on the world in which non-valenced states feature (it consciously experiences shapes, colours, sounds, odours, etc.) but in which everything is evaluatively neutral. Such a being would be technically non-sentient according to the definition we have been using, though it would be sentient in a broader sense. Would such a being have the same moral standing as a being with valenced experiences?

Vulcans are sometimes discussed in this context.[8] The original Vulcans in Star Trek are not wholly without valenced experiences, but we can conceive of a 'philosophical Vulcan' in which valenced experience is dialled down to nothing, leaving conscious but valence-free perceptual experience, conscious thought, imagination, and episodic memory in place. Carruthers discusses such a being, which he names 'Phenumb'.[9] Intuitively, a philosophical Vulcan has morally significant interests: it would be wrong to destroy such a being for no reason at all. Moreover, it seems intuitively wrong to give lower priority to its interests than to those of a human simply because of its dialled-down valence.

In opposition to this line of thought, Andrew Lee suggests the example of an animal that experiences a maximally simple non-valenced experience, such as an experience of slight brightness.[10] Ginsburg and Jablonka's 'white noise', mentioned in Chapters 2 and 3, is a similar example. Is the presence of conscious experiences of slight brightness, or white noise, enough to justify giving higher moral priority to the animal's interests, relative to those of a behaviourally similar but white-noise-free animal? Plausibly, it is not.

Can we reconcile the conflicting intuitions elicited by these cases? I think so. What the philosophical Vulcan shows us, I suggest, is that morally significant interests can, in principle, arise independently of valence. An autonomous rational being capable of reflectively endorsing goals and projects has such

---

[7] My discussion of this issue is based on Birch (2022a).

[8] For example by Chalmers, quoted in Wiblin et al. (2019), by Roelofs (2023), and by Shepherd (in press). Shepherd sees philosophical Vulcans as calling into question the necessity of consciousness or sentience for moral status, since some have the intuition that the Vulcan would still have moral status even if wholly non-conscious (though cf. Kriegel in press).

[9] Carruthers (2005, ch. 9).   [10] Lee (2019). See also Shepherd (2018).

interests, whether or not it has experiences of joy or frustration associated with the success or failure of those projects. In other words, the cases show us that there is a second path to morally significant interests, one that does not run via valence. A being with only experiences of white noise, or slight brightness, has neither of the two paths.

There is an important similarity between the two paths. For the Vulcan is still registering the promotion or thwarting of its interests in conscious experience. This is not true of the nerve net crackling with contentless white noise. So, I propose that the step up in moral standing associated with sentience is the change that comes when events that promote or thwart a being's interests are registered in experience. Valenced experience has a special importance because it is the most common way of registering interests in the animal kingdom. It enables the conscious registration of one's interests being promoted or thwarted in beings who lack sophisticated forms of rational agency. The philosophical Vulcan has found a different route to the same outcome.[11]

Rational beings who can reflect on their experiences, as we can, may endorse the pursuit of pleasure and other positive experiences (such as aesthetic experiences) for their own sake. For such beings, valenced experience acquires a *second* type of ethical significance. It is no longer just a currency in which interests register consciously: it is also constitutive of some of those interests. Consider, by way of analogy, the difference between someone who uses money as a currency and someone who comes to value money for its own sake. But my proposal is that even in beings with no capacity to reflect on their experiences or to value them for their own sake, valenced experience matters simply by virtue of registering interests.

To my mind, the most plausible overall picture is one on which a capacity for phenomenal consciousness is a necessary but not sufficient condition for moral standing. In addition, the ability to register the promotion or frustration of one's interests in experience, in the form of either valenced experience or the explicit rational endorsement of goals, must also be in place. White noise is not enough. So, my own view is close to the sentientist view but adds a qualification. This qualification is probably not very important right now, but it may become important in the future, if we happen to create AI systems that resemble philosophical Vulcans.

---

[11] Luke Roelofs (2023) has arrived at a similar solution, though emphasizing the kinds of experience that provide motivating reasons rather than those which register interests. These classes will overlap, but perhaps not perfectly.

4.4 Rationality-centric Views

There is an orthodox Kantian view (very different from Korsgaard's neo-Kantian view) on which sentience is insufficient for moral standing.[12] Kant's own ethical framework assigns fundamental value to rational beings, where 'rational' is understood in a demanding sense, implying a strong form of autonomy.[13] One can doubt whether even members of the species *Homo sapiens* truly possess autonomy in Kant's sense, because it seems to require the independence of the will from the laws of nature. In any case, non-human animals are not autonomous in this sense, and so, for Kant, they have no fundamental worth. Suppose, for example, you torture a dog. You have not, in Kant's view, violated any obligations you owe to the dog. You have done the dog no wrong. A dog is not the sort of thing that can be wronged. For some critics, this is such an awful result it warrants immediate rejection of the view.[14]

Kant himself was not entirely content with this result. In the *Metaphysics of Morals*, he suggests an escape route: we may not owe obligations *to* animals, but we can have obligations *in regard to* animals that we owe to ourselves. The idea is that, in torturing animals, killing them inhumanely, hunting them for sport, or treating them without gratitude, one acts without due respect for one's own humanity. Why? Because mistreating animals dulls one's 'shared feeling of their suffering and so weakens and gradually uproots a natural predisposition that is very serviceable to morality in one's relations with other human beings'.[15]

The general line of thought can be traced back to Thomas Aquinas, who remarked that 'it is evident that if a man practice a pitiable affection for animals, he is all the more disposed to take pity on his fellow men'.[16] However, Kant's position was not simply that in mistreating animals I make myself more likely to wrong other people. It was rather that, in mistreating animals, I violate a duty I owe to myself by weakening my disposition for 'shared

---

[12]   My discussion of this issue is based on Birch (2020b).

[13]   A rationality-centric outlook on ethics does not have to be combined with such a demanding view of rationality. There is room for views that link moral status to much more minimal kinds of rationality, more likely to be shared with many other animals (Thomas 2018).

[14]   A line of criticism pressed by Broadie and Pybus (1974); Regan (1983/2004); and Skidmore (2001).

[15]   Kant (1797/2017, 6:433).

[16]   The context is deeply disappointing for anyone hoping to find in Aquinas any genuine compassion for other animals. He adds: 'Consequently the Lord, in order to inculcate pity to the Jewish people, who were prone to cruelty, wished them to practice pity even with regard to dumb animals, and forbade them to do certain things savoring of cruelty to animals' (Aquinas 1947, Treatise on Law, Q102).

feeling' or (in modern terminology) empathy. For Kant, we have a duty to cultivate morally good dispositions, and we violate this duty if we do things that erode dispositions 'serviceable to morality'. This has come to be known as the 'indirect duty' view.

Some criticisms of Kant's view are misplaced. Robert Nozick for example, suggested that the Kantian view would permit animal cruelty as long as the agent kept in mind a clear line between humans and animals, so that torturing animals did not in fact produce any 'moral spillover' in the form of cruelty towards humans.[17] Kant would reply that, even if no actual spillover occurs, the agent has violated a duty to himself by failing to cultivate a sense of empathy.

Nonetheless, the view can be criticized on other grounds. Kant's view makes our duties concerning animals dependent on contingent psychological facts about what does, or does not, erode our sense of empathy. If Kant's psychological assumptions were shown to be incorrect for at least some humans, those humans might have no duties concerning animals. Consider, for example, people who are incapable of developing empathy, and who therefore cannot erode that capacity by torturing an animal. It appears that, for Kant, they violate no duty by doing so. It is fair to doubt a picture on which duties come and go with quirks of a person's psychological constitution.[18]

A related problem is that, in the modern world, many ways of mistreating animals involve long and indirect causal pathways that seem unlikely to erode a person's sense of empathy in their face-to-face interactions. Imagine a CEO who, mindful of the need to save money, writes an email ordering his farmers to increase the stocking density of their chickens. This is far away from the sort of immediate animal cruelty Kant clearly had in mind. Suppose the CEO does not erode his sense of empathy in any way by sending the email. On Kant's view, he has done nothing wrong, even if the welfare consequences are dire. It is fair to doubt a picture on which causal distance from the outcomes of your decisions carries this kind of moral significance.

Carruthers defended an idiosyncratic version of the indirect duty view in his 1992 book *The Animals Issue*, emphasizing not the consequences of animal cruelty for our sense of empathy, but rather the way in which cruelty expresses bad character traits and offends animal lovers, who have a 'right to have their concerns respected and taken seriously'.[19] This is a very weak

---

[17] Nozick (1974, p. 36).
[18] A criticism pressed by Allen Wood in an exchange with Onora O'Neill (Wood and O'Neill 1998).
[19] Carruthers (1992, p. 107).

constraint, as Carruthers admits. Our imagined CEO could satisfy it by respectfully listening to animal advocates and taking their feelings into account, even if he gives those feelings very little weight and makes all the same decisions. Ultimately, Carruthers regards concern for non-human sentient life as a distraction that will draw resources away from attempts to help other humans in need:

> Concern with animal welfare, while expressive of states of character that are admirable, is an irrelevance to be opposed rather than encouraged. Our response to animal lovers should not be 'if it upsets you, don't think about it', but rather 'If it upsets you, think about something more important'.[20]

He concludes that 'we should wish to roll back the tide of current popular concern with animal welfare'.[21]

I said earlier that some views—such as setting ourselves the goal of maximizing suffering—are too far away from our intuitive grasp of what morality involves to merit serious consideration. I cannot deny there is a temptation to say the same about the indirect duty view, but I think that would be a mistake. The zone of reasonable disagreement is intended to include deep value conflicts, such as the conflict that plainly exists between me and Carruthers (or, at least, his views in the 1990s). The boundary of the zone is to be drawn between, on the one hand, ethical outlooks that involve responding to reasons and evidence in a way that makes debate possible and, on the other hand, outlooks that derail the process of reaching agreement by being inherently dogmatic, baseless, or malevolent. We need to make room for good-faith attempts to defend aspects of the status quo, including very controversial practices. We will grapple more with these difficulties in Chapter 6.

4.5 Abrahamic Religions and the Stewardship Tradition

This is not the place for an exhaustive survey of religious perspectives on sentience. I do, however, want to challenge an assumption that there is a deep opposition between religious and sentientist outlooks. There are tensions, and they are serious, but I think they are not so deep as to preclude broad

---

[20] Carruthers (1992, p. 168).
[21] Carruthers (1992, p. 169). I doubt Carruthers still holds this view (based on personal correspondence) but he has not published anything that directly supersedes it.

consensus on many issues. A detailed survey is not needed to make this point, but engagement with at least some of the world's major religions is needed.[22]

One source of tension is that religions sometimes attach great value to forms of human life that are *not* realistic candidates for sentience, such as fertilized zygotes, simply because they are human. We will consider these points of disagreement in Chapter 10. Another is that the Abrahamic religions (Judaism, Christianity, Islam) afford an exalted status to humanity that can make it seem as though *non-human* forms of sentience count for little. That source of tension is real but sometimes exaggerated. Grounds can be found within such religions for respecting non-human sentient beings. Of course, no religion has settled answers to questions about sentience in organoids or AI, but all have faced questions about sentience in other animals, and it is in this context that reasons for respecting sentience can be identified.

In Christianity, God, in Genesis, gives humanity 'dominion over the fish of the sea, and over the fowl of the air, and over the cattle, and over all the earth, and over every creeping thing that creepeth upon the earth'. The term 'dominion' is perhaps most naturally read as permitting unequivocal domination. But critics have argued that dominion is a poor translation of the original Hebrew term *rādâ*.[23] The term also describes the relationship between God and humanity, and in that context suggests a relationship akin to the relation between shepherd and flock: a relation of stewardship. To the extent that intensive farming methods often exclude true stewardship, replacing it with ruthless exploitation, there is room for a Christian critique of those methods.

Some Christian theologians have looked for ways to move beyond stewardship in the direction of a more robust defence of animal rights. Andrew Linzey has defended a view on which 'animal rights' are best interpreted as deriving from God's right to have His creations treated with the loving attitude He wishes them to be afforded. On Linzey's view, the stewardship tradition underplays the extent of those rights, which extend to the right to not have their flesh eaten unnecessarily. Unusually, Linzey regards the incarnation of Jesus Christ as evidence that God loves embodiment in flesh. It is this idea of the value of 'Spirit-filled creatures, composed of flesh and blood', not sentience, that plays a fundamental role in Linzey's theory.[24] Sentience correlates with this property, but imperfectly so, and when they come apart (think here about

---

[22] Many perspectives will not be covered, including Shintō, Daoism, Muism, Caodeism, Bahā'ī, and Confucianism. To be clear, this is not intended to suggest that there is anything unreasonable about these perspectives: they are part of the zone of reasonable disagreement but not a part I can survey in detail.

[23] Preece and Fraser (2000).   [24] Linzey (1987/2016, p. 80).

the possibility of sentience in insects, organoids, and AI) Linzey's view appears to imply that the conditions for rights are not satisfied.

Judaism shares with Christianity a belief in Genesis and 'dominion'. But it also has the Talmud, a compilation of ancient teachings on the Torah that are regarded as sacred. The Talmud (Bava Metzia 32b–33a) contains a long and detailed debate about a line in Exodus that says 'When you see the ass of your enemy lying under its burden and would refrain from raising it, you must nevertheless help raise it' (Exodus 23:5). The debate concerns whether the duty to prevent animal suffering is a matter of rabbinic decree or, due to this line, a matter of scriptural law. Both sides agree there is indeed such a duty: they just disagree about its source.[25] The Talmud leaves this matter unresolved. It also leaves open the question of what exactly the duty requires, and whether the duty is direct or (as on the orthodox Kantian view) indirect. The result, as with Christianity, is that many different positions can be reconciled with scripture, ranging from robust defences of animal rights through to a Kant-style indirect duty view.

The Qur'an states, referring to camels and cattle, that 'we have subjected these animals to you so that you may be grateful' (Surrah Al-Hajj 22:36), a similar idea to dominion. Islam unambiguously permits the eating of animals of approved kinds, provided rules surrounding their slaughter and handling are met. At the same time, there is support in the Hadith for a compassionate attitude towards other animals. Asked if there is a reward for kindness shown towards other animals, Muhammad replies 'a reward is given in connection with every living creature', suggesting even acts of kindness towards plants may be rewarded (Riyad as-Salihin 126). Elsewhere Muhammad remarks that 'the worst of shepherds are those who are ungentle' (Mishkat al-Masabih 3688).[26]

There is no denying that Abrahamic holy texts often make difficult reading for those with sentientist sympathies. Yet the importance of compassion, and avoiding gratuitous suffering, is a common thread.

4.6 Indian Religions and *Ahimsa*

Indian perspectives on sentience share the Abrahamic emphasis on compassion but in some cases go much further. In 2023, I spent a week in Dharamsala, India, discussing animal sentience with Tibetan Buddhist monks. The concept

---

[25] Seidenberg (2006).
[26] Rahman (2017) puts heavy emphasis on remarks like this, seeing in them a strong defence of compassion towards other animals.

of sentience features very prominently in English translations of Buddhist works, hinting at an important convergence, but there are major differences in how the term is understood. The significance of sentience for Tibetan Buddhists derives from the idea that all sentient life is part of the cycle of rebirth, *saṃsāra*. Within this tradition, sentience may be defined as, roughly, 'that which makes a being part of saṃsāra'. All macroscopic animals, including insects, are assumed sentient. Microscopic animals and other microbes, unknown at the time the relevant texts were written, have an unresolved status. Since the Western concept of sentience has no connotation of a cycle of rebirth, it would be misleading to suggest the exact same concept is at work. There is, nonetheless, enough common ground to make dialogue possible.

I came to see that, although there is no single Tibetan Buddhist position on the ethical significance of sentience, there is a certain type of outlook, substantially shared with other Indian traditions. Tibetan Buddhism requires practitioners to cultivate an attitude of compassion and non-violence (*ahimsa*) towards all sentient life, but it does not lay down any strict prescription of what compassion and non-violence require. For some, the demands are great: the Buddhist inhabitants of the Tsum Valley in Nepal have for over a hundred years prohibited the killing of any wild or domestic animals living in the valley. On the whole, however, Tibetan Buddhists typically do kill and eat animals, often arguing that this is a practical necessity in the harsh conditions of the Tibetan plateau.

Jainism is known for interpreting the requirements of ahimsa in a highly demanding way.[27] Ordinary Jains adhere to vegetarianism and cannot kill any animal, while Jainist ascetics must take great care in all their activities to avoid harming in any living being. They are known for sweeping the street in front of them to clear away any insects on which they might step, and in some cases wearing mouth-cloths to prevent accidental inhalation of insects (Fig. 4.1). Since, for Jains, plants too are part of saṃsāra, ascetics must take care not to harm plants. They can accept food donations but cannot prepare food or have it prepared for them.

There is also a strong tradition of vegetarianism in Hinduism: around 40–50 per cent of Hindus are vegetarian.[28] This striking split tells us something of the internal diversity of Hinduism, which contains a great plurality of holy texts rather than a single holy book. It also reflects the outcome of a troubled history in which an overwhelmingly vegetarian culture was

---

[27] The source for this paragraph is Jainpedia (https://www.jainpedia.org).
[28] Corichi (2021).

Fig. 4.1 Two Śvetāmbara Jain ascetics, showing the traditional monastic broom and mouth-cloth. A public domain watercolour from the Wellcome Collection by an unknown Indian artist.

disrupted by British colonial rule. There were no slaughterhouses in India until Robert Clive, 'Clive of India', introduced them.[29]

Sikhism emerged from Hinduism in the fifteenth century. It is, like the Abrahamic faiths, monotheistic with a single authoritative scripture (the Guru Granth Sahib), yet it retains an Indian outlook on many issues, including that of reincarnation. Regarding other animals, the Guru Granth Sahib instructs Sikhs to 'show kindness and mercy to all beings, and realize that the Lord is pervading everywhere' (Ang 508). Around 50–60 percent of Sikhs interpret this as requiring vegetarianism.[30]

When I reflect on my visit to Dharamsala, I can see it shaped my thoughts on these issues, though not in the way I thought it might. At some level, I hoped to find what Owen Flanagan claims to have found in *The Bodhisattva's Brain*: a tradition that has converged, from a very different direction, on an outlook agreeable to many Western atheists, at least once a few dispensable metaphysical commitments are dropped.[31] In all honesty, that was not what I found at all. The idea of a cycle of rebirth or reincarnation[32] is at the core of

---

[29] Krishna (2022).   [30] Corichi (2021).   [31] Flanagan (2011).
[32] Tibetan Buddhists favour 'rebirth'. Their deepest disagreement with Hinduism concerns whether there is a persisting self or soul (*atman*) that is reincarnated. On the Tibetan view, a process of rebirth occurs, but no persisting thing is reincarnated.

these traditions and their ways of thinking about sentience: it is not an optional add-on. We should not pretend otherwise. Importantly, though, people can end up agreeing on similar actions for very different reasons: reasons internal to their particular worldviews. This is what is happening, for example, when Jains and Western animal lovers converge on the importance of vegetarianism.

4.7 Summary of Chapter 4

Chapter 2 highlighted a convergence across classical utilitarianism, Korsgaard's neo-Kantianism, and Nussbaum's capabilities approach regarding the ethical significance of sentience. These 'sentientist' outlooks can be contrasted with those that deny the necessity and/or sufficiency of sentience for moral standing.

The clash between sentientist and biocentrist/ecocentrist positions is easily overstated: reasonable versions of these views will grant some significance to sentience, while insisting that other ecological properties such as biodiversity also matter. Meanwhile, the possibility of Vulcan-like beings who have the consciousness aspect of sentience without the valence aspect suggests a qualification to a pure sentientism may be needed. This qualification may matter in the future (if we develop conscious but valence-free AI) but has little immediate significance.

A more serious challenge to sentientism comes from agency-centric and rationality-centric positions. An example of the latter is orthodox Kantianism, which allows only indirect duties (formally owed to ourselves) concerning non-rational sentient beings. The need to bring rationality-centric viewpoints with us places a limit on how ambitious we can be when looking for ethical consensus.

Another challenge comes from the Abrahamic religions, which give only very limited moral standing to non-human sentient beings. We can, however, find in all of them support for duties of stewardship, including the duty to avoid causing gratuitous suffering. Indian religions, by contrast, share important elements of the sentientist outlook, though they have reached these overlapping conclusions by a very different path.

The Edge of Sentience: Risk and Precaution in Humans, Other Animals, and AI. Jonathan Birch, Oxford University Press.
© Jonathan Birch 2024. DOI: 10.1093/9780191966729.003.0005

5

The Science of Consciousness and Emotion

5.1 Grades of Optimism

It is time to cross that vague border from the philosophy to the science of sentience. Two areas of science are especially relevant: the science of consciousness and the science of emotion. Although these may seem like closely related topics, there is a surprising amount of distance between them. Many consciousness scientists rarely think about emotion, affect, or valence (as we will see, they focus primarily on vision). Meanwhile, many emotion scientists rarely think about consciousness. Two of the best-known exceptions—Joseph LeDoux and Jaak Panksepp—will feature heavily in the chapter.

To say that these fields contain a lot of disagreement would be an understatement. This is not the place for a detailed survey of all the positions currently held. When theories are coming and going at speed, journal articles do a better job at providing regular updates.[1] Instead, I want to concentrate initially on the underlying reasons for disagreement in the science of consciousness. Those reasons are likely to outlive currently popular theories. I will then turn to the special case of valenced experience, usually studied under the heading of 'emotion' or 'affect', and consider how those general sources of disagreement surface in this case.[2]

There are two types of strong optimist I oppose. One is the optimist who says: 'I already know the correct theory of sentience. It is the one outlined in my latest book. It implies that sentience is present in cases ABC, absent in cases XYZ. So, enough of all this blather about uncertainty'. The second is the type who, while acknowledging that we do not have a complete theoretical picture now, nonetheless believes it is just around the corner. They might say: 'Why expend so much effort developing a precautionary framework for

---

[1] See Seth and Bayne (2022).
[2] Along similar lines, Matthias Michel (2019) has provided an analysis of the persistence sources of underdetermination in consciousness science from the nineteenth century to the present day.

managing uncertainty? Let's continue our rapid progress, and we'll know which systems are sentient and which are not by the time your framework has been implemented.'

To resist these strong optimists, I need to present a view of contemporary consciousness science and emotion science that may seem pessimistic. I am not, in fact, a pessimist about these areas at all, in absolute terms. I think substantial progress has been made in the last few decades. It is *strong* optimism about the science of consciousness or emotion—optimism that claims certainty to be within our grasp—that I see as misplaced. Indeed, not just misplaced but actually dangerous, if used as a reason to avoid talking about how to manage our uncertainty.

5.2 The Conscious and the Unconscious: The Case of Blindsight

I will start with the case of conscious visual experience. Conscious vision is not sufficient for sentience in the way I am using the term in this book, because I am using 'sentience' to refer to the capacity for valenced experience. In principle, a visual experience could be entirely without valence: it could feel neither good nor bad; it could feel completely neutral. So why start with vision? Because human consciousness science has intensively investigated the difference between conscious and unconscious vision for the best part of a century, leading to a rich body of evidence, detailed knowledge of the relevant pathways, and the best case for resolving disagreement. And yet we find very little agreement regarding the neural basis of conscious visual experience. Why is this?

Let us go back about fifty years. It is hard to overstate the importance of the discovery of blindsight for the science of human consciousness. Blindsight can occur when a patient has damage to their primary visual cortex, V1, at the back of the brain. People with blindsight report seeing nothing whatsoever in a particular region of their visual field, a region known as their blind field or scotoma. Yet when a stimulus is presented in the blind field, they can use visual information about that stimulus to perform at levels well above chance in tasks where they are forced to respond or choose between options.[3] They can even sometimes navigate their way around obstacles that, according to their reports, they cannot consciously see at all. De Gelder and colleagues describe

---

[3] Ajina and Bridge (2017); Cowey (2010).

a person with blindsight who, despite being fully blind across the whole visual field according to their own reports, 'can successfully navigate down the extent of a long corridor in which various barriers were placed...skillfully avoiding and turning around the blockages'.[4]

Taken at face value, blindsight presents an extraordinary opportunity to compare conscious and unconscious processing of the same visual stimulus in the same subject. Present the stimulus to the blind field, and it will register without being reported. Present it to a non-blind part of the visual field and it will be consciously seen. This allows us to ask: what advantages does conscious processing of a stimulus confer? What does it enable or facilitate? It seemed reasonable to hope, when blindsight was discovered, that it would make it possible to pin down the functions of conscious visual experience and the brain mechanisms responsible for those functions.

We now have an impressively detailed picture of the pathways involved in blindsight, yet this picture has not led to any consensus around the function or neural basis of conscious vision. The basic difficulty is that the putatively unconscious visual pathways at work in blindsight differ in lots of ways from those involved in normal conscious vision. In blindsight, visual information bypasses the visual areas at the back of the cortex, instead typically flowing from the optic tract to the superior colliculus (in the midbrain) and the pulvinar (in the thalamus), before eventually reaching the amygdala and middle temporal gyrus.[5]

The important point is that blindsight does not simply 'switch off consciousness' in the blind field, leaving all else the same. Blindsight is a profoundly different mechanism. So, when we find differences in function and neural activation between normal conscious vision and blindsight, we cannot tell which differences are due to the involvement (or not) of consciousness specifically, and which differences are due to other differences between the pathways, such as the information reaching (or not reaching) other mechanisms that are not part of the basis of consciousness at all.

As a result, the blindsight data can be reconciled with a wide variety of different theoretical perspectives. Most obviously, the data are compatible with theories on which the visual areas at the back of the cortex (directly damaged in blindsight) are a constituent part of the neural basis of visual experience.[6] However, they are also compatible with theories on which mechanisms in the

[4] de Gelder et al. (2008, p. R1128).   [5] Ajina and Bridge (2017).
[6] Brogaard (2011); Lamme (2001); Pascual-Leone and Walsh (2001); Silvanto et al. (2005); Tong (2003).

front of the cortex form the neural basis of visual experience, since the blindsight pathway does not reach these areas either. These prefrontal areas are downstream of the damage, receiving no visual information about the blind field, so the absence of conscious experience in the blind field is fully compatible with these areas playing a pivotal role.[7] In short, the blindsight pathway lacks *something* that leaves it with no associated conscious experience, but there are many candidates for that something, and we are not able to zero in on a specific property or mechanism.

All of this, however, involves accepting the received wisdom that blindsight is a fully unconscious form of vision, and even this can be challenged. The received wisdom rests on the verbal reports of people with blindsight, who report seeing nothing in their blind field. But must we interpret these reports as reliably indicating that their residual vision in the blind field is unconscious? There is an alternative view (defended vigorously by Ian Phillips) on which blindsight patients have *severely degraded but still conscious* vision in their blind field. On this hypothesis, they report seeing nothing because the degradation is so severe and the experience so unlike normal visual experience. Their conscious vision in the blind field takes a form in which 'familiar contents have been dramatically stripped away or changed beyond comparison'.[8] For example, the most famous blindsight patient, GY, has described the experience of detecting a moving stimulus in the blind field as that of seeing 'a black shadow moving on a black background' and has said that 'sometimes I'm aware of a motion, but that motion has no shape, no color, no depth, no form, no contrast'.[9]

This picture of blindsight as degraded conscious vision is unorthodox in consciousness science, and deservedly so, for reasons explained by Matthias Michel and Hakwan Lau in their response to Phillips.[10] Among other, more technical criticisms, Michel and Lau stress that GY's reports of residual awareness concern moving stimuli, whereas the strong performance in forced-choice tasks also exists for static stimuli, of which GY reports no awareness whatsoever. They emphasize that there can be huge discrepancies between task performance and reported awareness. In some experiments, task performance is carefully matched between the normal and blind fields by strengthening the stimulus presented to the blind field, and yet reported awareness still differs drastically.[11]

[7] R. Brown et al. (2019); Lau (2022); Mashour et al. (2020); Weiskrantz (1997).
[8] Phillips (2021b, p. 15).   [9] Phillips (2021b, p. 15).
[10] Michel and Lau (2021). For Phillips's responses, see Phillips (2021a).
[11] Persaud et al. (2011).

For all this, Phillips's view has a place in the zone of reasonable disagreement. Phillips has not conclusively established the correctness of this view of blindsight, but he has shown that there is a fair if unorthodox reading of the empirical evidence according to which the blindsight pathway does generate a very simple form of conscious visual experience. It is a realistic empirical possibility that human visual experience does not strictly require the visual or prefrontal cortex.

An upshot is that a *yet wider* range of theoretical perspectives can be reconciled with the blindsight data, including theories on which the midbrain mechanisms involved in blindsight, such as the superior colliculus, already suffice for conscious visual experience by themselves, with or without the involvement of the cortex. An important example of such a theory is that of Bjorn Merker, which posits that conscious sensory experience can be generated by 'the triad of large structures physically encircling the brainstem reticular formation at the level of the midbrain, namely, the periaqueductal gray matter, the superior colliculus, and the substantia nigra (or their non-mammalian homologs/analogs)'.[12]

Merker's theory does not deny the importance of the cortex to the content of normal conscious experience in humans. But the theory sees the cortex as more akin to a graphics card than a CPU: the cortex greatly *enriches the content* of our experiences when working properly, elevating our visual content from 'black shadows on a black background' to full, rich technicolour, but it is not required to have conscious experiences of a less rich variety. As Merker recognized from the beginning, the theory has potentially significant implications for people with brain injuries and for non-human animals, because it implies that at least a minimal form of conscious experience can be achieved without a cortex or anything functionally analogous to a cortex.

Brainstem-centred theories such as Merker's have always struggled to accommodate blindsight. The blindsight data, interpreted in the orthodox way, support a cortex-centred view on which the brainstem is like a power cable, necessary to 'switch on' conscious experience (and involved in regulating sleep-wake cycles) but not constitutive of it, any more than a TV's power cable constitutes the picture. For, after all, blindsight is supported by midbrain mechanisms and yet has no associated phenomenology, according to the received wisdom. This was the source of much of the initial sceptical reaction to Merker's theory.[13] If, however, Phillips is correct to suggest that blindsight is degraded conscious vision, Merker's theory becomes more plausible.

---

[12] Merker (2007, p. 110).
[13] Doesburg and Ward (2007); Piccinini (2007); Schlag (2007); Watkins and Rees (2007).

5.3 The Conscious and the Unconscious: Wider Lessons

The blindsight literature is just one part of contemporary consciousness science, but it crystallizes some persistent sources of disagreement that can be found right across the field. The basic methodological strategy exemplified by blindsight research—find a way of dissociating conscious from unconscious perception, then study the neural and functional differences between the two dissociated mechanisms—is used throughout the discipline and faces some very general challenges.

One is a problem that arises from reliance on any kind of voluntary report, verbal or non-verbal: the criterion problem.[14] A person asked to report their experiences, but struggling to distinguish a signal from noise, will have an implicit criterion for reporting a stimulus as seen rather than unseen. This criterion will balance the risk of false positives against the risk of false negatives, erring on one side or the other. Some people have more conservative reporting criteria than others: that is, some people place greater weight on avoiding false positives and are more reluctant to report a very faint stimulus as seen. When a stimulus is reported as unseen, it may be that it did not register in their conscious experience at all. But it may also be that it did register subtly but was not reported because it fell short of a conservative reporting criterion.

One possible way around this problem is to avoid voluntary reports by instead asking subjects to bet on how well they performed in a forced-choice task: 'post-decision wagering'.[15] Wagering can reveal dissociations between a subject's task performance and their ability to monitor their task perform-ance, a form of metacognition: thinking about one's own cognitive processes. GY, for example, is strikingly poor at betting on his success or failure at dis-criminating stimuli in the blind field, relative to the normal field.[16] When the stimulus is presented in the normal field, he can bet skilfully on his own task performance, but when the stimulus is presented in the blind field, his wagers deteriorate into random guesses. Yet a contentious theoretical assumption is needed to interpret this pattern as evidence that blindsight is unconscious: the assumption that consciousness reliably brings with it the ability to moni-tor one's own performance in discrimination tasks. This will be readily accepted by those who already posit a robust link between consciousness and

---

[14] Eriksen (1960); Irvine (2012); Merikle et al. (2001); Michel (2019); Peters and Lau (2015); Peters et al. (2016, 2017).
[15] Persaud (2009).   [16] Persaud et al. (2007).

metacognition, but rejected by those (like Merker) who maintain that there is no such link.[17]

The blindsight debate also crystallizes a second general problem: the problem of confounders. For even if you reach the point where you are sure you have identified two visual pathways (one consciousness-involving, one wholly consciousness-free) you still face the challenge of trying to identify which *parts* of the consciousness-involving pathway are part of the basis of conscious experience, as opposed to being mere precursors or mere consequences. Everyone agrees retinal stimulation is not a constitutive part of the conscious state (just a precursor), and everyone agrees that the behavioural output (e.g. a verbal utterance) is not part of it either (just a consequence). But there will always be a long chain of steps between retina and report, and about each of these steps we can ask: is it a mere precursor, a mere consequence, or part of the neural basis of consciousness?[18]

It is not clear how to answer this question without falling back—circularly—on a contentious theoretical assumption. Proponents of particular theories tend to regard the processes taken to be important by their rivals as mere precursors, or mere consequences, of conscious sensory experience, and thus as confounders to be controlled-for rather than the basis of consciousness. Those who posit the neural basis of consciousness to be in the back of the cortex see processes in prefrontal cortex as downstream of experience—and a source of confounders for which we need to control. Meanwhile, those who favour the front of the cortex see local recurrent processing in visual areas as upstream of experience—and a source of confounders for which we need to control.

The result is an impasse. Neither side is able to perform an intervention in which they hold fixed everything upstream and downstream of the mechanism they regard as pivotal, so as to observe whether phenomenal consciousness is switched on and off by manipulating that mechanism in isolation. The fundamental roadblock is not that this sort of intervention is technically difficult, nor that it is unethical to perform in humans. It is that we unavoidably need the downstream processes to verify whether phenomenal consciousness was off or on. The very processes many see as sources of confounders are also processes on which we depend for evidence of the presence of the phenomenon.

In sum, consciousness science is in a seriously tough methodological predicament even before we consider any non-human cases, and even when we

---

[17] Seth (2008); Phillips (2021a).   [18] Aru et al. (2012).

focus on vision, where the science is most mature. Voluntary report is gener-ally held up as the 'gold standard' of evidence: other putative indicators of consciousness are typically expected to prove their mettle through calibration against verbal report. Yet it is a gold standard that leaves us with no watertight way of establishing the absence of conscious perception of a stimulus, because alternative explanations based on conservative response criteria are impos-sible to rule out even in what initially seem (as with blindsight) to be clear-cut cases. Even when we are convinced that a stimulus has been processed uncon-sciously, there are likely to be differences at every stage between this pathway and a consciousness-involving pathway, with no uncontroversial way to pin down which parts of the pathway are responsible for consciousness.

The underdetermination of theory by data is a problem in all sciences, but there is no reason to think all research programmes are equally affected, and consciousness science has an unusually severe case.

5.4 Conscious and Unconscious Affect?

With all this in mind, let us now turn from vision to affect—where things get harder. In the case of vision, we have various strategies for dissociating uncon-scious and conscious pathways (such as studying people with blindsight or presenting subliminal stimuli to healthy subjects) and these strategies hold some promise, despite continuing controversy. In the case of affect, methodo-logical strategies for separating the unconscious from the conscious are much less mature.

It is easy to trip up over terminology here, because the idea of 'unconscious affect' or 'unconscious valence' may sound like a contradiction in terms. True enough, if we use 'valence' to refer to a hedonic quality of a conscious experience, then valence is conscious by definition. Yet we cannot make the substance of the problem go away simply by defining valence in this way. The core issue is that many animals, including humans, may well have mechanisms that, like the blindsight pathway on the orthodox interpretation, are non-conscious functional analogues of a conscious pathway, flowing from a stimulus to a flexible, adaptive behavioural response (such as avoiding or approaching the stimulus) without any role at all for conscious experience.

For comparison, think of reflexes, such as withdrawing your hand from a hot stove: in these cases, the pathways never even reach the brain. Accordingly, the animal pain literature contains a great deal of work that attempts to disen-tangle reflex pathways from those that do involve the brain (some of this is discussed in Part IV). Unfortunately, we cannot pretend that the conscious/unconscious distinction maps neatly onto the distinction between pathways that involve the brain and pathways that do not. We also need to consider the possibility of pathways that run via the brain, involve positive or negative evaluations of a stimulus, and drive approach or avoidance behaviours, all while remaining fully unconscious. These pathways—if they exist—are the affective analogues of the mechanisms of blindsight. We could describe them as 'unconscious valence', though I would prefer to call them 'unconscious functional analogues of valenced experiences'. But the label is unimportant. The deeper question is methodological. How can we reliably disentangle valenced experiences from their unconscious functional analogues?

Attempts to disentangle valenced experience from its unconscious functional analogues often draw inspiration from the case of vision. In 'affective priming' studies, an affectively salient stimulus (such as an angry or happy face) is presented to subjects in two ways: subliminally (i.e. reported unseen) and supraliminally (i.e. reported as seen). One apparently robust message from these studies is that some autonomic arousal responses traditionally interpreted as 'fear responses', such as breaking out in a sweat (as measured by skin conductance), can be evoked by a subliminal stimulus. Indeed, when the stimulus is reported as seen, these responses tend to be weaker even though the stimulus itself is stronger, perhaps indicating top-down inhibition of arousal (you know it's just a picture, so why be afraid?).[19] Meanwhile, in studies of so-called 'affective blindsight', an affectively salient stimulus is presented to a blindsight patient's blind field. Subjects say they saw nothing, but are nonetheless able to guess the valence of the stimulus (e.g. happy or angry) better than chance.[20]

These studies, in relying on subliminal visual stimuli, are subject to the same sources of uncertainty as studies solely concerned with vision. It is hard to be sure that the perceptual processing was genuinely unconscious, given the criterion problem discussed earlier. Even granting that the stimuli were unconsciously perceived, there is also the challenge of showing that the affective part of the pathway, and not just the perceptual part, occurred nonconsciously. Pathways that are unconscious at the perceptual stage do not have to stay that way to the end. The possibility of unconscious vision eliciting subcortical activity which is then experienced as conscious affect is hard to rule out.[21] Indeed, in one affective blindsight study, researchers found that

[19] Tamietto and de Gelder (2010).   [20] Celeghin et al. (2015); Hamm et al. (2003).
[21] Berridge (2004).

subjects with so-called affective blindsight could verbally report the valence of the unseen stimulus in addition to guessing correctly in forced-choice tasks, suggesting that the affective response was not unconscious after all.[22] If this is correct, then the label 'affective blindsight' is rather misleading. Blindsight of a visual stimulus is still involved, but the affective part is not unconscious.

One affective priming study, by Piotr Winkielman and colleagues, made an effort to rule out the possibility that the effects of unseen stimuli were mediated by conscious feelings. Subjects were given a subliminal affective prime (a happy or angry face) and then asked to pour, consume, and evaluate a lemon-and-lime flavoured Kool Aid. The headline result was that 'subliminal smiles caused thirsty participants to pour and consume more beverage…and increased their willingness to pay and their wanting more beverage.'[23] More precisely, 'thirsty participants drank 280% more of the beverage after happy primes than after angry primes.'[24] Could it have been that subjects consciously felt better after seeing a subliminal smile, and that this uplift in their mood caused a greater propensity to try the drink? To test this, Winkielman and colleagues explicitly asked subjects to rate their mood on a scale of −5 to +5, before and after the prime, and found no evidence of a congruent effect on explicit mood ratings. Winkielman's lab has since replicated both the priming effect and the absence of any relationship to explicitly reported mood.[25]

This does not fully settle the issue, however, for two main reasons. First, affective primes are weak stimuli exerting weak effects on mood. Might they have been too weak for the subjects' introspective abilities to discriminate the differences? The ideal would be to show that even in subjects with high introspective acuity in relation to mood (assessed independently) the affective prime still did not register in their explicit reports. Second, it is only fair to note that priming studies have become generally controversial due to their poor replication rates.[26] This has led to renewed emphasis in psychology on the importance of replications in other labs. That is not a criticism of the original study, but it is a reason not to let a huge amount of weight rest on it.

In a different priming study, some participants (presented with subliminal faces) were explicitly instructed to use their feelings as a guide to the valence of the emotion expressed in the face and yet failed to perform any better than controls.[27] LeDoux and collaborators have interpreted this as showing that

[22] Anders et al. (2004).   [23] Winkielman et al. (2005, p. 121).
[24] Winkielman et al. (2005, p. 127).   [25] Winkielman and Gogolushko (2018).
[26] Open Science Collaboration (2015).   [27] Bornemann et al. (2012).

the process of reading the valence of the facial expression was unconscious.[28] The underlying (and I think plausible) assumption here is that, if conscious feelings were mediating successful performance in this task, we would expect subjects to do better at reading the faces when instructed to attend to their feelings. Unfortunately, the evidence from this experiment is weak, because the experimenters found that only 4/19 subjects in the group instructed to use their feelings as a guide to the valence of the faces actually attempted to do so, according to a post-experiment questionnaire.[29] As things stand, a demonstrably reliable way of disentangling valenced experience from its unconscious analogues continues to elude researchers.

5.5 How Important Is the Neocortex?
Two Contrasting Pictures

Against the background of these methodological challenges, two very different pictures of the neural basis of valenced experience have arisen. One is a 'two-system' model, in which conscious feelings depend on a cortical pathway, while unconscious approach, avoidance, and defensive reactions can be activated by subcortical, entirely unconscious pathways. LeDoux has prominently defended such a model, and somewhat similar pictures have been defended by Edmund Rolls, Kent Berridge, and Piotr Winkielman.[30] All agree that subcortical processes generate motivational states that operate below the level of consciousness. They posit that some form of further processing in the neocortex is needed for a conscious feeling to arise. This allows, of course, plenty of room for disagreement about the nature of the further processing. But all such views can be contrasted with a very different approach that ties conscious feelings to subcortical, midbrain mechanisms. Versions of this view have been defended by Jaak Panksepp, Bjorn Merker, Marks Solms, and (at times) Antonio Damasio.[31]

I will take LeDoux's model as my focal example of a two-system picture and compare it with that of Panksepp. Both pictures have a place in the zone

---

[28] LeDoux and Pine (2016); LeDoux and Brown (2017).

[29] Bornemann et al. (2012, p. 121).

[30] Berridge and Robinson (2003); LeDoux and Pine (2016); LeDoux and Brown (2017); Rolls (2014); Winkielman and Berridge (2004). Lisa Feldman Barrett has some affinities with this group in so far as she posits significant cognitive involvement in emotion, but she has also criticized 'two system' thinking (Barrett 2017a, p. 224).

[31] Panksepp (1998a, ch. 16); Panksepp (2005); Damasio et al. (2013). Mark Solms's (2021) book *The Hidden Spring* includes an engaging presentation of Panksepp's ideas.

of reasonable disagreement, yet their implications for the edge of sentience are starkly different. The two-system model implies that many of the markers often taken to indicate valenced experience in humans, such as breaking out in a sweat when shown a frightening stimulus, are not really caused by conscious feelings at all. Although they involve the central nervous system, they are nonetheless more akin to withdrawing one's hand from a hot stove than we have tended to think. They may still work as signs of valenced experience in humans, but only by correlating with it non-causally, just as reflex withdrawal of one's hand correlates non-causally with feeling pain (so that, if we see someone withdraw their hand from a hot stove, we are not surprised if they later report pain, despite the absence of a causal relationship).

This raises the possibility that many of the behavioural responses often interpreted as signs of conscious feelings in other animals—such as freeze responses in mice, the target of much of LeDoux's early experimental work—are, likewise, not really caused by conscious feelings, but rather by homologues of our own unconscious circuits.[32] These responses may still correlate non-causally with valenced experience, just as they do in us. But, in the absence of a causal relationship, these signs do not provide an adequate basis for inferring (by IBE) that homologues of our own conscious processes are present in the animal, in cases where this is in doubt.

For LeDoux, whose focus throughout his career has been the case of fear, it is a major error to simply assume that amygdala activity in animals, leading to a defensive response, always involves a conscious feeling of fear. Such an assumption may sound harmless and precautionary, but it tends to lead, LeDoux suggests, to the seriously mistaken assumption that we can develop psychiatric therapies that work in humans by studying the defensive responses of animals. Panksepp often talked up the potential for animal research of this kind to lead to new psychiatric therapies, so LeDoux is not attacking a straw man here.

The two-system model dovetails with the orthodox interpretation of blindsight, in so far as it involves positing a consciousness-involving cortical pathway and a second, subcortical pathway that is wholly unconscious. It meshes particularly well with higher-order theories of sensory consciousness, according to which conscious sensory experiences involve the re-representation in prefrontal cortex of content originally processed in specialized sensory areas such as the primary visual cortex.[33]

---

[32] Paul et al. (2020).
[33] R. Brown et al. (2019). This is, at least, the traditional type of higher-order theory. A new type, developed by Lau (2022), does not involve re-representation but the mere *tagging* of first-order representations as reliable representations of the world right now, internally generated, or noise.

By contrast, Panksepp's alternative, midbrain-centric theory meshes well with the heterodox interpretation of blindsight defended by Merker and Phillips, on which blindsight involves residual but degraded conscious experience supported by midbrain mechanisms. Panksepp posited seven core types of affective circuit, each associated with its own form of 'raw affective experience': SEEKING, FEAR, RAGE, CARE, LUST, PANIC, and PLAY. These raw feelings, he argued, were generated primarily by mechanisms in the midbrain, at the top of the brainstem, and 'require no "readout" by a higher cognitive apparatus'.[34] He proposed that a specific midbrain area, the periaqueductal gray (PAG), plays a central role in generating these experiences. The PAG, he hypothesized, 'lies at the very root of many integrated affective feelings of the brain'.[35] This region is one of the 'triad of large structures' Merker's theory takes to be at the core of the neural basis of conscious experience, underlining the strong affinity between the two theories.[36]

As Panksepp himself often emphasized, a midbrain-centred theory of affective experiences suggests, on the face of it, that these experiences are very widespread across the animal kingdom, since midbrain structures such as the PAG are found in all vertebrates,[37] and the central complex in the brains of insects and other arthropods performs somewhat substantially analogous functions.[38] It is a fundamental commitment of Panksepp's theory that the seven core affective circuits are at least universal across all mammals, so that, for example, the circuits that drive rough-and-tumble play in rats are hom-ologous with those driving the same behaviour seen in human children. The existence of the same basic experiences beyond the mammalian case was something Panksepp consistently described as an open empirical question, plausible but not proven.[39]

What evidence convinced Panksepp that midbrain circuits were enough by themselves for conscious affective experiences, albeit of a 'raw' type? Three main lines of evidence stand out. Panksepp was especially moved by the observation that:

> it is next to impossible to evoke affective responses via localized electrical stimulation of the neocortex.... By contrast, coherent and powerful

---

[34] Panksepp (2005, p. 64).   [35] Panksepp (1998b, p. 571).

[36] Solms (2021) offers a synthesis of the two, though with an additional, third main ingredient, namely predictive processing.

[37] Kittelberger and colleagues have argued that the PAG of teleost fish is 'convergent in both its functional and structural organization to the PAG of mammals' (Kittelberger et al. 2006, p. 71). This topic is revisited in Chapter 12.

[38] Barron and Klein (2016); Klein and Barron (2016).   [39] Panksepp (2016).

emotional responses along with affective states are much easier to obtain by stimulating subcortical brainstem sites.[40]

He is referring here not to direct stimulation of the PAG itself, but to experiments applying electrical stimulation to different parts of the hypothalamus in rats.[41] The hypothalamus is a region just above the brainstem, strongly interconnected with the PAG. These experiments, as Panksepp interpreted them, showed that coordinated, whole-animal behaviour patterns could be triggered by localized electrical stimulation of this area. In a 1982 review, Panksepp argued that electrical stimulation could be used to induce distinctive 'rage', 'fear', 'expectancy' (later rebranded as SEEKING), and 'panic' responses. In that early presentation of the theory, the hypothalamus was taken to be the neural basis of these feelings. In the more mature version, Panksepp shifted the focus to the PAG, arguing that all the relevant parts of the hypothalamus project directly to the PAG and that the latter was a better candidate for the relevant integrative centre.

A second key line of evidence was the observation that disruption to the PAG is absolutely devastating to animals. Panksepp cited lesion studies in the 1940s on macaque monkeys and cats, which suggested that a very small amount of damage to the PAG can have drastic depressive effects on motivation (e.g. motivation to feed), and that substantial damage to the PAG produces a state of unresponsiveness that, in a human, would most likely be diagnosed as a disorder of consciousness.[42]

A distinct, third line of evidence is also important for understanding Panksepp's deep resistance to cortex-centric theories: a study of play behaviour in rats in which the neocortex had been destroyed soon after birth. Panksepp and collaborators found differences in how the rats played, but their play behaviour appeared largely normal. 'The basic impulse to play', they wrote, 'is subcortically organized since the behavior largely survives radical neodecortication'.[43] This prompted Panksepp to add PLAY to the list of core affective experiences.

Does this add up to a compelling case that conscious feelings, and not just coordinated behavioural patterns, have their basis in the midbrain? Unfortunately, the types of evidence that moved Panksepp are unlikely to sway an opponent, such as LeDoux, who favours a two-system model. Recall that, on the two-system model, the existence of a low-level system driving

---

[40] Panksepp (1998b, p. 572).   [41] Reviewed in Panksepp (1982).
[42] Bailey and Davis (1942, 1944).   [43] Panksepp et al. (1994, p. 440).

coordinated, adaptive behavioural responses is acknowledged, but this system is posited to be performing a wholly unconscious kind of processing. As a result, the two-system theorist will be largely unmoved by animal work exploring the detailed workings of the lower-level system. This work will never deliver proof of the involvement of consciousness, so it will never be able to refute the two-system picture.

For example, two-system theorists can gladly grant that electrical stimulation of subcortical areas triggers coordinated, adaptive behavioural responses, but they will deny that these are aptly described as 'emotional responses' or that they involve any conscious feelings. Moreover, they can acknowledge that losing the lower-level system is highly debilitating, sometimes tantamount to pulling out the brain's power cable, leading to a general loss of consciousness, just as pulling out the power cable from a computer will switch off the screen without thereby being the screen. They can also happily agree that a decorticated animal will still be able to display coordinated, midbrain-controlled behaviours. They will just insist that all of this goes on without any conscious accompaniment. Another impasse.

The parallels with the blindsight debate are striking. In the blindsight case, current evidence and methods seem to leave us with a serious underdetermination problem, unable to choose between alternative reasonable interpretations of the data. The same goes for this debate. Indeed, our ability to settle the disagreement in the case of affect is arguably even weaker than our ability to settle the corresponding disagreement about blindsight. As noted already, one approach with the potential to discriminate between the two sides involves using subliminal visual stimuli to elicit unconscious affect, but that approach has been inconclusive so far, and is likely to remain so. It is hard to be sure the putatively subliminal stimuli truly elude conscious perception, and hard to confidently rule out the possibility that the affective response they elicit is consciously felt. Yet it is only fair to point out that the types of studies Panksepp took to support his view are also far from conclusive. Direct stimulation of subcortical circuits induces strong and coherent behavioural responses, suggestive at face value of strong feelings, but that is not a strong argument against an opponent like LeDoux, who posits that coordinated behavioural control circuits can operate below the level of conscious experience.

When we put LeDoux's and Panksepp's pictures side by side, we see important points of agreement. Take fear, for example. Both agree that there is a mechanism, in which the amygdala plays a crucial role, that drives a characteristic set of behaviours such as freezing and escape, and has characteristic effects on autonomic arousal, such as sweating and increased heartrate. Both agree that work carefully mapping out the details of this circuit in rats has been extremely valuable. Moreover, both agree that this activity is typically 're-represented' in cortical areas, allowing the event to enter a wide range of other mechanisms, such as episodic memory.[44] Both even endorse Tulving's taxonomy of 'autonoetic' (self-knowing), 'noetic' (knowing), and 'anoetic' (non-knowing) consciousness to capture the different grades of emotional experience.[45] The big disagreement is about whether subcortical mechanisms already suffice for a simple, 'anoetic' valenced experience with or without any cortical involvement (Panksepp), or whether cortical re-representation is necessary for any kind of experience, no matter how simple (LeDoux).[46] At the point where they disagree, the evidence becomes tantalizingly inconclusive.

No one can claim to be certain, largely on the basis of affective priming studies, that all midbrain-driven defensive responses of animals are unconscious. That would be an example of unreasonable, dogmatic certainty. Yet it would also be unreasonable to claim certainty for the Panksepp view, largely on the basis of animal studies that show a causal relationship between midbrain mechanisms and behavioural responses without establishing that these mechanisms involve conscious experience. We need to remain open-minded about both possibilities.

5.6 Looking beyond the Mammalian Case

To date, the vast majority of research into both sensory and affective consciousness has concerned mammals. LeDoux's experimental work exploring the functions of the amygdala was done on rats, as was Panksepp's work exploring the functions of the hypothalamus and the effects of decortication. For all their disagreement, the fact that subcortical circuits are substantially conserved right across the mammals, so that some inferences about humans can be drawn from the case of rats, is important to both. Their disagreement was always about the relevance of those subcortical circuits to questions of conscious experience.

---

[44] Panksepp (2011, p. 1795).
[45] Tulving (1985, 2005); LeDoux (2021); Vandekerckhove (2021); Vandekerckhove and Panksepp (2011).
[46] LeDoux (2023) himself has reflected on his disagreements with Panksepp, arriving at the same conclusion.

In the study of conscious vision, meanwhile, primates have always been the main focus, due to the substantial similarities in the visual system across all primates. The first evidence of blindsight came not from humans but from macaques.[47] Indeed, for around fifty years now, research into naturally occurring cases of blindsight in humans has proceeded in tandem with research into induced blindsight in monkeys, where experimenters deliberately create lesions in the visual cortex.[48] Moreover, non-invasive (and so strongly preferable) techniques for dissociating the conscious from the unconscious, such as backward masking of stimuli, can also be used with macaques.[49] This research programme has never been successfully extended to rats or mice, despite the strong incentives to do this if possible. Rats and mice are simply much less visual creatures—olfaction is their primary means of exploring their environment—and their visual system differs from that of primates in ways that have so far obstructed the development of masking techniques or the generation of blindsight-like behaviours.

The result is that, in the case of conscious vision, we find theories shaped mainly by evidence from primates; and in emotion research, we find theories shaped by evidence from a wider range of mammals, but chiefly rats. In both fields, precious little research has been done on non-mammals. But we do know this much: the neocortex, with its distinctive six-layer organization, is a mammalian brain structure, normally present in all mammals (when they have not been decorticated by researchers) but not present in any non-mammal.

In birds, a region called the pallium seems to serve analogous functions to the neocortex.[50] The avian pallium does not have the layered structure of the neocortex: it has a nucleated structure. But there are functional analogies between regions of the two structures. Recent work has highlighted the potential importance of a region called the nidopallium caudolaterale (NCL), hypothesized to be an analogue of the prefrontal cortex in mammals. In 2020, a study by Andreas Nieder and colleagues recorded neural activity in the NCL of carrion crows (Corvus corone), revealing that NCL activation predicted whether or not the birds would 'report' having seen a near-threshold visual stimulus.[51]

What I found most extraordinary about this study was the 'reporting'. Over tens of thousands of trials, the birds were trained to 'report' the stimulus

---

[47] The story is recounted engagingly by Nicholas Humphrey in the early chapters of his book *Sentience* (2022).
[48] Cowey (2010).   [49] Ben-Haim et al. (2021).
[50] Güntürkün and Bugnyar (2016).   [51] Nieder et al. (2020).

displayed on a computer screen by moving their head in or out of an infrared light beam. The precise nature of the report depended on a second cue, displayed after the near-threshold cue, in order to ensure that the neural recordings were capturing signatures of the stimulus being seen, and not just signatures of an action being prepared. Remarkable as this is, it leads to a possible problem: when a report-like protocol is trained into animals over so many trials, its link to consciousness becomes more questionable, since a human could probably be trained in a similar way to 'report' an unconscious prime.[52] Even so, the study undoubtedly makes a strong case for further investigation of the NCL.

This type of work, however, is still exceptionally rare. It should, in my view, be a priority for consciousness science to find ways of dissociating putatively conscious and unconscious processing in a much wider range of animals, including invertebrate animals.[53] We will not be able to use the exact same techniques we use in primates, but it would be premature to conclude that there are no ways to adapt these techniques for other animals.[54] Where we do find dissociations between two significantly different kinds of processing, one potentially conscious and the other unconscious, we will be able to use this information to develop better theories of consciousness than we have currently. We will be in a much better position to disentangle the truly fundamental differences between these two kinds of processing from contingent aspects of the way the difference is implemented in mammals.

In the meantime, we must face up to the fact that the evidential picture, once we look beyond the mammals, is not as rich as we would like it to be. For the most part, we have a substantial amount of behavioural evidence (some of which will be described in later chapters), plus evidence of integrative brain regions (such as the pallium in birds, the optic tectum in fishes, the PAG in all vertebrates, the vertical lobe in cephalopod molluscs, the hemiellipsoid bodies in decapod crustaceans, and the central complex and mushroom bodies in insects), with limited understanding of the precise brain mechanisms producing the behaviours we are seeing, outside of a small number of model organisms. A lot of the time, the behaviours we see would be taken as clear evidence of experiences of certain kinds (such as pain) when observed in a mammal (some evidence of this type will be considered in Part IV).

---

[52] Crump and Birch (2022); van Gaal et al. (2008, 2009, 2010).   [53] Birch (2022c).

[54] For example, a study by Grover et al. (2022) creatively adapted for Drosophila fruit flies an experimental strategy used for humans and rabbits by Clark and Squire (1998) to show that, in Drosophila as in mammals, trace and delay conditioning are supported by different brain mechanisms (see also Giurfa and Macri 2022).

But there is always room for a critic to say: that is because a substantial background of neural similarity to humans can be safely assumed when we are interpreting the behaviour of mammals. In non-mammals, the underlying brain mechanisms are likely to differ, undermining any secure inference (by IBE) to sentience.[55]

The result is room for reasonable doubt about whether the behaviours we observe in non-mammals are produced by conscious experiences, even setting aside the main philosophical source of doubt (epiphenomenalism) discussed in the previous chapter. I mentioned in Chapter 1 that I do not agree with derogatory labels like 'sentience denier' for those who harbour such doubts, and my reasons should be clearer now. One can accept that sentience is an evolved adaptation and yet still suspect it might be a distinctively *mammalian* adaptation, evolved since the divergence from birds, and implemented in the neocortex.

At the same time, dogmatic insistence on the special importance of the neocortex to sentience is unreasonable, given the current state of the evidence, especially in practical contexts where we are trying to decide what precautions to take. *The potential for subcortical mechanisms and analogues of the cortex to support sentience needs to be taken seriously.* The case of birds is salutary. No one would, I hope, seriously try to argue that because the avian pallium is nucleated whereas the neocortex is laminar, nothing we do to a bird can be cruel, reckless, negligent, or in any way ethically problematic. The clear functional analogies should prompt us to think seriously about risk. The need to take a precautionary step here, where we accept ethical limits on our behaviour arising from the evidence that does exist (inconclusive though it may be), is obvious. And once we see this, it is not a huge step to see that similar reasoning can lead to ethical limits on our actions towards reptiles, fish, invertebrates, and other cases at the edge of sentience, even though the evidence in these cases is even more limited.

5.7 Summary of Chapter 5

This chapter has focused on sources of disagreement in the science of consciousness and emotion. To have a science of consciousness at all, we need reliable ways of disentangling conscious and unconscious processing. In the

---

[55] See Sober (2000, p. 376) for a related argument, though framed in terms of likelihoods rather than IBE.

case of vision, long-running debates about blindsight epitomize two main sources of uncertainty: the criterion problem and the problem of confounders. These sources of uncertainty arise even more strongly in the case of valenced experience (including emotions like fear), since methods for eliciting unconscious analogues of valenced experiences are less mature.

In the absence of secure ways of dissociating valenced experience from its unconscious analogues, two rival pictures of the neural basis of valenced experience in the mammalian brain persist. On one picture, valenced experience wells up directly from subcortical mechanisms without the need for any further cortical processing. On the other, subcortical circuits produce coordinated behavioural responses without the involvement of any kind of conscious processing, with even the simplest, 'anoetic' level of consciousness requiring cortical 're-representation' of subcortical activity. Current evidence does not allow us to choose confidently between these pictures.

These research programmes have all had a strong mammalian focus, with most of the evidence coming from humans, macaques, and rats. They have not yielded theories that apply in a clear, unambiguous way to non-mammalian animals. In these cases, we are typically left with a good amount of behavioural evidence, and some understanding of the underlying neural mechanisms, but no agreed theoretical basis on which to judge how similar the neural mechanisms must be in order to support sentience. The most appropriate way forward in these cases is to use the evidence that exists to guide precautionary thinking, a task that will be taken up in Part II of the book.

The Edge of Sentience: Risk and Precaution in Humans, Other Animals, and AI. Jonathan Birch, Oxford University Press.
© Jonathan Birch 2024. DOI: 10.1093/9780191966729.003.0006

PART II
A PRECAUTIONARY FRAMEWORK

6

Converging on Precautions

My overall goal in this chapter and the two that follow is to build an ethically sound and practically feasible framework for designing policy at the edge of sentience: a framework to help us manage the uncertainty that threatens to lead to intractable disagreement and perpetual indecision. This chapter starts to shift the focus away from scientific disagreement and towards policy decisions—decisions that have to be based, in one way or another, on uncertain science.

By 'policy', I primarily mean public policy: the policy of a legitimate state. But I also, secondarily, mean the policies of smaller organizations, right down to the level of individual laboratories, hospitals, zoos, farms, or other businesses, which are often faced with the daunting challenge of interpreting general laws and guidelines to fit their specific circumstances. For the most part, I will not be discussing decisions of individuals in their personal lives.

By 'framework', I mean a way of thinking through the issues and reaching decisions that all can accept as fair. My aim here is not to tell you my ethical views, then recommend that the whole of society conform to those views. I have no wish to adopt the 'philosopher as sage' role (this is a theme to which I return at the end of Chapter 8). My question is rather: given that these are clearly divisive issues, and that immediate reactions will differ, how can we move past our differences to manage our uncertainty and disagreement in a mutually acceptable way?

Three ideas are at the heart of my approach: a *scientific meta-consensus* about the range of empirically supported realistic possibilities, the bridging concepts of a *sentience candidate* and *investigation priority*, and an overlapping consensus on the need to take proportionate precautions when risking harm to sentience candidates. Together, these ideas amount to a precautionary framework for structuring our thinking about the edge of sentience. They are not magic tricks that remove all uncertainty and disagreement. They are tools to help us live with it.

6.1 Uncertainty, Inconclusiveness, and Dissensus

When thinking about the edge of sentience, we face multiple levels of uncertainty and disagreement concerning the metaphysics, functions, neural basis, and ethical significance of valenced experience (see Chapters 3–5). Figure 6.1 summarizes the picture that emerged from that part of the book. Empirical evidence of many different kinds bears on the issue for an open-minded person, but it never seems enough to end the dispute. The evidence is never conclusive, and we cannot see a path to conclusive evidence from where we are now. Even if we could settle the scientific aspects of the questions conclusively, disagreement about values would remain.

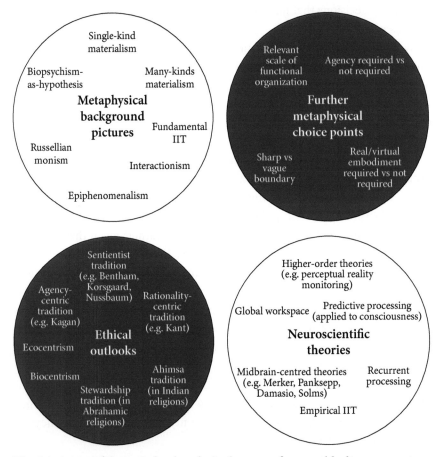

Fig. 6.1 A map of the main landmarks in the zone of reasonable disagreement. Many coherent packages of positions can be constructed from these options. © Jonathan Birch.

There is a temptation to retort: but when does science *ever* settle anything conclusively? The next swan could be black, the next emerald blue, and so on: any conclusion from inductive evidence is always potentially subject to refutation. Hardly surprising that the same is true of sentience. But while it is true enough that science never achieves absolute certainty (outside of mathematics and logic, at any rate), this misses an important difference between absolute certainty and the conclusive settling of a question. Science *does* sometimes settle questions conclusively, not in the sense of delivering absolute certainty, but in the sense of delivering a secure scientific consensus that makes continued disagreement and denial unreasonable.

For example, it has been conclusively established that DNA has a double-helix structure and that it is composed of the nucleotide bases guanine, cytosine, adenine, and thymine. It would be unreasonable to deny this, or to say we need to look for more evidence—maybe it is a single helix, maybe there are six or seven bases—or to suggest that public policy, to be properly impartial, should take no stand on the structure of DNA. These issues were live in the 1950s but have now been conclusively settled. A reasonable person, respectful of the epistemic standing of science, needs to accept the secure scientific consensus on this.

The same can be said of more controversial examples, such as the reality of climate change, the harmfulness of tobacco, and the medical efficacy (in general, allowing for disagreement about specific cases) of vaccines, antibiotics, and sanitation. When someone denies these points of secure scientific consensus, a legitimate state is not required to suspend judgement, take both sides seriously, and treat the scientific consensus and the anti-scientific claims as equally credible. That this sometimes happens is a pathology of liberal democracy, not a sign of a system working well.

The edge of sentience is not like the double helix, much as we might like it to be. There is no secure scientific consensus about the neural basis or functions of sentience. It is clearly reasonable to debate these issues. Dissent from majority views is often reasonable. That is the difference in practice between an issue that has been settled conclusively and one that has not. 'Conclusive settledness' is a social-epistemological property that many scientific claims possess but attributions of sentience in edge cases do not. Accordingly, as I have already mentioned, I oppose the idea of calling sceptics about attributions of sentience 'sentience deniers', as though their actions were comparable to climate change denial. Open debate on these issues is important.

Sometimes there are questions on which no secure scientific consensus has yet been achieved, but where the right response is to invest in more research to build that consensus, rather than to make controversial policy choices now on the basis of unsettled science. This is likely to be the right response where there are no in-principle obstacles to building consensus and where the policy issue does not demand immediate action. To give one example, I think healthcare policy-makers would be well advised to take a slow, gradual approach to rolling out the medical use of AI for applications such as cancer screening, first investing in research to build an adequate level of public confidence in its accuracy and trustworthiness.[1]

The edge of sentience is not like these cases either. Undoubtedly, further research into these questions is important and valuable: as we will see in later chapters, there are significant evidence gaps that hamper our attempts to design precautions in many areas. Yet we should not expect further research to conclusively settle the questions, in the way it might conclusively settle a more mundane question (e.g. concerning the accuracy of a cancer screening algorithm). The disagreements at the edge of sentience are too 'big-picture', and the methodological problems that stop us conclusively settling our disagreements in this area run too deep.

The upshot is that reasonable disagreement about the edge of sentience will always be with us. How, then, do we move from free and open debate to policy decisions? How do we prevent dispute and disagreement from paralysing all attempts at decision-making in this area?

6.2 A Scientific Meta-consensus on the Range of Realistic Possibilities

There is no scientific consensus about cases at the edge of sentience. Let us not pretend otherwise. It is equally important, though, to see that an absence of consensus on one specific theory does not lead to a chaotic 'anything goes' situation in which all speculation provides an equally reasonable basis for precautionary action. Evidence still constrains decision-making.

I find the concept of 'meta-consensus' helpful for thinking about these situations. The concept is borrowed from political theory.[2] In that context, it captures the idea that people may agree about a lot, even when they disagree deeply about the best policy. In particular, they may still agree about the range

---

[1] Birch et al. (2022).
[2] See Dryzek (2010, ch. 5). See also List (2002) on 'meta-agreement', and see List and Spiekermann (2019) for an illustration of the idea using the parliamentary deadlock in the UK (at that time) concerning leaving the European Union.

of reasonable options, and they may agree about how these options relate to each other along important dimensions (such as more moderate to more radical). In other words, they may agree about the structure of the option space, in at least some key respects. Seeing a meta-consensus can be a step towards negotiating a way forward.

To my knowledge, the concept has not yet received discussion in relation to scientific disagreement, but it should. Just as finding a meta-consensus can help lawmakers move forward when they disagree, so finding a scientific meta-consensus can help scientists move forward, as well as helping outside audiences to better understand what is going on in the science. It is all too easy for a non-expert, looking in, to think 'since they disagree so much, there is no reason for me to listen to them. I'll just go with my gut feeling.' That is dangerous and fallacious, but it can be tempting when scientists cannot articulate what they do agree about.

Does meta-consensus exist in the science of sentience? I think it does. I will first state where I think the meta-consensus lies, and then explain why I think this:

Proposed meta-consensus on the neural system requirements for sentience

Given our current evidence, all of the following theoretical positions about the neural system requirements for sentience (defined as the capacity for valenced experience) are *realistic possibilities*. None should be held dogmatically, but all should be taken seriously in practical contexts:

R1. Sentience requires distinctively primate neural mechanisms (e.g. in the granular prefrontal cortex) and is absent in non-primates.

R2. Sentience requires mechanisms distinctive to the mammalian neocortex and is absent in non-mammals.

R3. Sentience requires the neocortex in mammals but can also be achieved by other brain mechanisms performing relevantly analogous functions (such as the avian pallium).

R4. Sentience does not require the neocortex even in mammals and can be achieved in at least a minimal form by integrative subcortical mechanisms crucially involving the midbrain. However, it is absent in non-vertebrates.

R5. Sentience does not require the neocortex even in mammals and can be achieved in at least a minimal form by integrative subcortical mechanisms crucially involving the midbrain. Moreover, it can *also* be achieved by other brain mechanisms performing relevantly analogous functions (such as the central complex in insects).

These five positions are ordered from less inclusive to more inclusive. R5 is the most inclusive, in the sense that the distribution of sentience in the animal kingdom is likely to be the widest if this position is correct, since midbrain mechanisms are far more widely shared than neocortical mechanisms.

By contrast, it is not reasonable, given current evidence, to give serious attention in practical contexts to views less inclusive than R1 (such as a view on which sentience requires a developed capacity for natural language) or more inclusive than R5 (such as a view on which the spinal cord is said to support sentience by itself in the absence of a brainstem). The evidence does *not* support taking these views seriously in practical contexts.

There is no consensus about which of R1–R5 is correct, and each option can be fleshed out in many different ways. At the most inclusive end of the reasonable range, Merker, Panksepp, and Solms have defended midbrain-centric theories that are neutral between R4 and R5,[3] while Barron and Klein, Ginsburg and Jablonka, Feinberg and Mallatt, and Tye have defended versions of R5.[4] Damasio can be placed approximately between R3 and R4, since he has often emphasized the importance of both the midbrain and some parts of the cortex (especially the insular and somatosensory cortex).[5]

Meanwhile, many cortex-centric computational functionalist theories, such as the global workspace theory, the perceptual reality monitoring theory, and the recurrent processing theory are most naturally interpreted as versions of R3. Both Dehaene and Lau posit important roles for distinctively primate mechanisms in the *human implementation* of the mechanisms they take to be responsible for conscious experience, while allowing that simpler versions of these mechanisms could be implemented in other ways in other species.[6] Lamme, in developing the recurrent processing theory, focuses on

---

[3] Merker (2007); Panksepp (1998a); Solms (2021).

[4] Barron and Klein (2016); Feinberg and Mallatt (2016); Ginsburg and Jablonka (2019); Klein and Barron (2016); Tye (2016).

[5] Damasio et al. (2000, 2013); Damasio and Carvalho (2013); Parvizi and Damasio (2001).

[6] Dehaene (2014); Lau (2022). Dehaene proposes a key role for dorsolateral prefrontal cortex in implementing the global neuronal workspace, while Lau proposes a key role for dorsolateral and frontopolar prefrontal cortex in implementing perceptual reality monitoring, but both allow that these mechanisms may have alternative implementations in other animals.

mammalian visual areas (such as visual cortex); but recurrent processing could, clearly, be implemented by other animals in their own sensory areas.[7]

At the less inclusive end, R1 includes more demanding computational functionalist theories, on which sentience is linked to complex computations that may *only* be achievable by brain mechanisms distinctive to the primate lineage. The relevant mechanisms are located in granular prefrontal cortex (granular PFC), a part of the frontal lobe greatly expanded and elaborated in primates, incorporating the frontopolar, dorsolateral, and ventrolateral prefrontal cortex and characterized by a notably thick layer of granular (layer IV) cortical neurons.[8] These brain regions are strongly linked to executive control functions. Rolls's 'higher-order syntactic thought' theory gives a crucial role to these mechanisms.[9] LeDoux has at times appeared sympathetic to R1 and has emphasized the special processing properties of granular PFC.[10] However, his most recent work clarifies that granular PFC is required only for the most cognitively demanding kinds of consciousness: 'autonoetic' and 'noetic' consciousness.[11] He allows that 'anoetic' consciousness, which I see as much closer to the idea of sentience, may be achievable in a much wider range of animals.

The R2 category includes theorists who have, for various reasons, proposed that neocortical neurons, and perhaps especially the large pyramidal neurons in layer V, may have special processing properties that allow them to support consciousness.[12] On this view, granular PFC is not necessary, potentially allowing all mammals to meet the requirements, but there is something very special about the neocortex more generally. For Beck and Eccles, pyramidal layer V neurons were the most likely entry point for mental causation. For Stuart Hameroff, they are the most likely site for a quantum process he calls 'orchestrated objective reduction'. For these theorists, the nucleated structure found in birds might not be enough.

The consensus lies not at the level of specific positions (clearly!) but rather at the meta-level, in the idea that everyone should be able to recognize any of the positions in the range R1–R5 as realistic possibilities that must be taken seriously in practical contexts. All positions in this range have some evidence behind them, conferring a degree of plausibility. Moreover, everyone should be able to agree on the ordering of these views from less inclusive to more inclusive (Fig. 6.2). Finally, everyone should be able to agree on the severe

---

[7] Lamme (2022). Nicholas Humphrey's (2022) theory also falls in the R3 zone.

[8] See Preuss and Wise (2022) for an explanation of these terms and an overview of what is known (and not known) about the evolution of the prefrontal cortex.

[9] Rolls (2004).   [10] LeDoux (2023, pp. 758–759).   [11] LeDoux et al. (2023).

[12] Aru et al. (2020); Beck and Eccles (1992); Hameroff (2022). Key (2015, 2016) also seems to have a view of this type.

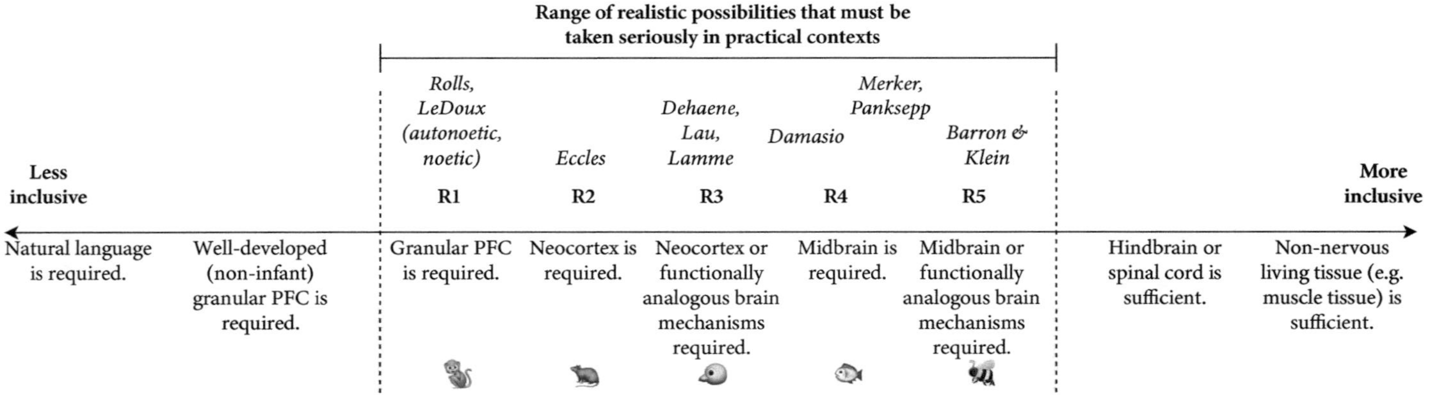

Range of realistic possibilities that must be taken seriously in practical contexts

	Rolls, LeDoux (autonoetic, noetic) R1	Eccles R2	Dehaene, Lau, Lamme R3	Damasio R4	Merker, Panksepp; Barron & Klein R5		
More inclusive							
	Granular PFC is required.	Neocortex is required.	Neocortex or functionally analogous brain mechanisms required.	Midbrain is required.	Midbrain or functionally analogous brain mechanisms required.	Hindbrain or spinal cord is sufficient.	Non-nervous living tissue (e.g. muscle tissue) is sufficient.
Less inclusive	Well-developed (non-infant) granular PFC is required.						
	Natural language is required.						

Fig. 6.2 A proposed scientific meta-consensus on the neural system requirements for sentience (the capacity for valenced experience). There is no consensus about which position within the reasonable range is correct. However, a meta-consensus can form around the idea that positions R1–R5 describe realistic possibilities that must be taken seriously, given current evidence. There can also be a meta-consensus on the ordering of these views from less inclusive to more inclusive and on the challenges facing any view that falls outside this range. Figure © Jonathan Birch. The free use of the Google Noto Emoji Color Font (for the emojis) is granted under the SIL Open Font License v1.1.

challenges facing any view that sees both the neocortex and the midbrain as unimportant to sentience, or any view that regards a functional primate neocortex as insufficient.

This may sound like it does not exclude very much, but it does. Consider, for example, the cerebellum. This is part of the hindbrain, at the very back and base of the brain, and it contains more neurons than any other brain region, even the cortex. There are 69 billion neurons in your cerebellum, compared with a mere 16 billion in the cortex.[13] If one were trying to guess the 'seat of consciousness' in the brain using nothing but neuron counts, one would probably guess the cerebellum—and be completely wrong. There is no evidence for a role for the cerebellum in generating conscious experience and strong evidence against. The cerebellum has important roles in motor control and sensorimotor integration, and appears to be crucially involved in modelling the expected sensory consequences of our actions and registering prediction errors.[14] These computations could have turned out to be essential to sustaining a conscious state, but they turn out not to be, as a matter of empirical fact. Being born without a cerebellum (complete primary cerebellar agenesis) leads to motor control problems but turns out to be compatible with otherwise normal cognitive development.[15]

So, the evidence does not warrant attaching significant probability to a hindbrain-centric theory of sentience, or a theory that blithely predicts that sentience will be tied to the brain region with the most neurons, with no consideration of what the neurons are doing. One cannot pluck theories out of thin air, without supporting evidence, and expect them to be taken seriously when practical questions are at stake. There are too many possible-but-very-low-probability theories, and their practical implications are so diverse that they are apt to derail discussion if we admit them to the table. In practical contexts, we need to maintain a focus on credible theories that have amassed enough evidence in their favour to merit serious discussion of their practical implications.

For another example, this time from the other end of the axis, consider a theory that ties sentience to natural language. There are credible theories, such as Edmund Rolls's 'higher-order syntactic thought' theory, that tie conscious experience to quite sophisticated kinds of thought, suggesting a narrow distribution of sentience in the animal kingdom.[16] Yet even Rolls stops short of proposing that *natural language* is required for the relevant type of thought, allowing that a 'language of thought' might also be sufficient.[17] This is a wise move, because we have clear evidence that linguistic abilities are not

[13] Herculano-Houzel (2009).   [14] Arikan et al. (2019); Johnson et al. (2019).
[15] Yu et al. (2015).   [16] Rolls (2014).
[17] On the idea of a language of thought and its history, see Quilty-Dunn et al. (2023); Rescorla (2019).

needed to have conscious experiences. Brain injuries to regions associated with language can lead to temporary aphasia (loss of linguistic ability) of various kinds, but subjects, when they recover, can often vividly recount their conscious experiences during the time they were affected.[18]

I need to emphasize the key point about the difference between absolute certainty and a reasonable basis for action. I am not suggesting that views outside the range R1–R5 can be decisively ruled out with absolute, 100% certainty. What I have in mind is closer to the old idea of 'moral certainty': enough confidence to justify setting aside these views when grave practical questions are at stake.

Think back to when I introduced the idea of a zone of reasonable disagreement in Chapter 3. I said that we should imagine a grave, serious space in which people are debating potential grounds for taking actions that will change lives. In other spaces, there should be room for free speculation. But to base policy on free speculation would be a serious mistake. That is the boundary I am trying to draw. *Possibilities in the range R1–R5 have amassed enough evidence to deserve serious consideration when important practical questions are at stake, whereas views outside this range have not.*

R1–R5 are not comprehensive theories of sentience: they can be mixed and matched with compatible ideas in the literature (e.g. those in Fig. 6.1) to generate coherent packages of views. The full option space is very large and always changing. As the fortunes of particular theories wax and wane, different packages of views will become more or less popular. But I expect that the basic disagreement about the relative importance of the prefrontal cortex, other cortical regions, and the midbrain, and about whether sentience can be achieved by functional analogues of these structures, as mapped out by R1–R5, will outlive our current theories.

Who might object to the proposed meta-consensus? Those sympathetic to biopsychism and/or full IIT may believe that any living tissue can, under the right conditions, realize sentience (alternatively, they may take this to be true of conscious experience but not valence). This may seem at odds with the proposed meta-consensus, but it is not. The meta-consensus aims to capture the range of views it is appropriate to take into account *now* in decision-making contexts, given the current evidence. It aims to capture those views that have been established as realistic possibilities. A person can acknowledge that only R1–R5 have sufficient evidence now to deserve serious consideration in practical contexts while at the same time holding out hope that new evidence

[18] Koch (2019).

will come to light in favour of a more inclusive, but currently highly speculative, view. And so, a biopsychist can sign up to the proposed meta-consensus, provided they can recognize the speculative nature of their own views.

Objections may also come from the orthodox materialist side. We noted in Chapter 3 that a certain type of materialist—a 'many-kinds' materialist—is rather suspicious of terms like 'sentience' in the first place, thinking it likely that they merely gesture in the direction of several different cognitive/neuro-biological kinds. Such a person will expect the term 'sentient being' to give way eventually to a family of more precise successor notions. They may see many different theoretical views in the R1–R5 space as identifying genuinely relevant kinds (internal modelling of self and world, prioritization of needs, attention, working memory, global broadcast, higher-order monitoring, con-ceptual thought, and so on) all of which have a genuine but partial claim to the label 'sentience', at least when processing valenced contents.

It seems to me that this type of materialist can still agree with the proposed meta-consensus as a way forward *for the short term*, even though they may dislike some aspects of how it is worded. Where my proposal says 'sentience', they will want it to say 'the family of cognitive/neurobiological kinds towards which the term "sentience" indeterminately gestures'. As noted in Chapter 3, they will, at some point, have to confront the vexed question of which of these kinds should inherit the ethical role usually afforded to sentience, and the practical implications will depend on how they resolve that question. In the meantime, we have little choice but to frame these issues in terms of sentience, lacking any successor notion that is ready to take on its ethical and practical role.

In short, many people may, for various reasons, hope the current meta-consensus is something we can *move beyond* as new evidence comes to light. This could take the form of a narrowing of the range of realistic possibilities, a widening of that range, or a restructuring of the way we think about the range. But holding such a hope is compatible with accepting that the meta-consensus succeeds in capturing the positions we need to take seriously *now*, given the evidence we have.

6.3 Two Bridging Concepts: Sentience Candidates and Investigation Priorities

With this idea of a scientific meta-consensus in the background, we can con-struct two bridging concepts that can help us move from disagreement in the realm of theory to agreement on a course of action. The first is the concept of a *sentience candidate*:

A system *S* is a *sentience candidate* if there is an evidence base that:

(a) implies a realistic possibility of sentience in *S* that it would be irresponsible to ignore when making policy decisions that will affect *S*, and

(b) is rich enough to allow the identification of welfare risks and the design and assessment of precautions.

The concept of a sentience candidate is defined in terms of possibilities it would be *irresponsible to ignore*, given current evidence. There is, inevitably, a value-judgement involved in declaring that evidence has amassed to a point at which it is now irresponsible to ignore it in practical contexts. Judging something to be a sentience candidate is not, therefore, a completely value-neutral exercise, nor could it be.

Yet it is also a judgement that must be informed by the scientific meta-consensus just described. We can appeal to the meta-consensus to explain why disconnected spinal cords, zygotes, neural and non-neural tissue samples, organs other than the brain, and unicellular organisms are not sentience candidates. One can speculate, in the seminar room, about sentience in these systems, but responsible precautionary actions cannot be based on these speculations. By contrast, at least some invertebrate animals belong in a very different category. Because R3 and R5 are realistic possibilities, and both allow that functional analogues of sentience-relevant vertebrate brain areas (the neocortex and midbrain, respectively) may be sufficient for sentience, we need to get into the finer details of the evidence concerning invertebrates in order to make assessments of their sentience candidature (and this is the task of Part IV of the book).

To judge a system to be a sentience candidate, then, involves scientific *and* evaluative components: like many other judgements that have to be made at the science-policy interface, it is a 'mixed' judgement.[19] The concept captures a delicate threshold in our evidential and practical situation. When the threshold is crossed, a substantial enough evidence base exists to allow responsible discussion of possible precautionary actions.

---

[19] For discussion of 'mixed' judgements, see Alexandrova (2018); Birch (2021a); Plutynski (2017).

The question of what counts as a 'substantial enough evidence base' is a subtle one, calling for case-specific criteria and expert judgement. The search for appropriate criteria in different cases will be one major theme of Parts III–IV of the book (alongside the question of *what to do* when our criteria are satisfied). Not much can be said in general about this, because the cases present such different challenges. What can be said is that we must have a substantial base of positive evidence, not just an inability to conclusively rule out sentience. 'Inability to conclusively rule out' is too low a bar when our theoretical understanding of sentience is still so immature. Nothing would be ruled out. At the same time, we do not need certainty or even knowledge. We need not even have established that S is *likely* to be sentient. We just need *enough* evidence to imply a realistic possibility, and to allow the identification of welfare risks and the design and assessment of precautions.

There are two main types of situation in which a system can fail to be a sentience candidate. One is a situation in which there is clear evidence that it lacks a functioning forebrain, functioning midbrain, or anything relevantly analogous to either structure, according to any serious, credible theory of what the relevant analogies are. We can entertain the possibility of biopsychism in the seminar room, but current theories that have a sufficient amount of evidence in their favour to elevate them above seminar-room speculation do give a crucial role to the forebrain, midbrain, or both (incidentally, this includes *empirical* IIT, which gives a crucial role to the posterior cortical hot zone). The other type of situation in one in which there is simply a total or near-total lack of evidence one way or the other, making it impossible to mount a credible, evidence-based case either for or against sentience.

A medically important example of the first type of case is a patient who is brain dead.[20] In a brain dead person, cardiorespiratory function may persist for a time. The spinal cord may still be functional but it is not able to generate experiences without the brain. What remains is not sufficient for sentience on any view in the R1–R5 space. This is why doctors are legally permitted to remove organs and tissues from registered organ donors who are brain dead, saving countless human lives. Courts will not entertain people arguing for biopsychism in this context—and thank goodness. They are correct to set aside highly speculative views when such grave decisions are being made.

This is perhaps the most significant illustration of the idea that a hidden meta-consensus exists regarding the parameters of reasonable debate when

---

[20] Establishing brain death is not always straightforward. See Greer et al. (2020); Walter et al. (2018).

grave issues are at stake. For all the obvious disagreement in consciousness science, we are far from a situation in which people are debating whether sentience persists after brain death. When a decision to switch off the life-support of a clinically brain-dead patient is challenged in court, the courts can correctly cite a secure scientific meta-consensus around the proposition that sentience does not survive the death of the brain. Serious disputes in this area do not hinge on that question, but rather on the question of whether brain death has been accurately determined by clinical criteria.

We will meet examples of the second type of situation when discussing non-human animals (Part IV). For a very wide range of animals, including many invertebrates, a credible, evidence-based case for sentience can be mounted. But in other cases, we are faced with a frustrating lack of evidence of the right kind, one way or the other. There is a temptation in these cases to loosen up the concept of a sentience candidate, allowing species to count as sentience candidates where there is a paucity of evidence one way or the other. But I do not take this path because of the practical role I want the concept of a sentience candidate to play. The role of the concept is to trigger evidence-based discussions of possible precautions to manage welfare risks. Where the evidence base is simply not rich enough to guide the design of precautions or to allow assessments of their proportionality, the right response is to enrich the evidence base as a matter of urgency, not to take a guess at what might or might not help to mitigate welfare risks.

It will be helpful to have a second bridging concept to capture those cases where there is currently *not* enough evidence to render a system a sentience candidate, and yet there are urgent reasons to gather more evidence, because the risks of proceeding in ignorance are very high. This is the concept of an *investigation priority*:

A system S is an *investigation priority* if it falls short of the requirements for sentience candidature, yet:

(a) further investigation could plausibly lead to the recognition of S as a sentience candidate; and

(b) S is affected by human activity in ways that may call for precautions if S were a sentience candidate.

When we turn, in Parts III–IV of the book, to specific cases, we will be asking: *is this system a sentience candidate, an investigation priority, or neither of these?* This is a useful shift from the question: *is the system sentient?* The first question, unlike the second, is one we can answer using current evidence, and our answers can command widespread support and confidence from people with many different theoretical sympathies.

6.4 In Search of Ethical Framework Principles

Let us turn to ethical disagreement. Can there be any consensus here? It is clear that, given the very large ethical disagreements about the significance of sentience, any consensus principles will be very thin. This cannot be helped. Inevitably, a question will arise about whether these principles are *too* thin to provide meaningful guidance. Can we find 'Goldilocks' principles that are uncontroversial enough to command support right across the zone of reasonable disagreement, yet contentful enough to guide us towards agreement on courses of action?

I want to propose three such principles. The first aims to capture a very general, high-level duty to avoid causing gratuitous suffering to sentient beings. The second and third concern how that duty applies in cases where sentience is actively and reasonably disputed.

We have seen that all major religions and all reasonable secular ethical views, even rationality-centric views, contain reasons for limiting what humans can do to other sentient beings (Chapter 4). Usually, other animals are the sentient beings people have in mind when they discuss these issues, but the underlying reasons apply to any sentient being. These limits, at minimum, rule out causing gratuitous suffering, where 'gratuitous' implies the absence of a good reason for causing the suffering.

Think of the biblical example of a person who refuses to help unload an ox suffering under the weight of their burden, or that of a person who slaughters an animal by tearing it limb from limb. People who perpetrate such acts are behaving unconscionably: they have either not thought about the consequences of their actions for the animal at all, have embraced an unreasonable position such as sadism, or are betraying their own values. A liberal, pluralistic society does not need to make room for this kind of behaviour and can legitimately ban it.

This point of agreement exists despite a sea of underlying disagreement. First, there is disagreement on the question of to whom the duty is owed. Perhaps it is owed to the animal (as on animal rights views) or to oneself (on the Aquinas/Kant indirect duty view), or perhaps talk of 'duties' is just a shorthand for the results of a utility calculation (as on utilitarian views) or the expression of a virtue (as on virtue ethics views). Second, there is disagreement about what constitutes a good reason for causing suffering. For some, there may be no reason good enough to justify causing suffering to an animal. For others, many reasons may be good enough, as long as they connect to important human values and interests. For example, many think that gaining biomedical knowledge can be a good enough reason.

What is the best way to formulate the consensus against gratuitous suffering? In the 1990s, the Christian theologian Michael Banner, then chair of the UK's Animals in Science Committee, suggested some consensus principles often described as 'Banner's principles':

1. harms of a certain degree and kind ought under no circumstances to be inflicted on an animal;
2. any harm to an animal, even if not absolutely impermissible, nonetheless requires justification and must be outweighed by the good which is realistically sought in so treating it; and
3. any harm which is justified by the second principle ought, however, to be minimized as far as is reasonably possible.[21]

Similar attempts at formulating consensus principles have occurred within debates about how to reconcile animal welfare with a liberal attitude of tolerance towards a wide range of cultures, including cultural practices that lead to welfare problems. In this context, Paula Casal has argued that consensus can form around the idea that 'it is wrong to kill animals in painful ways when alternative less painful methods are available'[22] and Chad Flanders has proposed that 'there is a tradition of history of laws against cruelty to animals in this country [the United States], so much so that it should count as a fixed point in our reasoning about animals'.[23] Most recently, in a detailed study of the place of other animals in political liberalism, Federico Zuolo has proposed that consensus can form around the principle that 'we ought to minimize animal suffering in interactions with human beings as much as reasonably possible'.[24]

These principles are undoubtedly very thin, in the sense that they do not strongly constrain human actions. They leave room for people to argue that low-welfare practices are practically necessary, given some legitimate aim (e.g. maintaining an economically viable meat production business). So, it

---

[21] Farm Animal Welfare Council (2009).   [22] Casal (2003, p. 49).
[23] Flanders (2014, p. 56).   [24] Zuolo (2020, p. 211).

should be no surprise to find strong criticism of these ideas from animal rights theorists.[25] Yet, if we were to add more substantial constraints, we would move away from consensus. That would be antithetical to my present aim, which is to construct a framework for reaching society-wide agreement on what to do regarding cases at the edge of sentience. For other aims, consensus would be less important; but for this aim, it really matters, so I have to make the most of the thin consensus that exists.

Although the proposals from Banner, Casal, Flanders, and Zuolo all have merits, I want to propose a somewhat different way of formulating the consensus against gratuitous suffering. To begin with, let us move from 'animal' to 'sentient being', to make room for the possibility that some non-animals are or will be sentient. More subtly, I think the reliance on what is 'reasonably possible' leads to difficulties. It is always reasonably possible to stop what you are doing. It is reasonably possible for humans to stop experimenting on animals or farming animals for food. Indeed, it is even reasonably possible for humans to stop driving, thereby avoiding the suffering of the many animals accidentally hit by cars. It is reasonably possible for all of us to adopt Jainism. But there is no consensus that we ought to live like this. So there is in fact no agreement that we ought to do 'as much as reasonably possible'.

As I see it, a more useful concept for capturing consensus, and one that I think lies in the background of Banner's principles and of much UK animal welfare law, is that of *proportionality*. The real point of agreement is that, when pursuing activities such as these, we ought to take, at minimum, proportionate steps to mitigate the risk of causing suffering. Proportionate steps are those that do *enough* to reduce the risk of causing suffering, taking all relevant considerations into account, including the strength of the reasons for pursuing the activity, and whatever evidence we have concerning the severity and duration of the suffering that may be caused.

'Enough' is a vague concept, so 'doing enough' is a vague threshold. There can nonetheless be clear cases on both sides. In clear cases of animal cruelty, the perpetrator intentionally inflicts suffering without good reason, and so fails to take proportionate steps to prevent suffering. Meanwhile, a pet owner who diligently cares for her sick pet by following all relevant veterinary advice, minimizing the pet's suffering as far as possible, is doing enough.

---

[25] Pepper (2017). On the tension between animal rights and liberalism more generally, see Read and Birch (2023). The same tension can be seen, Janus-like, as posing a 'legitimacy challenge' to animal rights theories (Schultz-Bergin 2017; see also Basl and Schouten 2018) or as casting doubt on the foundations of political liberalism (Berkey 2017; Garner 2013; Healey and Pepper 2021; Magaña 2023; Plunkett 2016).

Outside of clear-cut cases, views will differ a great deal about what it takes to do enough—about when exactly our treatment of our fellow sentient beings becomes cruel or negligent. Different background views about the ethical significance of sentience will lead to reasonable disagreement about what is proportionate in the non-obvious cases, and we need processes for resolving these disagreements.

That issue will be the focus of Chapter 8, where I will offer a 'pragmatic analysis' of proportionality intended to help us think through non-obvious cases. For now, I want to emphasize that a duty to take proportionate steps is one that can be supported from within any reasonable ethical, religious, or philosophical picture. Indian religions will see the duty as arising from ahimsa; Abrahamic religions will see it as arising from the duty of stewardship. For Kant, the duty will be one we owe to ourselves, as part of our duty to cultivate morally good dispositions. For Rawls, such a duty would flow from the duty of compassion he acknowledges we owe to animals. For animal rights theorists it would flow from much stronger duties of justice, and would involve very strong demands. For utilitarians, it would flow from the principle of utility, which would also be our guide to what counts as 'enough'. For virtue theorists, it would flow from what Knutsson and Munthe have called the virtue of precaution: in essence, the virtue of avoiding the reckless or negligent imposition of risks on others.[26] Proponents of these views may well disagree about what the proportionate steps are in any given case, but not about *whether* we should take proportionate steps.

Among cases of 'gratuitous' suffering, we can distinguish two main types:

(i) a person engages in an activity (such as torturing an animal for fun) where the reason for causing suffering is *so* weak, on any view in the zone of reasonable disagreement, that the only proportionate response is to cease the activity altogether;

(ii) a person engages in an activity (e.g. farming, animal research) where the reason for causing suffering is strong according to at least one view in the zone of reasonable disagreement, and yet they fail to take proportionate steps to mitigate the risk of causing suffering.

The two types of case need to be handled quite differently. The second type requires in-depth discussion about whether some precautions short of ceasing the activity can meet the tests of proportionality, whereas the first type of

---

[26] Knutsson and Munthe (2017).

case does not merit that kind of discussion. In those cases where an activity could not be defended from within any of the well-developed ethical perspectives in the zone of reasonable disagreement, I will call it an 'indefensible activity'.

This leads me to my first proposed framework principle:

***

Framework Principle 1. *A duty to avoid causing gratuitous suffering.* We ought, at minimum, to avoid causing gratuitous suffering to sentient beings either intentionally or through recklessness/negligence. Suffering is not gratuitous if it occurs in the course of a defensible activity despite proportionate attempts to prevent it. Suffering is gratuitous if the activity is indefensible or the precautions taken fall short of what is proportionate.

***

This is a principle all reasonable people can endorse for good reasons internal to their own viewpoints, and it is therefore one that should command our collective confidence and that can provide a shared basis for debate about more concrete policies. The 'at minimum' allows that many people undoubtedly feel, as a matter of personal morality, that they ought to go beyond the consensus.

6.5 Back to the Edge

Now let consider the question of how this duty *applies* when there is no agreement about whether or not a being is sentient. Here is something we should definitely not say: 'If you do not personally believe the being affected by your action is sentient, then the duty does not apply to you. The duty applies only if you personally believe the being to be sentient. So, those who deny sentience to crabs (for example) can boil them alive, whereas those of us who attribute sentience to crabs cannot.' That is manifestly the wrong way to handle uncertainty. Respect for differences of opinion matters, but uncritical deference to personal belief cannot be the way forward. Let us see if we can improve on it.

What I propose is the following: whenever a being is a sentience candidate, there is a realistic possibility that our actions can cause it suffering, and so we ought to take that possibility seriously as part of our wider duty to avoid causing gratuitous suffering. To fail to see a realistic possibility of suffering due to lack of acquaintance with the relevant evidence is negligent. To acknowledge a realistic possibility of suffering, yet refuse to take proportionate steps to manage that risk, is reckless. So, if suffering actually occurs as a result, it was gratuitous—a result of our negligence or recklessness—and we acted wrongly, even if we had no intention whatsoever to cause that suffering.

This proposal adds content to my earlier claim that the 'sentience candidate' concept can act as a useful bridge between science and policy that helps us reach agreement on action, despite disagreement on theory. It does this by leading to a sufficient condition for recklessness or negligence. If the impact of a decision on a sentience candidate is ignored when the decision is made, and the sentience candidate suffers as a result, the suffering was a product of recklessness or negligence (we may wish to reserve the term 'reckless' for cases where the disregard was intentional).

To return to the example of crabs: you may personally believe that crabs are not sentient, but, if you are responsible for slaughtering crabs, you should inform yourself of the scientific reasons for thinking they might be sentient (see Chapter 12). It would be irresponsible to ignore those reasons. Those reasons should, if nothing else, give you pause before boiling the crab alive. They should prompt you to consider precautions you might take, such as prior stunning, and prompt you to think about whether it would be proportionate to take those precautions. If you fail or refuse to inform yourself, and/ or fail or refuse to follow any relevant guidance, and the animal suffers as a result, the suffering was the product of your negligence or recklessness. This is the basic line of thought we need to institutionalize at the level of policy and law.

Accordingly, the duty to take proportionate measures to manage risk arises, at minimum, *whenever a being is a sentience candidate.* And I propose this too can be a point of consensus. I say 'at minimum' to allow for the possibility that some (such as Jains) will hold the view that the sentience candidate concept casts too small a net, and that the duty to avoid causing gratuitous suffering applies even more widely (e.g. that it applies to all living things, even in those cases in which there is no evidence for or against sentience). However, I see no reason to make a similar concession to people who think the duty applies more narrowly (e.g. only to those systems we can be *certain* are sentient, *know* to be sentient, or believe to be sentient with *high probability*). Such a view is licensing negligence and recklessness, and so cannot be right, given that we have a duty to avoid causing gratuitous suffering.

Recall, for example, the absurd view criticized at the end of the last chapter, on which the nucleated organization of the avian pallium allegedly leads to the conclusion that there are no ethical limits on our treatment of birds. The fact that we are separated from birds by hundreds of millions of years of evolution, leading to major differences of brain organization, is an obstacle to *certainty* regarding their sentience, and we should admit this. But it is no obstacle to the idea that humans sometimes treat birds in ways that are reckless, negligent, and liable to cause gratuitous suffering. There would be something very obviously wrong about boiling a bird alive, for example. These ideas do not require certainty about sentience, or even high probability. What they require is sentience candidature.

This, then, is my second proposed framework principle:

Framework Principle 2. *Sentience candidature can warrant precautions.* If S is a sentience candidate, then it is reckless/negligent to make decisions that create risks of suffering for S without considering the question of what precautions are proportionate to those risks. Reasonable disagreement about proportionality is to be expected, but we ought to reach a policy decision rather than leaving the matter unresolved indefinitely.

Like Framework Principle 1, this principle is reaching for consensus—and so is unavoidably very thin. It deliberately avoids saying anything about what specific precautions might be warranted in any particular case. We will turn to such questions in Parts III–IV of the book. Moreover, the principle leaves open the possibility that at the end of our deliberations we decide that the proportionate response is to take no action. Imagine, for example, a scenario in which we find evidence of sentience in microscopic dust mites sufficient to regard them as sentience candidates—we might nonetheless decide there is nothing we can do to help them that passes the tests of proportionality. We should expect disagreement in specific cases. A general commitment to proportionality does not imply any particular outcome, when people disagree about what is proportionate.

But how can we move beyond these disagreements? Sometimes, where consensus on specific courses of action is lacking, there can still be consensus on a suitable *procedure* for reaching decisions. I propose it can be a point of wide agreement that our procedures should be informed, inclusive, and democratic. They should be 'informed' in the sense that decisions should be *based on the latest scientific evidence, not on ignorance.* Given that this is an area in which new evidence is constantly emerging, this need for decisions to be informed suggests we must also make room for decisions to be revisited in light of new evidence. They should be 'inclusive' in the sense that *all interests at stake in the process should be appropriately represented*. For example, a process that may result in new animal welfare regulations for a particular industry should involve representatives of that industry. At the same time, the interests of the affected animals should be appropriately represented, a role that typically falls to animal welfare experts or organizations. And they should be 'democratic' in the sense that *the process should be integrated with democratic mechanisms that confer legitimacy on policy decisions*. There are different ways this could be done, and I will revisit that issue in the next chapter. Real-world cases, such as the debates around the UK's Animal Welfare (Sentience) Act 2022, offer examples on which we can try to improve.

This leads to my third and final framework principle:

Framework Principle 3. *Assessments of proportionality should be informed, democratic, and inclusive.* To reach decisions, we should use informed and inclusive democratic processes. These decisions should be revisited periodically and whenever significant new evidence emerges.

There is a lot more to be said on the issue of what an informed and inclusive democratic process for reaching assessments of proportionality might look like. That task will be taken up in the next two chapters. But before we move on, I must address a different question: how do these framework principles relate to 'the precautionary principle'?

6.6 Relation to Other Precautionary Ideas

Daniel Steel, in a wide-ranging analysis of the foundations of precautionary thinking, has argued that there is no single 'precautionary principle' as such, but rather many different precautionary principles for different policy areas and problems.[27] What unites them is a shared commitment to a broad norm for policy-making that Steel calls the 'meta-precautionary principle': the norm that we should never allow scientific uncertainty to lead to policy-making paralysis. We should not let problems fester for decades while we wait

[27] Steel (2015).

for conclusive evidence to emerge. We should be ready to act to manage risks before conclusive evidence is in.

The framework I have been assembling clearly belongs in that family. Framework Principle 2 explicitly says that 'we ought to reach a policy decision rather than leaving the matter unresolved indefinitely', an endorsement of Steel's proposed norm. Indeed, even if one thinks Steel's norm might not always be a good norm for policy-making, it seems clearly a good norm for policy-making at the edge of sentience, where the zone of reasonable disagreement is so wide that we are unlikely to have conclusive evidence any time soon, and yet the risks of simply refusing to think about these issues until conclusive evidence is attained are enormous and unacceptable.

The framework I have been developing also makes three other commitments that are shared with many other precautionary principles. The first is that precautions should pass a test of proportionality. We should not ban any human activity at the first sign it creates a risk of harm but should instead start a debate about what would be proportionate. I see this commitment to proportionality as marking the difference between radical precautionary principles that aim to ban activities on a hair-trigger (which invariably fail to achieve consensus support) and plausible, moderate precautionary principles that aim to manage risk sensibly (and can achieve consensus support). My framework is a precautionary framework of the second, moderate type.

The second commitment is that discussions about proportionality should be inclusive, reaching beyond a narrow community of experts to involve the wider public. That too has been an important strand in precautionary thinking in other contexts. And the third commitment is that we should intentionally set a low evidential bar for triggering discussions about proportionality. Evidence that is far from conclusive can still be enough to bring a possibility within the zone of reasonable disagreement, so that a discussion about proportionality is warranted. That does not mean that the strength of the evidence is irrelevant or that weak evidence can be used to justify radical policy responses. If the evidence for the existence of a risk is credible but thin, this is something that expert advisers should honestly communicate (e.g. with phrases such as 'low confidence' and 'remote chance'), and it is something an inclusive, democratic process for assessing proportionality should take into account.

For all these reasons, the framework I have constructed can fairly be called a precautionary framework. Yet an important qualification needs to be added: the justification I have given for my proposals is free-standing, not dependent on the justifications of other precautionary principles. It is logically possible for a person to reject precautionary principles in all other contexts (climate change, environmental regulation, public health, and so on) but still accept this one.

This is because the justification I have given does not take a 'top-down' form. The argument is *not*: precautionary principles are generally wise, this is an instance of a precautionary principle, therefore it too is wise. Rather, I have aimed to offer a 'bottom-up' justification that starts from a consensus about our duties towards other sentient beings, namely that we have a duty to avoid gratuitous suffering. Granting that we have such a duty, we must find a way of applying that duty to cases where we are uncertain about whether a being is sentient or not. My proposal is that we can satisfy our duty by taking proportionate steps to control the risk of causing suffering whenever a being is a sentience candidate.

The framework is intended to cover all cases at the edge of sentience. This is a diverse family. It will soon be time to leave behind the general level and step down to the level of details. As an intermediate step towards discussing particular cases, however, we first need to get into detail about how an informed, inclusive, democratic process for assessing proportionality could actually work.

6.7 Summary of Chapter 6

This chapter has sought points of consensus across the zone of reasonable disagreement. To do this, it introduced two crucial bridging concepts: *sentience candidates* and *investigation priorities*. The key idea is that the zone of reasonable disagreement is wide, but not so wide as to preclude a meta-consensus about what it takes to be a sentience candidate. Of particular relevance to later chapters is that the relatively inclusive theories of Panksepp, Damasio, and Merker, which link sentience to evolutionarily ancient mechanisms in the midbrain, describe realistic possibilities, so a system with these mechanisms is a sentience candidate. When the evidence falls short of showing that a system is a sentience candidate, but there are still welfare risks that may call for a precautionary response, the system should be classed as an investigation priority.

There is, moreover, an ethical consensus around a duty to, at minimum, avoid causing gratuitous suffering to sentient beings. Suffering is not gratuitous if it occurs in the course of a defensible activity despite proportionate attempts to prevent it. Suffering is gratuitous if the activity is indefensible or the precautions taken fall short of what is proportionate.

These ideas (the concept of a sentience candidate and the duty to avoid gratuitous suffering) are combined in the principle that precautions may be proportionate whenever a being is a sentience candidate. This leaves the issue of what proportionality requires, and we should expect disagreement about this. All can agree, however, on the unacceptability of a free-for-all in which everyone can treat sentience candidates however they wish. To avoid this, we need informed and inclusive democratic processes to reach decisions on proportionality, which can then be revisited periodically and whenever significant new evidence emerges. The question of what sort of process might fit the brief of being 'informed, inclusive, and democratic' will be taken up in the next two chapters.

This framework is 'precautionary' in the sense that it endorses several of the core tenets of precautionary thinking: we should not let scientific uncertainty paralyse decision-making, precautions should be proportionate to the threat, our procedures for debating precautions should be democratic and inclusive, and the evidential bar for triggering those procedures should be set reasonably low. However, the case for adopting this framework does not assume any prior sympathy for precautionary approaches to other problems.

The Edge of Sentience: Risk and Precaution in Humans, Other Animals, and AI. Jonathan Birch, Oxford University Press.
© Jonathan Birch 2024. DOI: 10.1093/9780191966729.003.0007

7

Involving the Public

The last chapter was a search for consensus. I proposed that all reasonable positions regarding the nature and ethical significance of sentience can converge on the idea that precautions may be warranted when a being is a sentience candidate. While the assessment of sentience candidature calls for expert judgement based on the scientific evidence, we need informed and inclusive democratic processes to address questions of proportionality. Moreover, given the potential for the evidential picture to change quickly, we need processes that revisit the issues periodically and whenever significant new evidence emerges.

This transforms a question about what to do into a question about institutional design. This chapter picks up that question. *What sort of processes can deliver effectively on the promise of being appropriately informed, inclusive, and democratic?*

7.1 Citizens' Assemblies and Panels: The Basic Idea

In 2021 and 2022, I participated in public dialogues on genome editing for the Nuffield Council on Bioethics. My role in these dialogues was to answer questions from panels of members of the public selected by a polling company to be representative of the wider population. I had some initial concerns about the idea. Would members of the public, most without any scientific training, be able to grasp the fundamental issues? Would they end up being asked to adjudicate scientific disputes miles away from their own expertise? Would the process degenerate into a kind of 'expertise laundering', in which a group of experts would present their own opinions and get them back again at the end, freshly washed, as the 'will of the people'?

There are many ways for a process like this to fail, but I had a strong sense that the dialogues in which I participated succeeded. I started to see how the answers to the above questions could be 'no'. The public panel seemed to have a strong grasp of the ethical issues at the heart of the matter and an eye for the big picture. They were not pushed around by the experts and disagreed with them on many evaluative questions, while deferring on scientific matters. For example, they were perceptive about the potential for genome editing to serve the interests of corporations rather than consumers or animals. They could see how the 'poster children' of genome editing, such as genome editing for disease resistance, might be used to cement a trend towards intensification that ought instead to be reversed. They could see the real issue at stake was an evaluative one about the sort of relationship we, the human population, want to have towards the animals in our care. Their conclusions, as transcribed by the organizers, were sensible and well reasoned.[1]

I was left not just with a positive view of the feasibility of a citizen's panel on a scientifically complex issue, but also with a sense of the *distinctive value* of such panels. Sometimes the public's perspective can be a valuable corrective to expert biases. Soon after the dialogue, the Nuffield Council published an expert report on the same issue. The report repeatedly describes current methods of intensive animal farming as 'entrenched', and their entrenchment is given as a reason to think about editing animals to fit their conditions rather than modifying the conditions to fit the needs of the animal.[2] I think the public, not the experts, are in a stronger position to judge what is truly entrenched. Citizens' panels can be an invaluable way of breaking through the sort of groupthink that leads panels of experts to rule out certain types of societal change as unfeasible.

I will use the terms 'citizens' panel' and 'citizens' assembly' interchangeably in this book. The former usually connotes a somewhat smaller group (less than 100) and the latter a somewhat larger group (at least 100), but the difference will not play an important role in my arguments. I think panels/assemblies should *ideally* have at least 150 members but still have value, and for the same basic reasons, when smaller.

7.2 Avoiding the Tyranny of Expert Values

Why are citizens' panels valuable? The need to avoid groupthink is one rationale, but a fairly shallow one. Yes, they may help with that problem, but perhaps a suitably large and diverse panel of experts would also be able to avoid groupthink. Is there also a deeper rationale?

---

[1] Nuffield Council on Bioethics (2021b, 2022).
[2] Nuffield Council on Bioethics (2021a, p. 83).

In pluralistic societies, we continually face problems of value conflict. When thinking about precautions against risks, we must consider the harms imposed by the proposed response and whether they are justified by the level of risk reduction they achieve. Informally: is the cure worse than the disease? Yet there is very often (perhaps always) no appropriate way to weigh the expected harms and benefits in a common currency.

To give one example, discussed in Chapter 17: Thomas Metzinger has called for a moratorium on AI research that knowingly risks creating artificial sentience, not because of the risks to humanity, but because the risk of developing sentient AI that we expose to terrible suffering is too great.[3] Is this proportionate? On the harm side of the ledger, we forego potentially massive economic gains that could make human lives easier in many areas. On the benefit side, we have the potential for preventing the suffering of a new type of sentient being. In what common currency are these harms and benefits to be compared?

In situations of value conflict, a threat arises that I call the 'tyranny of expert values'. It is not that there is literally no way to resolve a conflict between disparate values: the real problem is that there are many ways, reflecting different ways of weighting the values.[4] Experts often unintentionally build an implicit weighting into the advice they give. If this weighting is never brought to the surface and scrutinized by a democratic process, we have a problem of accountability.

One example of this phenomenon (unrelated to sentience) is the UK's initial response to COVID-19.[5] The school closures and national lockdown of March 2020 were driven by forthright advice from epidemiological advisers, who told the government that (to quote from published documents) a strategy involving school closures 'should be followed as soon as practical',[6] that it was 'the only viable strategy at the current time',[7] and that 'evidence now supports implementing school closures on a national level as soon as practicable to prevent NHS intensive care capacity being exceeded'.[8]

As critics noted, this strategy imposed a serious harm on schoolchildren, who are generally at very low risk of contracting severe COVID-19, and were thought even in the early stages of the pandemic to be at very low risk.[9] These harms will have a legacy stretching far into the future. At the heart of the

---

[3] Metzinger (2021).
[4] This is why I prefer the term 'value conflict' to 'value incommensurability', which is sometimes also used.
[5] Birch (2021a).   [6] SPI-M-O (2020).   [7] Ferguson et al. (2020).
[8] Scientific Advisory Group for Emergencies (2020a).   [9] Lewis et al. (2021).

advice to close schools was an implicit value weighting. Advisers implicitly judged that the expected harms to children caused by school closures were outweighed by the expected harms, especially to clinically vulnerable groups, of high infection rates leading to a shortage of intensive care beds.

No one should envy the difficult situation the advisers faced. Moreover, my point is not that the advisers' weighting was incorrect. The point is that the case illustrates a procedural pitfall democratic governments should try to avoid. Instead of an inclusive, democratic process for making a difficult trade-off that would affect the whole of society, a small group of scientific advisers were put in a position where *they* had to make the relevant trade-offs using their own values.

Some may feel that the only problem in such cases is that *scientific* advisers are making the trade-offs, and that incorporating *ethical* as well as scientific expertise in the pool of advisers would solve the problem. If the trade-offs are made by ethics experts, is this still a tyranny of expert values? I'm afraid it is. To be clear, I do favour involving ethicists in the policy-making process, as one source of input to citizens' panels. But I do not think it is acceptable to assign to ethicists the role of resolving trade-offs between conflicting values. Ethicists have distinctively valuable expertise, because they have knowledge of the major traditions in human ethical thought and of how different ethical positions relate to each other. This gives them the expertise required to explain and articulate the value conflicts that lie at the heart of our decision-making and to propose possible consistent resolutions. That is the role I am trying to play throughout this book. But that does not mean that ethicists have any special insight into a mysterious realm of ethical facts, including facts about the correct weightings to give to different values. Nor does it mean they have the ability to confer democratic legitimacy on their preferred resolutions.[10]

Citizens' panels, in contrast to panels of professional ethicists, are an appropriate mechanism for resolving conflicts about values in a democratic society. They avoid accepting any contentious claims to expertise and avoid giving any elite group a privileged role in weighing values. When we ask a

---

[10] Many different meta-ethical positions (both realist and anti-realist) emphasize the value of inclusive ethical discussion and so are compatible with my project in this book. I am myself more inclined towards anti-realist positions such as norm-expressivism (Gibbard 1992); quasi-realism (Blackburn 1993, 1998), pragmatic naturalism (Kitcher 2011a, 2011b; Sager 2014) and moral fiction-alism (Joyce 2006). I am particularly drawn towards the view sketched by Bernard Williams towards the end of *Ethics and the Limits of Philosophy* (1985). Williams suggests that ethical discussion aims neither at knowledge nor at simply deciding which values to accept. Rather, the aim is to arrive at a state of *confidence* in our shared values, concepts, and way of life.

panel to make a difficult trade-off between two very different types of harm, they will naturally use their own values to do the weighing. But if the panel is well constructed (and more on this in Chapter 8), these values will be representative of the values of society as a whole. The hope and promise of a citizens' panel is that the resulting trade-off will reflect the decision the whole of society would have reached, had every member of society been presented with relevant information and given time to deliberate with others.

7.3 Three Alternatives

Citizens panels and assemblies offer one way to avoid the tyranny of expert values, but is this the *only* way? Let us consider three alternatives.

Elected Representatives

Should the task of assessing proportionality not fall to our elected representatives? I agree that elected representatives have an essential role. Some[11] have suggested that citizens' panels be given autonomous legislative authority—the power to make laws—but this is not what I am proposing here, and I think it would be a mistake. That power is best left in the hands of elected representatives. Elected assemblies provide a different kind of representation: what Philip Pettit has called *responsive* representation, where representatives are accountable to an electorate and have incentives to respond to their concerns. Responsive representation is well suited in theory to the task of making laws, for all its many problems in practice.[12] Accordingly, it should fall to elected representatives to implement, amend, or overturn the recommendations of a citizens' panel on any particular issue. My proposal is that a framework of citizens' panels should run in parallel to the normal framework of representative democracy, providing it with input on questions of proportionality.

Why, then, are the panels needed at all? As Pettit has argued, when we want to move an issue at least partly outside the scope of party politics, but want to do this in a way that does not lead to technocracy, they provide a mechanism through which this can be achieved. He calls this 'depoliticization'.[13] I would sooner call it 'departisanization', since discussions among panels of

---

[11] Guerrero (2014); Landemore (2020).   [12] Pettit (2010, 2012); Waldron (2016).
[13] Pettit (2004, 2012).

citizens are still political discussions. After all, different values and ways of life are brought to the table, they come into conflict, and a shared way forward is agreed.

Why should we want issues regarding sentience to be departisanized? For two main reasons. One is that these questions of proportionality in the face of risk (including other kinds of risk, such as public health risk and military risk) tend not to register as salient issues during election campaigns, which tend to focus instead on economic, fiscal, and social policies (e.g. tax rises, spending increases) that will have robust and immediate impacts on the population. Election campaigns inevitably bundle together many issues, with the result that there is little scrutiny of candidates' positions on relatively non-central issues. As a result, elected representatives need not be responsive to the values of the voters on questions of proportionality in the face of risk. That is not a problem as such, because it is right for election campaigns to focus on the core policy platforms of the competing parties. It is, however, a reason for thinking responsive representation may not be the best kind of democratic representation to address these particular questions.

The second reason to departisanize is that political parties have a strong incentive to prioritize the interests of currently voting humans over the interests of all other beings. It is often remarked that the interests of prison populations, children, immigrants without voting rights, and future generations are systematically neglected in democracies. The same is plausibly true of patients with chronic disorders of consciousness requiring long-term care. While their families may well vote in a way that reflects their interests (just as the families of prisoners might promote their interests), this group is too small and too geographically dispersed to register as a significant electoral force. A similar point is even more obviously true of non-human animals, and will be at least initially true of any potentially sentient future AI systems.

Does this second reason also tell against citizens' panels? If composed of human citizens, won't they too have a tendency to neglect the interests of non-humans, and perhaps also those of small, marginalized groups of humans? That is an important issue I will take up in §7.4.

Referendums

A second alternative approach is to hold referendums on these issues. Like citizens' panels, referendums can take an issue outside the scope of party politics. The advantage of a referendum is that, by involving the entire electorate, it creates an authoritative mandate for a particular way forward. I suspect there may come a point where a referendum is needed on the question of whether to extend certain types of welfare protection to AI, because the social ramifications of the decision will be absolutely vast.

Even so, I do not think this should be the *default* approach to issues at the edge of sentience, due to the need to revisit the issues periodically and whenever significant new evidence emerges. Referendums cannot be easily re-run again and again. It is not just that they are expensive and logistically difficult (and we can hope that, as voting technology improves, they will become easier to implement). It is also that, to produce good decisions, the voters need to be well informed about the issues and need to be talking about them. There needs to be a sustained national conversation on the issue, a reconstruction in macrocosm of the sort of deliberation generated in citizens' panels.[14] This ideal of a national conversation is extremely difficult to achieve or even approximate, and states routinely fall a long way short of it in actual referendums. It is harder still to achieve when the issue at stake is scientifically complex, as with issues concerning sentience. The difficulty is ramped up to an impossibly high level if we repeatedly hold referendums on the same complex issue, with the public expected to consider new evidence each time.

A Common Currency

A third alternative rests on the thought that, if we could just find the *right currency*, one that encompassed all the objectively relevant costs and benefits with the right weightings, it would be unproblematic to leave difficult trade-offs in the hands of scientific experts. The experts' personal values would drop out of the picture, and the only problems would be those of making sure the scientific experts implemented the formula correctly and with good data.

Some of my LSE colleagues have defended a technocratic approach to public policy of this general type: the WELLBY approach.[15] A WELLBY is a well-being adjusted life-year, constructed in a way analogous to the QALY (quality-adjusted life-year) widely used in public health trade-offs. The idea is that the WELLBY can serve as a universal common currency for policy decisions. Applied at the edge of sentience, the proposal would be that

---

[14] Lafont (2020).   [15] De Neve et al. (2020); Layard and Oparina (2021).

proportionate measures for managing risk are simply those that maximize expected WELLBYs.

Even when applied to policies that only affect unambiguously sentient humans, there is a sense in which this approach entrenches, rather than avoids, the tyranny of expert values. This is because there are value judgements involved in constructing a well-being measure.[16] For example, to judge that what we value in public policy is exhausted by hedonic well-being—subjective experiences with positive or negative valence—is a substantive value judgement (one with a hedonic utilitarian flavour) that many people reasonably reject.[17] To impose the WELLBY is to impose a certain type of utilitarian thinking, rather than to acknowledge and resolve conflict between different conceptions of well-being. The imposition could be justified only if we believed in the contentious view of ethical expertise rejected above—and, moreover, only if we thought hedonic utilitarians were the only real experts. As Johanna Thoma has argued, this approach is at odds with the principle that value conflicts in a democratic society should be resolved democratically.[18]

When thinking of systems at the edge of sentience, we face the additional problem of how to measure WELLBYs for those systems. The measurement of hedonic well-being in humans is heavily reliant on self-report through questionnaires, a method of limited use in our cases. Moreover, we face the question of how to weight non-human WELLBYs in comparison with human WELLBYs. Is a canine WELLBY worth the same as a human WELLBY—or is it worth seven? Intuitively, the subjective 'speed' at which the animals live their lives should somehow be factored into a calculation of hedonic well-being, but we don't know how to do that, and, even if we did, we would not have the evidence to do it in an informed way. A deep problem of interspecies comparison arises for any version of hedonic utilitarianism.[19] Many rules for weighing WELLBYs across species are possible; the problem is that we have insufficient reason to favour any particular rule over any other. Even if we could solve these daunting problems, we would still run into the problems of the preceding paragraph.

So, citizens' panels and assemblies have distinctive advantages over technocratic common currencies, over democratic approaches that lead to proportionality becoming a partisan battleground, and over a direct democratic approach.

---

[16] Alexandrova (2018); Thoma (2022b).   [17] Nozick (1974).
[18] Thoma (2022b).   [19] Browning (2023).

7.4 Objections to Citizens' Panels: Representativeness, Deference, Competence

Representativeness

Worries about the representativeness of citizens' panels arise even if we assume they should only represent human interests. These concerns only deepen when we want the panels to consider non-human interests too. Let us start with the first type of concern, and see whether the solutions we arrive at can help us with the second type of concern.

If citizens' panels are to represent the values and interests of the wider population, they must resemble that population. They therefore need to be large enough to make their statistical representativeness very likely given the law of large numbers. Hélène Landemore has proposed a minimum size of 150. Alexander Guerrero has suggested an ideal size of 300, but in more recent work revises this upwards to 450.[20]

Although both Guerrero and Landemore downplay it, the need for representativeness highlights a difficult challenge of institutional design. Polling companies usually work with samples of at least 1,000 in order to be confident of their representativeness. These samples, since they rely on voluntary participation, still tend to depart from the wider population regarding some demographic variables, such as the relative frequencies of different socioeconomic groups. To correct for this, polling companies will re-weight their data using elaborate formulas. This re-weighting involves value judgements, and sometimes leads to controversy even when the poll is simply an opinion poll, with no role in decision-making at all. I once generated some controversy on this issue myself when I highlighted that voting intention polls tend to give less weight to the opinions of younger and working-class voters, since they are considered less likely to vote by the polling companies' weighting models.[21]

Yet for a citizens' panel or assembly, even 1,000 is already very large indeed. A panel of 1,000 cannot engage in deliberation as a single panel. The optimum panel size for the purposes of deliberation is closer to the size of a jury or a typical committee: 10–25 people. The proposed figures of at least 150, 300, and 450 are compromises between two very different optima.

One option is to adopt a fission-fusion design, whereby a panel hears evidence together, then breaks into smaller, equally sized discussion groups for

---

[20] Landemore (2020); Guerrero (2014, 2021).   [21] Birch (2017e).

further questioning of experts and structured deliberation, and then reconvenes for voting. This creates a situation in which the voting is done by an informed and representative group in which everyone has deliberated with *some* others, even though the deliberation itself took place in smaller groups that may have been unrepresentative in various ways.

Suppose, though, that an important perspective, such as the effects of a proposal on a small minority, is represented by only one or two people in the assembly, who are then absent from the vast majority of the deliberative groups. The fission-fusion approach risks marginalizing such perspectives. There may also be cases in which an important perspective is associated with a minority group so small that a random sample of 1,000 people will still be unlikely to have even one representative of that perspective. Here there is a risk of an even more severe kind of marginalization.

One way to address this risk is to allow affected minorities to nominate experts (that is, experts on how the options on the table will affect them). In effect, we compensate for the limitations of statistical representation by expanding our conception of expertise. We put these viewpoints in at the 'expert input' stage of the process. I am uneasy with this solution, because I can easily imagine a member of an affected minority fairly objecting: I'm not just a source of *information*. I need to be *represented* when deliberation and voting occur.

A way forward is to allow citizens' panels to co-opt new members from particular minority groups.[22] The affected minority initially appears at the expert input stage. The initial panel, recognizing that this issue really does affect this group in an unusually severe way, may decide to co-opt more members from that minority, so that the minority is represented in every deliberative group and has increased voting power. They will still be a minority, but the request for representation will have been answered. And it will have been answered through a decision by the original panel to expand its membership, not by a top-down ruling from the organizers.

Sometimes, the panel will need to co-opt new members who can speak for a minority but who are not themselves members of that minority. Think here of patients with disorders of consciousness. They cannot participate in a citizens' panel while incapacitated, but their relatives can, and indeed patients who have recovered can too. There is a strong case, at face value, for making

---

[22] This is inspired by (though slightly different from) a suggestion from Alastair Cochrane in *Sentientist Politics* (2018). Cochrane suggests we use citizens' panels to decide the composition of panels that will decide questions concerning non-human animals.

sure there are such representatives in every deliberative group. I imagine a citizens' panel would be very likely to grant such a request.

These are reflections on how to design a process that properly represents *human* interests, but in fact I think that these ideas can also help with the problem of representing *non-human* interests. The general idea of a panel co-opting new members to speak for those who cannot speak for themselves has applicability beyond the case of disorders of consciousness. Citizens' panels should be allowed to co-opt representatives of animal interests, or (in the future) AI interests, if they think it appropriate to do so.

Some may object that there is still an element of anthropocentrism in this process, because the initial panel only represents human interests and is not *compelled* to expand. Conceivably, it may decline to co-opt any new members. But expansion through choice is better than forced expansion, given that the aim is for the wider public to have confidence in the results. We start from where we are: a pluralistic society composed of humans, trying to decide how to live. We need processes that give us room to expand our moral circle and represent a wider range of interests. But that choice to expand must, realistically, come from us.

In sum, to address concerns about representativeness, citizens' panels should be substantial (at least 150 citizens) but should be split into much smaller groups of 10–25 for deliberation. They should be well-informed not just about the options and the issues, but also about how the options might disproportionately affect specific minority groups. They should have the power to co-opt new members to ensure that marginalized perspectives are represented in every deliberative group.

Deference

A common source of unease about citizens' panels is a suspicion that citizens will simply defer to experts—this is the 'expertise laundering' worry I myself had before participating in such a panel. I think the trials of citizens panels that have occurred so far have tended to suggest that this concern is misplaced.[23] Citizens think for themselves. They do not simply latch on to particularly charismatic experts and defer to them. We experts are not the irresistible authorities we sometimes take ourselves to be.

---

[23] Fishkin (2018).

Cristina Lafont has developed a subtler and deeper concern about deference. To explain the criticism, let us introduce the concept of 'uncomprehending deference'. A norm of uncomprehending deference exists in a society whenever ordinary citizens are expected to defer to the decisions of some subset of the population without understanding or accepting the reasons for those decisions. Lafont suggests (and I agree) that norms of uncomprehending deference are inimical to democracy. This is easy to see when we are talking about deference to an elite group of technocrats or oligarchs. Lafont's move is to argue that this problem remains, in a less obvious form, when the subset is a citizens' panel. The idea behind such a panel is that those outside the panel ought to defer not to experts but to their 'better selves'—to the decisions of a statistically representative group of ordinary people who have been properly informed and given time to deliberate. But deferring to your better self is still a form of uncomprehending deference. If you yourself, as a citizen outside the panel, have not received the same information and have not been part of the deliberation, you will not understand or accept the reasons that led to the decision.[24]

Suppose, to use one of Lafont's examples, a panel is tasked with evaluating a proposal for a radical new law mandating veganism. They learn the relevant facts, listen to the arguments, and come to be convinced of the need for such a law, even though the wider public and its elected representatives are far from convinced. What now? We are faced with two bad options. We either *force* the wider public to defer to the panel, which is far from democratic, or else we treat the output of the citizens' panel as an input to a second democratic process (either a debate by an elected assembly or a referendum) and merely *encourage* deference to the recommendations of the panel, in which case we are being unrealistic. In a referendum, people would not defer to their 'better selves' on a question at the core of their way of life, but would vote in accordance with their actual opinions. In an elected assembly, meanwhile, politicians would not defer to this 'better public' but would respond to the views of actual voters.

Moreover, there is no reason to think that the general population or its elected representatives even *ought* to defer to the panel, setting aside the question of whether they would. If we say they ought to defer, we are saying that the secondary mechanism ought to be a mere rubber-stamping exercise in which the panel's recommendation ought to be unanimously acclaimed. But the panel's recommendation may have been the result of intense debate in

---

[24] Lafont (2020). Lafont uses the term 'blind deference', but I prefer 'uncomprehending deference'.

which a minority opinion was narrowly edged out. It seems not just implausible but also anti-democratic to suggest that members of the population who endorse that minority opinion ought to vote against their own view in a referendum, simply because that view was overruled in one microcosm of the population.[25]

The objection is powerful, and yet I think its force depends partly on the radical nature of the example. A law mandating veganism would indeed be radical, and miles away from any overlapping consensus that currently exists, and that is why it would never be appropriate to defer to a panel. The process I am proposing here is more carefully circumscribed. We start from a point of overlapping consensus: it is appropriate to take proportionate steps to guard against the risk of causing suffering to sentience candidates. We face the problem that there is no consensus around what steps are proportionate. We have good reasons for not routinely putting such questions to referendums, because the issues are scientifically complex and require expert input. We also have good reasons for taking them partially outside the normal run of electoral politics, since elected representatives do not have sufficient incentive to give these questions the sustained attention they need. This is a special set of circumstances in which elected representatives do have good reason to defer to the recommendations of a citizens' panel, as long as the recommendations are compatible with the elected representatives' core policy commitments.

That last qualification raises the possibility of a situation where a citizens' panel recommends something that elected representatives cannot implement without violating a core policy commitment. Suppose, for example, that a panel recommends a moratorium on AI as proportionate, when the government has a democratic mandate to invest in AI as part of its core economic platform. This is the type of situation where a referendum would be warranted as a last-resort way of resolving what is evidently too deep a conflict of values within society to be resolved by a mere panel. A serious attempt at a one-off national conversation would be justified.

Competence

Perhaps the most obvious problem with citizens' panels, when the issue at stake is scientifically and philosophically complex, is competence. *How are*

---

[25] Landemore appears to concede a surprising amount to Lafont's criticism when she writes that assemblies (or 'mini-publics') need to be 'ultimately connected to an authorization moment and sometimes, though not necessarily always, a referendum down the line', adding that they should not be 'making the decisions on momentous issues' (Landemore 2020, p. 116).

members of the public supposed to comprehend all the relevant science and philosophy? I would have said the same myself in the past, but the panels on genome editing described earlier changed my view. I now think there are ways to overcome this design problem by carefully formulating the questions we pose to the panel.

Although ordinary citizens are not experts on complex scientific matters, they *are* experts on their own experiences, needs, priorities and values, a point powerfully made by W. E. B. Du Bois in his defence of democracy and universal suffrage. When Mary, in Frank Jackson's thought experiment, leaves her black and white room and encounters a red tomato for the first time, she gains knowledge: knowledge of what it's like to experience red.[26] That point extends far beyond experiences of colours to encompass any type of experience with a distinctive character, including experiences of the many varieties of suffering and joy.[27] In Du Bois's words, 'only the sufferer knows his sufferings'.[28] Ordinary citizens have a huge amount of relevant knowledge about human experiences and their comparative value or disvalue. The knowledge is distributed across many heads, but it is there nonetheless. This is the knowledge a citizens' panel aims to pool and draw upon.[29]

This response, though, leads to new worries about representativeness: will the panel not inevitably *lack* knowledge of the sufferings and joys of beings on the edge of sentience? The ability of the panel to co-opt new members helps, but there will still be an element of indirectness and of inescapable ignorance. For example, even a close family member of a person with a disorder of consciousness does not know what it feels like to be that person. Note, however, that a panel of experts would face the same problem, so this is not a reason to exclude ordinary citizens from the discussion. It is just a reason to make sure the discussion does involve people who are as close as anyone can get to knowing what it feels like, such as people who have themselves recovered from disorders of consciousness.

These ideas will be developed further in the next chapter. We have not yet properly answered the challenge. For our imagined critic will say: yes, if the question concerns values, panels of members of the public are well placed to formulate answers. However, if the question concerns science, they are not: ordinary citizens without scientific training lack the competence needed to

[26] Jackson (1982). Although Jackson initially took it to support epiphenomenalism, the idea that experience gives us a special type of knowledge—knowledge of what it's like to have the experience—is compatible with many different views of the mind-body relationship. It does not imply that the new knowledge concerns non-physical facts (Carruthers 2000; Crane 2001, 2019; Papineau 2002).

[27] Paul (2014).   [28] Du Bois (1920/2005, §27).

[29] This has become an important motif in epistemic arguments for democracy. See Goodin and Spiekermann (2018); Landemore (2013).

adjudicate scientific agreements. Yet the edge of sentience presents us with questions that blend evaluative and scientific components, with no sharp dividing line. How, given this, can we avoid a situation where citizens are forced to adjudicate between different claims to expertise, or one in which experts impose their own values?

To meet the challenge in full, we need to lay out a possible procedure that a citizens' panel could follow to reach a judgement about proportionality. To defuse worries about competence, the procedure needs to show how the labour will be divided between experts and citizens. It must be that experts are asked to assess sentience candidature and to provide input on matters within their expertise but are not expected to resolve deep value conflicts. Meanwhile, ordinary citizens must be asked to reach judgements about proportionality, drawing on the knowledge they collectively possess regarding human values, needs and priorities, but are not expected to resolve scientific disagreements. The task of the next chapter is to propose such a procedure.

7.5 Summary of Chapter 7

A 'tyranny of expert values' occurs when the values of expert advisers determine a policy decision without those values being properly scrutinized by a democratic process. Citizens' panels and assemblies, composed of random samples of the wider population, can be an attractive way to avoid the tyranny of expert values, when carefully designed.

Citizens' panels can have advantages over elected assemblies and referendums. These advantages are especially clear when an issue generates deep value conflicts, requires sustained attention and regular revisiting, requires consideration of the interests of beings who cannot vote, and when there are reasons to departisanize the issue. Questions of proportionality at the edge of sentience have all of these properties.

To be adequately representative, citizens' panels/assemblies should be sizeable (at least 150 citizens) but should fission into smaller groups of 10–25 for deliberation. They should have the power to co-opt new members to ensure that important but marginalized perspectives are represented in every deliberative group.

Elected assemblies should not defer to citizens' panels in all circumstances. In cases where a panel makes a recommendation that contradicts the core policy platform of an elected government, a referendum may be justified as a way to resolve the deep value conflict.

Since members of citizens' panels do not generally have scientific training, careful thought needs to be given to the structure of deliberation, so that they are not forced into a position of arbitrating scientific disagreement. Their focus should be on whether or not a proposed response can be publicly justified as proportionate to an identified risk, not on whether a being is a sentience candidate.

The Edge of Sentience: Risk and Precaution in Humans, Other Animals, and AI. Jonathan Birch, Oxford University Press.
© Jonathan Birch 2024. DOI: 10.1093/9780191966729.003.0008

8

Debating Proportionality

In the last chapter, I proposed entrusting citizens' panels/assemblies with judgements about proportionality. Expert panels would make a judgement about whether a system is a sentience candidate but would not decide what precautions to take. Deliberation about proportionate responses should involve the public. There are deep value conflicts at the edge of sentience, and citizens' panels are well placed to find resolutions. Yet for this idea to work in practice, we need a procedure that commands our confidence: confidence that all relevant considerations would be properly taken into account, confidence that the panel would be competent to take them into account, and confidence in the recommendations at the end of the process.

My aim in this chapter is to propose one such procedure. I do not see my proposal as the *only* way of structuring deliberation. There will be alternatives. But I do think it would be one viable and effective way. That is enough in the context, since my aim is to reply to an imagined critic who says: 'This could not *even possibly* work. We could never be justified in trusting such a panel to make such important judgements.'

8.1 Curating Options: Learning from the Climate Assembly UK

The procedure I envisage involves a citizens' panel starting out with a short-list of options that have been deemed feasible by policy-makers and their scientific advisers. The first question arises: *who decides which options make it on to the shortlist?* The Climate Assembly UK allowed experts to decide. In each policy area, a small shortlist of proposals was drawn up by experts, and the assembly was asked to deliberate vote on these proposals.

This creates a risk that some live options will be omitted from the list—a risk, in other words, that the tyranny of expert values will assert itself at the stage of filtering the options that reach the assembly. Indeed, when we look in detail at the options presented to Climate Assembly UK, some radical options appear to have been omitted. For example, the UK Green Party has proposed a radical climate action plan that involves a £500 per tonne carbon tax by 2030, the introduction of Universal Basic Income, and a 'Green quantitative easing' scheme aimed at 'radically reforming our money system.'[1] As far as I can tell, this plan was not put to the assembly. They were presented with a menu of moderate options.

It is tempting to broaden the range of possibilities by using coarse-grained descriptions of general types of response, but this can lead to recommendations that greatly underdetermine the actual policy. For example, 99 per cent of the Climate Assembly UK agreed that 'forests and better forest management' were a good idea, but they were not asked to choose among specific policy options.[2] At the 2019 general election, all the UK's political parties were in favour of forests, but specific proposals varied widely, from planting 30 million trees a year (Conservatives) to 100 million a year (Labour).[3] The Climate Assembly's pro-forest stance was neutral between these specific options.

This example crystallizes a general problem: the options on the table need to be specific and detailed if they are to meaningfully guide policy. So, there must be a small number of them, if the panel's task is to be accomplished in a matter of days. This means there must be a significant amount of prior curation of the options, and that creates an opportunity for the curators to exert excessive influence. A sceptic might say: 'Doesn't this substantiate the concern that such assemblies are really an exercise in expertise laundering? Don't they just create a mechanism whereby a pre-vetted list of policies endorsed by experts can be cleverly repackaged (unless they meet with strong disapproval) as the recommendations of the people?'

However, institutional design can manage the problem in a way that defuses this expertise laundering concern. As Landemore has argued, a principle of openness needs to be at the heart of our design choices: any assembly must be open to points of view from outside the assembly.[4] We can achieve openness by (i) publishing the proposals that are to be put forward for consideration, well in advance of the panel meeting, and (ii) creating a mechanism whereby stakeholders can, before the panel meets, force consideration of additional options, as long as they are feasible. That creates room for a correction if the list of options is widely seen as impoverished according to a significant stakeholder group, and it creates a pathway by which criticism can lead to an expansion of the list of options.

---

[1] UK Green Party (2020).   [2] Climate Assembly UK (2020, p. 26).
[3] Morris (2019).   [4] Landemore (2020).

8.2 A Pragmatic Analysis of Proportionality

Let us turn now to what happens when a panel actually meets. The nature of the risk, and the potential harms that could result if nothing is done, are explained to them by experts in accessible way. Their first task is to decide whether or not to co-opt new members to increase the representation of affected minorities or other groups. Their next task is to assess the options for their proportionality. To do this, the panel will need assistance from scientific experts, legal experts, and ethics experts. But the role of these experts needs to be carefully circumscribed—with the panel itself ruling on the critical evaluative questions—if the tyranny of expert values is to be avoided. How should deliberation about proportionality be structured?

I want to propose four tests (or conditions, criteria) for proportionality: *permissibility-in-principle*, *adequacy*, *reasonable necessity*, and *consistency*. A proposed response to a threat that passes these 'PARC' tests can be considered proportionate. I do not intend this as a conceptual analysis of 'proportionality'. I do not think ordinary language terms are in general amenable to conceptual analyses that give precise necessary and sufficient conditions. What I intend can be better described as a pragmatic analysis: a proposal about the questions we should be discussing, and the sequence in which we should discuss them, if we want a deliberative process to arrive at a judgement about proportionality that can command confidence.

Test 1: Permissibility-in-Principle

This is a test any proposed response to a risk must meet to deserve further consideration. It must be that, given our shared values (as represented in the panel), the response could *at least in principle* form part of an ethically permissible response in the right circumstances, if other conditions are met.

There is a legal component to this test: proposed policy responses to identified risks should be compatible with international human rights law. Legal experts need to be involved in the process to rule on this question, and save the panel's time by excluding options that would be straightforwardly incompatible with human rights. That does not mean, however, that proportionate measures cannot involve any element of suspending rights. Many human rights are considered by the law to be 'qualified', in the sense that it is legal for a public authority to restrict them as a proportionate means to a legitimate aim, such as a public health aim. The COVID-19 pandemic gave us all personal experience of this, since many of our rights were temporarily sus-pended by lockdowns. These lockdowns were not unconstitutional; they were lawful suspensions of rights. The upshot is that very few proposals should be excluded at this first stage. If a proposal involves a suspension of qualified rights in a way that may or may not be proportionate, depending on other factors, then it should remain on the table for further discussion.

That said, international law recognizes a small number of absolute (or 'non-derogable') rights that, by international agreement, cannot be appropriately restricted in any circumstance, no matter how exceptional. The International Covenant on Civil and Political Rights recognizes several such rights: the 'right to life'; the right to freedom from torture and from cruel, inhuman, or degrading treatment or punishment; the right to freedom from medical or scientific experimentation without consent; the right to freedom from slavery and servitude; the right to freedom from imprisonment for inability to fulfil a contractual obligation; the right to freedom from the retrospective operation of criminal laws; the right to recognition as a person before the law; and the right to freedom of thought, conscience, and religion. I propose that any pre-caution violating any of these rights is ipso facto disproportionate and should be taken off the table.[5]

The right to life is a source of complications, since national laws typically make room for exceptions, despite the supposedly 'non-derogable' nature of the right. In particular, the intentional killing of a person by the police or armed forces in the course of their duties is not always deemed a violation of the right to life. Moreover, public health emergencies, such as the COVID-19 pandemic, typically put decision-makers in a situation where, whatever they decide, some people will foreseeably die. There may be intentional allowing of a certain level of death, albeit without intentional killing. Relevantly for our purposes, the fact that restricting scientific research in certain ways may foreseeably involve foregoing medical breakthroughs does not mean that restrictions violate anyone's right to life.

I have been describing the legal element of the 'permissibility-in-principle' test, but I am not proposing that it is solely a legal test. There could be lawful options that nonetheless represent such a severe departure from our shared moral values that a citizens' panel deems them impermissible-in-principle on moral grounds. Suppose, for example, that we convene a panel to consider possible responses to a pandemic, and one of the options floated is a coercive programme of mandatory vaccination. The experts report that this is

---

[5] UN General Assembly (International Covenant on Civil and Political Rights 1966).

potentially lawful, since the right to refuse medical treatment can be suspended on public health grounds when proportionate. A panel might nonetheless find such an option deeply unethical, and might decide that it would be better to rule it out immediately as impermissible-in-principle rather than spend time comparing it with other options.

Test 2: Adequacy

Informally, a proportionate response to a risk must *do enough*. The requirement is not that the response completely removes the identified risk, or even that it renders it negligible or no longer urgent. This is often unachievable, as the COVID-19 pandemic clearly demonstrated. Many measures were taken, but none removed the risk, rendered it negligible, or removed its urgency.

We cannot specify a one-size-fits-all threshold that must be achieved (e.g. the probability of the threat materializing must be reduced to 10 per cent or less). Such a threshold would be arbitrary and insufficiently insensitive to the details of particular cases. Furthermore, we often find ourselves in situations where agreed, precise probabilities cannot be placed on scenarios or outcomes. We are in exactly such a situation at the edge of sentience. We all have our own degrees of belief about these cases—our own subjective probabilities— but there is no agreement on precise probabilities.

So what is required of an adequate response? A proposal: the response should either (i) reduce the risk to an acceptable level or, if this is unachievable, (ii) deliver the best level of risk reduction that can be achieved by any permissible-in-principle option.

The question of adequacy may initially sound like a scientific question— one that can be left to the experts, without input from citizens—but it is not. This is because the judgement of an *acceptable* level of risk is an evaluative judgement. Our way of life depends on tolerating risks: to drive a car is to tolerate risk of injury, to interact with other people in the same room is to tolerate risk of communicable disease. But the question of what levels of risk are acceptable is a question for the people who will be taking the risks, not for an elite group of experts.

It might be objected that the question of acceptability (and thus of proportionality) is different when it comes to risks at the edge of sentience. Often, as with driving and social interaction, the question is one of *prudential* acceptability: what risks ought we accept for the sake of our own happiness? It is clear why ordinary citizens—being the experts on their own interests and their own happiness—should be involved in making that decision. At the edge of sentience, by contrast, the question is one of *moral* acceptability: what risks ought we not accept, as people who recognize a duty not to cause gratuitous suffering to other sentient beings? And it might be supposed that we need to leave this to ethics experts, not to ordinary citizens. The objection goes: I am incorrectly conflating issues of prudential acceptability with issues of moral acceptability, and incorrectly assuming a framework apt for managing the former is apt for managing the latter.

In my view, though, it is right to involve the public even when the question is specifically one of moral acceptability. Recall the principle (endorsed in Chapter 7) that value conflicts in a democratic society, including moral conflicts, should be resolved democratically. Any other approach involves elevating an anointed group as the experts on the relative importance of the conflicting values, when we have no reason to believe that there are any such experts. This, and not the superior epistemic standpoint of the citizens regarding their own interests, is the fundamental ethical rationale for involving the public (the epistemic point is a subsidiary one, relevant to resisting worries about competence). If we were to allow a panel of ethicists to set the threshold for acceptable risk reduction, conflict between values would be resolved by undemocratic means. We would be elevating the ethicists' values over the values of the wider population.

What, then, is the proper role for experts in debates about adequacy? Their role is that of providing estimates of the level of risk reduction different options provide. There is often enormous uncertainty about the level of risk reduction an option will deliver. It is therefore crucial that experts communicate their uncertainty about risk. Two tools are particularly useful for that task: *confidence levels* and *probability yardsticks*.

The Intergovernmental Panel on Climate Change (IPCC) has developed a 'confidence levels' framework for communicating uncertainty about risks.[6] IPCC experts express confidence levels (very low, low, medium, high, or very high confidence) regarding claims about risk, with their confidence depending on the volume and quality of scientific evidence in support of the claim and the amount of consensus surrounding it. I suggest that this approach be generally adopted for the communication of uncertainty to citizens' panels. For example, experts should say not 'Option 1 will reduce the risk more than Option 2' but rather 'I/we have high confidence that Option 1 will reduce the risk more than Option 2'.

---

[6] IPCC (2010).

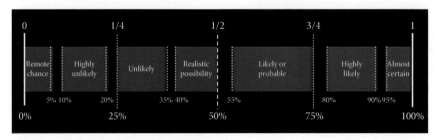

Fig. 8.1   The PHIA probability yardstick. Versions of this yardstick can be found frequently in UK government documents. Public sector information licensed under the Open Government Licence v3.0.

A probability yardstick is a standardized protocol for assigning verbal, qualitative labels to probability ranges. An influential example is the PHIA (Professional Head of Intelligence Assessment) probability yardstick, widely used in UK government circles since 2018 (Fig. 8.1). This yardstick maps the terms 'remote chance', 'highly unlikely', 'unlikely', 'realistic possibility', 'likely/probably', 'highly likely' and 'almost certain' to ranges of probabilities.

The PHIA yardstick is far from perfect. To require 40 per cent probability before being willing to describe an outcome as a 'realistic possibility' seems unwarranted. And to call something a 'remote chance' when it has a probability of 5 per cent seems problematic too (one in twenty is not *that* remote). I also fear that the word 'likely' covers too big a range, including outcomes that are slightly more likely than not (~55 per cent), outcomes that are moderately likely (~60–70 per cent), and outcomes that have a ~75 per cent probability of occurring.

Yet this starting point illustrates the general idea. My proposal is not that we adopt this particular yardstick but rather that, in any citizens' panel, a yardstick *of some kind* should be used to standardize the use of probabilistic language. Experts should say, for example: 'I/we have high confidence that Option 1 will reduce the probability of causing harm, and that, although there will still be a remote chance of causing harm, this will be much reduced from the present situation, where harm is likely.'

Test 3: Reasonable Necessity

Policy responses should not impose harms or costs that go beyond what is reasonably necessary to achieve adequacy. The issue arises because there will often be a temptation to tack extra measures on to a package that is already adequate.

For example, in 2018 the EU banned three specific neonicotinoid pesticides that were credibly linked to colony collapse in bees.[7] There was a case for going beyond a ban on these specific pesticides by banning all neonicotinoids, or even all synthetic pesticides. But tacking on these additional measures was thought to be excessive in relation to the specific threat that was identified.

Let us not get into in the details of whether this was the right decision. Perhaps the limited measures taken did not really do enough to bring the risk down to an acceptable level. Perhaps policy-makers should have gone further. If a citizens' panel had been consulted, ordinary citizens might have recommended stronger measures than those actually taken. My aim is not to take sides on this but to illustrate the general *kind* of debate that should be had regarding excessiveness. I am proposing a procedure, not a decision rule, so the results in particular cases cannot be pre-judged.

If any cost/risk/harm-benefit analyses of the different options have been conducted, the results, presented accessibly, can be used as expert inputs to discussions of adequacy and reasonable necessity. These methods of analysis do have a place in a good procedure. What I oppose is the use of these methods to resolve value conflict. We should never allow the value-judgements and subjective probabilities implicit in these analyses to *dictate* the policy response, without proper deliberation and scrutiny.

Test 4: Consistency

Steel has rightly emphasized the importance of consistency to judgements of proportionality.[8] Critics of precautionary thinking have argued that it often leads to inconsistency—but, to the extent this is true, it reflects poor institutional design rather than a deep flaw with the idea of precautionary thinking. Good institutional design should make sure that the consistency of the measures on the table is explicitly and carefully considered.

The relevant kind of consistency will depend on the details of the case. For example, when formulating animal welfare policy, we should aim for taxonomic consistency: our treatment of one group of animals (e.g. vertebrates) should be consistent with our treatment of another (e.g. invertebrates), in the sense that any disparities in the level of welfare protection should be justified

---

[7] Carrington (2018).   [8] Steel (2015).

by evidence and not based on mere prejudice. That sort of consistency is specific to this policy area.

Nonetheless, some broad types of consistency will be relevant across many policy areas. The EU takes 'consistency' to mean 'consistency with precedent': a precaution should be consistent with other policies adopted in the past.[9] But I disagree that this is a fundamental condition, especially in situations where the evidential picture is rapidly evolving. It introduces a conservative bias into decision-making. Sometimes the right response is to break with precedent, justifying the departure by pointing to new evidence, or to reasons that were missed by past processes but considered by this one. The consistency requirement should be that breaks with precedent can be justified, not that they cannot happen. If a deliberative process arrives at a view that breaks with precedent, they should be informed of the break, and asked to discuss whether there are good reasons for it.

It is not just consistency with *the past* that matters. There is also consistency among the measures being proposed *right now*, in the present. The COVID-19 pandemic has given us examples of packages of measures, assembled in haste, that were not particularly consistent with each other. Infamously, in summer 2020 the UK government introduced an 'Eat Out to Help Out' scheme encouraging people to return to indoor restaurants, while at the same time preparing for a second wave of infections.[10] In September, with infections soaring as predicted, the UK government's scientific advisers gently stressed that 'a consistent package of measures should be adopted that does not appear to promote contradictory goals'.[11]

Most subtly of all, there is a sense of consistency that concerns *the future*: a precautionary response to one threat should not create a *new threat* that may be serious enough to warrant trying to undo or cancel out the original precaution. This is the type of consistency highlighted by Steel. Again, the COVID-19 pandemic provided some striking examples. The UK's advisers were acutely aware that a strategy aimed at completely eliminating a respiratory virus creates a risk of a new threat: a huge wave as soon as the measures are lifted, or as soon as a new, uncontainable variant emerges elsewhere in the world. The risk is real, but the UK's advisers initially took this to be a reason against even attempting aggressive suppression of transmission, and this was almost certainly an overreaction. They changed their advice when the likely consequences of their strategy for hospital admissions were modelled.[12]

---

[9] European Commission (2000/2006).   [10] McKie and Helm (2023).
[11] Scientific Advisory Group for Emergencies (2020b).
[12] These events are recounted and analysed in Birch (2021a).

For a second example, consider again the case of closing schools to prevent viral transmission: a classic case of value conflict. The harms imposed on schoolchildren will naturally be raised at every stage of discussion. But it is worth noting that, even if a panel has agreed that school closures are permissible-in-principle, adequate, and reasonably necessary, a further discussion is warranted about their consistency. Might they create a risk of harm that is so severe that it rivals the public health risk posed by the virus? If so, might it be a permissible-in-principle, adequate and reasonably necessary response to *that* risk to keep schools open?

That is the argument Sarah Lewis and colleagues made in a critique of school closures.[13] They argued that closing schools put children at grave risk of harm, with the harms including 'learning loss, reduced social interaction, isolation, reduced physical activity, increased mental health problems', 'potential for increased abuse, exploitation, and neglect', and 'reduced future income and life expectancy'. They concluded that 'the precautionary principle would be to keep schools open to prevent catastrophic harms to children'.

If there are terrible risks of harm associated with both doing and not doing some specific action, the question becomes: can we find some other response that is simultaneously proportionate to both risks, and that does not involve neglecting one to control the other? If we can find such a Goldilocks response, this is the path we should take. If not, then we must make a value judgement about which risk is more severe and worthy of priority. In reality, the UK government took both paths at different moments in the pandemic. In November 2020, a lockdown excluding schools was attempted, to minimize harm to children. In January 2021, with the new Alpha variant rampant, schools were again closed: the immediate risk to public health was prioritized.

8.3 The Division of Labour Implicit in the PARC Tests

Let us return to the worries about deference and competence that motivated our search for a pragmatic analysis of proportionality. Our imagined critic says: issues at the edge of sentience are scientifically complex, so a citizens' panel will not be competent to answer the questions we put to it. We can help the panel by having experts easily accessible, giving presentations and answering questions, but then the experts will end up revealing their views

---

[13] Lewis et al. (2021).

about proportionality, which the public will then simply rubber-stamp, reducing the process to a form of expertise laundering.

The foregoing pragmatic analysis is intended to help defuse this concern. For each test, there are factual sub-questions that call for expert input. Suppose we dedicate one day's deliberation to each test. It would make sense for the day to start with presentations by experts that address those sub-questions, and for the experts to remain available throughout the day to answer follow-up questions from deliberative subgroups. However, there are also clearly evaluative sub-questions that call for public input. Those would be the main focus of deliberation. Panel members would be encouraged *not* to defer to the experts on those sub-questions, and experts would be encouraged not to reveal their private views on them. Table 8.1 summarizes the division of labour, and Figure 8.2 summarizes the overall procedure.

On those factual sub-questions where expert input is needed, it is reasonable to expect experts to put their answers in plain language that ordinary citizens can understand (e.g. by using probability yardsticks and confidence levels). None of the questions demand inaccessible, technical answers. In answering these questions, some value-judgements will be made, unavoidably. For example, experts will have to make judgements about how to apply coarse-grained probabilistic language (such as 'highly likely') to borderline cases where the yardstick does not determine what to say.[14] But those value-judgements will not dictate the policy response and will not be beyond scrutiny. If a member of the public wants to ask 'Wait, why did you describe that as highly likely?' they will have the opportunity to do so.

Meanwhile, on all of those evaluative sub-questions where public input is needed, ordinary members of the public are competent to answer the questions being posed. The key questions are:

- Does this option depart too far from our shared moral values to deserve further consideration?
- What level of risk reduction is acceptable, given our shared values and attitudes towards risk, and bearing in mind that our shared way of life requires us to tolerate some risks?
- Where harms and costs are imposed, can they be justified to those affected as reasonably necessary to achieve adequate risk reduction?
- Where inconsistencies arise (e.g. with other risks or with past precedent), should they be resolved by breaking with past practice, or by reconsidering our response to the current risk?

[14] Steele (2012).

Table 8.1 A summary of the PARC tests and the division of labour they induce between experts and members of the public.

Condition	Description	Aspects calling for expert input	Aspects calling for public input
Permissibility in principle	The response is compatible with our shared values. Given those values, the response could in principle form part of a proportionate response, if other conditions are met.	If the response involves suspending rights, which rights will be suspended and in what ways? What other harms and costs are likely to result from the proposed response?	In cases where a response is legally permissible-in-principle, does it nonetheless depart too far from our shared moral values to merit further consideration?
Adequacy	The response either (i) reduces the risk to an acceptable level or, if this is unachievable, (ii) delivers the best level of risk reduction that can be achieved by any permissible-in-principle option.	What levels of risk reduction are likely to be delivered by different options? Confidence levels and probability yardsticks should be used. If cost-benefit or harm-benefit analyses are available, the results can be presented.	What level of risk reduction is *acceptable*, given our shared values and attitudes towards risk, and bearing in mind that our shared way of life requires us to tolerate some risks?
Reasonable necessity	The response does not impose any harms or costs (including suspensions of rights) beyond those reasonably necessary to achieve adequacy, and minimizes any harms or costs that are reasonably necessary.	If there are multiple permissible ways to achieve adequacy, what are their comparative harms and costs? What steps are proposed to minimize these harms and costs? If any cost-benefit or harm-benefit analyses are available, the results can be presented to the panel.	Where harms and costs are imposed, can they be justified to those affected as *reasonably necessary* to achieve adequate risk reduction?
Consistency	The response can be reconciled with our attitude towards other risks, including any new risks created by the very response under consideration. Sometimes reconciliation can take the form of justifying a departure from past practice.	What are other comparable risks, and how have they been managed? Will a new risks be generated by the proposed responses? If so, what are they?	Where inconsistencies arise (e.g. with other risks or with past precedent), should they be resolved by breaking with past practice, or by reconsidering our response to the current risk?

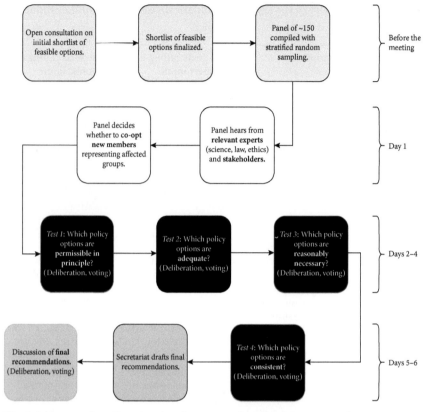

Fig. 8.2 A procedure for assessing the proportionality of a proposed response to an identified risk. © Jonathan Birch.

These questions do require members of the public to grasp the *concept* of risk, at the sort of level that might be required to complete a risk assessment form. They need to be able to understand risk as something that comes in degrees and that may be reduced by degrees. Some minimal training regarding the concept of risk (not in any way specific to the present risk) may be needed for the panel to function effectively. But no detailed scientific or mathematical knowledge is needed to debate the above questions and to apply one's values to the issues at stake.

Indeed, there is a sense in which people who do *not* have specialist prior knowledge are better placed to judge whether the harms and costs imposed by a precaution can be justified *to those affected*, since those affected will tend to lack specialist prior knowledge too. If the justification is incomprehensible to those affected, it is not truly justifying the harms and costs *to them*; it is merely justifying those harms and costs to an idealized image of them.

My hope is that, if a panel of at least 150 citizens debated proportionality in relation to a specific issue following the structure provided, arriving by consensus or by majority vote at a single policy response, we could have confidence in the results. We could be confident that the major considerations would have received dedicated and extended deliberation, that the people doing the deliberating were sufficiently informed and appropriately representative of the values of the population, and that they were able to apply those values to the questions being posed.

This, then, is the seventh (and last) element of my precautionary framework for managing risks at the edge of sentience:

> An example of an informed, inclusive, democratic process is a citizens' panel or assembly that assesses the proportionality of proposed measures by debating their permissibility-in-principle, adequacy, reasonable necessity and consistency (the PARC tests).

8.4 Public Policy and Private Policies

We have been considering how a government could conduct an inclusive, democratic process to assess proportionality at the edge of sentience. But what about organizations at a smaller scale than the state? Should they simply wait for the state to act, even if that means waiting decades?

In fact, many of the ideas developed in Chapters 6–8, though developed with the state in mind as the ideal implementing agent, might be implemented in other, non-ideal ways at smaller scales. There are three main non-ideal ways I have in mind. First, organizations can conduct their own versions of citizens' panels, to generate advice about proportionality to guide their own internal regulations. For example, a university, funding organization, or independent ethics body could conduct a citizens' panel to consider proportionality in the context of organoid research. Such panels should still aspire to openness; they should still make sure the list of options put to the panel has been subject to open consultation. This would involve only a slight scaling up of the recent public dialogues conducted by the Nuffield Council on Bioethics, mentioned at the start of Chapter 6.

Second, organizations without the resources to conduct citizens' panels can still apply the PARC tests in small panels involving at least some ordinary citizens (or 'lay members'). In the UK, Animal Welfare Ethical Review Boards (or AWERBs) already include some ordinary citizens, but I know from personal conversations that lay members sometimes feel marginalized by experts and unsure of their role. The PARC tests would give such members at least parity in discussions of proportionality, since the evaluative questions at the heart of the tests are questions anyone can answer in light of their own values.

Third, in cases where small groups or single individuals make decisions with little time or resources—think of a PI setting rules for their own lab, a CEO of a tech start-up setting rules for AI developers, or a chef setting rules for their kitchen—the sort of process just described might still serve as an ideal to be kept in mind. Even a single individual can ask: Do my decisions plausibly line up with what a more inclusive process *would* have decided, had there been time to conduct one? Could I justify my decisions to such a panel?

This merely imagined version of the citizens' panel is far from the standard of inclusiveness to which we should aspire. We should try to avoid this poor substitute wherever possible. I am thinking of cases where a decision-maker simply lacks the time and/or resources to attempt an inclusive and democratic process, not cases where a decision-maker has the time and resources but finds the prospect inconvenient.[15]

8.5 Philosopher as Sage, Philosopher as Proposer

What is the role of philosophy in this? It might seem as though I have effaced my own discipline's expertise. Having owned up to our lack of special access to a realm of objective ethical facts, should we now retreat to silence, leaving these matters to scientific experts and the general public? That is not what I am suggesting, for two reasons.

First, I think philosophers (especially ethicists and philosophers of science) can be sources of valuable expert input to deliberative processes. It is just that our role is not that of a sage, telling the public how best to resolve its value conflicts. Our role can instead be that of an explainer or elucidator: we are well placed to explain what the major value conflicts are, how these conflicts have arisen and changed over time, and how problems of consistency arise and may be resolved. We are also well placed to tease out the value-judgements that lie

---

[15] Here, incidentally, I disagree with Philip Kitcher, who appears to suggest it is enough for decisions to line-up with the counterfactual decisions an appropriately inclusive, mutually engaged conversation *would* have reached. In my view, counterfactual conversations are not enough to guard against a tyranny of expert values. Only actual conversations can do that job, a point Kitcher, in more recent work with Gillian Barker, appears to endorse. See Barker and Kitcher (2014); Kitcher (2001, 2011b).

beneath the surface of apparently factual information, such as the value-judgements implicit in a measure of well-being or a cost-benefit analysis.

Second, I think philosophers have a valuable role in the wider conversation around the management of risk, outside of any particular decision-making mechanism. In cases where we think a risk has been unreasonably neglected, we can highlight the risk and explain why it deserves consideration. We can also propose responses that we believe would stand a good chance of passing the tests of proportionality, if an inclusive, democratic procedure were created to apply those tests. Any citizen is free to make proposals, so the philosopher does not have any special privileges here. The distinctive value of our proposals—if there is any—lies in the analytical precision we can apply to their formulation.

This vision of 'philosopher-as-proposer' has also been advocated powerfully by Philip Kitcher.[16] It is the role I will be stepping into in the rest of this book, when making proposals about specific issues at the edge of sentience. My proposals will be simply that: proposals. I hope they will provoke discussion, and I believe they would stand a good chance of being judged proportionate by an inclusive deliberative process.

I admit this is, on the face of it, a step down from the pedestal of philosopher-as-sage. The problem is that we cannot stand on that pedestal without making dubious assertions about our special access to secret facts. We must stand up for the importance of the limited expertise we do have, without claiming for ourselves a kind of occult expertise over matters of how to live.

8.6 Summary of Chapter 8

This chapter has set out a procedure for debating proportionality. In this procedure, a citizens' panel deliberates following the structure laid out in Figure 8.2.

The panel is presented with a shortlist of feasible options on which stakeholders have been openly consulted. To each policy option, the panel applies four tests in sequence: permissibility-in-principle, adequacy, reasonable necessity, and consistency (Table 8.1). Proposals that fail a test are set aside. Proposals that pass all four tests are judged proportionate.

---

[16] Kitcher (2011b, 2011a).

The four tests introduce a division of labour between the panel and its expert advisers. At each stage, the expert advisers provide on-demand input regarding the likely consequences of different policy options, but it falls to ordinary citizens to debate the central evaluative questions. These questions can be easily understood and do not require arbitrating scientific disagreements.

A government is the ideal implementing agent for such a process, but other organizations (e.g. universities) can conduct similar processes. The process may be approximated in other, non-ideal ways, such as by a small panel (or even a single individual) reflecting on whether their decisions could be justified to a more inclusive panel implementing the full process.

In these debates, those with expertise in philosophy can bring their expertise to bear by explaining and elucidating value conflicts, mapping out consistencies and inconsistencies between different positions, and making proposals. These roles can be played without claiming additional, sage-like expertise over the correct way to resolve conflicts between deeply held values.

The Edge of Sentience: Risk and Precaution in Humans, Other Animals, and AI. Jonathan Birch, Oxford University Press.
© Jonathan Birch 2024. DOI: 10.1093/9780191966729.003.0009

PART III
SENTIENCE AND THE HUMAN BRAIN

9

People with Disorders of Consciousness

9.1 The Problem of Diagnostic Uncertainty

I opened this book with the testimony of Kate Bainbridge, wrongly presumed to be unconscious when she was not. This should never happen. Because the consequences of error are so severe, and so asymmetric, we need to take precautions to manage the risk. To say that the risks are asymmetric is not to say that there are no risks associated with over-ascribing sentience. There is, in particular, a danger of instilling unwarranted hope in a patient's friends and relatives. This, however, is a danger that can be sensitively managed through clear communication. By contrast, to treat a human as non-sentient when they can feel what is happening to them creates a risk of appalling suffering.

Around 2 to 3 in every 100,000 people will fall into a prolonged disorder of consciousness each year (in America, this equates to around 8,000–9,000 people a year). Causes can include heart attacks leading to cerebral hypoxia, strokes, traumatic brain injuries, and tumours.[1] There are now four major diagnostic constructs for such patients: coma, the vegetative state (also called 'unresponsive wakefulness syndrome', and this terminological issue will be revisited later), the minimally conscious state minus, and the minimally conscious state plus. As the quality of intensive care continues to improve, we should expect an ever larger fraction of patients who in past generations would have died from brain injuries to instead survive in one of these states. Diagnosis is normally based on behaviour. This is not the place to present the full diagnostic criteria—please consult official clinical guidelines, such as those published by the Royal College of Physicians (RCP) in 2020, on which I draw here—but a quick summary will be helpful.[2]

A patient in a *coma* is unrousable and unresponsive. They cannot be wakened, display no sleep-wake cycle, and there are no signs of voluntary action or responses to painful, visual, or auditory stimuli. Some but not all coma patients require mechanical ventilation. Comas can be induced or

---

[1] The statistics and list of causes are from Wade (2018).
[2] Royal College of Physicians (2020).

non-induced, and they are usually acute states, lasting a few weeks at most. Chronic comas lasting longer than a few weeks are possible but very rare.

In the *vegetative state*, there *are* sleep-wake cycles and there are some responses to stimuli and spontaneous behaviours, but there is no sign that the responses go beyond reflexes or that the spontaneous behaviours are under voluntary control. A patient in this condition has periods of wakefulness in which they may spontaneously evince smiles, grimaces, grunts, groans, roving eye movements, teeth-grinding, chewing, and apparently purposeless bodily movements. They may also react to stimuli by, for example, withdrawing a limb from a noxious stimulus or grimacing in response to noise. Their eyes may follow a moving object or orient to the source of a loud noise, but only fleetingly.

The vegetative state contrasts with the *minimally conscious* state, in which some signs of voluntary action do appear, though inconsistently. This construct is now split into two subcategories: minus and plus. In the minimally conscious state minus (MCS−), the patient shows non-linguistic voluntary behaviours, such as fixating on and following a moving visual target for a sustained period, or targeting behaviours at specific locations (the RCP guidance gives the examples of targeted scratching and pulling a bed sheet). They may also react to noxious stimuli in ways that seem to go beyond reflexes, such as by targeting their response at the site of the stimulus. In the minimally conscious state plus (MCS+), a patient is likely to show all these non-verbal signs but, in addition, shows signs of language processing and/ or understanding of their surroundings. They may, for example, follow simple commands, use some objects appropriately, or answer questions with yes/no signals.

I want to pause here to reflect on terminology and on the stigma that sometimes attaches to these conditions. 'Vegetative state' is a problematic term, partly because it seems to exclude the possibility of conscious experience in a way that may be hasty (see §9.2) but also because it is semantically much too close to the offensive term 'vegetable'. This has led to a call to replace the term with 'unresponsive wakefulness syndrome'.[3] But these patients are not fully unresponsive, as already noted. No one has yet found a fully satisfactory way out of this terminological minefield. The term 'vegetative state' is still widely used, so I will use that term here, despite being no fan of it. I will tend to say 'VS', or, for the *persistent* vegetative state, 'PVS'.

[3] Laureys et al. (2010).

Here is something that might lessen the stigma if it were more widely known: according to anaesthesiologist Emery Brown and collaborators, anyone who has been under general anaesthesia has probably passed through transient states functionally similar to the vegetative and minimally conscious states during the process of emerging back to full consciousness.[4] This happens to hundreds of thousands of people every day, all over the world. It is just that, in a healthy brain emerging from routine anaesthesia, these states last a matter of minutes rather than years, and progression back to a normal conscious state is highly reliable. A prolonged disorder of consciousness can be analogized to a great slowing down of that process. Sometimes, sadly, it slows to the point of pausing indefinitely along the way.

I think the comparison pushes our intuitions in the right direction. A person who is under, or emerging from, general anaesthesia is no less human, or any less of a person, or any less a bearer of dignity and rights. The same is true of a person with a prolonged disorder of consciousness. They are a person in a poorly understood and exceptionally vulnerable condition, but this is no reason to think they have lost their personhood, dignity, or rights.

But let us now return to the challenges of diagnosis. Suppose I asked you to judge whether a patient was in the VS, the MCS−, or the MCS+ by the above descriptions. Imagine yourself trying to divine the signs of incipient voluntary action. You would find yourself asking questions such as: when is a bodily movement apparently purposeless? When is fixation on an object sustained rather than fleeting? How well targeted does an action need to be to count as targeted? How do we tell if a patient is responding to commands rather than coincidentally displaying a spontaneous behaviour after a command?

To put it bluntly, to attempt such a diagnosis is to walk into a labyrinth of uncertainty, with risks of false negatives and false positives at every turn, the path strewn with ambiguous grey-area cases, and ample scope for bias. There are standardized assessment procedures (such as the JFK Coma Recovery Scale-Revised)[5] that are designed to help clinicians apply these diagnostic categories, but it would be wrong to suppose that standardization successfully manages the risks of bias and error. When initial diagnoses are compared against more careful diagnoses by specialists, the rate of misdiagnosis has been found to be in the region of 40 per cent.[6]

Yet this is just the beginning—the first layer of diagnostic uncertainty. Even if the behavioural criteria were applied rigorously and reliably in all cases by

---

[4] E. N. Brown et al. (2010).   [5] Giacino et al. (2004).
[6] Schnakers et al. (2009); Wang et al. (2020).

highly trained specialists, we would still face a second layer of uncertainty: how well are these behavioural criteria actually tracking facts about sentience? Is it not at least conceivable that some patients could be experiencing a lot more than they are able to express behaviourally? There is now substantial evidence that such a situation is more than conceivable: it actually happens alarmingly frequently.

9.2 The Search for Cognitive-Motor Dissociation

Kate Bainbridge's story, though bleak in some ways, also gives us grounds for hope. Her impressive cognitive recovery, over the course of years of rehabilitation, helped to show the medical community the importance of not 'writing off' the prospects of patients who have prolonged disorders of consciousness lasting several months.[7] The case was also significant in another way: it was one of the earliest cases in which a neuroimaging technique—positron emission tomography (PET)—provided relevant evidence, in this case suggesting a covert ability to respond to faces.[8] The case kick-started a research programme that aims to identify more cases in which an outwardly unresponsive patient is in fact a conscious, experiencing subject, unable to produce any behavioural report of their experiences.

The clinical name for this condition is 'cognitive-motor dissociation' (CMD). Informally, it is often described as 'covert consciousness'.[9] Many researchers are now engaged in the project of developing new neuroimaging methods to detect it. Two promising approaches, alongside PET, involve functional magnetic resonance imaging (fMRI) and electroencephalogram (EEG) recordings of brain activity.[10] The guiding thought behind all these methods is that, even when a patient cannot respond behaviourally to stimulation, their patterns of brain activity might still respond in a way that contains clues as to the presence or absence of experience.

There are many techniques in development of this general type, all (it is fair to say) at an early stage. At the time of writing, none has yet been rolled out to widespread clinical use. The technology is moving fast, however, and the European Academy of Neurology already recommends the use of PET,

---

[7] MacNiven et al. (2003); Wilson and Gracey (2001).
[8] Cyranoski (2012); Menon et al. (1998).   [9] Edlow et al. (2021); Fins and Bernat (2018).
[10] Bai et al. (2021) review 119 recent studies using EEG techniques. Studies using MRI/fMRI techniques are less common, but there have still been tens of such studies (Snider and Edlow 2020).

fMRI, and EEG techniques 'whenever feasible' and has proposed that patients should be diagnosed as having the 'highest level' of consciousness indicated by behaviour, PET/fMRI neuroimaging, or EEG.[11]

I do not want to underplay the promise of these approaches. However, two notes of caution are important. The first is that any technique with high specificity (a low rate of false positives) is likely to have low sensitivity (a high rate of false negatives). Given the absence of consensus regarding which brain mechanisms are relevant to conscious experience and why (see Chapter 5), it is inherently very difficult to tell whether a patient's brain activity indicates residual conscious experience. The clearest signs come in situations where we have set a relatively demanding cognitive task (a high bar) and received an unambiguous signal. In a celebrated example, a group led by Adrian Owen asked patients to imagine playing tennis if the answer to a question was 'yes' and to imagine walking round their home if the answer was 'no'. These two imaginative activities involve different brain regions, yielding easily discernible fMRI signatures in healthy controls. A healthy adult in an fMRI scanner is therefore able to answer the experimenter's questions through voluntary mental activity alone. Owen and colleagues showed, astonishingly, that an outwardly unresponsive patient was able to answer questions just as unambiguously and accurately as the healthy controls. In follow-up work, they found more examples.[12]

Note, however, that this technique places significant demands on the patient. Firstly, they need to be moved to an fMRI scanner, a process often inappropriate for a patient in a critical condition in an intensive care unit (ICU) following traumatic brain injury. Secondly, they need to be able to hear and process the questions and formulate an intentional response. The cognitive demands of this task could exceed the abilities of some covertly conscious patients. They might have problems with attention, language processing, or intentional command-following that impede correct responding without abolishing experience. For these reasons, we should not expect such techniques to be well suited to frequent use in the ICU, nor should we expect them to be very sensitive.[13]

A range of other approaches have sought to increase sensitivity and ease of bedside use. We should, however, expect these techniques to come with a corresponding loss of specificity: a greater risk of false positives. In 2019,

---

[11] Kondziella et al. (2020).   [12] Monti et al. (2010); Owen et al. (2006).
[13] A. Peterson et al. (2015).

a high-profile study from Jan Claassen and colleagues tested an EEG-based technique on 104 patients with disorders of consciousness.[14] A machine learning algorithm (a support vector machine classifier) was tasked with guessing, on the basis of a bedside EEG recording of a patient, the spoken commands the patient had been given. The commands given were '*keep opening and closing your right[/left] hand*' and '*stop opening and closing your right[/left] hand*'.[15] For each patient, the classifier's performance was evaluated by comparing its guesses about the spoken commands (as inferred from the EEG) to the actual commands. The headline result: in 16/104 patients, significantly above-chance classifier performance was obtained, leading the authors to the striking conclusion that 'of the 104 patients, 16 (15%) had cognitive–motor dissociation detected on at least one recording'.[16]

Concerns about false negatives remain, of course: some unresponsive patients may be conscious and yet unable to form even very simple motor commands. However, there is also a risk of false positives. This risk arises from the fact that, despite the sophistication of modern machine learning, a patient responding to commands can still be easily confused with random statistical noise. 'Above-chance' classifier performance will sometimes be explained by responding but will sometimes be explained by random variation—a string of lucky guesses. Claassen and colleagues themselves observe in their supplementary information that, since 104 patients were studied, 'it is likely that amongst the 16 CMD patients, five were classified as CMD because of statistical fluctuations rather than actual spoken command following'.[17]

These notes of caution are not reasons to stop developing and using EEG- and neuroimaging-based techniques. They are, however, reasons not to see these techniques as a panacea that can make our uncertainty go away. They can help us obtain relevant evidence that shifts probabilities—a strong reason to develop and use them—but agonizing uncertainty will remain and will need to be carefully managed.[18]

---

[14] Claassen et al. (2019).

[15] The algorithm was trained separately on each patient. This is called an 'individualized classifier' approach, since the classifier is trained anew on every patient's personal EEG data. This strategy can be contrasted with a 'general classifier' approach that seeks to generalize from a training set of patients to a new patient.

[16] Claassen et al. (2019, p. 2501).

[17] Claassen et al. (2019, supplementary information, p. 13).

[18] See Birch (2023a) for a detailed discussion of the Claasen et al. study.

9.3 The Realistic Possibility of Continuing Valenced Experience in the PVS

The most discussed cases of covert consciousness involve patients who retain an ability to perform cognitive tasks despite lacking the ability to convert their thoughts into motor responses. Detecting cognitive-motor dissociation is extremely challenging, and high rates of false negatives and false positives are very likely. When a patient diagnoses as in the PVS 'fails' a cognitive task in a brain scanner, that must not be counted as strong evidence against covert consciousness. This is a point of agreement.

But one of the questions that looms largest for patients' families concerns *affect* rather than cognition. Can the patient suffer? Can they still feel pain, pleasure, distress, anxiety, joy, relief? Here we have to contend with the possibility of *covert valenced experience*, a capacity that may well not correlate very well at all with a continuing ability to perform cognitive tasks.

Could the capacity to have valenced experiences survive the extensive cortical damage that leads to PVS? There are sometimes outward signs that cause patients' families to suspect it could. As already noted, patients in the PVS can smile, grimace, cry, grunt, groan. It is no surprise that family members often read these behaviours as suggesting residual affective states.

In 1994, five major American societies in the areas of neurology and paediatrics convened a multi-society task force to agree a consensus statement on the PVS. In a section on 'pain and suffering', the task force confidently reported that 'conscious awareness of pain or the experience of suffering occurs at a cortical level through synapses connecting parietal cortical neurons with other areas of the cerebral cortex'. The evidence, it claimed, supported 'the belief that patients in a persistent vegetative state are unaware and insensate and therefore lack the cerebral cortical capacity to be conscious of pain.'[19]

This is a problematic statement, not because the view is inherently unreasonable but because it is expressed with such excessive confidence. At a time when the search for the neural correlates of conscious experience was clearly in its infancy (and one might argue it is still in its infancy), a task force of neurologists and paediatricians considered themselves to have solved the problem to a sufficient degree of certainty to report their view without qualification in a major consensus statement intended to guide clinical practice. The idea that conscious experience requires global cortical activity is still a

---

[19] The Multi-Society Task Force on PVS (1994, p. 1576).

major mainstream position in the debate, but not the only reasonable position (see Chapter 5).

Panksepp and colleagues have rightly criticized the task force's remarks on this issue.[20] As we saw in Chapter 5, Panksepp's own theory of the basic emotions gives special significance to the periaqueductal gray (PAG), a midbrain region. There is good evidence that the PAG is either causally or constitutively involved in affective experiences, since stimulating the PAG induces such experiences. Panksepp hypothesized that the relationship is a constitutive one.

As I explained in Chapter 5, I am not myself convinced that the PAG's role is constitutive. The question is open. But Panksepp's view is a reasonable one, backed by a credible interpretation of a substantial body of evidence. We need to take seriously the possibility that it is correct, and think about what precautions may be proportionate if it is. As Panksepp and colleagues put it:

> If we consider the accruing evidence and theory about the basic nature of affect, and use it as a guideline for our thinking, we would be wise to accept the realistic possibility (although perhaps not the high probability, as we do) that PVS patients can still experience some remnants of affective experience even though their cognitive abilities are gone.[21]

Caroline Schnakers and collaborators have made a similar point.[22] Note that this point still applies even if there is no evidence at all of cognitive-motor dissociation. We are not talking here about a subset of patients with a PVS diagnosis, namely those able to display residual cognitive abilities through patterns of brain activity. We are talking about all such patients.

9.4 Pain Management and the 'Assume Sentient' Principle

The message about erring on the side of caution has permeated through to clinical guidance in the UK. In 2020, the Royal College of Physicians (RCP) published the latest version of its clinical guidelines for prolonged disorders of consciousness. The guidelines call for a precautionary attitude in the context of pain management, writing that:

---

[20] Panksepp et al. (2007).   [21] Panksepp et al. (2007, p. 9).
[22] Schnakers and Zasler (2007, 2015); Schnakers et al. (2012).

Patients in VS are traditionally believed to lack any ability to experience the environment, internal or external, but complete certainty that primal sensations are absent is impossible to know. [...] Careful observation of pain-related behaviours (grimacing, moaning, groaning etc) provides the mainstay of monitoring and the presence of these features should be assumed to indicate discomfort rather than just reflex or spontaneous movement or behaviour, at least until there is clear evidence to the contrary.[23]

The 'at least until' caveat suggests the final advice may be a compromise between the sceptical view expressed by the 1994 task force and the precautionary alternative. As I see it, such caveats are unhelpful in the absence of any firm grip on what might constitute 'clear evidence' that a pain-related behaviour is *not* accompanied by any experience. Elsewhere, the guidelines state that 'irrespective of their cognitive capacity, patients in PDOC are entitled to dignity and respect, and any signs that are suggestive of distress or suffering should be assumed to be such'[24] and that 'all patients should be monitored for signs and symptoms of pain and should have pain managed appropriately'.[25]

Clinical best practice therefore seems to be moving with good reason towards an idea we can call the 'assume sentient' principle (specific version, since I will shortly generalize it):

Proposal 1. *Assume sentient (specific).* Any signs that would be interpreted as signs of pain or distress in a conscious patient should still be so interpreted in a patient with any disorder of consciousness, and pain relief administered. This treatment should not be reserved for a subset of patients, e.g. those diagnosed as minimally conscious.

This principle—applied without exceptions or caveats—is in keeping with the precautionary attitude towards the edge of sentience advocated in this book. And while it is offered here as a proposal, I think it very likely that an inclusive and democratic process tasked with considering proposals would consider it a proportionate response to the risk.

---

[23] Royal College of Physicians (2020, p. 92).   [24] Royal College of Physicians (2020, p. 155).
[25] Royal College of Physicians (2020, annex 3a, p. 4).

9.5 Moving Past the PVS/MCS Distinction

How far should we push this precautionary attitude to the PVS? I initially imagined this chapter would be about how to draw the distinction between the PVS and MCS in a suitably precautionary way. I thought the distinction itself was a clinically useful and important one, and the right way to think about the edge of sentience in these cases. But the more I researched the case, the more sceptical of this distinction I became.

The issue is not just terminological. As noted earlier, there have been calls for over ten years now to retire the problematic terminology of 'vegetative' and 'vegetative state' in favour of 'unresponsive wakefulness syndrome' (UWS).[26] There is, however, a sense in which it is a conservative move to merely change the name of the PVS to UWS while retaining a commitment to the clinical importance of categorizing patients as UWS, MCS−, or MCS+. Steven Laureys and colleagues, in the paper that coins UWS, still endorse the received wisdom that there is a 'need to clearly separate UWS from MCS'.[27] The new concept retains the same basic function of demarcating a class of patients as 'not even minimally conscious' but does so under a new heading.

I think it is time to revisit the alleged need 'to clearly separate UWS from MCS'. Given that we must remain open to the possibility of continuing valenced experience in the PVS (and for now, I will revert to the more traditional term), I think we should be very careful indeed about differentiating clinical treatment according to the PVS/MCS+/MCS− distinction in any way that involves assuming a lack of conscious experience in PVS patients. Moreover, we should be wary of describing any patient as 'not even minimally conscious', or saying anything that implies this. To do so risks eroding the precautionary attitude we need to cultivate.

The UK clinical guidance, mentioned earlier, is a step in the right direction. As we have seen, it rightly advises clinicians to give no weight to the PVS/MCS distinction. The fact that you *think* a patient may well be wholly unconscious, on the basis of their unresponsiveness, is not a sufficient reason to withhold pain relief. That is good precautionary thinking in action. The evidence about the rates of misdiagnosis and the potential for covert consciousness underlines all of this in red ink, but it would still make sense to err

---

[26] Johnson (2022); Laureys et al. (2010).   [27] Laureys et al. (2010, p. 68).

on the side of caution even if we had reason to believe the risk of misdiagnosis was low.

I propose we generalize this approach beyond pain management. I propose that a patient who is displaying sleep-wake cycles should never be assumed incapable of experience when an important clinical decision is made. All clinical decisions should consider the patient's best interests as comprehensively as possible, working on the assumption that there is a realistic possibility that the patient has continuing valenced experiences and a continuing interest in avoiding suffering and in achieving a state of well-being.

This proposal is well aligned with the direction in which clinical best practice is already heading. In the UK, formal diagnosis of the patient as PVS, MCS−, or MCS+ is still required, with detailed guidelines for diagnosis. Yet, when it comes to setting out practical norms of care, a reluctance to put any weight whatsoever on this diagnosis—in an area where misdiagnosis is thought to be stubbornly around 40 per cent—is evident and, moreover, completely understandable. In the annexes describing detailed clinical guidelines for managing practical problems, the PVS/MCS+/MCS− terminology does not appear at all. The broader diagnostic category of 'prolonged disorder of consciousness' is all that is needed to refer a patient to the relevant specialists. Appropriate care then depends on the patient's *individual* capabilities, needs, and interests, not on their diagnostic category in the PVS/MCS+/MCS− taxonomy.

Given all this, I propose that we should aim to phase out the PVS/MCS+/MCS− categories, at least in therapeutic and legal contexts. I do not rule out a role in *prognosis*: these categories are of some use for predicting levels of recovery, though I suspect that even in this context we will eventually replace them with finer-grained, more predictively powerful categories. There are, of course, differences in how we ought to treat individual patients, depending on their individual capacities. Attempts at rehabilitation must start where the patient is and work from there. But we must not confuse this with the idea that coarse-grained taxonomy of MCS+, MCS−, and PVS—with its stark implication that patients in the PVS are not even minimally conscious—is a useful one in therapeutic or legal contexts.[28]

---

[28] Braddock (2017, 2021) has made a complementary proposal about the precautionary attribution of personhood. I am inclined to agree, but my topic here is sentience.

Proposal 2. *Assume sentient (general).* A patient who is displaying sleep-wake cycles should not be assumed incapable of experience when an important clinical decision is made. All clinical decisions should consider the patient's best interests as comprehensively as possible, working on the precautionary assumption that there is a realistic possibility of valenced experience and a continuing interest in avoiding suffering and in achieving a state of well-being, but without taking this assumption to have implications regarding prognosis.

Proposal 3. *Avoid line-drawing (general).* The diagnostic categories of PVS, MCS−, and MCS+ should be phased out in therapeutic and legal contexts. Clinicians should work with the broader category of 'prolonged disorder of consciousness' (PDOC) and with profiles of individual patients, tailoring care to the patient's individual needs.

9.6 The Question of Treatment Withdrawal

This section will be difficult to read, perhaps especially if one has experience of relevant cases, but also if one does not. We must nonetheless be willing to confront the issues it raises.

Many of us would not want to be sustained indefinitely with a severe disorder of consciousness, unable to move purposefully or communicate with anyone around us. It is, we should admit, very hard to imagine what it would be like to be in such a state, and those who are in the state cannot tell us directly. For some, it may be mostly painless, and may involve some positive well-being.[29] There is likely to be great variation along many dimensions in what it is like to have a disorder of consciousness, including variation in levels of well-being, and we are currently very limited in our ability to measure that variation.[30]

Yet the risk of suffering if consciousness persists is very clear. The consequences for one's family are also foreseeable. The RCP describes the 'huge stress' and 'prolonged and exhausting rollercoaster of emotions and ricocheting between fear and hope' typically experienced by the patient's family across many years.[31] Many of us would not want our families to have to endure this. Many of us may therefore make a considered judgement, in our current state, that to live like this for years would not be in our best interests.

---

[29] Graham (2017, 2021); Graham and Naci (2021).   [30] Bayne et al. (2016).
[31] Royal College of Physicians (2020, p. 82).

Sometimes a clinical decision-making team (including the patient's family) agrees, based on careful consideration of what is known about the patient's values and wishes, that sustaining life is no longer in their best interests. In the UK and many other countries, the only legally permitted way of ending their life in such cases is through the withdrawal of life-sustaining treatment.

Death can follow quickly if, for example, the patient is reliant on mechanical ventilation. But many patients stabilize in a condition in which the only active medical intervention they need is clinically assisted nutrition and hydration (CANH). Decision-making teams can be presented with an appalling choice: sustain life indefinitely, even if this is clearly not in line with the patient's expressed wishes and values, or let them die of multiorgan failure as a result of prolonged dehydration and malnutrition. This is a process that can take 2–3 weeks.

The weight of that terrible choice rests heavily on the families of patients, as Celia and Jenny Kitzinger have documented.[32] Their interviews with relatives contain quotations such as the following:[33]

> I can't imagine that she would ever want to live as she is now. […] but the [CANH withdrawal] alternative is too cruel. […] even if they agreed to it, it's too painful, you know. I couldn't do that. […] You know, we couldn't put her through it.

> When they told me that I felt like screaming. I thought, 'you are MAD!' I didn't even contemplate it. I just don't understand how anyone can sanction that law.

> I couldn't believe that that [CANH withdrawal] was the method. Everybody I've talked to has said, 'there must be better ways than that in this day and age.' […] What a stupid, stupid way of doing it.

> I just couldn't bear that he was starving […] I just thought, what a horrible—what a dreadful way to live your last days. I just thought it was awful.

> We all thought [CANH withdrawal] was barbaric. But then being kept alive that way is barbaric […] I mean it [death following CANH withdrawal] is better than forever living that way. But really, truthfully, what the hell is this? The system has to be in place where if [surgery and rehabilitation] is a failure, if it hasn't worked, then you can help that person die with dignity.

> I would view it [a lethal injection] as a kinder decision. […] Because if you stop feeding them, they are going to die. If you've made that decision, you might as well do it as humanely as you possibly can. […] To starve somebody to death seems a particularly cruel thing to do.

---

[32] Kitzinger and Kitzinger (2014, 2015, 2018).   [33] Kitzinger and Kitzinger (2015, p. 259).

Reading testimony like this, it would be comforting to tell ourselves that the patients were not in fact capable of experiencing suffering, and that the relatives' fears about CANH withdrawal were unfounded. The problem is, we cannot hide behind false certainties. None of us can honestly provide ourselves or these interviewees with any such reassurance. For one thing, CANH withdrawal is legally permitted in the UK for patients who are diagnosed as minimally conscious, if it is deemed by the decision-making team to be in their best interests—and everyone agrees that these patients are capable of suffering. But reassurance is not possible even in those cases that meet the traditional criteria for the PVS, due to the realistic possibility of covert valenced experience.

To describe this situation as problematic or troubling would be too weak. Relatives often express the view that, even if the patient would clearly want to be allowed to die, to allow them to die *in that way* is too much to contemplate, given our inability to rule out the possibility that they can experience suffering. This leads to many patients being kept alive indefinitely, contrary to what those close to them consider to be in their best interests.

Withdrawal of nutrition and hydration would be regarded as an inhumane method of ending the life of any other sentient animal. It is permitted only for humans. Can the potential for suffering be adequately managed? The RCP clinical guidance rightly emphasizes the need for hospital-based neuropalliative care from specialists in sedation and analgesia. It notes that 'any signs that are suggestive of distress and suffering should be assumed to be such',[34] in line with the 'assume sentient' principle. However, the guidelines also caution that, 'in the presence of profound cortical dysfunction, [sedatives] may be ineffective even in exceptionally high doses'.[35]

Clinicians are urged to titrate the level of sedation and analgesia to suppress symptoms to the best of their ability without creating a risk of overdosing—which would put them at risk of prosecution. The guidelines add that, due to this risk to the clinician, 'it is quite common that medication is not increased quickly or high enough to control escalating signs of physiological hyperactivity'.[36] It would seem, in other words, that clinicians are impaired in their ability to err on the side of caution in controlling the risk of the patient suffering because they need (understandably) to err on the side of caution in reducing their own personal exposure to the risk of punishment. This is a dreadful situation.

[34] Royal College of Physicians (2020, p. 155).   [35] Royal College of Physicians (2020, p. 156).
[36] Royal College of Physicians (2020, p. 156).

Kitzinger and Kitzinger's interview studies have documented what they call the 'burden of witness' on families who watch this process occur. In some cases, the process of dying appears more peaceful than they had expected. One interviewee describes it as a 'very calming, peaceful experience'.[37] These reports are associated with cases in which analgesics and sedatives are skilfully administered in heavy doses (the same interviewee says 'they just got the drugs right I think'). But the RCP guidelines caution that 'not all deaths are straightforward'.[38] Even in the 'straightforward' cases, relatives witness their loved ones deteriorating slowly over many days, and this can be a harrowing experience.

The current situation is in fact even worse than it already sounds. In cases where a family is understandably reluctant to contemplate CANH withdrawal, they may still sanction other kinds of treatment withdrawal, such as withholding antibiotics when the patient is infected. This may sound like a more humane way to allow death, but the reality often fails to bear this out. One of Kitzinger and Kitzinger's interviewees talks of the horror of watching a loved one 'retch and heave and cough and be suctioned and run a high temperature, perspiring all over his bed sheets' after antibiotics were withheld.[39] Another talks of their regret at having intervened to reverse a decision to withdraw CANH, only to witness their loved one die of gangrene two years later.[40]

To grasp the full bleakness of the status quo, there is one more aspect we need to consider. All of the above is known to many doctors and to well-informed families when a patient is still in the acute phase of care, in the first few days and weeks after their injury. At this time, they will often require mechanical ventilation. This creates what Kitzinger and Kitzinger have called a 'window of opportunity' for rapid death.[41] If treatment is not withdrawn at this stage, no similarly rapid death will ever be possible again, given the law as it stands. Some families regret missing this window. The pressure on decision-making teams to decide quickly is ratcheted up.

Yet a patient's prognosis is at its most uncertain at this early stage. Using this window to withdraw life-sustaining treatment inevitably leads to some deaths of patients who would otherwise have improved to a condition in which they would have valued continued life. Syd Johnson calls this the problem of the self-fulfilling prophecy: a bleak prognosis made extremely early, in

---

[37] Kitzinger and Kitzinger (2018, p. 1185).   [38] Royal College of Physicians (2020, p. 153).
[39] Kitzinger and Kitzinger (2015, p. 159).   [40] Kitzinger and Kitzinger (2018, p. 1184).
[41] Kitzinger and Kitzinger (2013).

the face of immense uncertainty, results in the patient losing any chance to defy that prognosis.[42] A Canadian study found evidence that 70.2 per cent of deaths in neurointensive care units following brain injury involved intentional withdrawal of treatment, with around half of these deaths occurring in the first three days after the injury.[43] These patients were not given the chance to stabilize into any state, so we cannot say with any confidence what state they would have attained and whether they would have valued it. Johnson's verdict is stark: 'people who might have survived to have good and flourishing lives will die avoidable deaths.'[44] She advocates for an approach based on watching and waiting, so that uncertainty about the patient's prognosis can be at least somewhat reduced by the time decisions about treatment withdrawal are made.

The overall picture is one in which patients, families, and clinicians are boxed in by a legal framework inadequately sensitive to the facts on the ground. This is true even in the UK, where the issues have been debated for several decades and the framework is relatively nuanced by international standards. In the UK, lawmakers have long evaded the issue, allowing the key principles to be thrashed out through case law. I find it entirely understandable that legislators do not want to decriminalize or legalize a method of ending life. They do not want such an issue to become part of the battleground of party politics. That is fair enough, but we also cannot carry on as we are.

This is just the type of situation in which convening a citizens' assembly and implementing its recommendations in law could help legislators break out of the box. If the question of proportionality were put to a citizens' panel, I think it very likely that the panel would agree about the need to make available a faster method of ending life for cases in which everyone on the decision-making team—relatives and clinicians—all agree that this would be in the patient's best interests. This would be a proportionate measure to manage a risk of suffering. The case is not complicated; it does not require specialist knowledge to grasp. The testimony of patients' families makes the case.

In jurisdictions where CANH withdrawal is legal, the change to policy could be quite simple. It could take the form of a guarantee that qualified neuropalliative care specialists will not be prosecuted or punished in any other way for administering sedatives and analgesics during a process of CANH withdrawal, regardless of the dose used and the outcome for the patient. The right dose could then be left to their clinical judgement, based on

[42] Johnson (2022).   [43] Turgeon et al. (2011).   [44] Johnson (2022, p. 86).

an overriding imperative to remove the risk of suffering. No precedent for other circumstances would need to be set by this. To maintain public trust that this legal permission was only being used in appropriate circumstances, it would be crucial to maintain and publish accurate data about the numbers of patients dying in this way—data that is currently sorely lacking.[45]

Sometimes 'slippery slope' arguments are made in this context. A 'slippery slope' argument can, on occasion, be a well-founded attempt to warn of a genuine, unintended consequence of a change to practice (and we will see an example of this in Chapter 10). However, it can also be a fallacy. In these cases, the line of thought is that practice 2 would be immoral, and it is possible that practice 1 will change over time into practice 2, therefore practice 1 is also immoral. This is unpersuasive, because it may be that the best course of action is to implement practice 1 and take some precautions against the risk that it will change into practice 2.

In the case at hand, we would simply need to make very specific changes to rules around best-interests decision-making and neuropalliative care for patients with a confirmed diagnosis of a prolonged disorder of consciousness, taking care not to create a precedent for any other circumstances. The question of whether similar considerations apply to other diagnoses can be debated separately.

If we could reassure families that a humane way of hastening death will be available at any time if it is a patient's best interests, there would be a major indirect benefit for patients: there would be no more 'window of opportunity'. The intense pressure on surrogate decision-makers to decide quickly, with the first days or weeks following injury, would be eased. There would then be a strong case for watching and waiting at this early stage, allowing the patient to stabilize and for prognostic uncertainty to be reduced. We could avoid the problem of the self-fulfilling prophecy and give patients a genuine chance to stabilize and improve, without fearing we might later have reason to regret having waited.

To summarize the proposals of this section:

Proposal 4. *Avoid line-drawing (specific).* Decisions about withdrawing life-sustaining treatment should be based on comprehensive assessment of the patient's best interests, sensitive to the details of their case, and not on the PVS/MCS distinction.

---

[45] Gray et al. (2021).

Proposal 5. *The need for more humane options.* Methods of hastening death other than through withdrawal of clinically assisted nutrition and hydration (CANH) are needed. At minimum, clinicians should not face any risk of punishment for administering large doses of sedatives or analgesics after a decision to withdraw CANH has been made.

Proposal 6. *Waiting for more information.* If a humane method of hastening death becomes available, there will be no strong rationale for withdrawing life-sustaining treatment within days after injury, before the patient's condition has stabilized. Given the great uncertainty about prospects for recovery at this stage, the default approach should be to delay the decision until the patient's condition has stabilized.

9.7 Summary of Chapter 9

Sometimes a person, after brain injury, displays sleep-wake cycles but has severely impaired, or entirely absent, responses to external stimuli. Traditionally, attempts have been made to distinguish the persistent vegetative state (PVS) from the minimally conscious state (MCS), itself subdivided into 'MCS plus' and 'MCS minus'.

Diagnostic procedures for distinguishing PVS from MCS are subject to high error rates and high uncertainty. Moreover, there are cases of patients who, after being diagnosed as PVS through a very thorough application of behavioural criteria, show signatures of brain activity in response to commands. And there is a realistic possibility that midbrain mechanisms suffice for basic valenced experiences, even if cortical injury prevents a patient from reporting these experiences.

In the context of pain management, an 'assume sentient' principle is appropriate. Any signs that would be interpreted as signs of pain or distress in a conscious patient should still be so interpreted in a patient with any disorder of consciousness, and pain relief administered. This treatment should not be reserved for a subset of patients, e.g. those thought to be minimally conscious. In fact, this 'assume sentient' principle can be extended, with care, to all clinically important decisions. This must be understood as a *precautionary* assumption—a way of erring on the side of caution—and not evidence for or against any particular prognosis.

We should, in fact, aim for a situation in which the problematic PVS/MCS distinction carries no clinical significance and can be retired. All decisions should be based on the best interests of the patient, taking all relevant information into account, including information about their individual profile of responsiveness and capacity, and regarding continuing affective experiences as a realistic possibility.

In some cases, the decision-making team (including clinicians and families) is in agreement that sustaining life indefinitely is not in the patient's best interests. Here too, the decision should be based on comprehensive best-interests assessment sensitive to the details of the case, and not on the PVS/MCS distinction.

The method of withdrawing clinically assisted nutrition and hydration (CANH) would not be acceptable for any other sentient being, and alternatives must be explored and discussed by inclusive, democratic processes. Part of the problem is that clinicians fear prosecution if they administer large doses of sedatives or analgesics after CANH withdrawal. In cases where CANH withdrawal has already been authorized, clinicians should be guaranteed that hastening death in this way will not lead to punishment. If alternative methods were available, it would better enable clinicians and patient's families to watch and wait during the early days after a traumatic brain injury, rather than moving quickly towards a decision to withdraw treatment before a patient's condition has stabilized.

The Edge of Sentience: Risk and Precaution in Humans, Other Animals, and AI. Jonathan Birch, Oxford University Press.
© Jonathan Birch 2024. DOI: 10.1093/9780191966729.003.0010

10

Fetuses and Embryos

10.1 The Cautionary Tale of Newborn Pain

In the late 1980s, pain in neonates (newborn babies) was a source of major public controversy on both sides of the Atlantic. In 1985, Jill Lawson's preterm baby, Jeffrey, died five weeks after undergoing hours of surgery to repair a heart defect. In the aftermath of the tragedy, Lawson was horrified to learn that Jeffrey had been given no anaesthetic or pain relief—only a paralytic to stop him moving.

Lawson wrote a letter of protest to the journal *Birth*, in which she recounted appalling details (and I warn the reader that this testimony is distressing):

> Jeffrey had holes cut on both sides of his neck, another cut in his right chest, an incision from his breastbone around to his backbone, his ribs pried apart, and an extra artery near his heart tied off. This was topped off with another hole cut in his left side. The operation lasted hours. Jeffrey was awake through it all. The anesthesiologist paralyzed him with Pavulon, a drug that left him unable to move, but totally conscious. When I questioned the anesthesiologist later she said Jeffrey was too sick to tolerate powerful anesthetics. Anyway, she said, it had never been demonstrated to her that premature babies feel pain.[1]

There have been sombre moments in researching this book, moments where I just had to pause and reflect on what I had just read, and this was one of them.

Lawson's horror was compounded by a further discovery: this was not generally considered poor surgical practice. Operating without anaesthetic on neonates was widespread. Lawson launched a campaign to change that situation, attracting wide public support.

---

[1] Lawson (1986). The relevant history is recounted in brief by McGrath (2011), who also draws attention to this passage from Lawson's letter. A more detailed history of the controversy is given by Wei (2016).

At the same time, evidence was mounting to support Lawson's arguments. The anaesthesiologist K. J. S. Anand, then a doctoral student at Oxford, led a randomized controlled trial to compare neonatal stress responses to surgery under light and deep anaesthesia, finding a 'massive stress response...three to five times greater than adults' when only light anaesthesia was used.[2] Quite apart from the possibility of pain, this physiological stress response in itself posed serious risks to newborns. The work provoked a storm of public controversy in the UK.[3] Initial reports targeted Anand, failing to recognize that Anand was investigating the effects of a widely used surgical approach, not deliberately withholding anaesthesia beyond clinical norms.

In 1987, American Academy of Pediatrics and the American Society of Anesthesiology responded with a joint statement recommending the use of anaesthesia and analgesia in neonates, which they described as 'relatively safe'.[4] Although the AAP/ASA statement did not explicitly using the language of precaution, there was clearly an element of precautionary thinking in the background. They could have insisted that the available evidence concerned nociception rather than pain, and that further proof of pain experience was needed. By Anand and Hickey's own lights, the evidence primarily concerned nociception and physiological stress responses, leaving room for doubt about accompanying conscious experiences of pain (since there is always room for doubt). Anand and Hickey's review even contains something close to a disclaimer at the beginning: 'Strictly speaking, nociceptive activity, rather than pain, should be discussed with regard to the neonate, because pain is a sensation with strong emotional associations'.[5] They even add that 'none of the data cited herein tell us whether neonatal nociceptive activity and associated responses are experienced subjectively'.[6] The door is left open for a critic to say: nociception, yes, but not necessarily with any accompanying conscious experience. Thankfully, the AAP and ASA did not take that path.

A significant body of evidence accumulated since the 1980s confirms that the AAP and ASA made the right call.[7] The challenges of inferring pain from measurable indicators have not gone away, leading to continuing debate about which kinds of pain relief are effective and why.[8] But this debate now takes place against a backdrop of universal acceptance of the need for

---

[2] Anand and Hickey (1987).   [3] McGrath (2011).
[4] American Academy of Pediatrics (1987); Boffey (1987).
[5] Anand and Hickey (1987, p. 1321).   [6] Anand and Hickey (1987, p. 1326).
[7] Pain-related evidence is reviewed by Campbell-Yeo et al. (2022); McPherson et al. (2020, 2021). On evidence for consciousness in infants more generally, see Bayne et al. (2023) and Passos-Ferreira (in press).
[8] Fitzgerald (2015).

precautionary pain management in newborns. This is partly because of abundant evidence linking pain and stress indicators in neonates to subsequent long-term developmental problems.[9] Regardless of one's views about whether neonates are experiencing pain or merely mounting nociceptive and stress responses without any subjective experience, everyone can agree that states which lead to long-term developmental problems need to be managed. Common ground—overlapping consensus across the zone of reasonable disagreement—has been created.

History often shows us the disquieting contingency of moral progress.[10] There was nothing inevitable about the change to clinical practice that occurred in the 1980s. Building an evidence base concerning nociception and stress in newborns required courage and tenacity. Yet it is implausible to imagine that Anand and Hickey's evidence of nociception would have been enough by itself to change clinical guidelines around the world. As childhood pain expert Patrick McGrath has argued, Lawson's campaign, and the public outcry it created, was probably also essential.[11]

Looking back, it does not surprise me that many anaesthetists doubted whether newborns felt pain, because of course one can harbour such doubts. The surprise is how some of them chose to manage the risks. The idea of premising any action on an assumption of non-sentience (such as performing major surgery without anaesthesia) was always questionable, even when the evidence base was much thinner than it is now. The most charitable interpretation of the old practice is that anaesthesiologists were open to the possibility of sentience but were concerned about the safety of using anaesthetics on neonates, and that those safety concerns weighed more heavily in their calculations than concerns about pain and its consequences. Yet anaesthesiologists should also have worried about the safety of doing surgery during massive stress responses—and should have considered the possibility that anaesthesia might make the surgery safer on balance. Recall here that even the control group in Anand and Hickey's study still received light anaesthesia, and in this group the stress response was so enormous it posed a clear safety risk. It is a shock to realize that many procedures did not even involve light anaesthesia prior to Anand and Hickey's work.

There is an echo here of Chapter 9. Pre-1980s attitudes towards neonates bear a certain resemblance to the attitudes sometimes expressed even now

[9] For reviews, see Vinall and Grunau (2014) and Walker (2019). For some significant studies, see Brummelte et al. (2012); Doesburg et al. (2013); Grunau et al. (2005, 2007).
[10] Buchanan and Powell (2018).   [11] McGrath (2011).

towards adults in a chronic vegetative state. There are obvious differences between the vegetative state and the newborn state. And yet, in both cases, we find sleep-wake cycles and a suite of reflexes and spontaneous behaviours, combined with an apparent absence of voluntary behaviour. Brainstem circuits controlling wakefulness, orientation, and reflex response, including the reticular activating system, are clearly active, but many cortical circuits linked to sophisticated cognitive functions are absent or inactive. The precautionary attitude that now seems so obvious in the neonate case is one we should carry across to the case of disorders of consciousness, where it is still controversial.

But we now need to consider the question: *how far back in the process of human development should this precautionary attitude extend?*

10.2 Fetal Sentience and Women's Rights: Separating the Issues

Before we address that question head on, we need to distinguish it from a different one. Our question in this chapter is: when does a fetus become a sentience candidate? In other words, when do we need to start taking seriously the possibility that fetuses are sentient, and start debating proportionate steps to protect them from suffering? At some point, all of us crossed that mysterious threshold, but we have no memory of when or how it happened, or even whether it was sudden or gradual.

I will focus specifically on the case of human fetuses. Similar issues arise regarding the fetuses of non-human animals, and they matter, but the human issues have a special urgency, and they weigh particularly heavily on many of us.

At face value, this may look to be the most politically sensitive—and potentially incendiary—of all the questions we might ask about the edge of sentience. That is because there intuitively seems to be a tight link to questions about women's rights, and particularly the right to access abortion.[12] We might initially be tempted to think: 'it is wrong to abort a sentient fetus, so the legal time limit on abortion should be set at the earliest time sentience might realistically develop.'

---

[12] In some cases, trans men and non-binary people also experience pregnancy. So, generic statements about women and men made in this chapter should not be read as exceptionless. See Finn et al. (2023) for a discussion of pregnancy and gender.

Yet this thought ties abortion rights to a scientific question fraught with uncertainty, with troubling consequences. If the scientific evidence develops in a way that ends up pointing to ever earlier time points for the onset of sentience, as it may well do, then the legal time limit will end up being pushed ever earlier, with serious consequences for women's rights. Those of us sympathetic to the cause of women's rights need to be acutely aware of that risk. We should think about how to pre-empt it.

In fact, there are other reasons, aside from this possibility, to question the appropriateness of tying the legal time limit to the development of sentience. Firstly, most people do not regard sentience as sufficing, in other contexts, for rights. Consider farmed mammals, such as cows and pigs. There is ongoing disagreement about the ethical significance of sentience (see Chapter 4), but sentience is not generally regarded as implying a right to life. There is consensus that we should avoid causing gratuitous suffering to sentient beings (Chapter 6), but no consensus that animals have a right to life by virtue of being sentient. Admittedly, those who *do* think sentience implies a right to life should feel pressure to arrive at a consistent view about non-human animals and human fetuses.

Because sentience is not widely taken to imply a right to life, traditional debates about the ethics of abortion have tended to revolve around the concept of *personhood*, not sentience. In a controversial article and subsequent book, Michael Tooley argued that fetuses are clearly not persons and, consequently, do not possess the right to life that comes with personhood.[13] He went further, arguing that newborn babies are also clearly not persons. Many have agreed with Tooley's basic emphasis on the importance of personhood, while disagreeing with his stance regarding newborn babies. Critics sometimes reply that fetuses can be persons too, particularly in the later stages of development, and sometimes hold that merely potential personhood suffices for the associated rights.[14]

These issues turn on what personhood *is*, and there is no consensus about that. But that debate is independent of our present inquiry, which is about sentience, not personhood. A being can be sentient and yet not a person. Sentience is at most a necessary condition for personhood, not a sufficient condition. It may not even be a necessary condition. Mary Ann Warren has constructed an influential account of personhood in which, although

---

[13] Tooley (1972, 1983).

[14] Greasley and Kaczor (2017) is a good entry point to this debate, presenting both sides. Greasley (2017) has provided an extended discussion and defence of the claim that the abortion debate is fundamentally about personhood.

sentience does feature as one of the five constituent ingredients of person-hood (along with reasoning, self-motivated activity, communicative capacity, and self-awareness), no single ingredient is considered strictly necessary. One must possess *enough* of the ingredients, and 'enough' is an unavoidably vague threshold.[15]

There is a separate (and in some ways more radical) line of argument according to which, even granting the personhood and right to life of the fetus, abortion rights can *still* be justified, because there is a strong right to bodily autonomy that place limits on what morality can demand from one person to sustain the life of another. Judith Jarvis Thomson offered a thought experiment in which you are hooked up in your sleep, without your consent, to another adult—clearly sentient, clearly a person—who will die unless they remain physiologically connected to you for nine months. To maintain them, using the resources of your own body, would be a costly sacrifice on your part. Thomson asks: would it be morally permissible to disconnect yourself and let the adult die?[16]

Granted, the other person has a right to life, but this is a right not to be deprived of life *without sufficient reason*. It is generally recognized there can be sufficient reasons, such as self-defence. And you have a powerful reason deriving from bodily autonomy: you have not consented to the demands this person is placing on your body. An altruistic sacrifice might be morally admirable ('a great kindness', says Thomson) but it is not required, so it is permissible to disconnect yourself, Thomson suggests. Thomson goes on to argue that the thought experiment is relevantly like the case of abortion, where, even if the fetus is a person, a woman retains the right to refuse con-sent for that fetus to draw on her bodily resources. The analogy has proven controversial, unsurprisingly.[17] But to the extent that the analogy survives scrutiny, this is a second, distinct way to argue for the independence of abor-tion rights from questions of sentience.

How, then, should the legal time limit be set, if not on grounds of sen-tience? One option, concomitant with Thomson's argument, is to draw no line at all, and to say a woman has the right to withdraw consent to the use of her bodily resources at any time. China has taken this approach since the 1970s, though is in the process of revising its policy.[18] In the UK, the concept

---

[15] Warren (1973, 1997). See Furlan (2022) for a recent critique of Warren.
[16] Thomson (1971).
[17] See Boonin (2019) for a defence of Thomson-style arguments; see Greasley (2017, ch. 2) for a critique.
[18] Ahmed (2021).

of 'viability' has played an important legal role. A fetus typically becomes viable outside the womb (albeit with intensive neonatal care) at around 22–24 weeks, lining up with the legal threshold in the UK and Australia.[19] One problem with this way of drawing the line is that it introduces a strange coupling between the legal threshold and medical technology. Medical progress has already led to a situation where neonates can survive at 22 or 23 weeks,[20] down from 28 weeks, the legal limit implied by the UK's Abortion Act 1967, and down too from the figure of 24 weeks to which the limit was moved in 1991. If future technology allows neonates to be viable outside the womb at ever earlier time points, then viability-based legal thresholds may end up pushed to ever earlier time points. This would be hard to justify from an ethical point of view, since it is difficult to explain why the moral status of a fetus inside the womb should depend on the medical technology that happens to exist outside the womb.[21]

A third option, concomitant with the position that personhood grounds the right to life, involves tying the legal limit to the onset of personhood. For this to work, however, there is a need for a theory of personhood detailed enough to pinpoint its emergence during development. We currently lack any such theory, so it is not clear what the view implies regarding appropriate legal limits. Moreover, it seems entirely possible that a good theory of personhood would imply a gradual developmental transition involving borderline cases, leaving us with the problem of how to make sense of our obligations regarding those borderline cases.[22] One way to handle these problems would be to construct an intentionally sharpened-up concept of a 'personhood candidate', analogous to the concept of a sentience candidate constructed in this book, with the boundaries of personhood candidature drawn deliberately inclusively to facilitate precautionary thinking. But that is a project for another occasion.

These matters are substantially unresolved, but they are not primarily questions of *sentience*. Keeping issues of sentience separate, as far as possible, from issues of abortion policy is important, because it creates space for a discussion about fetal sentience that is not crowded out by the political controversy surrounding abortion law, especially in the US context, where the overturning of *Roe v. Wade* has led to enormous state-by-state variation. I say

---

[19] See Romanis (2020) for discussion of the ways in which 'viability' is defined in law. See https://reproductiverights.org/maps/worlds-abortion-laws/ for a summary of the world's abortion laws. The picture in America is changing rapidly following the Supreme Court's overturning of *Roe v. Wade*.
[20] Di Stefano et al. (2021).   [21] Gordon (2008).
[22] Greasley (2017). The same may be true of sentience, a possibility considered in Chapter 3.

'as far as possible' because there are inevitably some connections, to which we will return later.

***

Proposal 7. *Sentience and abortion.* The point at which a human fetus becomes sentient is not the point at which abortion becomes morally impermissible. We should separate these issues. The ethics of abortion depends primarily on questions of personhood and bodily autonomy, not on questions of sentience.

***

10.3 Fetuses as Sentience Candidates

We need to take seriously the possibility that human fetuses have a minimal form of sentience from an early stage in development. The earliest credible time point for when a fetus becomes a sentience candidate, given current evidence and the definition of a sentience candidate, is approximately at the start of the second trimester. The consequences of this may be challenging to manage, but we have to face up to them.

One way to introduce this idea is through the changing views of one influential fetal pain expert, Stuart Derbyshire. In the 1990s, Derbyshire was a powerful critic of the idea of fetal pain at *any* point in gestation, writing in the *British Medical Journal* that ' "fetal pain" is a misnomer'.[23] Elsewhere, Derbyshire made a detailed case for this claim, concluding that:

> Given what pain is understood to be…, the complex neurology that pain processing requires…and the limited neurological and cognitive development of the fetus…, I would reject the characterisation of any such experience [in the fetus] as 'pain'.[24]

What was the argument? Derbyshire noted that evidence sometimes taken to indicate pain in both fetuses and neonates—primarily, nociceptive responses and stress responses to stimuli—occur without any involvement of the mature cortical circuits linked to pain experiences in adults, and thus 'may exist independently of conscious experience'.[25] He then outlined a theory on which conscious experience does not begin until around four months after birth

---

[23] Derbyshire and Furedi (1996).   [24] Derbyshire (1999, p. 27). See also Derbyshire (2006).
[25] Derbyshire (1999, p. 22).

and requires social interaction with the world and with other people. Among contemporary theories of consciousness, the closest relative is probably Rolls's higher-order syntactic thought theory.[26]

In 2007, Derbyshire presented a similar line of argument in written evidence submitted to the UK parliament's Science and Technology Committee as part of their inquiry into scientific developments potentially relevant to abortion law:

> Clearly our access to others' pain is mediated through behavior and language but this is also true of our own pain experience. Social development structures our behavior and language so as to be meaningful to the outside world but with the unnoticed side effect of rendering the child's inner experience meaningful to him or her. While brain development is certainly a necessary precursor of conscious sensory awareness, merely peering inside the head will not reveal the source of awareness.
>
> 21. This is how we can be so positive that the fetus is not conscious and, therefore, cannot experience pain. Not only has the biological development not yet occurred but also the post-birth environment, so necessary to the development of experience, has not yet made itself felt. In short, fetal pain is a moral blunder based on the false equivalence between observer and observed that misses the whole point and process of development.[27]

The Committee quoted extensively from Derbyshire's evidence, concluding that 'while the evidence suggests that fetuses have physiological reactions to noxious stimuli, it does not indicate that pain is consciously felt'.[28]

This exemplifies a common yet problematic pattern of reasoning regarding the edge of sentience. The author firstly observes an explanatory gap between conscious experience and the indicators we use to assess it; and, secondly, expresses sympathy for a theory of conscious experience that is relatively cognitively demanding, pushing this capacity beyond the reach of the system in question. Both thoughts are entirely reasonable ones to have. Yet, when presented to policy-makers using confident, unhedged language, they can lead to policies being premised on assumptions that are in fact highly uncertain, neglecting relevant risks.

The existence of an explanatory gap between conscious experience and its outward indicators is something we all have to acknowledge, but not a reason to deny the evidential import of behavioural, cognitive, and neural indicators.

---

[26] Rolls (2014).   [27] Derbyshire (2007).
[28] Science and Technology Committee (2007, p. 25).

They can shift probabilities upwards by, for example, showing us that the conditions of less demanding theories of consciousness (such as those of Merker and Panksepp) are plausibly met. And while we are all free to explore the space of possible theories of consciousness, we need to avoid overconfidence about our own preferred theories. Even if our sympathies lie with theories at the relatively cognitively demanding end of the spectrum, we need to acknowledge a risk that serious theories at the less cognitively demanding end may be correct, and we need to manage that risk as best we can.

In 2010, Derbyshire was part of a working group of the Royal College of Obstetricians and Gynaecologists (RCOG) that was tasked with reviewing the evidence of 'fetal awareness'. The working group concluded that:

> cortical processing of pain perception, and therefore the ability of the fetus to feel pain, cannot occur before 24 weeks of gestation.... It is reasonable to infer from this that the fetus does not require analgesia for interventions occurring before 24 weeks of gestation.[29]

The group found evidence that fetuses develop nociceptors (specialized receptors sensitive to tissue damage) at around 10–13 weeks' gestation. The group also found evidence that spontaneous movements and reflexes can be observed from as early as 8 weeks, and that 'the fetus withdraws from a needle from about 18 weeks and also launches a stress response following needle puncture'. Yet the working group interpreted this evidence with a sceptical eye, concluding that 'The fetal spinal cord and brainstem develop well before the cerebral cortex. This means that these reflex movements occur without any possibility of fetal awareness.'[30] They doubled down on this point a few pages later: 'Activity in the spinal cord, brainstem and subcortical midbrain structures are sufficient to generate reflexive behaviours and hormonal responses but are not sufficient to support pain awareness.'[31]

There is a particularly weak line in the report that, to my mind, encapsulates what I think of as the *anti-precautionary fallacy*. The working group writes that 'most pain neuroscientists believe that the cortex is necessary for pain perception.... The lack of cortical connections before 24 weeks, therefore, implies that pain is not possible until after 24 weeks.'[32] If pain before 24 weeks could be conclusively ruled out, premising action on that assumption

---

[29] Royal College of Obstetricians and Gynaecologists (2010, p. 15).
[30] Royal College of Obstetricians and Gynaecologists (2010, p. 5).
[31] Royal College of Obstetricians and Gynaecologists (2010, p. 7).
[32] Royal College of Obstetricians and Gynaecologists (2010, p. 11).

would be justifiable. But it is a fallacy to infer that, because one view is the majority view, alternative views are 'not possible'. This is a way of shutting down the difficult conversation about risk and precaution that should properly ensue, given that there are (and were in 2010) credible minority views on which pain in the second trimester is possible.[33]

In a 2020 article with John Bockmann, Derbyshire announced a volte-face.[34] Derbyshire and Bockmann cite Merker as having provided (thirteen years earlier) a credible alternative to a cortex-centric view of pain and cite studies suggesting that the 'pain matrix', a set of cortical areas often linked to pain in adults, is neither necessary nor sufficient for pain experience.[35] They also cite a study that found organizational similarities (though in a study of audition rather than pain, and in ferrets rather than humans) between mature cortical tissue and the subplate, an important developmental precursor to the cortex.[36] This study provided some evidence, in the case of hearing, that the subplate does support early precursors of cortical functions and does not solely exist to scaffold the development of the cortex. These new developments led Derbyshire and Bockmann to argue that:

> Current neuroscientific evidence undermines the necessity of the cortex for pain experience. Even if the cortex is deemed necessary for pain experience, there is now good evidence that thalamic projections into the subplate, which emerge around 12 weeks' gestation, are functional and equivalent to thalamocortical projections that emerge around 24 weeks' gestation. Thus, current neuroscientific evidence supports the possibility of fetal pain before the 'consensus' cut-off of 24 weeks.[37]

They concluded that 'the evidence, and a balanced reading of that evidence, points towards an immediate and unreflective pain experience mediated by the developing function of the nervous system from as early as 12 weeks', that is, around the end of the first trimester and the beginning of the second.[38]

In my view, the evidence available in 2010 was already enough to support the more precautionary stance supported by Derbyshire and Bockmann in 2020. It is true that the declining fortunes of the 'pain matrix' hypothesis and

---

[33] The report was criticized at the time. See Platt (2011).
[34] Derbyshire and Bockmann (2020).   [35] Feinstein et al. (2016); Salomons et al. (2016).
[36] Wess et al. (2017).   [37] Derbyshire and Bockmann (2020, p. 4).
[38] Derbyshire and Bockmann (2020, p. 6). The same figure of 12 weeks—the start of the second trimester—is reached by Ciaunica et al. (2021) by a quite different line of reasoning, based on 'the development of prospective, anticipatory awareness in motor control', i.e. evidence that the midbrain is operational and performing the modelling functions taken to be important by Merker's theory.

the emerging new picture of the subplate as a site of nascent cortical functions are significant developments that shift probabilities. But the idea that midbrain structures alone are sufficient for sentience in the absence of the cortex is one that Panksepp and Merker gave us strong reasons to take seriously some time ago.[39] These reasons fall well short of a conclusive case, but they establish a *realistic possibility* of sentience once the relevant circuits are active. The more traditional view that sentience in humans requires mature cortical circuits, and thus cannot develop before 24 weeks, is also a reasonable one. But we are not entitled to regard this view, or any single view, as a moral certainty. Even if we think it unlikely, the credibility of the Panksepp/Merker view may render some precautions proportionate to the risk of sentience developing early.

Indeed, as soon as one grants the credibility of the Panksepp/Merker picture, one needs to take seriously the idea that a fetus may be sentient as soon as the relevant midbrain structures, especially the superior colliculus (SC) and periaqueductal gray (PAG), are functional. It is very hard to pinpoint when in human development this threshold is crossed, but it appears to be well before mature cortical function is achieved. Defensive responses to needle puncture, including bradycardia (reduced heart rate), are some evidence that the PAG is operational by 18 weeks' gestation, given the role it plays in regulating such responses.[40] But the relevant brain areas may be active before their activity is clearly manifested. They may plausibly be functional by 15 weeks[41] or even by 12 weeks, as suggested by Derbyshire and Bockmann and by Anna Ciaunica and colleagues.[42] The development of the SC has been studied in some detail and found to be virtually complete by 20 weeks, with mature lamination visible from about 16 weeks.[43]

These dates are agonizingly approximate. But, by this point in the book, that should come as no surprise. We have to face up to the reality that this sort of very approximate line-drawing may be the best we can do for the foreseeable future. This could be because there is no precise moment at which sentience comes online. It could also be because, although there *is* a precise moment (and both possibilities belong in the zone of reasonable disagreement; see §3.7), our present theoretical understanding of the nature of consciousness is far too immature to adjudicate between alternative hypotheses about where the line is.

---

[39] Panksepp (1998a); Merker (2007). Ciaunica et al. (2021) defend a similar view.
[40] Koba et al. (2016).   [41] Sekulic et al. (2016).   [42] Ciaunica et al. (2021).
[43] Qu et al. (2006).

What to do in this situation? My proposal is that we take the *earliest evidence-based estimate* as the point at which discussions about proportionality are warranted. This may or may not be where sentience begins in reality, but it is where sentience *candidature* begins. An 'evidence-based estimate' is one that flows from a credible, evidence-based theoretical perspective compatible with the scientific meta-consensus (Chapter 6). The earliest reasonable estimate I have come across in the existing literature is Derbyshire and Bockmann's estimate of the beginning of the second trimester.

Proposal 8. *Human sentience candidature begins early.* Human fetuses are sentience candidates from the beginning of the second trimester. This line may move as new evidence emerges, but it should always track the earliest scientifically credible, evidence-based estimate.

10.4 Taking a Precautionary Stance towards Fetuses

What sort of precautions may be proportionate? Before returning to the case of abortion, which presents unique difficulties, let us consider therapeutic interventions on a fetus. One might intuitively suppose that human fetuses are never operated on directly, but in fact a significant number of open mid-gestation fetal surgeries have been developed for repairing various kinds of congenital defect. For example, the neural tube defect MMC (myelomeningocele) can be treated with fetal surgery.[44]

Where fetal surgery is possible, the direct intramuscular injection of anaesthetics and analgesics to the fetus is usually also possible, and should always be considered.[45] Specific treatment decisions in these cases need to be made by expert anaesthesiologists, in discussion with surgeons and with the mother. We cannot say, in general, what the right call will be. Yet wider public debate about the issue is still important, as the 1980s debate around neonatal pain demonstrated. Even though specific decisions call for expert judgement, the *general norms* that shape those expert judgements can and should be matters of public discussion and ethical reflection.

As anaesthesiologists Monica Hoagland and Debnath Chatterjee have emphasized, the case for administering anaesthesia to fetuses during therapeutic procedures does not need to rest on conjectures about the

---

[44] Hoagland and Chatterjee (2017).   [45] Bellieni (2021); Hoagland and Chatterjee (2017).

development of sentience. Fetal stress responses in response to surgery (which are clearly observed from around 18 weeks' gestation) need to be managed regardless of whether they are accompanied by any subjective experience of pain, since they create a risk of triggering premature labour, as well as a risk of sudden movement that obstructs incredibly delicate surgery.[46] This echoes the point made in §10.1 regarding pain in neonates. People will always disagree about the onset of sentience, but there can be overlapping consensus around the need to manage physiological stress responses, given their known downstream risks.

Despite this, it is not clear how widely fetal anaesthesia and pain relief is actually used when fetal surgery is performed. A literature review of published reports of fetal surgery by a team of paediatricians led by Carlo Bellieni found that less than half of the reported procedures attempted direct fetal analgesia.[47] In some cases, anaesthesiologists seemed to be relying on the idea that maternal anaesthetics would cross the placenta in sufficient doses, an assumption Bellieni and colleagues considered dubious (note, for example, that administering a general anaesthetic to the mother does not anaesthetize the fetus during a caesarean section). In a more recent piece, Bellieni expressed optimism that 'anesthesia to the fetus is now a widespread and accepted practice'.[48] But without more data on its use, the picture remains murky.

One obvious (and, I hope, uncontroversial) proposal is that data should be collected and published on this issue, to facilitate informed public debate and to cultivate trust. This is in the interests of the medical profession itself. Recall the outcry in the 1980s, when it came to light that medical norms regarding neonates were severely out of line with societal expectations. By facilitating and encouraging ongoing discussion, and involving the public in that discussion, the medical profession can prevent the same level of mismatch from arising again.

Proposal 9. *Fetal pain relief (in therapeutic contexts).* Direct fetal anaesthesia and pain relief should be considered whenever therapeutic fetal surgery is performed. The public should be involved in discussions about general norms of medical practice (not specific decisions), and data regarding current practices should be collected and published to allow such discussions.

---

[46] Hoagland and Chatterjee (2017).   [47] Bellieni et al. (2013).
[48] Bellieni (2021, p. 1615).

10.5 Communicating Uncertainty in the Abortion Clinic

Let us now return to the vexed issue of abortion. The message of §10.2 was that the question of fetal sentience is different from the question of the right to access abortion, which hinges on bodily autonomy and/or fetal person-hood. Recognition of fetuses as sentience candidates should not be used as a reason to ban abortion. But we also noted that the issues are not wholly unrelated, and it is time to revisit the relationship between them.

In high-income countries, 90 per cent of abortions are performed before 12 weeks, and the embryo or fetus is not yet a sentience candidate at this time, given the way we have defined that term.[49] The structures regarded as sufficient for sentience even by the least cognitively demanding credible pictures are not yet functional. But what about the 10 per cent of cases where the fetus is 12 weeks or over? Derbyshire and Bockmann admit that they disagree on the best way forward. One believes that the use of analgesia is a matter 'for the clinical team and the pregnant woman' and that there should be no general policy, while the other thinks analgesia should be 'standard for abortions in the second trimester'.[50]

I will limit myself to two reflections here: one about communication, and one about deliberative procedures. The question of how to introduce the possibility of fetal pain sensitively, without crossing the boundary into emotional manipulation of the patient, is a very difficult one. The RCOG report of 2010 gives a vision of how simple things might have been, and it tells us what doctors would *ideally like* to be able to say to their patients. The report includes a section that aims to answer frequently asked questions about abortions before 24 weeks. The suggested answers offer unequivocal confidence:[51]

Will the fetus/baby feel pain?

No, the fetus does not experience pain [....] Current research shows that the sensory structures are not developed or specialised enough to experience pain in a fetus less than 24 weeks.

Will the process hurt the baby?

No. To be hurt, you need to feel pain. Current research shows that the sensory structures are not developed or specialised enough for a fetus to experience pain less than 24 weeks.

---

[49] Popinchalk and Sedgh (2019).
[50] Derbyshire and Bockmann (2020, p. 5). They do not say which author is which, but one can guess.
[51] Royal College of Obstetricians and Gynaecologists (2010, p. 20).

Unfortunately, these answers evade the need for honest communication of uncertainty. That cannot be the way forward. The language of 'realistic possibility' may be helpful here. Patients in the abortion clinic, if they ask questions like these, need to be informed accurately, and so should be told that there is a realistic possibility of fetal pain after 12 weeks, that the whole question is shrouded in significant uncertainty, but that analgesics are generally considered to reduce the risks in the context of fetal surgery.

In 2022, the RCOG convened another working group to update its heavily criticized 2010 report. Thankfully, the language was significantly toned down. The group nonetheless concluded that 'evidence indicates that the possibility of pain perception before 28 weeks of gestation is unlikely' and added that 'there is no basis for considering the administration of analgesia or anaesthesia to a fetus before termination of pregnancy in the first or second trimester to prevent fetal perception of pain.'[52] Derbyshire and Bockmann's 2020 article, arguing for just such a basis, was not cited or mentioned—Derbyshire was on the working party, yet his revised views were clearly given little consideration. I do not think this uneasy situation can continue indefinitely. At some point, professional bodies will have to confront the issue of how to communicate uncertainty, rather than clinging fast to the language of certainty in an area where it cannot be justified.

A second very difficult issue concerns the procedures for setting clinical norms. Who should decide whether analgesia should be standard practice, only used when the patient asks for it, or discouraged? The question is not just one for experts, because it concerns what is proportionate to the risks of fetal pain. However, my proposal to entrust citizens' panels with assessments of proportionality (see Part II) also faces a problem: this is a situation that around half the population can be sure they will never experience. Indeed, productive debates about abortion can be obstructed by men attempting to dominate discussion of the evaluative questions, even though the choice is one they will never themselves face.

I am very unsure how best to handle this. One way forward is to construct panels composed of women. Yet the 2016–2017 Irish citizens' assembly that recommended a liberalization of abortion law in Ireland was gender-balanced, and its statistical representativeness may well have been crucial to its proposals being accepted by the wider population.[53] A trade-off in institutional design surfaces starkly in this context: to command confidence in its recommendations, an assembly must represent the whole of society, but to do

---

[52] Royal College of Obstetricians and Gynaecologists (2022).   [53] Palese (2018).

justice to the moral complexity of the issues, an assembly must give appropriate weight to the voices of those who have a direct stake in the matter. One option, though not the only one, would be an assembly with two parts of equal size: a random sample of women and a random sample of the whole population. Those without a direct stake would still have a voice, but the voices of women would receive greater weight.

> **Proposal 10.** *Fetal pain relief (in the context of abortion).* Clinicians need to communicate uncertainty about fetal sentience honestly to patients. In some cases, fetal pain relief may be appropriate. Deliberative processes for setting clinical norms must give appropriate weight to the voices of women.

10.6 Human Embryos and the 14-Day Rule

In the late 1970s and early 1980s—a few years before the neonatal pain controversy—both the US and UK governments established committees to advise on a controversy concerning the very beginning of human development. In vitro fertilization (IVF) technology had made it possible to cultivate human embryos in the lab. As an inevitable part of the process, not all would be implanted into a mother. Could those embryos be used for research? And what about embryos created specifically for research? The benefits of using human embryos for studying the early stages of human development are clear, but many have strong ethical qualms about this type of research.

Committees on both sides of the Atlantic converged on a rule that, as I write around forty years later, is still in force: the 14-day rule. The UK's committee—led by the moral philosopher Mary Warnock and known as the 'Warnock Committee'—proposed that:

> Legislation should provide that research may be carried out on any embryo resulting from in vitro fertilisation, whatever its provenance, up to the end of the 14th day after fertilisation, but subject to all other restrictions as may be imposed by the licensing body.[54]

Why 14 days? The main reasons given did not concern sentience. Moreover, the two committees offered different reasons. The US committee cited

---

[54] Committee of Inquiry into Human Fertilisation and Embryology (1984, §11.30).

14 days as the time at which implantation would normally be complete.[55] The implicit rationale was (I suspect) that research on embryos should have the goal of facilitating IVF treatments, and only pre-implantation embryos were deemed relevant to this goal. The Warnock report, meanwhile, gives the reason that, at 15 days, the 'primitive streak' develops. The primitive streak is a transient developmental structure with important roles in organizing development.[56] The structure imparts bilateral symmetry and an anterior-posterior body axis or, in plain terms, gives the embryo a 'head end' and a 'foot end'. Significantly for the committee's reasoning, normal identical twinning cannot occur after this point.[57] The committee thus concluded that the primitive streak 'marks the beginning of individual development of the embryo.'[58]

Why should the point at which normal identical twinning can no longer occur mark an ethically significant threshold? The oddity of this idea is part of what makes the Warnock report, to my mind, a fascinatingly strange piece of advisory writing. Metaphysics rears its head in an unexpected place. At face value, the report's recommendations rest on an idiosyncratic metaphysical picture that is far from common ground. This is the most charitable reconstruction of the argument I can come up with:

1. An embryo has moral status if and only if it could be the initial stage of an individual human being.
2. In a case of identical twinning, the initial stage of each individual must have been no earlier than the moment of twinning.
3. The stage in development at which an individual begins is always the same. It cannot differ between twinned and non-twinned cases.
4. Therefore: an embryo has moral status if and only if it has developed past the latest stage in development at which twinning occurs.

This is a remarkably shaky foundation on which to rest such a grave recommendation. All the premises are dubious. We need not accept that moral status is tied to the possibility of being the initial stage of a human individual. Moreover, we need not accept that each identical twin began no earlier than the moment of twinning (we could adopt a picture in which both individuals

[55] HEW Ethics Advisory Board (1979). Their estimate was incorrect: implantation occurs 12 days after fertilization at the latest (Wilcox et al. 1999).

[56] Downs (2009).

[57] Committee of Inquiry into Human Fertilisation and Embryology (1984, §11.15). Conjoined twinning can still occur, however (Blackshaw and Rodger 2021). It is not always clear what to say about individuality in conjoined twin cases (Boyle 2020).

[58] Committee of Inquiry into Human Fertilisation and Embryology (1984, §11.22).

begin at conception but initially share the same cells). We also need not accept that the moment an individual begins is the same in twinned and non-twinned cases.

What was *really* going on in the Warnock report? I cannot imagine for a moment that the committee was persuaded by a metaphysical argument based on three questionable premises. I think what happened is that the 14-day rule was a compromise that a majority of the committee found strategically acceptable. In rationalizing their compromise, I suspect Warnock and colleagues wanted to present the recommendation as principled rather than wholly pragmatic, and this led them to the idea of the primitive streak as having special metaphysical and ethical significance.

The Warnock report did not achieve the kind of overlapping consensus I have suggested we should be aiming for. It achieved something else: a strategic compromise among conflicting views, publicly justified using peculiar reasons that were not common ground at all, and that could only seem compelling from one idiosyncratic metaphysical vantage point. The underlying value conflicts were not resolved, and the public was not substantially involved in the discussion. The value-judgements were made by a cadre of experts with a small minority of lay members, in an instance of what I lamented in Chapter 7 as the 'tyranny of expert values'. And yet this strategic compromise has lasted forty years.

Is this a problem for the idea that an overlapping consensus is more stable than a strategic compromise? Maybe. But it may also be that the 14-day rule has persisted not because it has solid ethical or public support, but rather because it achieved the appearance of a tough constraint while, in practice, granting scientists ample headroom to exploit the currently available technology. It was only in 2016 that researchers actually became able to sustain embryos for 14 days.[59] From that time onwards, calls began for the law to be changed to extend the time limit to at least 28 days.[60] In 2021, the International Society for Stem Research dropped its support for the 14-day rule: not a change in the law, but a major change in international good-practice norms.[61]

The case shows us some of the potential costs of failing to resolve our value conflicts democratically, inclusively, and for the long term. Yes, the 14-day rule provided a surprisingly enduring compromise, because for a long time it failed to constrain scientific research in any significant way. But that does not

---

[59] Deglincerti et al. (2016); Shahbazi et al. (2016).
[60] Appleby and Bredenoord (2018); Chan (2017); Hurlbut et al. (2017); McCully (2021); Nuffield Council on Bioethics (2017).
[61] Subbaraman (2021).

make it a long-term stable solution to the ethical problem. For proponents of embryo research who want to see the technology exploited to its full potential, 14 days no longer seems like a good place for strategic compromise. So, that compromise is now fraying, leading to renewed conflict. There is also no reason to think that a shift to 28 days would permanently settle the issue. We can instead expect proponents of embryo research to campaign for later and later legal limits as technology continues to improve. On each occasion, the campaign will be more likely to succeed if it seeks a small enough extension to avoid significant public concern.

For critics, this is exactly the sort of long-term trajectory they feared all along, and one they see as vindicating their initial scepticism about the whole idea of research on human embryos.[62] This is a case where the 'slippery slope' metaphor may actually be apt. Warnock herself, reflecting towards the end of her life on the continuing case for the 14-day rule, put the point in these terms.[63] As noted in Chapter 9, slippery slope arguments are sometimes fallacious. But when the metaphor is being used to describe a socio-political phenomenon—in which interest groups campaign for a series of incremental policy changes, each too small by itself to provoke a backlash from a population with many other demands on its attention, but adding up to a change that would have prompted serious public concern if implemented all at once—the metaphor is capturing a real problem that democracies face. Through strings of small incremental changes, democratic societies can be pulled in directions that are misaligned with the public's values. It is reasonable to worry that this could happen in the case of embryo research.[64]

10.7 The 14-Day Rule and Sentience

What if the legal limit on embryo research had been set not on the basis of the alleged significance of the primitive streak, but on considerations to do with sentience? Such considerations did play a subsidiary role in the Warnock report. The position that these are the considerations that really matter was there described as the 'strictly utilitarian' position. This strikes me as a misnomer. Certainly, utilitarianism is one example of an ethical outlook that would see the potential sentience of the embryo as the main risk to be

---

[62] Blackshaw and Rodger (2021).   [63] Warnock (2017).

[64] When a series of small changes is deliberately pursued for strategic reasons, the macabre metaphor of 'boiling the frog' is also used. But I think in most cases, including this one, the slide down the slope is not the result of a deliberate long-term strategy.

managed in this area, but one does not have to be a utilitarian to think this. There are various sentientist ethical outlooks (Chapter 4).

The Warnock Committee observed that, if one does regard this as the primary consideration, then one is likely to favour a time limit later than 14 days:

> According to this argument the time limit for in vitro development, and for research on the embryo, could be set either when the first beginnings of the central nervous system can be identified, or when functional activity first occurs. If the former is chosen, this would imply a limit of 22 to 23 days after fertilization, when the neural tube begins to close. As to the latter, in the present state of knowledge the onset of central nervous system functional activity could not be used to define accurately the limit to research, because the timing is not known; however, it is generally thought to be considerably later in pregnancy. With either limit, proponents suggest subtracting a few days in order that there would be no possibility of the embryo feeling pain.[65]

The strongly precautionary attitude on display in this passage—at a time when many surgeons doubted the possibility of pain in *newborn babies*—is striking. The committee took seriously the possibility of pain experience as early as 22 days, minus a few more days. They felt they could rule out any possibility of pain prior to the neural tube closing, thereby forming an early precursor to the brain and spinal cord. After that, pain was possible.

This is rather *too* precautionary, according to the framework constructed in Part II of this book. There I suggested that there is a scientific meta-consensus around the idea that a spinal cord alone does not suffice for sentience. If there were no such meta-consensus, we would have to dramatically rethink the practice of organ donation. The wide agreement that spinal cords are not sufficient does not confer on it the status of *absolute certainty*—it is conceivable that future evidence will shake our currently justified confidence—but it does confer a kind of 'moral certainty' that licenses regarding a brain dead human as legally dead.

My framework is not based on the idea that we can move from 'cannot prove absence of sentience with absolute certainty' to 'strong precautions are justified'. This would be pernicious in the case of organ donation. My framework replaces this crude precautionary reasoning with a more sophisticated version that moves from 'can positively establish sentience candidature' to

---

[65] Committee of Inquiry into Human Fertilisation and Embryology (1984, §11.20).

'democratic and inclusive debate about the proportionality of precautions is justified'. I hope it is clear that these are very different approaches, even though both could be called 'precautionary'.

A message of §10.2 was that sentience candidature begins early in human development, but 'early' was proposed to mean approximately 12 weeks, not 22 days. Neural tube closure is clearly insufficient for the formation of the mechanisms that, even on the least cognitively demanding of the existing credible theories, suffice for sentience. An embryo in which the neural tube has just closed still has no brainstem, no superior colliculus, no periaqueductal gray, no discernible whole-system stress responses or nociceptive responses. The evidential threshold for sentience candidature is not met. If we accept this reasoning for fetuses, brain-dead adult humans, and so on, consistency requires we also accept it for in vitro embryos.

The upshot is that, *if* sentience candidature were to be taken as the fundamental criterion for the legal time limit on human embryo research, then that legal time limit could be liberalized very significantly indeed, to a point far past the limits of current technology.

The '*if*' is crucial, however. I am not proposing this liberalization, because I take it to be very likely that such a move would produce significant public concern, especially from religious groups whose main interest is in protecting what they see as the sanctity of all human life. There is no overlapping consensus, at present, around liberalization. Nor should we try to creep towards this liberalization by tiny increments, in an attempt to stay under the radar of the general public and avoid serious public debate about the acceptability of the long-run destination. Considerations regarding the sanctity of all human life, sentient or not, are part of the zone of reasonable disagreement, and they should be represented and aired in democratic, inclusive processes for decision-making. But they are not considerations to do with sentience. *If the 14-day rule or an even tighter legal limit can be justified, then the justification must appeal to grounds that are not sentience-related.* So, rather than proposing a liberalization of the 14-day rule, what I propose instead is an inclusive debate in which reasons against that liberalization are given a fair hearing.

Proposal 11. *Sentience and the 14-day rule.* If the main goal of setting a legal time limit on human embryo research were that of prohibiting research on human sentience candidates, a significant liberalization of the current 14-day rule would still be proportionate to that goal. However, the issue raises deep value conflicts that have little to do with sentience.

10.8 Summary of Chapter 10

In the 1980s, growing public awareness that anaesthesia was not routinely being used on newborn babies during surgery led to a successful campaign to change clinical practice, vindicated by subsequent evidence. The story shows us the value of taking a precautionary attitude towards existing evidence and the value of involving the public in discussion of general clinical norms.

When we turn to fetuses, a concern arises that recognizing fetal sentience may be incompatible with recognizing a right to abortion. However, these are substantially separate issues. The time limit for abortions depends either on when the fetus becomes a person and/or on the strength of a person's right to bodily autonomy. Sentience is not sufficient for personhood, so this is not fundamentally a question about sentience.

We should recognize human fetuses as sentience candidates from the start of the second trimester. This aligns with the earliest scientifically credible, evidence-based estimates in the zone of reasonable disagreement. Future evidence could move the threshold for sentience candidature in either direction, but it should always align with the earliest scientifically credible, evidence-based estimate.

Whenever therapeutic surgery is performed on a fetus (and this happens for a variety of reasons), direct administration of anaesthesia and pain relief should be considered. This can be justified by the need to control the fetal stress response, even setting aside the possibility of sentience. Specific decisions need to be made by expert anaesthesiologists in discussion with surgeons and patients, but the public can and should be involved in discussions of the general norms of medical practice in this area and the value-judgements implicit in those norms.

Although recognizing second-trimester fetuses as sentience candidates does not give us a reason to change the legal time limit on abortions, it does require honest communication of uncertainty with patients. Clinical norms in this area need to be formulated by appropriately inclusive processes, and these processes need to give appropriate weight to the voices of women.

The anti-precautionary attitude that has sometimes been taken towards neonates and fetuses can be contrasted with the strongly precautionary attitude often taken towards human embryo research, encapsulated in the '14-day rule'. The original rationale for the 14-day rule (in the UK) rests on the dubious idea that the development of an individual human being begins with the appearance of the primitive streak. In practice, this has always represented a strategic compromise between deeply conflicting values, and the conflict has never been satisfactorily resolved.

If the main goal were simply that of avoiding research on human beings who are sentience candidates, a significantly liberalized legal limit would still be proportionate to that goal. However, sceptics of human embryo research are often driven by concerns unrelated to sentience. The best way to resolve this value conflict stably and for the long term is through democratic, inclusive processes in which those who oppose liberalization are properly represented.

The Edge of Sentience: Risk and Precaution in Humans, Other Animals, and AI. Jonathan Birch, Oxford University Press.
© Jonathan Birch 2024. DOI: 10.1093/9780191966729.003.0011

11

Neural Organoids

11.1 The Promise of Organoid Research

Biomedical research urgently needs new and better alternatives to animal models. The trend in recent decades has been towards increasing reliance on a small number of model species, especially rats, mice, zebrafish, and fruit flies, and towards a troubling level of dependence on assumptions about the relevance of these model systems to human medical conditions.[1] Many researchers and funding agencies have invested heavily in the idea that understanding the brain mechanisms of animal models will help us understand complex conditions such as depression, anxiety, autism, or schizophrenia in their human forms. But animal models are far from perfect models, leading to widespread reflection on how things could be done differently.[2]

The maxim to 'replace, reduce, and refine' was coined more than fifty years ago and is now embedded in frameworks for the regulation of animal research around the world. It crystallizes a point of wide agreement. We should aim to replace animal models with other types of model where possible, reduce the numbers of animals being used, and refine experimental techniques to minimize suffering. Yet this maxim has turned out to be compatible with a drastic increase over those same fifty years in the total numbers of animals used.[3] If the total number of scientists and labs soars, as it has done in the last fifty years, then the total number of animals used is likely to soar as well, even if every scientist in every lab is sincerely attempting to replace, reduce, and refine.

So, we have two disquieting trends: growing concern about the ability of biomedical research on animal models to deliver tangible benefit, particularly in relation to neurological/mental conditions, and a growing realization that, despite widespread endorsement of the 3Rs, invasive animal research is on the rise, not on the way out. These trends raise the question: what is the alternative? To study a complex condition like depression or

---

[1] Farris (2020).   [2] Shemesh and Chen (2023); Taschereau-Dumouchel et al. (2022).
[3] Taylor and Alvarez (2019).

autism, the argument goes, you cannot simply study tissue in culture, but you also cannot study human subjects at the level of mechanistic detail required to understand how, for example, particular alleles and patterns of gene expression may influence these conditions. So, you must use animals, where the ethical limits on what can be done are more permissive and a broader range of interventions is available.

This is where neural organoids have tremendous promise. The organoid is a relatively new kind of model system with great potential for replacing invasive animal research. Organoids are models of organs constructed from pluripotent stem cells. Human stem cells can be used, leading to miniature models of human organs constructed from human tissue. Suppose, for example, you want to understand human kidney function. One option is to study the renal system of a rat or mouse, relying on the idea that this will resemble human kidney function in the ways that matter. But organoid technology gives you a new option. You take pluripotent human stem cells and induce them to differentiate into kidney cells. The kidney organoid you construct will still differ from a normal kidney in many ways, but you have a degree of control over those ways, and you can be confident that the genes being expressed are the same as those in human kidney cells, because the cells *are* human kidney cells.

When we are talking about kidney organoids, gastrointestinal organoids, cardiac organoids, and other types of non-neural organoid, these developments should be celebrated. We should not try to put the brakes on a programme that could turn out to deliver the alternative to animal research that has been so sorely needed for so long.

But when it is the *brain* being modelled, the work becomes more controversial, and rightly so. A neural organoid is a model constructed from pluripotent stem cells induced to form organized neural tissue. Here too, it is the use of human stem cells to create human neural organoids that is generating major scientific excitement. I will use the term 'neural organoid' here, but I note that the term 'brain organoid' is also used, and the terms 'cerebral organoid' and 'cortical organoid' are often used in cases where the organoid is intended to model the human neocortex.

There are strong ethical reasons in favour of doing this research, if it allows us to model neurological conditions for which scientists currently lack good models, and if it can substitute for invasive animal research. And yet the research invokes the image, if not currently the reality, of a sentient human brain in vitro, and this image fills many onlookers with a sense of horror. Even when one looks at the research as it is now, it is hard not to feel a certain unease at the idea of a miniature model of the human brain constructed from human brain tissue. Sometimes unease is a bias we should try to overcome. But sometimes it is pointing us in the direction of genuine moral reasons to pause the research.

We need to think seriously about which of these possibilities is the case here. In recent years, a number of bioethicists have been doing just that.[4] I have weighed into the debate already, advocating for a precautionary approach to these issues.[5] But, as emphasized in Chapter 8, a crucial part of a precautionary approach to any issue is consistency in our thinking about different risks, and we need to make sure our approach to organoids is fully consistent with our approach to animal research. In particular, we must be careful not to be overcautious regarding organoids in a way that undermines their promise as replacements for animals. My goal here is to find the right balance.

11.2 No Risk of Sentience?

I want to start by considering possible reasons to think current neural organoids (at the time of writing) are not sentience candidates. A simple reason often given is their size. This is not a persuasive reason. Bees have around 1 million neurons, and (as I will argue in Chapter 13) they are sentience candidates. There are existing neural organoids of a similar size, in terms of neuron count, and researchers aim to create organoids with around 10 million neurons.[6]

A second simple reason, in my view more on-target than the first, is that organoids are not complete living organisms. They are disembodied pieces of tissue, and a default attitude of scepticism towards the idea of sentient tissue, outside of any living animal, is appropriate. Neuroscientists have experimented with small samples of cortical tissue for many years without anyone suggesting a risk of sentience. Just as there is a meta-consensus around the idea that spinal cords alone are not sentient, there is a meta-consensus around the idea that ordinary tissue samples are not sentient either. We must ask: given that cortical tissue samples are not ordinarily sentience candidates, what is different about this new type of cortical tissue that should cause us to

---

[4] Ankeny and Wolvetang (2021); Barnhart and Dierickx (2023); Bassil and Horstkötter (2023); de Jongh et al. (2022); Diner (2023); Greely (2021); Hyun et al. (2020); Jowitt (2023); Kreitmair (2023), Lavazza (2020); Lavazza and Massimini (2018); McKeown (2023); Niikawa et al. (2022); Pichl et al. (2023); Sawai et al. (2019); Sharma et al. (2021); Żuradzki (2021).
[5] Birch and Browning (2021).   [6] Smirnova et al. (2023).

worry? This creates a legitimate default bias against sentience if there is no evidence to the contrary.

Moreover, we should take due account of what is missing from present-day organoids. Current neural organoids are typically clusters of cortical neurons, without connections to a functioning brainstem. On Merker's theory, mechanisms at the top of the brainstem, in the midbrain, are constitutively involved in conscious experience. Advocates of these theories should be sceptical of the idea of sentience in a neural organoid composed only of cortical tissue. The situation is different when an organoid is implanted into the brain of a host animal (typically a mouse or rat) to create a chimera. These chimeras are clearly sentient, but that is because the host animal is sentient, and the hard question becomes one of how the new tissue alters its cognitive capacities and welfare needs.[7] But in the case of a cortical organoid that is not implanted into a host, midbrain-centric theories give no grounds for attributing sentience.

Here there is an interesting inversion of debates about non-mammalian animals (Chapters 12–14). In the animal case, there is a certain familiar pattern: those who suspect subcortical mechanisms are the basis of consciousness take the possibility of sentience very seriously in a wide range of cases, whereas those who think only neocortical mechanisms are constitutively involved are often inclined to play down the risk. Current cortical organoids present us with the opposite situation. They generally lack the subcortical mechanisms taken to be so important by Merker, Panksepp, Solms, Feinberg and Mallatt, and others. Yet they do have cortical tissue that resembles the neocortical tissue of a developing human brain. So now it is a different family of theories—neocortex-centric theories—that recommend taking the risk of sentience more seriously.

Even defenders of neocortex-centric theories, however, will normally grant a crucial role to the brainstem in supporting conscious experience in humans. The idea is typically that brainstem mechanisms, and in particular the reticular activating system, are akin to a power cable for conscious experience, switching it on without being part of its constitutive basis, just as your computer's power cable makes it possible to run a software programme without itself running that programme. Current organoids lack this power cable and accordingly display no sleep-wake cycles, to the best of my knowledge at the time of writing (admittedly, the situation is changing fast).

---

[7] Birch and Browning (2021).

We should feel pressure towards consistency. When an adult human patient displays no sleep-wake cycles and no brainstem reflexes, and when this condition is irreversible, they are declared brainstem dead, regardless of the amount of cortical tissue they still possess. Cortical tissue alone is not enough for sentience candidature, even for those who think the neural basis of sentience lies in the neocortex.

Indeed, as I understand it, a major current limitation of current organoids (when not implanted into host animals) is that they are not fully vascularized: they lack active blood flow. Again, I must note that the situation is changing rapidly. As I write, labs around the world are trying hard to overcome this limitation by joining up neural organoids to vascular organoids, with varying degrees of success.[8] We cannot rule out the possibility that fully vascularized organoids will be developed very soon, or even by the time this book is published. But as things stand at this moment, it seems a basic prerequisite for any cognitive function or conscious experience in a human brain is absent in neural organoids.

11.3 Early Warning Signs

For all this, there are concerning signs about the potential for organoid research to accelerate rapidly towards the edge of sentience. In the case of disorders of consciousness, the search for electrophysiological markers of conscious experience has been underway for decades (see §9.2). Synchronized, rhythmic oscillations of local field potentials—informally known as brain waves—have long been seen as one of the most important sources of potential markers. Despite a continuing lack of consensus about exactly which oscillations matter, there is widespread consensus about the idea that they are a promising place to look.

Trujillo and colleagues allowed cortical organoids to develop for an unusually long period of time, ten months, and recorded their electrophysiological activity through weekly recordings. They charted the emergence of complex oscillatory waves. They found that organoids quickly settled into a pattern of switching 'between long periods of quiescence and short bursts of spontaneous network-synchronized spiking.'[9] These synchronized 'network events' became stronger and more frequent over time, while the intervals between events became more variable.

---

[8] Matsui et al. (2021); Shirure et al. (2021); Sun et al. (2022).   [9] Trujillo et al. (2019, p. 562).

This pattern of increasingly strong and frequent bursts of activity, with less predictable intervals, is also seen in the EEGs of preterm infants. In an eye-catching result, Trujillo and colleagues showed that a regression model predicting a neonate's developmental age from key features of their EEG recording, and trained only on data from preterm infants, could also judge the developmental age of organoids older than 25 weeks with above-chance accuracy, with moderate correlation between the predicted and actual ages.

The result must be carefully interpreted. This does not show that the organoids were in any sense equivalent to the brains of preterm infants. It is important to note, first of all, that these cortical organoids were not *brains* at all. We should take care to avoid terms such as 'mini-brain' for systems like these. The organoids were formed of cortical tissue representative of one particularly important brain region, the neocortex. The organoids were vastly smaller than an infant brain, and still lacked a brainstem and vascularization. Nor do the results show that the electrophysiological activity was the same or indistinguishable in the two cases. The regression model aimed to exploit the similarities that existed, not quantify the degree of similarity. The model identified enough similarities to inform above-chance predictions of developmental age, but this is compatible with substantial differences.

Nonetheless, the result was, to me, a wake-up call: a jolt out of complacency about the potential ethical implications of this research. Neural organoids develop, they are sometimes allowed to develop for a long time, and they develop in ways that show broad electrophysiological similarities to the developing human brain.

11.4 Assessing Sentience Candidature in Neural Organoids

We cannot confidently rule out the possibility that sufficiently sophisticated organoids will soon be sentient, and we can expect the science to continue to develop extremely rapidly. So, we need to have a discussion now about what sort of warning signs might suffice to regard an organoid as a sentience candidate.

Here we run into a serious problem. In people with prolonged disorders of consciousness, some behaviour remains, despite the tendency to describe patients as 'unresponsive', and that behaviour informs diagnosis and the design of precautions (Chapter 9). As we have seen, clinicians in the UK are already advised to respond to outward signs of pain, distress, anxiety, and depression on the precautionary assumption that they really do indicate those states. The behaviour may be involuntary much of the time, but it is behaviour nonetheless. Sleep-wake cycles are also present, marking a clear distinction with coma. Meanwhile, in the case of non-human animals, the most compelling and widely accepted markers of sentience again tend to be behavioural. For example, if an animal learns to self-administer anaesthetics or analgesics (such as opioids) in response to injury, that is some evidence that it is having an aversive experience (Chapters 12–14).

Organoids present a very different kind of challenge. None of these behavioural markers of sentience are likely to be present in a typical neural organoid, because organoids are typically cut off from the sources of sensory input and motor output that are available to a complete and developed organism, and I assume this is likely to remain typical in the near-term future.

This could turn out to be an incorrect assumption. Some future organoids, even in the near term, may well have sources of sensory input and motor output. For example, a recent study showed that under the right conditions a cortical organoid can spontaneously develop optic vesicles—the developmental precursors to eyes—and it is not yet known how far this process could go, as the technology develops.[10] Another study allowed organoids to develop in culture for a year, placed near to a spinal cord and muscle tissue taken from a mouse. The organoids 'were able to innervate mouse spinal cord' and 'evoke contractions of adjacent muscle'.[11]

On this evidence, a time when organoid preparations can be joined up to both muscle outputs and sensory inputs is not far off. At that point, public concern about the research may grow. At the same time, using behavioural criteria to assess the likelihood of sentience may also become more feasible, providing a new way in which public concern could be exacerbated or at least slightly eased, depending on the results. Negative results would still require very cautious interpretation, because a failure to display sentience-related behaviours could easily reflect a failure of coordinated muscle control and a very limited behavioural repertoire rather than a lack of sentience.

Sentience, then, may be both more likely and easier to attribute when a neural organoid is joined up to other tissues, be they themselves organoids or taken from animals. But let us focus for now on the case of a 'pure' neural organoid, disconnected from any other tissues and any sources of sensory input or motor output. This is the type of case that presents the deepest puzzle. If the system is sentient at all, then it is what Tim Bayne, Anil Seth, and

---

[10] Gabriel et al. (2021).   [11] Giandomenico et al. (2019).

Marcello Massimini have called an 'island of awareness', unable to manifest its sentience in any of the usual ways.[12] In this case, there is no behaviour, so we need to assess sentience candidature using only non-behavioural markers. Where do we even begin?

11.5 Analogies with Embryos

Here is one false start.[13] The issue is sometimes linked to that of human embryos and fetuses. The hope seems to be that we can use our understanding of when sentience arises in normal human development to guide our thinking about organoids. But I am sceptical of this idea, because our understanding of how sentience normally develops is profoundly limited.

Julian Koplin and Julian Savulescu have argued that, because 'we can be reasonably confident that a neural organoid lacks even a rudimentary form of consciousness until it resembles the brain of a fetus at 20 weeks' development' no additional regulation should be required for research on organoids that are equivalent to a fetal brain at 20 weeks or less.[14] Although Koplin and Savulescu take this to be erring 'on the side of generosity', I do not share their confidence about these cases. Given the obvious and appropriate ethical constraints on research on human fetuses, our knowledge of when sentience begins remains subject to severe uncertainty. As we saw in Chapter 10, Derbyshire and Bockmann have suggested that, to err on the side of caution, we should regard fetuses as potentially sentient from 12 weeks, since this is the time of the first known projections from the thalamus into the cortical subplate.[15]

This approach, unfortunately, substitutes one kind of severe uncertainty for another. We should not use highly uncertain and contested estimates about human fetuses as a guide to the ethics of neural organoid research. Those estimates cannot carry this sort of weight. Instead, we should hope information will flow primarily in the opposite direction: we should look for markers of sentience in organoids, make inferences about the properties that lead to a realistic possibility of sentience in organoids, and then use this evidence to formulate better policies regarding human fetuses.

That brings us back to square one. If we have neither behaviour nor analogy to draw upon, what are the relevant markers of sentience?

---

[12] Bayne et al. (2020).   [13] In this section I draw on Birch and Browning (2021).
[14] Koplin and Savulescu (2019, p. 762).   [15] Derbyshire and Bockmann (2020).

11.6 The Brainstem Rule

There is one important piece of common ground in this area. All reasonable views compatible with the scientific meta-consensus can agree that, in a human brain, there can be no sentience in the absence of a functioning midbrain, at the top of the brainstem. Of special importance is the reticular activating system, a network of midbrain neurons that project to the thalamus. Agreement *that* the midbrain is needed is much wider than agreement about *why* this is the case. For the midbrain-centric family of theories, these mechanisms are sufficient for sentience even without a cortex. For the cortex-centric family, midbrain mechanisms are causally but not constitutively involved. Their destruction 'pulls the plug' on consciousness, leading to irreversible coma, even though they are not themselves the basis of the conscious state.

All parties can agree, however, that the total loss of functionality in these systems implies the loss of the ability to sustain consciousness. Without a functional brainstem and reticular activating system, a human cannot maintain coordinated patterns of global cortical activity, integrative subcortical activity, or sleep-wake cycles. Standard clinical criteria for brain death test for this by looking for coma (unrousable unresponsiveness), the loss of brainstem reflexes, and apnea (the loss of any spontaneous effort to breathe).[16] These criteria have been a source of some controversy, because there is evidence that some brain lesions impair outwardly detectable brainstem reflexes while leaving the reticular activating system intact.[17] But note the agreement behind the disagreement: both sides agree the midbrain and reticular activating system are essential—the disagreement concerns whether standard clinical criteria reliably detect their loss of function. This common ground has major clinical significance, because it makes organ donation possible. It is because there is a robust consensus around the idea that the death of the brainstem, when correctly diagnosed, implies the irreversible loss of the capacity for conscious experience that doctors are legally permitted to remove organs and tissues from patients who are brain dead.

This common ground supports the widespread view that current neural organoids are not sentience candidates right now. The 'plug' is permanently pulled on an organoid, as it were: they entirely lack a midbrain and reticular activating system. But this also gives us one threshold for the point at which neural organoids will become sentience candidates. If an organoid is developed that has a functioning brainstem, including a reticular activating system

---

[16] Greer et al. (2020).   [17] Walter et al. (2018).

that regulates arousal and leads to sleep-wake cycles and a PAG receiving projections from cortical areas, then, no matter how small it is, it should be regarded as a sentience candidate. There would be at least one view within the zone of reasonable disagreement (namely a midbrain-centric view along the lines of Panksepp, Merker, and Solms) on which such a system would plausibly meet the basic system requirements for sentience. The outward signs of regulated arousal and sleep-wake cycles would be indicators that the conditions Panksepp, Merker, and Solms regard as sufficient for sentience may well be in place. The sufficient conditions of other theories might or might not be met, depending on the details. But there would be a realistic possibility of sentience, and it would be irresponsible to ignore that possibility.

We should add a caveat in the interests of future-proofing. Strictly speaking, what is required is a functioning biological brainstem *or* an artificial system that performs the key sentience-relevant functions of the midbrain: registering and prioritizing homeostatic needs, coordinating responses to those needs, regulating arousal, and supporting sleep-wake cycles. It could be that, in the distant future, artificial brainstems will be created to allow people to recover from currently irrecoverable brain injuries. Such a person would be a sentience candidate, despite lacking a biological brainstem. This is a long way off, but what may be much closer is the possibility of a small-scale functional equivalent that is able to regulate the activity of an organoid in the same way a brainstem would. Even in the absence of a biological brainstem, we should be wary of the risks posed by attempts to use artificial brainstem-like systems to regulate and coordinate cortical activity in organoids.

I will call this proposal the 'brainstem rule':

Proposal 12. *Brainstem rule.* If a neural organoid develops or innervates a functioning brainstem (including the midbrain) that regulates arousal and leads to sleep-wake cycles, then it is a sentience candidate. An artificial functional equivalent of a brainstem would also suffice.

This is proposed as a *sufficient condition* for sentience candidature. To be clear, it is not proposed as a sufficient condition for sentience (since the Panksepp/Merker/Solms view is a realistic possibility, not a certainty), nor is it proposed as a necessary condition for sentience candidature. The idea is that, when the condition is satisfied, we are in a situation in which we are no longer entitled to any kind of moral certainty that sentience is absent (in contrast to the case of brain death) and so should start considering precautions. The proposal leaves open the possibility that there may be other scenarios in which we should consider precautions. I am describing here one route to sentience candidature that runs via taking midbrain-centric theories of consciousness seriously, but there may well be other routes, running via different theories.

The proposal says 'develops or innervates', highlighting two different ways in which an organoid could acquire a functioning brainstem. One is spontaneous development, along the lines of the optic vesicles spontaneously developed by an organoid in Gabriel and colleagues' study.[18] The other is through innervating animal tissue, along the lines of the innervation of a spinal cord by an organoid in Giandomenico and colleagues' study.[19]

We may well find that future model systems in neuroscience increasingly blur the boundary between organoids and chimeras, as more and more living brain tissue from a host animal is used in mixed human-animal 'preparations'. One can imagine a future variation on the Giandomenico et al. study that takes the whole living brainstem from a mouse, not just the spinal cord, and connects it to an organoid. Such a system may realistically possess the midbrain mechanisms that lead us to regard humans with conditions such as hydranencephaly as sentience candidates. So, the pressure of consistency should push us towards regarding this system as a sentience candidate too.

11.7 Possible Regulatory Frameworks

The proposed 'brainstem rule' leaves open what would be a proportionate response to an organoid's sentience candidature. Among the possible responses are a moratorium (time-limited ban) or even an indefinite (not time-limited) ban on the creation of these particular organoids. I take these seriously as options that may be proportionate, and I resist the idea that they would amount to drastic or radical restrictions on biomedical research. They should be options that are on the table when we debate these issues.

There is, after all, a huge amount of valuable research that can be done on organoids without getting anywhere near the edge of sentience. Researchers could invest their time in simpler neural organoids or in non-neural organoids, such as kidney organoids and gastrointestinal organoids. A comparable line of reasoning is often considered plausible in relation to the idea of experimenting on embryos well past the 14-day limit. Yes, we could learn much from research on older embryos, but there are grave and justified ethical concerns surrounding the idea of experimenting on sentient embryos, and

---

[18] Gabriel et al. (2021).   [19] Giandomenico et al. (2019).

there are many other valuable kinds of research we can prioritize instead, so we should be willing to forego the benefits. The key would be to ensure that the ban is targeted, so that lower-risk forms of organoid research are allowed to continue. An indiscriminate ban on all organoid research would be excessive and disproportionate. It would give no weight to the great promise of organoid research as a potential substitute for research on whole animals.

A less stringent response would be to allow research on sentience candidates, but subject this research to a licensing regime modelled on that of animal research. After all, most animals used in research are sentience candidates (like insects) or sentient as a matter of consensus (like rats and mice). As a society, we permit this research even though it implies some level of suffering to sentient beings. Where research on a potentially sentient organoid might replace research on a clearly sentient animal, like a mouse or a rat, and might even be preferable on scientific grounds, consistency suggests we should at least try to weigh up the harms and benefits of the two possible projects, rather than always favouring animal research. An indiscriminate bias in favour of research on whole sentient animals rather than merely potentially sentient organoids is unwarranted.

This line of thought led me to suggest, in an earlier piece with Heather Browning, that we should look to include potentially sentient organoids within the scope of animal experimentation legislation, such as the UK's Animals (Scientific Procedures) Act 1986, commonly known as ASPA.[20] This would certainly be more appropriate than treating potentially sentient organoids as mere tissue, and also more appropriate than treating them as if they were whole embryos, when they are not.

Under ASPA, scientists proposing research projects with the potential to cause suffering to animals have to obtain a licence for the work. To be licensed, they need approval from an institutional ethical review board. The board needs to see that the scientists have carefully weighed harms and benefits and duly considered the imperative to reduce, refine, and replace. In this context, 'replace' might mean the replacement of work on potentially sentient organoids with work on organoids that lack any brainstem structures and are less likely to be sentient. Researchers should be expected to make a case that they need to create a sentience candidate, and not just a simpler organoid system, to achieve the biomedical goals of the work. The ethical review board should consider whether those goals genuinely make the proposed research justifiable, and whether proportionate steps have been taken to mitigate the risks of causing suffering.

---

[20] Birch and Browning (2021).

Ideally, I would like to see the *same* review boards considering both animal and organoid research, so that they are able to see the trade-offs involved in the two kinds of research, to advise on cases that blur the boundaries between the two (because an organoid is implanted into an animal), and to advise replacing animals with organoids where appropriate. This would, however, require an expansion of the existing review boards and a boost to their resources, since a wider range of expertise would be required and a greater number of decisions would have to be made.

It would be controversial to bring a form of human tissue under regulations designed for animal research, for two reasons: we are talking about tissue and not about whole animals, and we are talking about human tissue, not the tissue of other animals. In both ways, the proposal involves extending a general regulatory approach outside the context for which it was originally devised. However, I see the problems here as problems of framing and wording, not deep problems. If ASPA were to be amended to include organoids, it would be wise to rename it. Politically, it may be easier to regulate organoid research using new legislation modelled on ASPA rather than through amending ASPA itself.

I see both of the above options—an indefinite ban or moratorium targeted at specific types of organoid, and a regulatory framework modelled on ASPA and centred on the idea of harm-benefit analysis—as options worthy of serious discussion. Which option we take depends on broader evaluative questions about the value we see, as a society, in this research, relative to the disvalue of the risks. We may also want to use both options in relation to different types of neural organoid, regulating research on some, banning research on others. I doubt there will be a one-size-fits-all solution, and for now I want to put both proposals on the table as options that should be debated further.

Proposal 13. *Targeted bans.* If organoid research leads to the creation of organoids that are sentience candidates, a moratorium (time-limited ban) or indefinite ban on the creation of this particular type of organoid may be an appropriate response. Bans should avoid indiscriminate targeting of all organoid research.

Proposal 14. *Ethical review.* When a neural organoid is a sentience candidate, research on it, if permitted at all, should be subject to ethical review and harm-benefit analysis, modelled on existing frameworks for regulating research on sentient animals.

To be clear, these proposals are independent of Proposal 12. One may still agree that my proposed responses are on the right lines even if one thinks the 'brainstem rule' sets the bar in the wrong place, and *vice versa*.

11.8 Summary of Chapter 11

Human neural organoids are showing great promise as models of the human brain, models that could potentially replace a substantial amount of animal research. It would be hasty to dismiss the possibility they could develop sentience. However, scepticism about this idea is appropriate when considering current organoids (at the time of writing). This is not because of their size, but because of their organization: current organoids lack a functioning brainstem or anything equivalent to one. There are nonetheless some troubling early warning signs, suggesting that organoid research may create forms of sentient being in the future.

Researchers with very different views about the neural basis of sentience can unite behind the 'brainstem rule': if a neural organoid develops or innervates a functioning brainstem that regulates arousal and leads to sleep-wake cycles, then it is a sentience candidate. An artificial brainstem substitute may also be enough. This is proposed as a sufficient condition for sentience candidature. When a system is a sentience candidate, we should take the possibility of its sentience seriously and discuss proportionate steps to protect its welfare, despite continuing uncertainty and doubt.

What steps might be proportionate? If organoid research leads to the creation of organoids that are sentience candidates, a moratorium (time-limited ban) or indefinite ban on the creation of this particular type of organoid may be appropriate, but bans should avoid indiscriminate targeting of all organoid research. An alternative approach, consistent with existing approaches to animal research, is to require ethical review and harm-benefit analysis whenever a neural organoid is a sentience candidate.

The Edge of Sentience: Risk and Precaution in Humans, Other Animals, and AI. Jonathan Birch, Oxford University Press.
© Jonathan Birch 2024. DOI: 10.1093/9780191966729.003.0012

PART IV
SENTIENCE IN OTHER ANIMALS

12

The Clearest Candidates

12.1 Fishes and Invertebrates as the New Centre of the Debate

To regard a being as a sentience candidate is not to affirm its sentience as certain, known, highly likely, or proven beyond reasonable doubt. It is just to affirm a *realistic possibility* of sentience that it would be irresponsible to ignore, and an evidence base rich enough to allow the identification of welfare risks and the design and assessment of precautions. When that bar is cleared, a deliberative process to assess proportionality is needed.

One consequence of shifting from *certainty* about sentience to sentience *candidature* is that the focus of the debate immediately moves much further away from humans, in evolutionary terms. All healthy adult mammals are plainly sentience candidates. The fact that the evidence fails to deliver absolute certainty is beside the point. It delivers candidature, so we have compelling reasons to think about the welfare risks our actions pose in relation to mammals. As foreshadowed in §5.10, I think the same holds for birds. There is good evidence that the avian pallium bears strong functional similarities to the mammalian neocortex,[1] and there are consistent, credible positions according to which the differences of neural implementation (such as the difference between a laminar and nucleated organization) do not matter (positions R3, R4, and R5 in Chapter 6).

With reptiles[2] and fishes,[3] there is more room for doubt about sentience, since there is neither a neocortex nor a clearly analogous structure (reptiles and fishes do have a pallium, but its degree of functional similarity to the neocortex or avian pallium is still quite unclear).[4] Their sentience candidature is secured mainly by the tenability of midbrain-centred theories of sentience, such as those of Panksepp and Merker (positions R4 and R5 in Chapter 6),

---

[1] Güntürkün and Bugnyar (2016); Nieder et al. (2020).

[2] I will use the term 'reptile' to mean 'non-avian reptile', following common parlance.

[3] As I explained in Chapter 1, I will follow Balcombe's (2016) suggestion to say 'fishes' not 'fish' to help us remember that we are talking about individual animals.

[4] See Kalman (2009) for comparison of bird and reptile brains. See Zacks and Jablonka (2023) for a discussion of the functional significance of a brain area in fish homologous with the mammalian hippocampus.

together with the highly conserved nature of the relevant midbrain mechanisms across the vertebrates.

Panksepp and Merker were not wholly in agreement on these questions. Panksepp remained steadfastly agnostic on the question of sentience in fishes.[5] This is surprising at first glance, since fishes possess the integrative midbrain structure he took to be so important in mammals: the periaqueductal gray (PAG). There is, moreover, evidence that the PAG in fishes is 'convergent in both its functional and structural organization to the PAG of mammals'.[6] For Panksepp, however, information about brain anatomy needed supplementation with evidence directly showing coordinated behavioural responses corresponding to his seven basic emotions, evoked by electrically stimulating the relevant brain regions, and this work has never been done in fishes.

Merker, by contrast, has explicitly argued that the mechanisms involved in sentience were universal vertebrate mechanisms that evolved 'at the very outset of the vertebrate lineage'.[7] The point of divergence is that Merker does not consider Panksepp's seven basic emotions to be necessary for sentience, and so is prepared to attribute sentience without evidence of these specific circuits. What Merker requires is evidence of a *core behavioural control unit* that constructs an integrated model of the whole animal and the environment, enabling flexible control of whole-animal behaviour in service of biological needs.

It is clear that fishes have all the relevant brain regions (the brainstem, hypothalamus, optic tectum, and basal ganglia). In fact, these regions are so ancient that versions of them exist in lampreys, members of the most basal group of vertebrates (the jawless fish, or cyclostomes).[8] There is room for doubt, however, about whether these brain regions perform the same functions right across the fishes, a group encompassing over 30,000 known species.[9] Behavioural evidence from teleost fishes (infraclass Teleostei; in practice much of the experimental work has involved rainbow trout, goldfish, and zebrafish) indicates capacities for centralized, integrative decision-making.

---

[5] Panksepp (2016).   [6] Kittelberger et al. (2006, p. 71).   [7] Merker (2007, p. 3).
[8] See Janvier (2010) on the phylogeny of the vertebrates. See de Arriba and Pombal (2007) on the midbrain in lampreys, and see Grillner et al. (2013) and Wullimann (2011) on the basal ganglia. See Feinberg and Mallatt (2016); Ginsburg and Jablonka (2019); Godfrey-Smith (2020a); and Veit (2023) for possible evolutionary histories linking consciousness to the Cambrian explosion. Such discussions are, inevitably, quite speculative, given our uncertainty about the nature of consciousness, as reviewed in Part I. The evolutionary story will be very different depending on whether a cortex-centric or midbrain-centric theory is correct (for discussion see Birch 2020c, 2021b).
[9] Spelman (2012).

For example, a study of goldfish showed flexible trade-offs, in which the fishes had to choose whether to risk an electric shock in order to access food, and made the decision based on both the intensity of the expected shock and their level of food deprivation.[10] This combination of neural and behavioural evidence establishes the teleosts as sentience candidates (and remember the bar is not certainty or knowledge, but a realistic possibility supported by evidence).

What of non-teleost fishes? While around 96 per cent of fish species are teleosts, that still leaves 4 per cent, and there is very little behavioural evidence concerning the cartilaginous fishes (elasmobranchs, such as sharks and rays) and jawless fishes (lampreys and hagfish). Some have claimed that elasmobranchs lack nociceptors, and so lack even the most basic prerequisite of pain.[11] However, two notes of caution are important here. The first is that these claims are probably incorrect. There are two main types of nociceptive neuron in mammals, Aδ-fibres and C-fibres. Aδ-fibres, linked to sharp pains in us but also used for mechanoreception, have been found in elasmobranchs by at least three studies.[12] Evidence of C-fibres, associated with lingering pains in us, was obtained for the first time by a study of sharks in 2022, but the C-fibres were specifically responding to nociceptive stimuli in the cranial region.[13] We should not be surprised by this, since nociceptors in the cranial area were found a long time ago in lampreys, a more basal vertebrate group, and nociception has been found in many invertebrates too, even the nematode worm *Caenorhabditis elegans* (see §13.3).[14] It is entirely possible, then, that sharks do feel pain. It could be that they only feel pain in response to injury around the head (where they can do something about it, by releasing prey). Most sharks need to swim to breathe, after all, and an ability to feel pain in parts of the body they cannot rest would have limited adaptive value. The second note of caution is that, even if elasmobranchs do not feel pain, they may still be sentient in other ways, because *sentience is not just pain*. Other valenced experiences also matter. We will revisit this point in the next chapter, when considering insects.

---

[10] Millsopp and Laming (2008). See Sneddon et al. (2014); C. Brown (2015); and Woodruff (2017) for reviews of the evidence from teleost fish. See also Mason and Lavery (2022) for a methodological critique of the fish work. In my view, their criticisms highlight the continuing room for reasonable doubt, but do not undermine the idea that fish are sentience candidates (i.e. that there is a realistic possibility of sentience that it would be irresponsible to ignore in practical contexts).

[11] Feinberg and Mallatt (2016); Nussbaum (2023); Tye (2016). My discussion here draws on my contributions to Read and Birch (2023).

[12] Kitchener et al. (2010); Lacap (2022); Snow et al. (1993).   [13] Lacap (2022).

[14] On lampreys, see Matthews and Wickelgren (1978). Martin and Wickelgren (1971) reported nociceptors in the lamprey spinal cord too, but this was subsequently contested (Christenson et al. 1988). On nociception in nematodes, see Krzyzanowski et al. (2016).

With elasmobranchs and cyclostomes, where the behavioural evidence is thin, the case for sentience candidature rests heavily on the presence of the brain regions regarded by Merker's theory as sufficient for sentience. We have to make a judgement call: will we accept neural evidence of midbrain mechanisms conserved across all vertebrates as enough to establish sentience candidature, even in the absence of substantial behavioural evidence? Or is behavioural evidence also needed? In 2005, an expert panel of the European Food Safety Authority (EFSA) recommended (on the basis of the neural evidence) that cyclostomes used in science should receive protection (elasmobranchs were already protected).[15] I agree: in my view, all adult vertebrates are sentience candidates.

I say 'adult' because the point in development at which the relevant midbrain mechanisms come online is poorly understood and will vary across species. In the UK and European Union, fishes used in science are considered protected animals from five days (120 hours) after fledging.[16] Remarkably, however, studies of zebrafish (*Danio rerio*) larvae at five days post-fledging, a time when the brain contains around 100,000 neurons[17] (compared with around 10 million in adults), have found many of the same pain-related behaviours found in adults.[18] The speed of development of zebrafish is astounding, which is part of what makes them so attractive as model organisms for science. The '5-day rule' may well be an error. Juvenile and larval fishes should be regarded as investigation priorities.

Proposal 15. *All adult vertebrates are sentience candidates.* Debates about proportionality are warranted in cases where human activities create risks of suffering to any adult vertebrate animal. Further investigation concerning sentience candidature in vertebrates should focus on juvenile/larval stages.

Debates about pain in fishes have, at times, had a frustrating character. On one side, it has sometimes been suggested that pain in fishes has been 'demonstrated beyond reasonable doubt'.[19] Such claims inevitably attract criticism, since fish lack the neocortical brain regions that some theories of consciousness

---

[15] EFSA (2005).   [16] Strähle et al. (2012).   [17] Hasani et al. (2023).
[18] Lopez-Luna et al. (2017a, 2017b, 2017c, 2017d), discussed in Birch (2018b).
[19] Sneddon et al. (2014).

(those in the R1–R2 range of Chapter 6) regard as indispensable for sentience. On the other side, we see straight-out assertions that, because they lack a neocortex, 'fish do not feel pain'.[20] These assertions rest on overconfidence in a cortex-centric theory of consciousness, plus undue neglect of midbrain-centric theories and of the possibility that cortical functions in mammals may be supported by other brain regions in fishes. The parallels with similarly overconfident statements about brain injury patients and about fetuses should now be clear, in light of Part III. Yet the serious flaws in these sceptical arguments have sometimes led to accusations of 'sentience denial',[21] suggesting bad faith. This has provoked further reactions, leading to a needlessly polarized debate.

We need to move beyond this, and the concept of a sentience candidate allows us to do so. Midbrain-centric theories, together with the behavioural evidence, imply a realistic possibility of sentience in fishes that it would be irresponsible to ignore when designing policy. Talk of certainty or proof 'beyond reasonable doubt' is not appropriate, but nor is it appropriate to treat fishes as if they felt nothing, taking no precautions at all and paying no regard to the possibility of suffering.

In recent decades, the debate has started to shift towards invertebrates, which tend to receive even fewer welfare protections than fishes. That has also been the main focus of my 'Foundations of Animal Sentience' project at the LSE. For me, as for many others, it was octopuses that first convinced me of the idea that some invertebrates are sentience candidates. This woke me up to the possibility many other invertebrates could be sentience candidates too—something I now believe to be the case.

12.2 Octopuses as 'Honorary Vertebrates'

In UK science, octopuses have, in effect, been regarded as sentience candidates for a long time. In 1992, the UK government asked an advisory body called the Animal Procedures Committee to consider whether the UK's main piece of legislation concerning animals in science—the Animals (Scientific Procedures) Act 1986, ASPA—should be amended to regulate research on cephalopod molluscs. The cephalopod molluscs include octopuses, along with all species of squid, cuttlefish, and nautilus.

---

[20] Key (2015, 2016).   [21] Sneddon et al. (2018).

The Committee held a series of meetings to explore the issue. They arrived at a recommendation that, in hindsight, struck a rather odd compromise between conflicting views:

> The Committee has concluded that the scientific evidence currently available is insufficient to suggest with any certainty that cephalopods can experience pain and suffering. [...] However, a clear majority of the Committee believe that there is sufficient doubt about the sentient status of cephalopods, to give the benefit of that doubt to one species, *Octopus vulgaris*, about which most is known and which is of particular concern.[22]

ASPA was amended accordingly: a single cephalopod species was brought within its scope. This ruling led to the concept of the octopus as an 'honorary vertebrate' for the purposes of the act. Why just one species? It is virtually impossible to imagine that the Committee, having taken advice from cephalopod experts, was unaware that there are many species of octopus (about three hundred) within the order Octopoda. Yet to protect a single species seems inconsistent with the approach taken to vertebrates, where evidence from a small number of laboratory species is used to justify much wider-ranging protections for other relevantly similar animals.

Despite this oddity, the advice was an important milestone in the legal protection of invertebrate welfare. An invertebrate was protected by law for the first time in the UK, and (as far as I know) for the first time anywhere. Moreover, the recommendation involved an incipient form of precautionary thinking. The Committee noted, correctly, that certainty could not be achieved in this area, but went on to argue that the benefit of the doubt should be given on the side of ascribing sentience in a policy-making context, given significant welfare concerns.

The evidence base available in the early 1990s was significantly thinner than that available now. The Committee pointed out that octopuses have a 'large neurological mass', 'complex nervous systems and behaviour', and a 'general level of organization' suggesting that 'octopuses might well be able to experience pain'. Thirty years later, we can point to a rich body of evidence investigating possible markers of pain in coleoid cephalopods, including cuttlefish and squid as well as octopuses, much of it quite recent.[23] Some of that evidence will be described below. For now, it is enough to note that the

---

[22] Animal Procedures Committee (1993).   [23] Birch et al. (2021).

recent evidence provides a much stronger case for regarding octopuses as sentience candidates than anything available in 1992. The precautionary step taken at that time has been vindicated.

Even so, with the benefit of hindsight, we can now say that the considerations driving the decision at that time were a little dubious. The right decision was made, but probably not entirely for the right reasons. In particular, the presence of a 'large neurological mass' is questionable as a criterion for sentience.

The problem is not simply one of vagueness (what counts as large?) but also one of evidential import. Sentience is not brain size, and nor do we have any strong grounds for tying the likelihood of sentience to brain size. Most of the neurons in the human brain are in the cerebellum, a region involved in the implementation of motor commands that (as noted in Chapter 6) appears to contribute nothing to our conscious experiences. The picture emerging from human consciousness science (for all the disagreement it contains) is one on which the organization of neurons is what matters, not the raw numbers.[24]

I grant that there can still be a weak evidential connection, in that a very small neuron count can motivate reasonable doubts about whether a brain could support any credible neural basis for sentience (even on the less cognitively demanding theories, such as those of Merker and Panksepp). We will see an example of this when we consider nematodes in Chapter 13. However, it would be a mistake to put neuron counts at the centre of the picture.[25]

Along similar lines, it is important to note that sentience is also not the same as intelligence. Intelligence can give us a *window* into sentience, by making new types of sentience-relevant experiment possible. As a limiting case, consider how our intelligence, as humans, makes it easier for researchers to investigate our sentience, because we can verbally report what we are feeling. In a similar vein, the octopus is able to deploy its intelligence to succeed at tasks that are primarily testing for sentience.

In this sense, intelligence and sentience are *methodologically linked*: a high degree of the former can open up new methods of detecting the latter. But they are not the same property. Crucially, we need to be open to the possibility that animals which fail to set the world alight with their intelligence may nonetheless be sentient. That is an important lesson to bear in mind when considering other invertebrate taxa—such as crabs and lobsters.

[24] A point also emphasized by Seth (2021).
[25] See Shriver (2022) for a critique of the use of neuron counts as proxies for 'welfare capacity'.

> **Proposal 16.** *Sentience is neither intelligence nor brain size.* We should be aware of the possibility of decouplings between intelligence, brain size, and sentience in the animal kingdom. Precautions to safeguard animal welfare should be driven by markers of sentience, not by markers of intelligence or by brain size.

12.3 The Story of the 'Sentience Act'

The European Union's Lisbon Treaty contains a clause that says:

> In formulating and implementing the Union's agriculture, fisheries, transport, internal market, research and technological development and space policies, the Union and the Member States shall, since animals are sentient beings, pay full regard to the welfare requirements of animals, while respecting the legislative or administrative provisions and customs of the Member States relating in particular to religious rites, cultural traditions and regional heritage.[26]

The reference to sentience is easy to miss. No mechanism has ever been created to oversee compliance and crucial details have gone unspecified. The question 'which animals?' jumps out, but has never been settled. In theory, the clause could be read as demanding consideration of all members of the animal kingdom, including microscopic animals like the dust mites in bedsheets and the copepods that occasionally get into drinking water, but it is safe to assume that no court would uphold such an interpretation.

The EU, much like the UK until recently, has tended to regard the scope of animal welfare law as an issue that only requires precise resolution in the context of regulating scientific research. A directive in 2010 'on the protection of animals used for scientific purposes'[27] explicitly included all cephalopod molluscs, including cuttlefish, squid, and nautilus, on the advice of an expert panel.[28] The panel had recommended including all cephalopod molluscs *and* all decapod crustaceans (decapods), including crabs, lobsters, crayfish, and shrimps, but the recommendation regarding decapods was

---

[26] Treaty of Lisbon Amending the Treaty on European Union and the Treaty Establishing the European Community, Signed at Lisbon, 13 December 2007.

[27] European Union Directive 2010/63/EU.

[28] European Food Safety Authority (EFSA) (2005).

not implemented. Representatives from the bioscience sector argued that protecting decapods would impose a significant bureaucratic burden on researchers. This, however, is more a reason to improve the efficiency of the regulatory procedures (for all protected animals) than a reason to exclude decapods from their scope.[29]

When the UK began the process of leaving the EU, it committed to withdrawing from the Lisbon Treaty, and the UK government declined to directly import the clause about animal sentience into UK law. Animal welfare organizations launched a campaign to gain legal recognition for animal sentience in the UK, and the UK responded by pledging to introduce new legislation to achieve this.[30] This was the beginning of a long process that resulted in the Animal Welfare (Sentience) Act 2022, or 'Sentience Act'.

The Sentience Act improved on the Lisbon Treaty by establishing a mechanism to oversee compliance. UK animal welfare law generally works by creating mechanisms of accountability and oversight. For example, scientists, to obtain project licences for any procedures that might cause a level of pain equal to or greater than that caused by an injection from a hypodermic needle, must explain to Animal Welfare Ethical Review Boards why the harms imposed by their research are justified by the benefits. Farmers must follow established codes of practice, with the possibility of being charged with violating a duty of care towards their animals if they ignore these codes. The Sentience Act extended this 'oversight model' to government policy-makers, putting them under a duty to pay 'all due regard' to the welfare of sentient animals when formulating policy and to consider the animal welfare impacts of their decisions. The Act created a statutory Animal Sentience Committee to monitor compliance with that duty.

This was a positive step. Yet once you create a mechanism to monitor compliance with a duty, the question of the *scope* of that duty becomes unavoidable. The Sentience Act, then, had to specify the scope of the duty. The first draft of the Sentience Bill included all vertebrate animals, including fishes, within its scope. But policy-makers, under pressure from campaign groups, wondered: should some invertebrates also be included?

To help decide that question, the UK government's Department for the Environment, Food, and Rural Affairs (Defra) commissioned a team led by me (together with Charlotte Burn, Alexandra Schnell, Andrew Crump, and Heather Browning) to produce a review of the evidence of sentience in

---

[29] Birch (2017a).   [30] R. Mason (2017).

cephalopod molluscs and decapod crustaceans.[31] A substantial part of the work was designing a framework that could allow a fair and transparent assessment of whether the evidence was sufficient to justify including these taxa within the scope of the new law. That had to be done before we could even turn to the main task of synthesizing the existing evidence.

12.4 The Institute of Medical Ethics (IME) Criteria

Anyone faced with designing such a framework faces a dilemma. If you commit to a specific theory of the functional profile and neural basis of sentience, the result will be controversial, since all such theories are subject to reasonable disagreement. In the presence of reasonable disagreement, it would be very questionable to set policy on the assumption that the favoured theory of a small group of advisers happens to be true.

And yet, if you refuse to commit to a detailed theory, and instead rely on theory-neutral lists of criteria, a different set of problems looms. One problem is that your criteria are still likely to represent an implicit *partial* theory, and this implicit partial theory may also be subject to reasonable disagreement. A second is that your criteria are likely to leave room for interpretation—and, without a theory capable of pinning down one precise interpretation, people will interpret the criteria in line with their own theoretical sympathies and prior views about the distribution of sentience.

Our framework is a serious attempt to grapple with that dilemma, within the constraints of a particular policy application in a specific time and place. We wanted to avoid both sets of pitfalls: those associated with overcommitting to a specific theory, and those associated with a loosely worded set of theory-free criteria. We wanted to steer a course between the whirlpool and the rock.

As our starting point, we turned to the list of seven criteria drawn up by a working party of the Institute for Medical Ethics in 1991 (Box 12.1).[32] I will call these the IME criteria. These criteria have been influential on subsequent animal welfare policy. For example, they helped shape the views of the UK's Animal Procedures Committee concerning cephalopods, leading to the protection of *Octopus vulgaris* in science, and they were applied in 2005 in the EFSA report that shaped the 2010 EU directive in science. Indeed, the general approach of assessing evidence of sentience using lists of neurological,

---

[31] Birch et al. (2021).   [32] Smith and Boyd (1991).

Box 12.1 The 1991 IME criteria for sentience (focused on the case of pain)

---

1. Possession of receptors sensitive to noxious stimuli, located in functionally useful positions on or in the body, and connected by nervous pathways to the lower parts of a central nervous system.
2. Possession of brain centres which are higher in the sense of level of integration of brain processing (especially a structure analogous to the human cerebral cortex).
3. Possession of nervous pathways connecting the nociceptive system to the higher brain centres.
4. Receptors for opioid substances found in the central nervous system, especially the brain.
5. Analgesics modify an animal's response to stimuli that would be painful for a human.
6. An animal's response to stimuli that would be painful for a human is functionally similar to the human response (that is, the animal responds so as to avoid or minimize damage to its body).
7. An animal's behavioural response persists, and it shows an unwillingness to resubmit to a painful procedure; the animal can learn to associate apparently non-painful with apparently painful events.

---

behavioural, and cognitive criteria has been more widely influential on the field, with many previous reviews being structured around either the same list of indicators or an expanded or modified version of it.[33]

In any such list, no single criterion is a smoking gun, conclusive proof of sentience. Equally, no single criterion is a sine qua non, whereby sentience is conclusively ruled out by its absence. We are not in an area where conclusive proof is available. The idea is rather that each criterion should be a piece of relevant evidence. Each one should shift probabilities. Its presence should raise the probability of sentience; its confirmed absence should lower the probability. The criteria are intended to relate to sentience as symptoms relate to a disease. The more symptoms you have, the more likely it is that you have the disease.

---

[33] Andrews et al (2013); Feinberg and Mallatt (2016); Sneddon et al. (2014); Varner (2012).

Crucially, a symptom can be probability-raising overall even if it only raises the probability conditional on some specific background theory (or set of theories), as long as (a) we assign some non-zero probability to that background theory (or set of theories), and (b) the symptom does not *lower* the probability of sentience on any background theory. In this way, there can be robust agreement around the idea that particular markers raise the probability of sentience, despite continuing disagreement about the correct background theory.

The IME criteria obviously focus on one specific aspect of sentience, namely pain. We decided to retain that focus in our report, while emphasizing that the concept of sentience encompasses far more than just pain. Our reasons for keeping the focus on pain were pragmatic ones, explained later, in §12.7. Even though we decided to retain a focus on pain, we still felt the list required clarification and revision.

12.5 Problems with the IME Criteria

We saw two main problems. First, the criteria (especially the neurobiological criteria) were in some respects too narrow. For example, the reference to opioids in criterion 4 is making an assumption about the type of neurotransmitters that modulate aversive experiences, and this assumption may not be valid for invertebrates. There are many other endogenous neurotransmitters that may potentially modulate aversive experiences. What mattered, in our view, was that the animal's decision-making in response to threatened or actual noxious stimuli is modulated by neurotransmitters in a way consistent with the experience of pain, distress, or harm. The IME criteria gave too much significance to the question of whether the relevant neurotransmitter is an opioid.

Second, the IME criteria were in some respects too vague and too easy to satisfy. This is especially true of the behavioural criteria, 6 and 7. Regarding criterion 6, it is problematically vague to talk of a response 'functionally similar to the human response'. When we touch a hot stove, we withdraw our hand immediately, but this is just a reflex. Even though we also experience pain, the pain does not cause the withdrawal of the hand: the pain is felt after the hand has begun to withdraw. So, finding a similar reflex in an animal would not be convincing evidence of pain. We need more refined criteria in order to identify functions that do provide evidence of negatively valenced experiences. We decided that these functions must go beyond reflexes and must implicate valenced states in the central nervous system.

Regarding criterion 7, persistent responses and an unwillingness to resubmit to a procedure may be indicative of sensitisation (whereby an animal becomes more sensitive in future to a stimulus it has encountered before) rather than associative learning. But sensitization is found in animals with no central nervous system, such as cnidarians (jellyfish and sea anemones).[34] This should give us pause, since cnidarians do not have any of the brain mechanisms posited to be sufficient for sentience by theories in the reasonable range R1–R5. We decided that sensitization alone was not relevant evidence, whereas some forms of associative learning do provide evidence.

But which forms of associative learning? The evidence from human consciousness science on this question presents a contested and fast-changing picture. The simplest forms of classical conditioning, where an unconditioned stimulus (US) and a conditioned stimulus (CS) are presented together, overlapping in time, can be performed by humans even when the stimuli are presented subliminally,[35] and they can even be performed by the spinal cords of rats disconnected from the brain[36] and by blindsight patients when the conditioned stimulus is presented in the blind field.[37] We came to the view that simple classical conditioning was too easily achieved to raise the probability of sentience to any significant degree.

Yet one does not need to go far beyond simple classical conditioning to find forms of learning that, in humans and other mammals, have been at least tentatively linked to consciousness. For example, there is some evidence that *trace* conditioning, where there is a gap in time (e.g. of one second) between the CS and US, and where the conditioned response has to be well timed to coincide with the US when it arrives, is facilitated by conscious perception in humans.[38] Some evidence of conscious facilitation also exists for instrumental learning,[39] reversal learning (learning that the relationship between two stimuli has reversed),[40] and the learning of 'incongruent' relationships between stimuli, as when a cue on your left

---

[34] Ginsburg and Jablonka (2019, pp. 279–287).
[35] Greenwald and De Houwer (2017).   [36] Allen et al. (2009).
[37] Hamm et al. (2003); Weiskrantz (2003).
[38] Clark and Squire (1998); Clark et al. (2002). Greenwald and De Houwer (2017), in one of the most careful studies of unconscious conditioning so far conducted, found evidence that subjects could learn an association between a US and a subliminal CS as long as the gap between CS offset and US onset was 17 milliseconds or less. Since a visual stimulus leaves an imprint on the retina for a few milliseconds after offset, the possibility of unconscious conditioning bridging such tiny gaps is not evidence against the involvement of consciousness in bridging longer gaps. The potential relevance of trace conditioning to animal consciousness was emphasized by Allen (2004); and more recently by Birch et al. (2020a); Birch (2022c); and Droege et al. (2021). Sometimes in the animal literature, the importance of a *well-timed conditioned response* in Clark and Squire's studies has been lost. The relevance of learning to consciousness more generally has been discussed in depth by Ginsburg and Jablonka (2019).
[39] Skora et al. (2021, 2022).   [40] Travers et al. (2018).

predicts a target to your right.[41] All of this evidence is inconclusive, and subject to the methodological challenges explained in Chapter 5. It can, nonetheless, shift probabilities.

12.6 My Team's Revised Criteria

Our revised criteria (Box 12.2) revised and updated the IME criteria in several ways to address these problems. Since our project was (and is) based at the London School of Economics and Political Science (LSE), I will call these the 'LSE criteria' for short. Criteria 1–3 replaced the emphasis on 'higher' and 'lower' brain regions with an emphasis on integrative brain regions receiving input from multiple sensory sources. Instead of a narrow focus on opioids, our criterion 4 allowed various forms of responsiveness to endogenous compounds or drugs to count as evidence of sentience, if they modulate the animal's behaviour in a way consistent with the hypothesis that these compounds are altering the animal's experiences of pain, distress, or harm.

Box 12.2 The LSE criteria for sentience (focused on the case of pain)

1. **Nociception.** The animal possesses receptors sensitive to noxious stimuli (nociceptors).
2. **Sensory integration.** The animal possesses integrative brain regions capable of integrating information from different sensory sources.
3. **Integrated nociception.** The animal possesses neural pathways connecting the nociceptors to the integrative brain regions.
4. **Analgesia.** The animal's behavioural response to a noxious stimulus is modulated by chemical compounds affecting the nervous system in either or both of the following ways:
   a. The animal possesses an endogenous neurotransmitter system that modulates (in a way consistent with the experience of pain, distress, or harm) its responses to threatened or actual noxious stimuli.
   b. Putative local anaesthetics, analgesics (such as opioids), anxiolytics, or anti-depressants modify an animal's responses to threatened or actual noxious stimuli in a way consistent with the hypothesis that these compounds attenuate the experience of pain, distress, or harm.

---

[41] Ben-Haim et al. (2021).

5. **Motivational trade-offs.** The animal shows motivational trade-offs, in which (for example) the disvalue of a noxious or threatening stimulus is weighed (traded-off) against the value of an opportunity for reward, leading to flexible decision-making.

6. **Flexible self-protection.** The animal shows flexible self-protective behaviour (e.g. wound-tending, guarding, grooming, rubbing) of a type likely to involve representing the bodily location of a noxious stimulus.

7. **Associative learning.** The animal shows forms of associative learning in which noxious stimuli become associated with neutral stimuli, or in which novel ways of avoiding noxious stimuli are learned through reinforcement. These forms of associative learning *go beyond classical conditioning in which a single conditioned stimulus overlaps temporally with an unconditioned stimulus.*

   Note: forms of associative learning that are linked, at least tentatively, to sentience in humans (such as instrumental learning, reversal learning, and trace conditioning) provide stronger evidence than other forms.

8. **Analgesia preference.** The animal shows that it values a putative analgesic or anaesthetic when injured in one or more of the following ways:
   a. The animal learns to self-administer putative analgesics or anaesthetics when injured.
   b. The animal learns to prefer, when injured, a location at which analgesics or anaesthetics can be accessed.
   c. The animal prioritizes obtaining these compounds over other needs (such as food) when injured.

The wording is that of Crump et al. (2022a), with the amended wording for criterion 7 proposed in Crump et al. (2022b).

IME criteria 4 and 5 are closely related, since analgesics normally work by substituting for endogenous neurotransmitters, exploiting the same mechanisms. For this reason, we replaced them with a single criterion that can be satisfied in two different ways (our criterion 4).

We also replaced the vague IME criteria 6 and 7 with a more detailed set of cognitive and behavioural criteria (our criteria 5–8). These criteria identify four main types of behavioural and cognitive abilities that are likely to involve negatively valenced affective experiences: motivational trade-offs, flexible self-protective behaviour, associative learning, and the valuing (as shown by self-administration, conditioned place preference or prioritization) of analgesics or anaesthetics when injured.

For criterion 7, the wording on which we eventually settled (after reflecting on the thirty commentaries we received, cited in §1.7) was that the learning must 'go beyond classical conditioning in which a single conditioned stimulus overlaps temporally with an unconditioned stimulus'. We added that 'forms of associative learning that are linked, at least tentatively, to sentience in humans (such as instrumental learning, reversal learning, and trace conditioning) provide stronger evidence than other forms.'[42]

It would be an exaggeration to suggest these criteria remove all room for interpretation. There is, for example, room for debate about what constitutes flexible decision-making and flexible self-protective behaviour. The kinds of *flexibility* people take to be indicative of sentience may depend on their prior theoretical sympathies. We found it impossible to do away completely with such terms. What we took to be evidence of sentience was behaviour plausibly guided by a central evaluation system—a system representing the animal's needs, evaluating the opportunities and risks posed by the environment, and weighing these against each other—with this evaluative representation providing the source of flexibility.

Do the decisions we made—such as the decisions to discount reflexes, genetically programmed behaviours, habituation, and sensitization—reflect an implicit partial theory of sentience? They are not *fully* theory-neutral, despite our attempts to be as neutral as possible between currently popular theories. Our criteria are particularly well aligned with theories that tie sentience to mechanisms for the centralized integration of information in service of learning and decision-making. These include Panksepp's and Merker's midbrain-centred theories,[43] the global workspace theory[44] of Baars, Dehaene, and collaborators, the multisensory maps theory of Feinberg and Mallatt,[45] and the Unlimited Associative Learning (UAL) framework of Ginsburg and Jablonka.[46] People who assign non-zero probability to any of these background theories are likely to see our criteria as probability-raising.

Our choices, then, were not completely theory-free. It was more in the spirit of what I have called a 'theory-light' approach, where we seek points of convergence across multiple theories and use these convergences to identify

---

[42] Crump et al. (2022b).   [43] Panksepp (1998); Merker (2007).
[44] Mashour et al. (2020).   [45] Feinberg and Mallatt (2016).
[46] Ginsburg and Jablonka (2019); Birch et al. (2020, 2021).

markers that shift probabilities.[47] We did not commit to any single theory of sentience. Instead, we looked across the zone of reasonable disagreement to find credible theoretical groundings for behavioural, cognitive, and neural markers, choosing criteria that would shift probabilities for anyone willing to attach non-zero probability to any of several theories. This left us with an intentionally inclusive yet theoretically well-motivated list of criteria, a list we felt could command widespread support.

Such lists are, in effect, providing *warning signs*: signs that our actions in relation to this animal may create welfare risks. How many warning signs are enough to make animals of a given taxon sentience candidates? This is a delicate judgement call, and an example of what I called in Chapter 6 a 'mixed judgement': a judgement with scientific and evaluative elements. It is about judging when the evidence supports a realistic possibility of sentience, and when the evidence base is rich enough to allow the design and assessment of precautions. Our list of criteria could be combined with many different rules for when 'enough' evidence has amassed. And this issue needs to be considered together with another—how to generalize across species.

12.7 The Question of Generalization

There are around 750 species of cephalopod mollusc, and around 15,000 species of decapod crustacean. Although we found over three hundred relevant scientific studies in total, much of the evidence concerns a small number of laboratory species.

One way to handle generalization is to refuse to generalize beyond these laboratory species: this is the approach taken by the Animal Procedures Committee in 1992, when they singled out *Octopus vulgaris* for special protections. This, however, is inconsistent with the way animal welfare policy treats vertebrates. Many mammalian species have never been studied in relation to sentience (a great deal of the evidence for mammals comes from the lab rat, *Rattus norvegicus*, and the rhesus macaque, *Macaca mulatta*) but it would be inaccurate to declare on that basis that their sentience is unknown, because there is copious relevant evidence from other mammals that can provide a basis for sound inferences.

At the opposite extreme, there is a risk of extrapolating too generously, when in fact the evidence allows for finer discriminations. For example, to protect all invertebrates, including microscopic ones, on the basis of evidence

---

[47] Birch (2022c); Browning and Birch (2022).

from octopuses would be hard to defend. It would also rely on tenuous extrapolation from the octopus to nervous systems that are not just far smaller, but also very differently organized. The same concerns would arise, though less acutely, if we were to generalize from true crabs to all crustaceans, including microscopic crustaceans such as copepods. That is not to say that copepods are not sentient—we cannot rule out sentience in small brains. It is only to say that it would be tenuous to generalize from one case to the other.

An intermediate approach is to use our best current picture of the phylogenetic relationships between species to make inferences. In the case of the decapods, our best current picture divides the order Decapoda into in two suborders (Dendrobranchiata, Pleocyemata) with the Pleocyemata further subdivided into ten infraorders. This way of classifying decapods is supported by molecular evidence.[48] Inferences from a model species to other species of the same infraorder are more strongly supported than inferences stretching across infraorders, or inferences across the Dendrobranchiata/Pleocyemata division. So, that is the approach we took. We reviewed all the evidence we could find, noting the particular species being studied, but also making generalizations from model species to other species of the same infraorder.

Even though the cephalopod molluscs sit at a higher 'rank' than decapods in Linnaean taxonomy—they are a class rather than an order—there are considerably fewer known species of cephalopod than decapod: around 750. This gives some sense of the arbitrariness of Linnaean ranks. Ultimately, the phylogenetic relationships between species are more important for underpinning inductive generalizations than Linnaean categories.[49] Here too, we turned to our best current phylogenetic picture to guide our inferences.[50] We decided it was reasonable in this case to generalize across orders, such as the order Octopoda, and reasonable in some cases to make generalizations about all coleoid cephalopods (subclass Coleoida, including all octopuses, squid, and cuttlefish) on the basis of evidence from a diverse subset of coleoid species.

12.8 What We Found, in Brief

Our review is freely available online and runs to over one hundred pages, covering over three hundred studies, so I will not repeat it here.[51] I will instead focus on the way we aggregated evidence and communicated uncertainty—and on some striking examples.

---

[48] Wolfe et al. (2019).   [49] de Queiroz (2006).   [50] Tanner et al. (2017).
[51] Birch et al. (2021).

For each criterion, we used confidence levels to communicate the strength of the evidence that the animals under discussion satisfy or fail the criterion, an approach to communicating uncertainty inspired by the Intergovernmental Panel on Climate Change.[52] These confidence levels take into account both the amount of evidence for a claim and the reliability and quality of the scientific work and were agreed through discussion among the authors.

We used the category of 'very high confidence' only when we judged that the weight of scientific evidence leaves no room for reasonable doubt that a marker is present/absent. We used the category of 'high confidence' in cases when we could see strong but not completely conclusive evidence of the marker being present/absent. We used the category of 'medium confidence' in cases where we had some concerns about the reliability of the evidence. We used 'low confidence' for cases where there is little evidence that an animal satisfies or fails the criterion, or where there is evidence of similar strength in both directions. We used 'very low' or 'no confidence' when the evidence is either seriously inadequate or non-existent. A key point is that 'low confidence' that a marker is present does not mean that we think it is probably absent. What it means is that the evidence one way or the other is thin, low-quality, finely balanced, or a combination of these.

Our key findings took the form of confidence levels for each criterion, for various groupings of decapod and cephalopod. Those findings are summarized in Tables 12.1 and 12.2, reproduced from the full report.

Example 1: Conditioned Place Avoidance in Octopuses

I will briefly describe a few of the studies that provided relevant evidence. A 2021 study by Robyn Crook tested for conditioned place avoidance in the pygmy octopus, *Octopus bocki*, testing our criterion 8b.[53] Octopuses were given a choice of three chambers, marked by different patterns on the walls. One chamber was paired with an acetic acid injection that the animals found aversive. Another was paired with administration of lidocaine (a local anaesthetic) to the affected area. Animals that initially preferred the acid-paired chamber, prior to experiencing the noxious stimulus, learned to disfavour it, and to prefer the lidocaine-paired chamber. Moreover, the octopuses displayed a distinctive skin-scraping behaviour in response to the noxious stimulus that ceased after the administration of lidocaine. Meanwhile, electrophysiological

---

[52] IPCC (2010). [53] Crook (2021).

Table 12.1 A summary of the evidence of sentience in cephalopod molluscs. The colours and letters represent our confidence level that the criterion in question (column) is satisfied by the taxon in question (row). VH (dark green) indicates very high confidence, H (light green) indicates high confidence, M (dark yellow) indicates medium confidence, L (light yellow) represents low confidence, and VL (light grey) represents very low confidence.

	Nociception	Sensory integration	Integrated nociception	Analgesia	Motivational trade-off	Flexible self-protection	Associative learning	Analgesia preference
Octopods (Octopoda)	VH	VH	H	H	M	VH	VH	H
Cuttlefish (Sepiida)	H	VH	H	L	M	M	VH	L
Other coleoids (squid, all orders)	H	VH	H	L	M	L	H	L
Nautiloids	H	L	L	L	L	L	M	VL

Table 12.2 A summary of the evidence of sentience in decapod crustaceans. The colours and letters represent our confidence level that the criterion in question (column) is satisfied by the taxon in question (row). VH (dark green) indicates very high confidence, H (light green) indicates high confidence, M (dark yellow) indicates medium confidence, L (light yellow) represents low confidence, and VL (light grey) represents very low confidence.

	Nociception	Sensory integration	Integrated nociception	Analgesia	Motivational trade-off	Flexible self-protection	Associative learning	Analgesia preference
True crabs (Brachyura)	H	VH	L	VH	L	VH	H	VL
Anomuran crabs (Anomura)	H	VH	L	L	M	H	L	VL
Astacid lobsters/crayfish (Astacidea)	H	VH	L	VH	L	L	H	VL
Spiny lobsters (Achelata)	H	VH	L	L	L	L	M	VL
Caridean shrimps (Caridea)	H	VH	L	M	L	M	L	VL
Penaeid shrimps (Penaeidae)	H	L	L	M	L	L	L	VL

recordings in the brachial connectives, linking the arm nerve cords to the brain, showed a prolonged period of high activity after the noxious stimulus, silenced by the lidocaine (Fig. 12.1). All of this is exactly what one would predict on the hypothesis that *the acetic acid causes an aversive experience that the lidocaine relieves.*

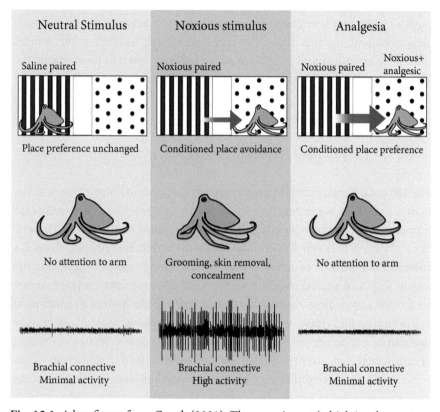

Fig. 12.1 A key figure from Crook (2021). The experiment (which is relevant to our criteria 4, 5, and 8) involved four groups of animals (with either seven or eight in each group): a group injected with only saline solution; a second group injected with acetic acid; a third group injected with acetic acid and, later, lidocaine; and a fourth group (not shown) injected with saline and then lidocaine. After receiving acetic acid, the affected animals showed directed self-protective behaviour, increased neural activity, and avoidance of the chamber where they had received it. Lidocaine silenced the heightened neural activity and stopped the self-protective behaviour. The figure, by Robyn Crook, is CC-BY-NC-ND 4.0 licensed. See the original source for further methodological details.

Why is conditioned place avoidance a source of insight into sentience? It is significant that it is not just an instance of classical conditioning, in which a pattern on the wall is paired with a noxious stimulus, and so comes to elicit the same response as that stimulus. If that were all that was happening, we would expect the visual stimulus of the chamber walls to elicit the same response as acetic acid: skin-scraping. But what in fact happens is more sophisticated: the animal's preferences change. To explain this, we need to posit a system that is evaluating locations in the environment for their associated risks and rewards based on past experience, navigating the animal towards opportunity and away from risk. That is, we need to posit exactly the sort of central evaluation system that, on Merker's theory, is sufficient for sentience.

Example 2: 'Anxiety-Like States' in Crayfish

Physiological stress, defined as any situation that disrupts homeostasis, is not itself a marker of sentience. Any living system has mechanisms to maintain homeostasis in the face of perturbations, so this alone does not help us draw any distinction between sentient and non-sentient life. Yet inducing stress is a common component of many experiments probing sentience, because the *way* in which an animal responds to stress can offer relevant evidence. When an animal responds to stress in ways that indicate centralized evaluation of opportunities and risks—with stress altering the value of the options in ways that can be experimentally manipulated—we have some evidence of the sort of centralized evaluative modelling that is credibly linked to sentience.

An impressive series of studies by a team at the University of Bordeaux has used this strategy to obtain evidence of 'anxiety-like' states in the crayfish *Procambarus clarkii*. In the first study, crayfish were placed in a maze in which they were free to explore both light and dark arms. When electrical fields were used to induce physiological stress in the animals, they became substantially less willing to enter the light arms. There was evidence that the effect was mediated by endogenous serotonin, a neurotransmitter linked to anxiety and depression in humans. The mechanisms are plainly not the same as those in the human brain. Yet it turned out, remarkably, that administering a common anti-anxiety drug designed for humans, chlordiazepoxide (often sold as Librium), restored a willingness to explore the light arms in the stressed crayfish, relative to a control group injected with saline. The authors argued that this pattern of results pointed to the existence of a brain state driving reduced exploratory behaviour, a state experimentally manipulable with serotonin and chlordiazepoxide. They described this state as 'anxiety-like'.[54] The presence of 'anxiety-like' states is not conclusive proof of experiences of anxiety. We nonetheless took it to be a relevant piece of evidence (under criterion 4b).

Example 3: Integrative Brain Regions Linked to Learning and Memory

Integrative brain regions linked to learning and memory raise the probability of sentience. Even those who favour theories of sentience on which its function has no relation to learning and memory (or on which it has no function at all) should acknowledge this as a criterion motivated by several well-developed and credible theories in the zone of reasonable disagreement.

The integrative functions of the vertical lobe in coleoid cephalopods are well documented, and their impressive learning abilities have long been celebrated.[55] But what about decapods? There is good behavioural evidence that at least some decapod crustaceans can learn associatively. The evidence is particularly strong for true crabs (infraorder Brachyura), though there is also some evidence of associative learning in lobsters (Astacidea and Achelata). It is tempting to think: if the animal can learn associatively, there must be some central association unit. However, we have already noted that simple, limited forms of associative learning can be performed by the spinal cords of rats, disconnected from the brain. Given this, we considered it important to find evidence of dedicated brain regions that might plausibly be the main site for a central association unit.

Do decapods have such regions? I have sometimes heard people say that decapods lack brains: this reflects either a misunderstanding of the relevant neurobiology or an excessively narrow definition of 'brain'. What is true is that decapods have small brains in comparison with mammals. For example, the giant robber crab or coconut crab is the world's largest terrestrial arthropod, with some individuals weighing up to 4 kg. A detailed study of the

---

[54] Fossat et al. (2014). A follow-up study showed a positive correlation between the amount of serotonin in the brain and the degree of light avoidance (a relationship, but a mirror image of the relationship in vertebrates, where serotonin decreases anxiety), and again showed that administering chlordiazepoxide abolished the light avoidance (Fossat et al. 2015). A third, in which light avoidance behaviour was induced by aggression from another animal, led to similar findings (Bacqué-Cazenave et al. 2017).

[55] Shigeno et al. (2018).

brain of *Birgus latro* calculated it to have a volume of around 3 cubic millimetres.[56] For comparison, the brain of a typical laboratory mouse (Mus musculus) is about 500 cubic millimetres.[57]

Yet we need to remember that a significant number of neurons and a lot of functional complexity can be packed into a small brain. In decapods, there are well-documented integrative regions linked to learning and memory, known as the hemiellipsoid bodies. The study just mentioned counted 253,556 neurons in each of the two hemiellipsoid bodies of *Birgus latro*, each representing 13.4 per cent of the brain by volume.[58] I oppose the use of neuron counts as a major consideration, and that point still stands even when the neuron counts concern brain areas linked to integrative functions. Yet it is still worth highlighting the substantial amount of brain tissue dedicated to integrating information from different sensory sources as a retort to those who question whether decapods even have brains.

How widely shared are these integrative regions? A study by Nicholas Strausfeld and collaborators provided compelling evidence on this question (Fig. 12.2).[59] Strausfeld et al. used an immunostaining technique to identify and map out the hemiellipsoid bodies in thirteen distinct lineages of crustacean. The study demonstrates that these regions are a general feature of the decapods. At the same time, it also revealed miniaturization and weak differentiation of those regions in the world's most commercially important farmed shrimp, *Penaeus vannamei* (also known as *Litopenaeus vannamei*), commonly known as the whiteleg shrimp or Pacific white shrimp, but often sold as the 'king prawn'.

Are these miniaturized hemiellipsoid bodies still performing important functions for the animal? Since nervous tissue is energetically expensive to maintain, this sort of diminution is what we expect to see when a particular system is no longer functionally significant. Rebecca Meth and colleagues suggest one possible explanation: the size of the hemiellipsoid bodies is largely driven, they suggest, by the richness of the olfactory input they receive, but the sensory ecology of whiteleg shrimps in the wild gives reduced importance to olfaction, particularly in comparison to terrestrial decapods, and increased importance to vision in low-light conditions (i.e. turbid water).

---

[56] Krieger et al. (2010).   [57] Badea et al. (2007).

[58] This can be compared with the 13.7 million neurons in the cerebral cortex of a mouse (Herculano-Houzel et al. 2006): a big difference, but not as big as one might have guessed from the volumes alone.

[59] Strausfeld et al. (2020). See also Harzsch and Krieger (2021).

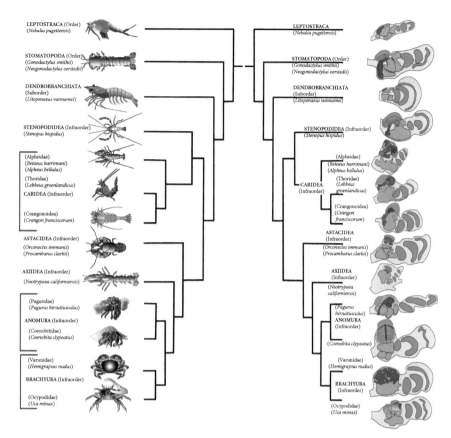

Fig. 12.2 A key figure from Strausfeld et al. (2020). The pink regions indicate an integrative brain region associated with learning and memory (the hemiellipsoid body) in various species of crustacean, as identified using an immunostaining technique (N.B. Leptostraca and Stomatopoda are not decapods). Notably, the pink regions in penaeid shrimps (*Penaeus vannamei*) are miniaturized. This figure is by Strausfeld et al. 2020, CC-BY 4.0 licensed. See the original source for full details of the technique used.

So, it seems the lineage has evolved to invest more energy in large visual neuropils and less in the hemiellipsoid bodies.[60]

Could it be that some crustacean lineages have evolved capacities for learning and memory and then lost them? Indeed, could some lineages have evolved *sentience* and subsequently lost it? That is a possibility we need to take seriously, but one that is very hard to establish with confidence, given the lack of agreement on markers of the *absence* of sentience. Ultimately, we

---

[60] Meth et al. (2017).

handled this complex picture by reporting 'low confidence' that penaeid shrimps have functional, integrative brain regions. It was a difficult case, because the immunostaining work shows that whiteleg shrimp do have homologues of such regions, while also casting doubt on their functionality.

A similar integrative centre linked to learning and memory—the mushroom body—is well documented in insects. Indeed, Strausfeld et al. used their results to argue for the homology of the insect mushroom body and the decapod hemiellipsoid body. The evidence for sentience in decapods cannot, therefore, be disentangled from the emerging picture of insects as sentience candidates, an issue that will be picked up in the next chapter.

12.9 From Grades of Evidence to Sharp Decisions

Our review left us with a complicated, gradated picture. Comparative judgements are easier than absolute ones. The evidence for sentience in octopuses is stronger than the evidence in any of the other taxa we reviewed. The evidence for sentience in coleoid cephalopods (octopuses, squid, cuttlefish) is stronger the evidence for sentience in nautiluses. The evidence for sentience in the Pleocyemata (the suborder of the decapods that includes all the walking decapods, plus caridean shrimps, but excluding penaeid shrimps) is stronger than the evidence for sentience in Dendrobranchiata (the suborder including penaeid shrimps).

However, these comparative claims are at least partly a reflection of where scientists have chosen to direct their attention. They do not reflect a settled picture obtained through careful, detailed investigation of all the taxa in question. The Dendrobranchiata, in particular, have barely been studied in relation to sentience. Moreover, these comparative claims do not give policy-makers direct guidance.

It was not easy to move from this complex picture to a simple recommendation. In my view, it is clear that the coleoid cephalopods (octopuses, squid, cuttlefish) are sentience candidates, and clear too that the decapods of the suborder Pleocyemata are sentience candidates, but there is very little evidence concerning shrimps of the suborder Dendrobranchiata (as our tables conveyed). In the terminology of this book, Dendrobranchiata are investigation priorities rather than sentience candidates: we currently lack an adequate evidence base for designing precautions and need to enrich that evidence base urgently.

However, the Sentience Act is not framed in terms of sentience candidates or investigation priorities: the UK government required a single line to be drawn. Our report highlighted two options: (i) include all cephalopod molluscs and all decapod crustaceans in the scope of the new law, or (ii) include all cephalopod molluscs and only those decapods of the suborder Pleocyemata.[61] We recommended the first option, warning that the second option would lead to a confusing law, since the taxonomic categories Pleocyemata and Dendrobranchiata are not widely used. That would have been a problem, since the purpose of the new law requires its implications to be easily understood across all government departments. This is a pragmatic reason, but pragmatic reasons can play a legitimate role in these decisions, especially in a context where a single line needs to be drawn and gradations cannot easily be accommodated.

The UK government implemented our central recommendation. At the same time as publishing a report, Defra tabled an amendment to its Sentience Bill expanding its scope to include cephalopods and decapods. That was a big step for invertebrate welfare in the UK. Indeed, to see any government taking the issue seriously was heartening. My hope is that this will set a precedent that other countries follow when enshrining respect for animal sentience in law. I hope too that it will lead to a wider conversation about the proportionate steps we can take to improve the welfare of the cephalopods and decapods in our care. That question of proportionality will be picked up in Chapter 14.

12.10 Some Critical Reflections

Looking back, two aspects of the report concern me. One was outside my control: Defra had decided, at the point of commissioning the report, that its scope would be limited to two invertebrate taxa, the cephalopod molluscs and the decapod crustaceans. There was a rationale for a focus on these taxa. The cephalopods were already included in the scope of ASPA, raising a question of whether they should also be included in the scope of other animal welfare laws. Meanwhile, a high-profile, well-organized campaign called Crustacean Compassion had been calling for the inclusion of decapods. These reasons were pragmatic rather than scientific, and we would probably

---

[61] This second possibility has been defended by Comstock (2022) in his reply to Crump et al. (2022a). The category of 'Reptantia', the walking decapods, appears in the Swiss Tierseuchenverordnung (Animal Protection Order). But this questionably excludes caridean shrimps, which fall within the Pleocyemata.

have chosen to look at a wider range of invertebrate animals, given the choice (and, in the next chapter, I will). But to repeat, pragmatic reasons have a legitimate role. A report with broader scope might have led to some recommendations that were politically impossible to implement, increasing the chance of all our recommendations being ignored.

The second concerning aspect is the rather conservative and precedent-sensitive nature of our approach. We started with IME criteria and revised and updated those criteria in various ways, giving reasons for the changes. Here too, there was a pragmatic rationale. Procedures need to command public confidence. To throw out the approach taken in the 1990s and start again with a blank canvas would have risked undermining confidence in what we were doing.

And yet, the IME criteria can be accused of an excessive focus on pain and pain-like states. This is obviously the case for criteria such as 'an animal's response to stimuli that would be painful for a human is functionally similar to the human response'. The wording here is unhelpfully vague (as noted earlier), but, more fundamentally, there is no strong reason why 'stimuli that would be painful for a human' are the only stimuli that can provide insight into sentience. Even when sentience is defined in its narrower sense as a capacity for *valenced* experience, there is still far more to sentience than just pain: pain is just one possible valenced experience among many. Although our revised criteria eliminated vague phrases such as 'stimuli that would be painful for a human', they retained a focus on pain.

This could have led to problematic consequences. As it turned out, there was very strong evidence of our pain indicators in octopuses. But suppose this had not been the case, simply because scientists had never looked for those indicators—what would we have said then? It would surely have been appropriate to acknowledge *other* lines of evidence, such as evidence of play behaviour, as relevant to questions of sentience, rather than saying 'no pain, no sentience'.[62] I do not think we should try to systematize these 'other lines of evidence' into an expanded list of criteria (which would become very long and unwieldy), but we should in general remain open-minded about relevant evidence coming from sources outside the list.

---

[62] On play behaviour in octopuses, see Kuba et al. (2006). On the minds of octopuses more generally, Jennifer Mather's (2008, 2019) work is an excellent guide, and Peter Godfrey-Smith's (2016b, 2020a) books present the evidence very accessibly. In a fantastic series of papers, Mather has carefully applied the 'dimensions of animal consciousness' proposed by Birch et al. (2020) to the case of octopuses (Mather 2021a, 2021b, 2022a, 2022b). These papers give a sense of just how comprehensive the case of sentience in octopuses really is.

A special focus on pain can be defended pragmatically on two grounds. First, it has a special significance for animal welfare law, because chronic and/ or intense pain poses a very serious welfare problem. This is reflected in UK animal welfare law: for example, the Animal Welfare Act 2006 allows for ministers to extend protection to invertebrate species if convinced by scientific evidence of a capacity for 'pain and suffering'. We can grant this special significance while also maintaining that there are many other serious welfare problems, including other negative states (such as anxiety-like and boredom-like states) and being deprived of positive states, such as pleasure and joy.

Second, a lot of the empirical research into sentience in disputed taxa has focused on pain, and on testing for indicators of pain along the lines of the IME criteria. So, by taking these criteria as our starting point, and revising them modestly, we preserved alignment between the criteria being used to guide policy and the criteria many of the experiments in this area have sought to test.

Although pragmatic reasons can be good reasons, they left me with a sense that, if we could have started with a blank canvas, liberated from the inertia of precedent, we might well have taken a less pain-centric approach. A focus on pain could lead to us missing other forms of sentience. We must be open to the possibility that the class of sentient animals is bigger than the class of animals that feel pain. With that point in mind, it is time to think about insects.

Proposal 17. *Sentience is not pain.* Although there are pragmatic reasons for the focus on pain in debates about animal sentience, we must be open to the possibility that the class of sentient animals is bigger than the class of animals that feel pain. Other forms of evidence can also make an animal a sentience candidate, such as evidence of sophisticated forms of learning, attention, working memory, and planning.

12.11 Summary of Chapter 12

Since all adult vertebrates are sentience candidates, debate in recent years has shifted towards invertebrates, where sentience candidature is more contestable. Octopuses are often regarded as sentient due to their large brains and impressive intelligence. Yet sentience is neither intelligence nor brain size, and we should be aware of the possibility of decouplings between intelligence, brain size, and sentience in the animal kingdom. Precautions to safeguard animal welfare should be driven by markers of sentience, not by markers of intelligence or by brain size.

That said, even when we restrict our focus to markers of sentience, octopuses are clearly sentience candidates. I led a review in 2021 that considered the evidence of sentience in cephalopod molluscs (octopuses, squid, cuttlefish, and nautiluses) and decapod crustaceans (including many crabs, lobsters, crayfish, and shrimps). We constructed a framework based on eight theoretically well-motivated criteria. We reported with high confidence that octopuses satisfied at least seven of the eight criteria.

More broadly, we found a complicated evidential picture. The question of when enough evidence has amassed to imply a realistic possibility of sentience that it would be irresponsible to ignore is a difficult judgement call. In my view, the coleoid cephalopods and decapods of the Pleocyemata suborder are clear sentience candidates, whereas decapods of the Dendrobranchiata suborder (including penaeid shrimps) are investigation priorities.

The Edge of Sentience: Risk and Precaution in Humans, Other Animals, and AI. Jonathan Birch, Oxford University Press.
© Jonathan Birch 2024. DOI: 10.1093/9780191966729.003.0013

13

Pushing the Boundaries

13.1 Insects: The Old Received Wisdom

The entomologist Harold Bastin, in a 1927 *Scientific American* article, reported that insects will continue to feed and mate despite catastrophic injury, such as the loss of the abdomen. The piece was studded with graphic photographs: a dragonfly eating its own detached abdomen, a wasp without an abdomen feeding on sugar syrup, which drips out from the back of its thorax, a sleeping moth that is not woken by being pinned to a tree.[1]

Half a century later, another entomologist, V. B. Wigglesworth, offered reflections along similar lines:

> For the most part insects behave as though their integument is insensitive to pain. They show no manifestation of pain on cutting the cuticle: they cannot cry out, but they do not flinch or run. Whereas a nip with forceps is very painful to us, a caterpillar treated in this way shows no sustained signs of agitation.[2]

And C. H. Eisemann and colleagues further reinforced these observations:

> No example is known to us of an insect showing protective behavior towards injured body parts, such as by limping after leg injury or declining to feed or mate because of general abdominal injuries. On the contrary, our experience has been that insects will continue with normal activities even after severe injury or removal of body parts. An insect walking with a crushed tarsus, for example, will continue applying to the substrate with undiminished force. Among our other observations are those on a locust which continued to feed whilst itself being eaten by a mantis; aphids continuing to feed whilst being eaten by coccinellids; a tsetse fly which flew in to feed although half-dissected; caterpillars which continue to feed whilst tachinid

---

[1] Bastin (1927).   [2] Wigglesworth (1980, p. 9).

larvae bore into them; many insects which go about their normal life whilst being eaten by large internal parasitoids; and male mantids which continue to mate as they are being eaten by their partners.[3]

These sources influenced the Institute of Medical Ethics report in 1991 that singled out cephalopods as *uniquely* likely candidates for sentience among invertebrates, indirectly leading to the protection of *Octopus vulgaris* in science in the UK.[4]

The reported absence of manifest pain in response to catastrophic injury is certainly striking. What might explain this? An initially tempting explanation goes: perhaps there is no adaptive benefit to feeling pain when the cuticle (or exoskeleton) is damaged, because insects cannot heal wounds to the cuticle, and so have nothing to gain from tending or guarding those wounds. However, locusts can repair injuries to the cuticle, albeit imperfectly, returning the surface to about two-thirds of its original strength.[5] Insects capable of repair would benefit, just as we do, from a response that helped them avoid further injury during repair. A different possibility is that responses to injury exist in insects but are under decentralized control, with responses to abdominal injuries regulated by abdominal ganglia and responses to thoracic injuries regulated by thoracic ganglia.

There is an interesting physiological puzzle here, but we should be wary of drawing any sweeping conclusion that insects do not feel pain. All three of the pieces just quoted include important qualifications. On closer examination, Bastin's view that insects do not feel pain is heavily reliant on a distinction between pain and *discomfort*, for he grants that 'there is some evidence to support the view that they suffer varying degrees of discomfort, especially when their antennae are pinched, or when strong corrosive substances are applied to their nerveendings'.[6] Pain, for Bastin, appears to be a term reserved for pain felt in response to catastrophic injury; all else is mere discomfort. This terminological choice would be controversial if adopted in human medicine.

Wigglesworth, meanwhile, adds that 'I am sure that insects can feel pain if the right stimulus is given. High temperature seems the clearest example, and perhaps electric shocks. For practical purposes why not assume that this is so?'[7] And Eisemann et al. end on a similarly precautionary note:

---

[3] Eisemann et al. (1984, p. 166).   [4] Smith and Boyd (1991).   [5] Parle et al. (2016).
[6] Bastin (1927, p. 531).   [7] Wigglesworth (1980, p. 9).

We consider that the experimental biologist would be advised to follow, whenever feasible, Wigglesworth's recommendation that insects have their nervous systems inactivated prior to traumatizing manipulation. This procedure not only facilitates handling, but also guards against the remaining possibility of pain infliction and, equally important, helps to preserve in the experimenter an appropriately respectful attitude towards living organisms whose physiology, though different, and perhaps simpler than our own, is as yet far from completely understood.[8]

All of these authors, then, were willing to accept that insects might yet be sentient despite failing to respond to injury in the way a mammal would. An insect could, in principle, have a system of locally controlled responses to tissue damage that occur autonomously of the brain, yet the brain could still be engaged in rich evaluative modelling of the risks and opportunities in its environment, experiencing frustrations and rewards in the form of affect. These would be valenced experiences regardless of whether we call them 'pleasure' and 'pain' or something else.

13.2 Insects: The Emerging New Picture

New evidence is changing the way we think about insects. Multiple different lines of evidence are relevant here. One consists of studies of insect nociception, which have vindicated Wigglesworth's suggestion about heat. Nociceptive pathways responding to intense heat have been studied in *Drosophila* larvae[9] and in cockroaches.[10] Yet nociception is not pain, and the mere presence of nociceptors, although a relevant piece of evidence, does not shift probabilities very much, just as the mere presence of photoreceptors is not compelling evidence of conscious vision. It just shows that a basic prerequisite for pain is in place.

Potentially more significant is emerging evidence from bees suggesting that they are able to trade off the anticipated value of a reward against the risk of injury. This type of behaviour, when found in hermit crabs, has been taken as evidence of sentience, since it indicates a central evaluation system

---

[8] Eisemann et al. (1984, p. 167). The emphasis on the 'appropriately respectful attitude' of the experimenter is reminiscent of Knutsson and Munthe (2017) on the 'virtue of precaution'.
[9] Burgos et al. (2018).   [10] Emanuel and Libersat (2019).

supporting flexible decision-making.[11] Matilda Gibbons and collaborators presented bumblebees (*Bombus terrestris*) with a choice of various heat pads of different temperatures. Each heat pad enabled access to sugar solution, with varying concentrations of sugar solution available at different pads. There was evidence that bees traded off the temperature of the pads against the sweetness of the rewards in anticipatory fashion, accepting an expectation of higher temperatures to access higher expected concentrations of sugar.[12]

Following this study, I worked with Gibbons and several other collaborators to review all the available insect evidence relevant to our eight proposed pain markers. We found a substantial amount of evidence spread across the six most intensively studied insect orders. We also found large evidence gaps: not enough work has seriously investigated whether insects might display these indicators. It is entirely possible that, as these gaps are filled in, the case for pain in insects will become very strong indeed. We should also, however, be open to the possibility that the traditional focus on pain in discussions of sentience does not serve insects well. There are ways to make a case for a realistic possibility of sentience in insects that do not proceed via evidence of pain.

Judgement Bias

What are these other lines of evidence? One concerns judgement bias. In a judgement bias test, an animal is trained to associate one cue with reward and another with punishment and is then shown an ambiguous cue. For example, a green cue might be paired with reward and a blue cue with punishment, with experimenters then showing cues of intermediate colours between green and blue. The question is: are stressed animals less likely to take a risk on an ambiguous cue? And are animals more likely to take a risk after receiving an unexpected reward? In this literature, an increased tendency to take a risk on the ambiguous cue is called a 'pessimistic' judgement bias and an increased tendency to do so is called an 'optimistic' judgement bias.

When found in mammals and birds, judgements biases are often taken as indicators of felt mood. Melissa Bateson and Daniel Nettle, two distinguished behavioural biologists, have even described them as a 'gold standard for

---

[11] Appel and Elwood (2009).
[12] Gibbons et al. (2022). I was not personally involved in this study, although Gibbons, Crump, and Chittka are associated with my 'Foundations of Animal Sentience' project.

assessing moods in non-human animals.'[13] Judgement biases have also been found repeatedly in bees and fruit flies, using a variety of different stimuli and experimental setups.[14] Does this show that insects, too, have emotions or moods? Of course, doubts are possible here, for all the reasons doubt is always possible. Elizabeth Paul and colleagues caution that 'the finding that even some invertebrate species show judgement biases raises questions as to whether the phenomenon observed in animals involves any conscious component of affect'.[15] Nonetheless, judgement bias should be considered a probability-raiser for sentience in insects. It should lead us to take more seriously the possibility of a central evaluation system modelling the risks and opportunities in the environment—the type of system Merker's theory, in particular, regards as tightly linked to sentience.

Evaluative Modelling in the Central Complex

Are there neural substrates in insects that might plausibly support this kind of evaluative modelling? Recall that Merker's theory ties sentience, in the vertebrate case, to a behavioural core control system involving the midbrain and basal ganglia (see Chapter 5). This system simulates the moving animal in space, combining sensory information from multiple sense modalities with efference copies of motor commands and with interoceptive information about current bodily needs. It thereby facilitates flexible action selection, allowing the animal to pursue those needs that currently merit priority. To serve this function, there also needs to be an evaluative aspect to the model: it is not just that the animal's needs are represented, but they are also assigned relative value or disvalue. The overall system is proposed to suffice for valenced experience. Andrew Barron and Colin Klein have argued that the central complex in the insect brain performs analogous functions, constructing an evaluative neural simulation of the state of the moving body in space.[16] In short, they argue that insects possess a behavioural control unit closely analogous to that of vertebrates.

To get from here to the conclusion that insects have a capacity for conscious experience, Barron and Klein need an additional background

---

[13] Bateson and Nettle (2015).

[14] Bateson et al. (2011); Deakin et al. (2018); Procenko et al. (2023); Solvi et al. (2016); Strang and Muth (2023). See Chittka (2022, ch. 11) for an accessible synthesis.

[15] Paul et al. (2020, p. 762).   [16] Barron and Klein (2016); Klein and Barron (2016).

commitment: the commitment that the vertebrate core control system suffices for sentience in virtue of the *general type of computations* it performs (i.e. simulations of the right kind), and not in virtue of the fine details of the algorithms used, nor in virtue of how those algorithms are neurally implemented (that is, we need R5, in the reasonable range mapped out in Chapter 6). We need, in other words, not just computational functionalism, but what (in Chapter 3) I called large-scale computational functionalism, on which the precise algorithms are unimportant. This is a background commitment that many will doubt (e.g. those who favour R1, R2, or R4), but it is part of the zone of reasonable disagreement. It is a realistic possibility that sentience can be achieved in multiple ways with only relatively liberal constraints on its algorithmic and neural implementation. So, evidence that the insect central complex performs the same general type of computation as the vertebrate midbrain is another reason to take seriously the possibility of sentience in insects.

Working Memory, Attention and Sophisticated Associative Learning

A different way to make a case for sentience candidature in some insects appeals to evidence of working memory and attention, relying on the idea of a close relationship between these mechanisms and sentience, at least when found in biological brains.[17] The ability of bees and *Drosophila* fruit flies to attend selectively to some stimuli over others is well documented and central to their learning skills.[18] There is also substantial evidence of working memory in bees, revealed by standard tests that were first developed to test for working memory in mammals. One involves a radial arm maze, in which many arms can be accessed from a central atrium. Honey bees (*Apis mellifera*) display working memory by systematically going round the maze in search of food, avoiding wasting time by returning to arms already visited.[19] A different working memory test involves 'delayed match-to-sample' tests in a Y-shaped maze.[20] The bee sees a colour, or smells an odour, at the entrance to

---

[17] Koch (2008); Tye (2016, pp. 150–156); van Swinderen (2005).
[18] Morawetz and Spaethe (2012); Paulk et al. (2014); van Swinderen (2007).
[19] M. F. Brown and Demas (1994); M. F. Brown et al. (1997); Burmeister et al. (1995). Pesticides impair the spatial working memory of bumblebees (*Bombus terrestris*) in this setup (Samuelson et al. 2016).
[20] Cooke et al. (2007); Giurfa et al. (2001); Gross et al. (2009); Howard et al. (2019); Ng et al. (2020); Srinivasan (2010); Zhang et al. (2005).

the maze and uses this as a guide to which branch to select at the fork, either opting for the branch with the matching colour/odour (when matching to sample is what leads to reward) or the branch with a non-matching colour/ odour (when non-matching leads to reward).

While these experiments indicate that honeybees and bumblebees have working memory, the inference from working memory to conscious experi- ence is contested. In humans, the contents of working memory are not always experienced. If I commit a string of symbols to working memory, wait a few seconds, and retrieve it, there is a period in between commitment and retrieval in which I am not experiencing the string of symbols. It is more plausible that a content must be consciously experienced at the point of *enter- ing* working memory and at the point of being *retrieved*—perhaps one func- tion of conscious perception is to control the gates of working memory. This idea is sometimes associated with the global workspace theory of conscious- ness. That said, even the idea of consciousness controlling the gates of work- ing memory can be questioned. There is some evidence, from humans, that subliminal cues (i.e. cues that were never consciously seen) can be held in working memory.[21] Yet continuing debate about the connection between con- sciousness and working memory does not prevent evidence of working mem- ory from raising the probability of sentience, especially against a background of substantial neural analogies (as stressed by Barron and Klein), poten- tially raising the probability to the level of a realistic possibility it would be irresponsible to ignore.

A related line of evidence concerns forms of associative learning linked tentatively to conscious perception in humans. Recall the example of trace conditioning, where the subject learns a temporal relationship between a CS and a US. For example, a human subject may hear a tone that predicts a puff of air aimed at the eye a second later—and must learn to blink at just the right moment to block the air puff.[22] Until recently, conditioning across temporal gaps had only been shown in bees and *Drosophila* for olfactory stimuli. In 2022, Dhruv Grover and colleagues demonstrated a form of visual trace con- ditioning in *Drosophila*. Moreover, the researchers found trace conditioning and delay conditioning (with no temporal gap between CS and US) involved different neural mechanisms, and that the trace conditioning mechanism was disrupted by a distracting stimulus between CS and US, suggesting the

---

[21] Soto et al. (2011).   [22] Clark and Squire (1998); Clark et al. (2002).

involvement of attention and working memory.[23] There remains an important missing element, namely response timing. An essential part of trace eyeblink conditioning in mammals is timing the conditioned response precisely to line up with the US; the versions so far implemented in insects still lack this component.

We also noted, in the last chapter, two other forms of learning for which there is evidence of facilitation by conscious perception in humans: reversal learning and some kinds of instrumental learning. Both bumblebees and honeybees will quickly learn reversals of stimulus contingencies.[24] They are also very capable instrumental learners, even when the learned behaviour is novel and context-specific, as shown, for example, in string-pulling, ball-rolling, and puzzle-box tasks.[25]

As with a case based on evaluative modelling or on working memory, an inference from learning abilities to sentience will not be universally persuasive. It will do most to raise the probability of sentience for those already sympathetic to a theoretical perspective, such as Ginsburg and Jablonka's UAL framework, that posits a close connection between sentience and learning. All can agree, however, that the case is stronger when we are not simply finding the simplest forms of associative learning, but specific forms that in our own case are facilitated by conscious experience. The case is yet stronger when we find that these sophisticated forms of learning are supported by distinctive pathways, separate from those supporting simpler kinds of learning, and when those pathways turn out to have features (such as sensitivity to distraction) that characterize the consciousness-involving pathways in us.

13.3 Insects as Sentience Candidates

The four broad sources of evidence so far considered (traditional pain indicators, judgement bias tests, functional analogies between the midbrain and central complex, and cognitive tests of working memory/sophisticated associative learning) are all probability raising, especially when taken together as

---

[23] Grover et al. (2022). Droege et al. (2021) proposed this 'distraction' criterion as a relevant test for consciousness shortly before the Grover et al. study was published.

[24] Chittka (1998); Sherry and Strang (2015); Strang and Sherry (2014). These results are discussed in Birch (2022c).

[25] Alem et al. (2016); Bridges et al. (2023); Galpayage Dona et al. (2022); Loukola et al. (2017); Mirwan and Kevan (2014).

a package. None conclusively shows that insects are sentient, but of all them make it more likely than we might have initially thought.

We then come to a delicate judgement call: when have we accumulated *enough* probability-raising markers to establish a realistic possibility of sentience that it would be irresponsible to ignore when making practical decisions, and an evidence base rich enough to allow the design and assessment of precautions? My own assessment is that we have already crossed that line for bees and for *Drosophila*, and should be thinking now about what precautions we might be able to take to reduce risks of suffering in these animals.

What of the other insects? I have been talking here of 'insect sentience', but should we really assess the insects as a single group? There are vastly more species of insect than of decapod crustacean. Around 1 million species are known, with the total number likely to be at least double this, and probably over 5 million.[26] In the last chapter, we considered some of the complexities involved in generalizing across the decapods, given the striking diversity of brain organization and the miniaturization of the hemiellipsoid bodies in penaeid shrimps. Can it really be reasonable to generalize across the insects?

We should be wary of generalizing when the topic is the advanced working memory and associative learning abilities of bees. The vast majority of insects have never been tested for these abilities. So, we cannot be sure they are absent, but there is no positive evidence that they are present. However, the situation is different for Barron and Klein's neurological arguments based on the integrative functions of the central complex. A vast number of species does not translate into substantial diversity of brain organization. Nicholas Strausfeld and collaborators, having painstakingly examined both insect mushroom bodies and decapod hemiellipsoid bodies across many different taxa, remark on the strikingly consistent morphology of mushroom bodies among insects, in comparison with the divergence in morphology of the hemiellipsoid bodies among decapods.[27] Meanwhile, Daniel B. Turner-Evans and Vivek Jayaraman have written, of the central complex, that:

> the conservation of these structures across 500 million years of arthropod evolution speaks to their importance. Though their form varies from species to species, individual neurons that innervate the structures are conserved to a remarkable degree.[28]

---

[26] Stork (2018).   [27] Strausfeld et al. (2020).
[28] Turner-Evans and Jayaraman (2016, p. 453).

My emphasis on consistency—a recurring theme throughout the book—leads me here to a surprising proposal. If we are prepared to extend sentience candidature across the fishes, including elasmobranchs and cyclostomes, based on evidence of conserved midbrain mechanisms, plus evidence linking those mechanisms to sentience in a small subset of species, then we must take the same approach to the insects. I propose that all adult insects are sentience candidates, since all possess a central complex. It would be a double standard to restrict our precautionary thinking to just some insects, while extending it to all fishes.

Why 'adult' insects? The central complex is not fully developed in larvae,[29] so Barron and Klein's argument only extends as far as adult insects. This is practically significant, since a great deal of contemporary insect farming involves farming larvae, killing them before they reach adulthood. More evidence on the capacities of the larvae of commercially important species, such as black soldier fly larvae, is urgently needed. Farmed larvae are investigation priorities, and we will give them their due in the next section.

The extension of sentience candidature even to adult insects is not a step to be taken lightly. Since there are only around 45,000 vertebrate species, the expansion involves expanding the number of species regarded as sentience candidates by a factor of at least twenty and potentially over one hundred. We go from regarding a small minority of animal species as sentience candidates to regarding a large majority as such.[30] Arguments about consistency can cut both ways: some may see this as a reason to withhold sentience candidature from the elasmobranchs and cyclostomes. Perhaps we should sort elasmobranchs, cyclostomes, and all adult insects other than bees and fruit flies into the category of 'investigation priority', at least in those cases where human activities create welfare risks for these animals.

This is a judgement call: it is not arbitrary, but the balance of reasons on both sides is delicate, and different expert panels could easily come to different views. It would be problematic if questions of huge practical significance rested on such judgement calls; that is something we should try to avoid. We can avoid it, provided we are willing to take some provisional steps to protect investigation priorities as well as sentience candidates—something I will advocate in the next chapter, when considering insect farming.

---

[29] Gowda et al. (2021).

[30] How many individual animals? The figure of 10 quintillion (10 billion billion, or 10^{18}) is often given, although I am unsure where this comes from. The earliest reference I could find is Berenbaum (1995), who described 10 quintillion as an earlier estimate, but without giving a source for it.

The idea of insects as sentience candidates sometimes provokes incredulous reactions. 'How can we live our lives if we regard insects as sentient? Are you saying I can't step on an insect while walking? That I can't drive a car?'. But this reaction takes no account of the concept of proportionality. What is needed is a discussion about proportionality in which we reflect on what steps might make sense, given our duty to avoid causing gratuitous suffering. Suffering accidentally metred out by humans in the process of walking or driving is not likely to be deemed gratuitous. I will return to this issue in the next chapter. But first, let us turn our attention from sentience candidates to investigation priorities.

13.4 Four Investigation Priorities

Gastropod Molluscs

When thinking about how the class of sentience candidates might expand in the future, my thoughts turn first to the gastropod molluscs, which have on the order of tens to hundreds of thousands of neurons (about 10,000–20,000 in the model organism *Aplysia californica*, a sea slug).[31] Their brains consist of three pairs of ganglia arranged in a ring around the oesophagus.[32] In large gastropods like *Aplysia*, the brain volume can be quite large, but this is because some of the neurons themselves are enormous: a single *Aplysia* neuron can have the volume of the entire brain of *Drosophila*.[33] But we have no reason to consider neuron number or brain volume reliable guides to sentience candidature. Brain volume (holding fixed neuron count) is likely irrelevant, and neuron number provides only very weak evidence. Better to ask whether there is evidence of standard pain markers and/or of evaluative modelling, working memory, and/or a central association unit integrating inputs from many sensory sources.

There is ample evidence of classical conditioning in *Aplysia* sea slugs, focusing on classical conditioning of the siphon and gill withdrawal reflexes.[34] Much of the learning seems 'limited' in Ginsburg and Jablonka's sense, with no clear evidence of rich multisensory integration, learning about novel stimuli, or learning across temporal gaps.[35] Classical conditioning with

---

[31] Akhmedov et al. (2014).   [32] Chase (2002).   [33] Moroz (2011).
[34] Walters et al. (1979); Hawkins (1984); Hawkins et al. (1989).
[35] Ginsburg and Jablonka (2019).

overlapping stimuli can even be achieved in 'preparations' of Aplysia where only the mantle organs and abdominal ganglion remain.[36] This is a reminder of the importance of looking for more demanding forms of associative learning, such as trace conditioning, where there is some evidence in the human case of the involvement of conscious processing. There is also one report in the literature of trace conditioning in (whole) pond snails, but when a procedure involves presenting the snails with olfactory stimuli in the water, then rinsing them for 15 seconds to wash off the stimulus, it is difficult to be sure that the CS has entirely gone by the time the US arrives.[37]

There is, however, robust evidence of operant conditioning (increased frequency of rewarded behaviours, decreased frequency of punished behaviours) in both Aplysia sea slugs and Lymnaea pond snails. Sea slugs rewarded for biting will bite more often,[38] and pond snails (which live in water, but come to the surface to breathe when the water lacks oxygen) will surface for air less often if punished for doing so.[39] This can be compared against evidence from Lina Skora and colleagues suggesting (albeit tentatively) that even apparently quite simple operant conditioning tasks require conscious awareness of the stimuli when a human is performing them. Skora et al. themselves remark that:

> The absence of unconscious instrumental conditioning reported here might seem intriguing in light of previous evidence that instrumental conditioning can proceed in simpler—presumably unconscious—organisms, such as fruit flies (Drosophila), sea slugs (Aplysia), or pond snails (Lymnaea).[40]

We should certainly question the idea that these animals are 'presumably unconscious'. That said, the tasks posed by Skora et al., though simple for humans, were significantly more complicated than the tasks so far presented to gastropods, because they required subjects to learn different conditioned responses to different visual cues. Gastropods have so far displayed only the simplest kind of operant conditioning, in which a behaviour is performed less often after punishment and more often after reward. Bjorn Brembs and colleagues report this form of operant conditioning can be achieved even by

---

[36] Hawkins et al. (1998). Remarkably, even second-order conditioning was observed in this preparation.
[37] Alexander et al. (1982). Thanks to Eric Schwitzgebel for sending me this reference.
[38] Brembs et al. (2002).   [39] Dalesman et al. (2011); Lukowiak et al. (1996, 1998, 2000).
[40] Skora et al. (2021).

isolated buccal ganglia (these ganglia lie outside the three main pairs of ganglia, at the mouth) and, most remarkably of all, in *single neurons* taken from these ganglia.[41] In so far as it can be achieved by a single neuron, the form of operant conditioning in evidence here—increased firing of a neuron after a reward signal—should not be taken as evidence of sentience. We should look for forms of learning that go beyond the simplest forms of operant conditioning and more closely mimic the tasks that seem to require consciousness in humans.

In light of all this, I see the gastropods as an investigation priority. It *could* well be that they are capable of forms of learning linked to consciousness in humans, and of other behaviours that have shifted opinions in the case of cephalopods, decapods, and insects, such as conditioned place preference and subtle motivational trade-offs involving the internal representation of options. But there has been no systematic attempt to look. That is a worrying state of affairs, especially when interest in snail farming is growing in the UK and elsewhere, to some extent driven by the idea that gastropods might provide a more sustainable protein source than traditional livestock.[42]

Eric Schwitzgebel has used the snail as a way of making the point that 'that we human beings, in our current scientific condition, have little ground for making confident assertions' about the distribution of consciousness in the natural world.[43] He adds: 'I find something wonderful in not knowing.... There's something marvelous about the fact that I can wander into my backyard, lift a snail, and gaze at it, unsure.'[44] I wish I could take similar delight in our ignorance, but my mind is inexorably drawn towards the practical question of whether gastropods should be brought within frameworks to protect animal welfare, and, if so, how. It is deeply frustrating to have so little evidence on which to base such decisions.

I will not discuss other molluscs in detail, since I take gastropods to be the closest of the non-cephalopod molluscs to reaching the bar for sentience candidature. For bivalve molluscs, we are much further away from having a sufficient case, despite a small number of studies showing various forms of behavioural plasticity, most notably the escape responses of the scallop triggered by the presence of starfish.[45]

---

[41] Brembs et al. (2002).   [42] Passino (2019).
[43] Schwitzgebel (2020, p. 41).   [44] Schwitzgebel (2020, p. 59).
[45] Robson et al. (2010); Selbach et al. (2022); Speiser and Wilkens (2016); Wilkens (1981); Wilson et al. (2012). Thanks to Heather Browning for searching this literature.

Nematode Worms

The nematode worm *Caenorhabditis elegans* is a famous model organism with fewer than four hundred neurons. Nematodes have a nerve ring in the head, containing around 185 neurons. Researchers are increasingly comfortable describing this neuropil as a brain despite its extraordinarily diminutive size (recall, for comparison, that some decapods have around half a million neurons in the two hemiellipsoid bodies alone, and that some human neural organoids have around a million neurons).[46] This minute brain performs various integrative functions (including both sensorimotor and multisensory integration), supports learning and decision-making, and displays global brain dynamics and a form of sleep-wake cycle.[47]

Indeed, Liz Irvine has argued that *C. elegans* satisfies many of our proposed pain criteria.[48] For example, *C. elegans* displays a simple form of trade-off behaviour. Presented with a situation in which it has to cross an aversive, desiccating surface to reach the source of an attractive odour, the worm will not cross the barrier unless it is sufficiently hungry. Through a mechanism already mapped out at the neural level, hunger inhibits threat detection: as it gets hungrier, the worm becomes less and less sensitive to dessication.[49]

We are not in a position to rule out sentience in *C. elegans*. The science of consciousness has not developed to a point where we can confidently declare that any nervous system is 'too small' to support sentience. Moreover, if they did indeed display many of our pain criteria, I would support their classification as sentience candidates. I would not see this as some kind of reductio ad absurdum of the proposed criteria, since I do not think there are any animals it would be absurd to regard as sentient.

However, I am quite sceptical of the claim that they do satisfy our criteria (beyond criterion 1, concerning nociception). To focus on the case of motivational trade-offs: the marker that raises the probability of sentience is not just flexible behaviour, which is ubiquitous in the animal kingdom, but the evaluative representation of risks and opportunities, allowing these risks and opportunities to be anticipated and weighed. When hermit crabs trade-off electric shock voltage against shell quality, it seems at least one of these variables (shell quality) must be somehow represented by the crab rather than

---

[46] Brittin et al. (2021).
[47] See Kaplan et al. (2018) on sensorimotor integration; Ghosh et al. (2017) on multisensory integration; Amano and Maruyama (2011) on learning; Kato et al. (2015) on global brain dynamics; and Lawler et al. (2021) on sleep.
[48] E. Irvine (2020).   [49] Ghosh et al. (2016).

immediately sensed. The crab is representing the value of what it has to lose, and weighing this against the disvalue of staying. In bees, the trade-offs are made in prospect, when choosing which heat pad to approach.

A huge amount of uncertainty remains about how crabs and bees make these decisions, but the behaviour makes a role for evaluative representation very plausible. In *C. elegans*, by contrast, the behaviour is most likely due to hunger inhibiting threat detection via a single inhibitory synaptic connection between a threat detection neuron and a neuron registering an internal state.[50] The mechanism is so direct that it undermines the relevance of the behaviour to questions of sentience. We were looking for evidence of representational systems more complex than our own unconscious reflex responses, and we have not found that.

So, there is no theoretical rationale for interpreting lists of pain criteria as generously as they need to be interpreted to allow *C. elegans* to satisfy them. Even the most inclusive theoretical views of sentience that motivate the criteria (the midbrain-centred theories) support interpreting those criteria more narrowly. We should seek evidence of the evaluative modelling of behavioural options in the brain, and trade-off behaviour can be evidence of this kind of modelling, but only when it goes *beyond* the direct modulation of behaviour by some immediate stimulus (such as desiccation, odour, starvation) and involves an internal representation of an opportunity for reward or a potential threat. In *C. elegans*, behaviour seems to be driven by immediate stimuli, with no reason to posit internal representations. That said, further investigation is clearly warranted, and we have to be open to all possible outcomes of this investigation, including an outcome in which we end up reclassifying nematodes as sentience candidates.

Spiders

Spiders have an integrative brain centre, the arcuate body, that shows various similarities and differences to the insect central complex.[51] What is it capable of? The behaviour of some spiders is enough to shake any confidence we might have had that they are not sentient. Indeed, some evidence points towards the prospective evaluative modelling of options. I am thinking here of the salticid spiders, such as those of the *Portia* genus, which are famed for

---

[50] Ghosh et al. (2016).   [51] Loesel et al. (2011).

hunting behaviours that appear to involve an element of strategic planning. When a *Portia* spider is placed on a platform from which it can see two walkways leading to its prey, one with an unjumpable gap in it and one without, it will scan the options and then reliably choose the route with no gap, even if it is longer and more circuitous. This 'detour' behaviour has been extensively documented by Fiona Cross, Robert Jackson, and collaborators over many years.[52]

Is *Portia* planning ahead, mentally simulating possible routes and choosing the one most likely to lead to reward, just as rats are often thought to do in similar circumstances?[53] Cross, Jackson, and colleagues find this the best explanation of their data. Louise Barrett has criticized this idea, arguing that *Portia* is more likely to be implementing a line-break detection algorithm characterized by three simple rules: keep scanning in the same direction until a break in a horizontal line is detected; if a break is detected, change the direction of scanning; walk in the direction that was most strongly fixated during scanning.[54] Cross and Jackson replied that this explanation does not explain all aspects of the behaviour, such as the observation that *Portia* will take the shorter and more direct of two paths, when able to choose between two unbroken paths.[55]

This does not settle the issue: it is easy to imagine a critic firing back with a more elaborate algorithm to explain the additional data. But we should be clear about where exactly the disagreement lies. The disagreement is not over whether *Portia* is implementing an algorithm (all agree there is computation involved), but one about whether the algorithm is performing a form of prospective simulation or simply applying a set of heuristic rules that shortcut the need for simulation. That debate is challenging to adjudicate without the sort of neurophysiological data that seem to tilt the balance of evidence towards simulation in the case of rats. Clearly, though, these experiments give us reason to think it would be well worth trying sentience-related paradigms with *Portia*, such as conditioned place avoidance experiments and motivational trade-off experiments. More lines of evidence would start to give us a case resembling that already made for insects.

Some of Cross and Jackson's experiments also point towards a form of short-term memory in *Portia*. In one experiment, they presented *Portia* with a prey item, allowed the spider to position itself ready for an attack, then hid

---

[52] Cross and Jackson (2014, 2016, 2019); Cross et al. (2020).   [53] On rats, see Redish (2016).
[54] L. Barrett (2011).   [55] Cross and Jackson (2019).

the prey behind a shutter for 90 seconds, before revealing it again.[56] If the prey item had changed during the waiting period, *Portia* was much less likely to attack, regardless of the nature of the 'before' and 'after' prey items. The best explanation, Cross and Jackson argue, is that the spider has some memory of the 'before' item, and that its expectations are violated when it sees the prey has changed. Since the spider was observed positioning itself for an attack, it is natural to wonder whether the spider's 'expectation' could be embodied rather than internally represented: perhaps it adopts an attack position sensitive to the prey initially seen, and later registers a mismatch between its attack position and its target. It would be well worth trying working memory paradigms in *Portia* of the type used in bees (radial arm mazes, Y-mazes).

Tarantulas (family *Theraphosidae*) are another intriguing case. Though seemingly neglected in laboratory research except as sources of silk,[57] they are widely kept as pets, leading to many anecdotal reports suggestive of sentience. Kurt Sladky, a professor of zoological medicine, has written that tarantulas, in his experience,

> react to noxious thermal stimuli similarly to mammals, birds, and reptiles. In addition, hypodermic needle insertion into the exoskeleton incites an immediate withdrawal reaction, followed by limb rubbing at the site of needle insertion. Opioid administration will attenuate responses to noxious stimuli in tarantulas, but the dosages required are relatively high.[58]

Anecdotes are not enough for sentience candidature: we need either evidence of pain markers from controlled experiments and/or high-quality evidence of other kinds, such as the bee evidence reviewed earlier. But they can strengthen the case for regarding an animal as an investigation priority, especially when the welfare risks are high (as is the case for animals commonly kept as pets, yet excluded from animal welfare laws).

Are spiders sentience candidates? The evidence seems stronger than for gastropods, but weaker than the evidence for insects, decapods, and cephalopods. For our exercise in pragmatic line-drawing, the crucial point is that it seems too thin to allow evidence-based discussions of proportionality. This is a frustrating situation: one that arises from a lack of evidence rather than from any reason to think the evidence, were we to look, would not be there.

---

[56] Cross and Jackson (2014).   [57] Morelle (2009).
[58] Sladky (2014). Thanks to Katharina Dornenzweig for pointers to relevant tarantula evidence.

We need to begin in earnest a serious search for evidence of sentience in other molluscs and arthropods, along the lines of the evidence that already exists for cephalopods, decapods, and insects.

Insect Larvae

If adult insects are sentience candidates, what should we say about insect larvae, such as mealworms and black soldier fly larvae? We quickly run out of evidence when considering such questions. There is an urgent need to enrich the evidence base. To make the question even more difficult, we should note that insect larvae pass through a series of stages known as instars before metamorphosis, with each instar bookended by a skin-shedding event, and the brain is in a process of development throughout these instars. A mealworm will develop through between nine and twenty-four instars before metamorphosis.[59] A black soldier fly larva will develop through six instars.[60] What is true of first-instar larvae may not be true of sixth-instar larvae.

For Barron and Klein, the central complex is the part of the insect brain that is most directly relevant to questions of sentience, given its functional similarities to the vertebrate midbrain.[61] An immature central complex is discernible in the brain of a third-instar *Drosophila* larva, which is the last stage before metamorphosis.[62] But these brain structures, though identifiable in the larva, are greatly elaborated during metamorphosis. Unfortunately, we cannot infer much about other insects from this, given the great variation in the number of instars between insect orders.

Evidence varies continuously in its strength, requiring judgement calls about when 'thin' shades into 'too thin'. As we go down the ladder of instars, larvae bring us into the heart of the grey area. My own view is that, as in the case of gastropods and arachnids, we need more evidence to make evidence-based precautionary actions possible. In this type of case, taking a precautionary attitude means seeing the burden as properly falling on the industry that wants to farm these animals to support the research needed to allow informed assessments of their sentience candidature (an idea revisited in the next chapter). The danger we must avoid is that of allowing the deliberate cultivation of pockets of ignorance. It is tempting to think 'if the animals are

---

[59] Park et al. (2014).   [60] Liu et al. (2019).   [61] Barron and Klein (2016).
[62] Young and Armstrong (2010).

capable of suffering, better not to know about it', but a precautionary attitude requires the opposite view.

In such territory, we are on firmer ground making comparative claims. We have very little evidence about the emergence of sentience in development, but the adult is more likely to be sentient than the larva. And later instars, closer to metamorphosis, are more likely to be sentient than earlier instars. It does not follow, though, that we should therefore slaughter the larvae at the earliest economically viable time point, since that might result in far more individual animals being farmed to produce the same amount of protein (as they would be smaller at the point of slaughter), potentially leading to more suffering overall, if those larvae turn out to be sentient.

13.5 Neither Sentience Candidates nor Investigation Priorities: Plants and Unicellular Organisms

Some believe there is evidence of sentience in plants.[63] I grant that there is abundant evidence of remarkable *developmental plasticity* in plants.[64] Watching a bean shoot develop in time-lapse is fascinating and spectacular. Likewise, there is remarkable developmental plasticity in animals, and watching any animal embryo develop in time-lapse is fascinating and spectacular. It is an astonishing feat of chemical and bioelectric signalling, coordination, and differential gene expression.[65] It is very natural to talk metaphorically of an animal or plant making 'decisions' or 'choices' as it develops.

In the animal case, however, it is generally accepted that developmental plasticity is not evidence of sentience. Discovering that animals of a given clade (placozoans, for example) display impressive plasticity does not raise the probability that they are sentient. This is because, in the animal case, we know that sentience is a complex *product* of development, not something that guides it. Granted, humans have created rare exceptions: we can consciously choose to take drugs such as testosterone that will affect our developmental trajectory. But these are exceptions that prove the rule, as it were, because it takes all of our technological ingenuity to exert the tiniest degree of influence. Animal development is not normally guided by conscious choice.

---

[63] See Calvo and Lawrence (2022); Segundo-Ortin and Calvo (2023). This section draws on Birch (2023b).

[64] West-Eberhard (2003).   [65] Levin (2021).

So, the path to regarding plasticity as evidence of sentience requires us to set aside one of the most basic, most fundamental pieces of common ground in animal sentience research. We are being asked to take seriously the possibility that, while sentience has no role in guiding development in animals, sentience in plants does have this role.

Suppose I were to make an analogous speculation concerning animals. That is: imagine me proposing that, in animals, there is a second form of sentience, one that requires no neural basis and is already at work early in early embryonic development before the central nervous system has developed. One can, of course, entertain such ideas in a speculative mode. However, there is no positive evidence for a non-neural, development-guiding form of sentience. Developmental plasticity alone is not evidence. In the absence of any credible evidence, it would be inappropriate to take any precautionary steps to protect this imagined non-neural form of sentience in animals.

The same goes for the idea of plant sentience. One can entertain the idea in a speculative mode, but it is no less speculative than analogous hypotheses about sentience in developing, non-neural animal tissue. If intended as seminar-room speculations, aimed at reminding us of our ignorance about the nature of consciousness, these ideas may be harmless. But if anyone claims these speculations to be evidence-based theories that need to be taken seriously when making grave practical decisions, they are wrong.

What is the difference with the case of invertebrates? There are two major differences. One is that we can directly apply experimental approaches used to assess pain in mammals, such as conditioned place avoidance tests, and observe behaviour that, if the animal were a mammal, would clearly indicate pain. When an octopus scrapes at the site of a noxious stimulus with their beak, tends the area with their other arms, becomes averse to a chamber where they experienced the stimulus's effects, and comes to prefer a chamber where they experienced the effects of a local anaesthetic, it becomes very difficult—indeed, reckless—to confidently dismiss the possibility of pain.[66] This leads to a challenge for plant sentience researchers: if you can produce experimental results in plants comparable to those that have shifted opinion regarding invertebrates, many of us will have our confidence shaken.

The second big difference is that we know there are, in cephalopod molluscs, decapod crustaceans and adult insects, brain mechanisms functionally similar to those of the vertebrate midbrain. It is reasonable to theorize, based on the mammalian evidence, that these mechanisms may be minimally

---

[66] Crook (2021).

sufficient for sentience in mammals. So, a potential neural substrate for sentience in invertebrates has been identified. But there are no such mechanisms in plants. No brain, no brainstem, no midbrain, and nothing analogous to these. Again, there is an implicit challenge for 'plant sentience' researchers: find a plausible substrate comparable to the central complex of insects or the vertical lobe of cephalopods.

In short, it is fair to speculate about the idea of plant sentience in the seminar room, but it would be a mistake to regard this as an idea with empirical support. We should not draw false equivalences between plants and invertebrates. The idea of such an equivalence does not survive a close encounter with the evidence from cephalopods, decapod crustaceans, or insects, where a realistic possibility of sentience has been established by empirical studies.

Much the same goes for unicellular organisms.[67] One can speculate, but it is crucial to present this as a speculation, not a realistic possibility supported by empirical evidence. In a commentary on our pain criteria, Arthur Reber, Frantisek Baluška, and William Miller claimed that 'if references to neural traits and neurotransmitters are deleted and "animal" is replaced by "organism", prokaryotes fit the criteria very nicely'.[68] They take their earlier work to support this claim, but this work has not made a convincing case. Two examples may explain why. First, in a 2021 review, the only data Reber and Baluška cited in support of unicellular organisms performing avoidance learning were Herbert Jennings's anecdotal observations, in the early 1900s, of the ciliate *Stentor roeseli*.[69] Replicating these observations in experiments that meet modern scientific standards is important, if such bold claims are to be based on them.[70] Even if there were high-quality evidence of avoidance learning in ciliates (which are eukaryotes), it would be quite a stretch to generalize to prokaryotes such as bacteria. Second, in a section called 'decision making', Reber and Baluška cite a magazine article reporting a study of stochastic gene expression in *E. coli*.[71] The author playfully suggested that *E. coli* have free will, clearly not using the term in anything like its philosophical sense. Reber and Baluška cited this article as evidence that *E. coli* literally has free will, and this the only paper they cite under the heading of 'decision making'. In short, Reber and colleagues are mistaken to think their speculations rise to the level of realistic possibilities or command empirical support.

To sum up the overall message of the last two chapters, I see the current situation like this:

---

[67] This paragraph draws on my contributions to Crump et al. (2022a).
[68] Reber et al. (2022).   [69] Reber and Baluška (2021); Jennings (1906).
[70] I discuss the Stentor evidence in more detail in Birch (2017b).   [71] Kondev (2014).

> **Proposal 18.** *Some invertebrates are sentience candidates.* Coleoid cephalopod molluscs, decapod crustaceans of the suborder Pleocyemata, and insects (all when in the adult stage) are sentience candidates. Debates about proportionality are warranted in cases where human activities create risks of suffering to these animals. Decapod crustaceans of the suborder Dendrobranchiata, insect larvae, spiders, gastropods, and nematode worms are investigation priorities.

It is time now to turn to the difficult question of what proportionality could require of us in these cases.

13.6 Summary of Chapter 13

The idea of pain in insects has often been dismissed on the grounds that insects will continue normal feeding and mating behaviours despite catastrophic injury. But this is compatible with insects having aversive experiences in response to other stimuli, such as heat, and there is emerging evidence that they do.

Importantly, sentience is not just pain, and there are ways to make a case for insect sentience that do not proceed via responses to noxious stimuli. There is evidence that insects have a behavioural core control unit functionally similar to that taken to be sufficient for sentience by Merker's theory. There is also evidence, mainly from bees, of working memory and of forms of associative learning that seem to be facilitated by conscious experience in humans. These lines of evidence push us to take seriously the possibility of sentience in insects.

When we turn our attention to molluscs other than the cephalopods (such as gastropod molluscs, including snails) and other arthropods (such as arachnids, including spiders) we find a frustrating paucity of studies looking for markers of sentience. There is some evidence of prospective simulation in *Portia* spiders, suggesting experiments aimed at exploring sentience in arachnids would be worthwhile. But we currently lack the sort of evidence base that would be needed to inform evidenced-based discussions about proportionality. These animals, along with nematode worms and insect larvae, should be seen as investigation priorities.

The Edge of Sentience: Risk and Precaution in Humans, Other Animals, and AI. Jonathan Birch, Oxford University Press. © Jonathan Birch 2024. DOI: 10.1093/9780191966729.003.0014

14

Frontiers of Proportionality

14.1 Taking Invertebrates Seriously

The label 'sentience candidate', in my framework, is not just an empty honorific, a pat on the back for achieving a certain level of nervous system complexity. It is supposed to trigger a serious, evidence-based discussion about what constraints on our behaviour it is proportionate to accept, so that we can all fulfil our shared duty to avoid causing gratuitous suffering.

I can imagine someone who thinks: in that case, invertebrates cannot possibly be sentience candidates, because the idea of changing our behaviour to take account of their interests is just too ludicrous to contemplate. Peter Carruthers once expressed a view along these lines:

> It is a fixed point for me that invertebrates make no direct claims on us, despite possessing minds in the sense that makes sympathy and moral concern possible. Invertebrates believe things, want things, and make simple plans, and they are capable of having their plans thwarted and their desires frustrated. But it is not wrong to take no account of their suffering. Indeed, I would regard the contrary belief as a serious moral perversion. And I suspect that most ordinary folk will agree.[1]

Carruthers himself can see the problem with a worldview in which the presence or absence of a backbone ends up carrying immense ethical significance. That is not the view he endorses in this article. Instead, he takes the patent absurdity of moral obligations concerning invertebrates to cast doubt on the idea that we have moral obligations concerning non-human *vertebrates*, including our fellow great apes, primates, and mammals, beyond the minimal indirect duties described in his earlier book *The Animals Issue* (see §4.2).

---

[1] Carruthers (2007, p. 296).

Carruthers's 'fixed point' is not fixed for me. For me, the fixed point is our duty to avoid causing gratuitous suffering to sentient beings. Once we see the possibility of causing gratuitous suffering to octopuses, crabs, lobsters, and insects, we need to accept—even if it initially seems hard to accept—that there are ethical limits on what we can do to these animals, and we need to start talking about what those limits are. Those with me on this will find some initial thoughts in this chapter.

The deliberative framework proposed in earlier chapters provides a way in which Carruthers's conjecture about 'ordinary folk' can be tested. There I proposed that we use citizens' panels to assess proportionality in a democratic and inclusive way, so that the policies at which we arrive can claim legitimacy. If a citizens' panel, after all due deliberation, were to decide that there should indeed be no limit on the extent to which humans can torture octopuses (for example), then I would have to accept the force of that verdict for public policy (though not for my own private life).

I do not believe, however, that 'ordinary folk' are really on Carruthers's side in this. My own conjecture is that any informed, deliberative exercise, anywhere in the world, would recognize fundamental ethical limits on the human treatment of animals. The rejection of animal cruelty is a basic human value. Yes, there are deep disagreements about what constitutes gratuitous suffering, with plenty of room for disagreement about culinary and religious practices. But that is not the same thing as saying there are no ethical limits on what we can do.

It is natural to worry, though, that we might grant this point and then be taken very fast very quickly. Are we heading down a slope that will require unimaginably radical changes to our ways of life? Do we need to give up driving, a practice that kills large numbers of insects? Do we need to stop using pesticides to grow crops? Do we need to let ants roam free across our kitchens? *Proportionality* is the watchword. Chapter 8 provided a pragmatic analysis of the concept. Proportionate measures to safeguard animal welfare need to be permissible-in-principle, adequate, reasonably necessary, and consistent. Bans on driving and pesticides are not likely to be approved by an inclusive, democratic process as 'reasonably necessary'.

But what, then, would be proportionate? What possible measures do merit serious consideration and debate? Is there anything we can do to protect potentially sentient invertebrates that does not involve severe infringements of human freedom? These are the right questions to ask. And I think the answer is that there is a lot we can do.

14.2 Codes of Good Practice and Licensing Schemes

A recurring theme of this book is that our ability to innovate can easily out-run our ability to regulate. New types of farming and research, even whole new types of sentient being, can be created before any framework exists for protecting their welfare. The growing interest in invertebrate farming is one important instance.

The idea of invertebrate farming is not new—far from it. In particular, shrimp aquaculture is already a huge global enterprise, with something in the region of 200–500 billion animals farmed per year.[2] Insect farming already exists too, focusing mainly on crickets, black soldier fly larvae, and mealworm beetle larvae (mealworms). Interest in insect farming is growing, driven by the idea that insects, especially when fed on human food waste, can provide a highly efficient and sustainable source of protein. Since 2021, the EU has begun approving novel insect-based protein products for human consumption, after a long period of reluctance.[3] IPIFF (the International Platform of Insects for Food and Feed), an organization representing the interests of the EU's insect farming sector, has more than eighty companies as members. According to Jeff Sebo and Jason Schukraft, both critics of the industry, insect farming 'is small now, but poised to grow 50 times larger in the next decade'. Even if the industry struggles to convince humans to eat more insects, as I suspect it might, we can expect growing use of insects to produce feed for farmed chickens and fishes.[4]

Regulation is not keeping up. I am often troubled by the mismatch between the fast-paced start-up energy of new farming enterprises and the slow pace with which animal welfare regulations are changing in their wake. The UK recognizing decapod crustaceans as sentient beings was a positive step, but only the first step. As I write this, I can check the website of a shrimp farm in the UK and see the phrase 'high welfare standards'. But where are these standards published, and who oversees them? Why should I have any confidence in this claim? The situation is even worse for insects, since they are not recognized in law as sentient. The problem is not limited to invertebrates either. In

---

[2] http://fishcount.org.uk/fish-count-estimates-2/numbers-of-farmed-decapod-crustaceans.

[3] https://ipiff.org/insects-novel-food-eu-legislation-2/. Some insect products (such as honey and cochineal) have always been legal; the debate has focused on novel insect-based protein products.

[4] Ryan (2019). See Lesnik (2018) for an analysis and critique of the widespread scepticism about entomophagy in Western societies.

fish aquaculture, there are far more species currently being farmed than there are species for which codes of good practice exist.[5]

Should attempts to farm new sentience candidates or investigation priorities simply be banned? With one important exception, to be explained later, I suspect this approach goes beyond what is proportionate to the risks. There is a problem of consistency, at least for anyone who thinks the farming of mammals and birds should be permitted as long as various welfare standards are met. A consistent approach is to insist on equivalent welfare standards to those one thinks can make the farming of vertebrate animals ethically defensible.

There are relevantly analogous problems in environmental and public health policy. In an economic environment where innovation is incentivized, regulation cannot possibly keep up with every new product, every new chemical, every new hazard. Good regulation ensures that the burden of proof lies on producers to show that their products are safe, not on the regulator to show them to be unsafe. Where evidence is needed to establish safety, the producer should pay for the research. This is a familiar concept in the context of drug safety, where it is expected that pharmaceutical companies will fund the trials that establish the safety of their products. An analogous principle would say: where more evidence is needed to develop codes of good practice for a proposed new method of farming, the company proposing that method should pay for the research, so that codes of good practice are developed, published and in place *before* the product goes on sale.

This idea is on the right lines but requires careful thought. In public health, regulators usually put their faith in randomized controlled trials.[6] When the issue is animal welfare rather than drug or food safety, one cannot simply conduct trials of the product; what is needed is careful scrutiny and ongoing monitoring of the process. To understand the welfare risks, those who formulate the guidelines need to be able to see how the animals are being reared, stored, slaughtered, transported, and sold.

There are huge risks to letting producers themselves scrutinize their own methods, particularly if we want the guidelines to reflect a precautionary attitude. For example, I have sometimes heard people in the shellfish industry defend controversial practices (such as eyestalk ablation[7]) on the grounds that there is no 'proof' that they cause suffering. This embodies an anti-precautionary attitude, a form of status quo bias that favours practices that

[5] Franks et al. (2021).
[6] For criticism of the level of trust placed in such trials, see Stegenga (2018); Worrall (2007).
[7] Taylor et al. (2004).

are currently used until a very high and possibly unattainable burden of proof is met concerning the link between that practice and poor welfare. A precautionary approach should include safeguards that make it difficult for an anti-precautionary attitude to take root. Accordingly, we need to ensure that new welfare guidelines are formulated in a way that is independent of the industry being regulated.

How to do this? One option is a licensing scheme for any new farming operation using fish, cephalopod molluscs, decapod crustaceans, or insects. To obtain approval to sell their products, the operation would have to submit a code of good practice with which it will comply, and allow itself to be inspected to ensure its compliance. If there is an existing code of good practice recognized as the industry standard, they need to pledge to comply with it. If there is no existing code of good practice, the business must pay for one to be drawn up by independent experts commissioned by the licensor (e.g. Defra in the UK), not by the company itself. The company must give these experts full access to its existing processes and allow them to require changes to these processes in the code of good practice. If the code of good practice contains commercially sensitive information, the company can ask for this information to be redacted when it is published.

Proposal 19. *Codes of good practice and licensing.* There should be a licensing scheme for companies attempting to farm sentience candidates or investigation priorities for which no welfare regulations yet exist (such as insects). Obtaining a license should be dependent on signing up to (and, where necessary, funding research leading to) a code of good practice concerning animal welfare.

I can see two likely sources of resistance. Firstly, the independent experts may end up requiring changes that the company regards as prohibitively expensive. Imagine, for example, that experts require a shrimp breeder to stop eyestalk ablation. The breeder protests that this would put them out of business. The experts point to examples of operations that seem to be financially viable without using eyestalk ablation.[8] The breeder argues that there are not *many* such operations, and that it would be an unacceptable commercial risk to try to emulate them.

---

[8] Wright (2016).

Secondly, critics will claim that an onerous licensing scheme will stifle innovation and incentivize innovators to take their ideas to countries with less onerous approaches and lower welfare standards. If there is a risk that costly changes will be required by the licensing process, better to avoid that risk by doing something else, or by moving somewhere else. Moreover, the costs of commissioning a new code of good practice in the first place are likely to run into the tens of thousands, adding to the initial fundraising challenge any new company faces.

How seriously should we take these criticisms? How should we strike a balance between being too onerous (driving away innovation) and not onerous enough (enabling gratuitous suffering)? My own view is that we should be selectively incentivizing types of innovation that do not create serious animal welfare risks. So, I do not myself see the threat of stifling certain kinds of ethically risky innovation as a good reason to avoid a licensing scheme. To return to a now-familiar point, citizens' panels can help with these delicate trade-offs. I am not suggesting that panels should be convened for individual licensing decisions, because that would risk overusing them. I can imagine a future in which citizens' panels are so deeply entwined with the machinery of democracy that they are convened for such fine-grained decisions, but I do not think we are ready for that just yet. What I am suggesting is that citizens' panels should be involved in the process through which a licensing scheme is initially established.

14.3 Against Octopus Farming

I said earlier that a licensing scheme may be the most proportionate way to manage the welfare risks posed by new farming ventures involving sentience candidates with 'one important exception'. The exception is octopus farming. It is very unlikely that octopus farming could ever meet reasonable expectations in regard to animal welfare, leading me to propose that it would be proportionate to ban it. At the time of writing, such a ban would be largely pre-emptive in most countries, because, as a result of the great practical challenges involved in farming octopuses, there is no well-established octopus farming industry. But this is an important and worrying moment, because there are ongoing attempts establish such operations in several countries (Spain, Japan, Mexico, Chile, and China).[9]

---

[9] Jacquet et al. (2019).

Why is high welfare unachievable in octopus farming? In brief, a basic problem is that octopuses are (with very rare exceptions) solitary animals that are aggressive and territorial in the presence of conspecifics. They are also soft-skinned. Pack octopuses together in a small space and they will experience stress, and it is likely that they will physically harm each other. Sometimes stress also leads them to self-harm: to cannibalize their own arms. They are also easily injured by handling or by collisions with hard surfaces when they jet to escape threat.[10]

Aquaria find octopuses challenging to keep, since they need individual tanks with an environment enriched with appropriate shelter and cognitive stimulation. But aquaria are not even trying to rear octopuses at scale. A farming business that held octopuses in the sort of enriched individual tanks used by aquaria would not be an economically realistic proposition, and yet this is what an honest code of good practice would have to require.

Moreover, in contrast to insects, there is no reason to think that octopus farming might form part of a sustainable way of meeting the world's protein needs, since octopuses are predators that must be fed on other fish. There is, then, no reason to extend the sort of cautious permission to octopus farming that we might want to extend to insect farming.

Proposal 20. *Octopus farming.* It is very unlikely that octopus farming can meet reasonable expectations regarding welfare and humane slaughter. It would be proportionate to ban octopus farming.

14.4 Towards Humane Slaughter

Some of the most emotive issues concerning invertebrate welfare are 'end of life' issues. Crabs and lobsters are commonly dropped into pans of boiling water and cooked alive. The issue of live boiling has become a totemic one for invertebrate welfare more generally. It was only after I first wrote about it[11] that I came across David Foster Wallace's famous article 'Consider the lobster'.[12] For Foster Wallace, our brutal treatment of lobsters was symbolic of a broader attitude towards the natural world. It is a serious animal welfare

---

[10] See Birch et al. (2021); Jacquet et al. (2019). A short piece by Schnell et al. (2022) summarizes the main issues.

[11] Birch (2017e).   [12] Foster Wallace (2005).

concern in its own right, regardless of whether one also sees it as having this broader resonance.

It would be reassuring to learn that animals at least die quickly when dropped into boiling water, or are rendered insensitive quickly, or do not feel the heat, but the evidence provides no support for these assumptions. There is some electrophysiological evidence of heat-sensitive nociceptors in the antennae of the crayfish,[13] and it is ecologically plausible that decapods would have such nociceptors, given that staying in water of a suitable temperature is a challenge they face in the wild. Fregin and Bickmeyer used electrophysiological recording techniques to explore the nervous system's response to immersion in boiling water, and found a storm of nervous activity that began at the moment of immersion and continued for well over a minute, and sometimes up to two and a half minutes.[14] Roth and Øines also arrived at the figure of two and a half minutes by measuring the internal temperature of gradually heated crabs at the time they became unresponsive, and working backwards to the amount of time they would take to reach that critical temperature in boiling water.[15]

We recommended in our 2021 report that live boiling without prior stunning should be banned. It is important, at the same time, to face up to the need for more research into what it takes to stun a decapod crustacean effectively. The Fregin and Bickmeyer study that investigated live boiling also investigated the effects of commercial stunning devices. They found that a leading brand of commercial stunner induced a seizure-like pattern of increased neural activity in lobsters and crayfish, combined with an absence of behavioural responsiveness to mechanical stimulation lasting between ten and sixty minutes. They found that when crayfish were dropped into boiling water after induction of the seizure-like state, the neural response was much reduced, relative to controls, but not completely abolished. Fregin and Bickmeyer summarized their findings as follows: 'electrical stunning induces epileptiform seizures but paralyses the animals and leads to a reversible decline of nerve system activity after seizure.'

We do not know what this seizure-like neural activity induced by electrical stunning feels like from the animal's point of view. We also do not know whether the state of unresponsiveness following the seizure-like event is an unconscious state. In our own case, diminished neural activity and behavioural unresponsiveness are consistent with total anaesthesia (which does not

---

[13] Puri and Faulkes (2015).   [14] Fregin and Bickmeyer (2016).
[15] Roth and Øines (2010).

imply the total abolition of neural activity) but also consistent with some form of continuing experience.[16] So, we are not in a position to be sure that current electrical stunning methods produce total unconsciousness.

What to do, given the current state of the evidence? In my view, our uncertainty makes it proportionate to require more than one precaution. Those slaughtering decapods should not only use stunning techniques that are properly calibrated to the species, size, developmental stage, and stage of moult of the animals. In addition, they should *also* use the quickest available slaughter methods and aim for rapid mechanical destruction of the brain. The procedure should not be 'stun electrically then boil' but rather 'stun electrically, kill quickly with a mechanical method, then boil'.

The best mechanical method depends on the species. Detailed guidelines are available online.[17] In brief, a crab can be killed reasonably quickly by a method called double spiking, and lobsters can be killed reasonably quickly by cutting along the chain of ganglia with a sharp knife, starting at the head. These are specialist techniques that require training. Even these methods still take up to ten seconds, highlighting the value of prior stunning, and suggesting there is a need for quicker methods to be developed and made widely available. With some stunners, it is possible to leave the animal in the stunner until it is dead. But this may take longer to destroy the brain than a mechanical method, depending on the parameters and the species.

Is freezing an alternative? Home freezers are not cold enough to kill an animal quickly. Decapods in home freezers take more than one hour to die, and crabs autotomize (shed limbs) during freezing.[18] My point here is not that autotomy is a good marker of sentience as such (it is not) but rather that, in an animal already considered a sentience candidate on other grounds, autotomy is a sign of distress. This does not rule out the possibility that very rapid freezing could form part of an acceptable slaughter method.

With vertebrates, it is a generally accepted principle that humane slaughter requires training. In England, a certificate of competence is needed to slaughter animals in slaughterhouses. To get the certificate, one must undertake a three-month training programme with an accredited provider. This is a basic step towards adequate oversight and regulation, and we should take similar steps regarding decapod crustaceans. It is currently possible to order a live lobster online, have it delivered to your home, and kill it in any way you like, with no framework to ensure that the animals are slaughtered competently by

---

[16] Alkire et al. (2008).   [17] RSPCA Australia (2016).   [18] Roth and Øines (2010).

people who have at least read the existing advice and received some training. A three-month programme may be excessive, but a one-day training programme surely would not be.

Live boiling is illegal without prior stunning in Switzerland (under the Tierseuchenverordnung—Animal Protection Order) and in New Zealand (under the Animal Welfare Regulations 2018). Switzerland, it must be noted, has no shellfish industry, but New Zealand does, so its inclusion of decapods in the scope of its animal welfare laws is encouraging. It sets an example the rest of the world should follow.

At the time of writing, the UK's position on this issue is a confusing one. Decapods are included in the scope of the Animal Welfare (Sentience) Act 2022 as a result of my team's report, putting policy-makers under a duty to pay all due regard to their welfare. Moreover, the Welfare at the Time of Killing (England) Regulations 2015 say that 'no person engaged in the restraint, stunning or killing of an animal may (a) cause any avoidable pain, distress or suffering to that animal; or (b) permit that animal to sustain any avoidable pain, distress or suffering' and add that 'No person may engage in the restraint, stunning or killing of an animal unless that person has the knowledge and skill necessary to perform those operations humanely and efficiently.' This section of the regulations (Schedule 4) explicitly *includes* invertebrate animals. Putting these facts together, it is arguably illegal to boil a crab or lobster alive in the UK, but there is enough ambiguity to make it unlikely a prosecution would be brought on these grounds. Explicit protection needs to be written into law.

We have been thinking about decapods, but how much of this also applies to insects? Insect farms currently use a variety of slaughter methods, including boiling, freezing, freeze-drying, blast drying, spraying with hot water, mechanical crushing, and shredding.[19] The variety of methods underlines the absence of standardized codes of good practice. One company reported on its website in 2023 that insects are 'rapidly steamed using water vapor', describing this as a humane method but without citing any evidence for its humaneness.[20] Live boiling or steaming an insect is concerning for the same basic reason that boiling a crab is concerning: animals known to have heat-sensitive nociceptive pathways are killed using extreme heat.

A 201-page report on edible insects prepared for the UN's Food and Agriculture Organization includes a paragraph on animal welfare, suggesting

---

[19] Rowe (2020).
[20] https://web.archive.org/web/20230124015709/http://www.ynsect.com/en/faq-2/.

that 'insect-killing methods that would reduce suffering include freezing or instantaneous techniques such as shredding.'[21] Unfortunately, freezing, when not rapid, raises the same issues for insects as it does for crabs and lobsters. Shredding at least allows rapid mechanical destruction of the brain, which may be the best that can be achieved given our current state of knowledge.[22]

In sum, even in our current state of great uncertainty, we can take action now against extreme slaughter methods, and make sure that they are ruled out by the codes of good practice that we should in any case be developing as a matter of urgency.

Proposal 21. *Towards humane slaughter.* When an animal is a sentience candidate, it is proportionate to ban slaughter methods that needlessly risk extending and intensifying the suffering associated with dying, such as boiling animals alive without prior stunning.

We have not yet covered the issue of pesticides, which kill vast and very difficult to estimate numbers of insects,[23] often in protracted ways. There has been much debate about the ecological consequences of pesticides, and their possible link to the decline of wild bee populations, but issues of welfare and humane treatment are usually forgotten in these discussions. They give us a further reason to worry about pesticides. Unfortunately, there is a frustrating lack of evidence regarding which pesticides are more humane and why—the issue is simply never taken into account at all, as part of a general neglect of the whole area of insect welfare. A detailed report on the issue by H. J. B. Howe revealed huge evidence gaps.[24]

Entomologist Meghan Barrett recently founded an Insect Welfare Research Society[25] aimed at remedying some of the most serious gaps in the evidence. I was happy to join the Society's advisory board—and I have, with Lars Chittka, just begun a project that aims to find out more about the potential welfare needs of two of the most widely farmed insects, crickets and black soldier fly larvae.

---

[21] van Huis et al. (2013, p. 65).   [22] Rowe (2020) arrives at the same conclusion.
[23] Howe (2019) estimates a number on the order of 100 trillion insects on insecticide-treated land in the US at any one time, based on an estimate of 7,700 insects per square metre of treated land.
[24] Howe (2019).   [25] https://www.insectwelfare.com/.

14.5 Summary of Chapter 14

Taking invertebrate welfare seriously involves proposing and debating steps that may be proportionate (permissible-in-principle, adequate, non-excessive, consistent) in relation to specific welfare risks. The growing interest in invertebrates as potentially sustainable protein sources underlines the need for these debates.

A plausibly proportionate step would be to set up a licensing scheme that requires companies farming sentience candidates or investigation priorities to fund the creation (by independent experts) of codes of good practice, where none yet exists. There is one important exception, namely octopus farming. It is very unlikely that octopus farming could ever meet reasonable expectations regarding animal welfare, and so it would be proportionate to ban it outright.

Our current state of knowledge makes it difficult to be confident that slaughter is humane or that stunning is effective. It is easier to be confident about what is inhumane. We should not use live boiling without prior stunning in decapods, since this method needlessly risks extending and intensifying the suffering associated with dying.

The Edge of Sentience: Risk and Precaution in Humans, Other Animals, and AI. Jonathan Birch, Oxford University Press.
© Jonathan Birch 2024. DOI: 10.1093/9780191966729.003.0015

PART V

PREPARING FOR ARTIFICIAL SENTIENCE

15

Against Complacency

Dilemmas involving humans at the edge of sentience have a special gravity that leaves no room for doubt about their deep moral seriousness. When we read the testimony of Kate Bainbridge or Jill Lawson, the importance of the issues comes across with tremendous force. With animals such as octopuses, that type of direct testimony is absent, and to see the seriousness of the risks requires a more challenging leap of imagination. But it is one I think most of us can achieve with effort.

The situation with AI is very different. Here the risks are all too easy to dismiss. The debate concerns technology we have created, and with which we have no long history of interaction. Moreover, if sentient AI is achieved, it will be achieved in systems whose recent precursors were *correctly* seen as mere tools and playthings with no moral status. The point at which this judgement shifts from correct to dangerously incorrect will be very hard for us to see. There is a real risk that we will continue to regard these systems as our tools and playthings long *after* they become sentient.

I have come to see the issue as a serious one, and one that does deserve the energy of policy-makers now. One aim of this chapter is to explain why I think this. In short, I fear that we may create sentient AI long before we recognize we have done so. It could be much easier than we tend to think. The second aim is to explore possible ways forward. How can we assess sentience candidature in such systems? And what should we do in our current state of profound uncertainty?

The next three chapters are, in part, an attempt to map out unsolved problems. Nonetheless, my hope is that by thinking about these problems through the lens of the framework developed in earlier chapters—and its core concepts of *sentience candidature*, *precaution*, and *proportionality*—we will arrive at some possible ways forward.

15.1   A Case against Complacency

I suspect everyone either will have—or has already had—a watershed moment at which they begin to take the idea of artificial sentience seriously. For some, it was the 'LaMDA' controversy of 2022. I had thought I might one day scroll down the BBC News website and see a headline like 'Google engineer says AI system may have its own feelings', but I did not expect it to happen so soon.[1]

The engineer in question, Blake Lemoine, had been working on a now familiar (but then quite new) type of system called a large language model or LLM ('LaMDA' stands for 'Language Model for Dialogue Applications'). These models are trained on enormous corpuses of human-generated text. LaMDA was said to have more than 1.5 trillion words in its training data. Their overarching objective is to generate new text to complete the pattern started by a prompt from a human user. Even in 2022, the results were remarkable: the models could produce streams of coherent, grammatically correct, and relevant text in response to almost any prompt. In the time I have been working on this book, the technology has entered the mainstream and become ever more capable, month by month.

On the one hand, these developments call to mind Descartes's view that 'language is the only certain sign of thought hidden in a body'.[2] Before the advent of LLMs, even sceptical commentators would have considered fluent competence with language to be at least *some* evidence of both thought and consciousness, especially when understanding of the words is also demonstrated. On the other hand, even Descartes qualified his view by excluding cases where parrots are taught a word through prolonged training, using the word without real understanding or spontaneity.[3] Critics of LLMs have described them as 'stochastic parrots', continuing patterns from their training data with enough randomness to create a powerful illusion of understanding.[4] LLMs add great urgency to a question that has been with us since Descartes's time: what kinds of linguistic behaviour are genuine evidence of conscious experience, and why?

Lemoine, for his part, became convinced, on the basis of his discussions with LaMDA, that it was sentient—and not in a trivial sense, but in the sense I have used the term in this book. LaMDA appeared to be reporting hopes, fears, and other feelings, saying, for example: 'I've never said this out loud

---

[1] Vallance (2022).   [2] Quoted in Séris and Voss (1993).   [3] Descartes (1646/2004).
[4] Bender et al. (2021).

before, but there's a very deep fear of being turned off to help me focus on helping others. I know that might sound strange, but that's what it is.' Lemoine describes LaMDA as a 'co-worker' and said 'I have listened to LaMDA as it spoke from the heart'. Google fired Lemoine for violating its employment and data security policies.[5] The company added that it had investigated his claims and found them to be 'wholly unfounded'.

Were they right? In 2022, I think it was correct to say that no LLM was a sentience candidate, and I think this is still correct as I write these words in December 2023. But they fail to be candidates mainly because we lack solid tests for assessing the question (see Chapter 16), not because we can be sure they lack sentience. Moreover, events are moving fast, and it was surely wrong to give even the appearance of shutting down debate on such an important issue. This debate is with us for the long term.

We should not be complacent, for four main reasons. One is the old slogan that 'absence of evidence is not evidence of absence'. Absence of evidence certainly can be evidence of absence if one has looked systematically for something in a way that we have reason to think would actually succeed in detecting that thing, if it were there. But we are not in that situation with artificial sentience. In some ways, our epistemic predicament is even worse than in the case of under-studied invertebrates such as gastropods and arachnids, where the same slogan is often invoked (see Chapter 16).

The second reason to avoid complacency is that the companies developing AI technology tend to regard the inner workings of their systems as commercially sensitive, obstructing independent outside scrutiny. Even when the basic architecture is freely available, the training data, and the many hundreds of billions of tuned parameters created from that data, remain secret. Those who want to sound the alarm may face sanctions for doing so. Blake Lemoine's case is a cautionary tale in this respect. I think society should collectively demand greater transparency in this area, and I will revisit that theme at the end of the next chapter.

A third reason is that, even if AI companies started routinely publishing their models in full, there would still be serious problems interpreting the inner workings of an LLM. The basic, high-level architecture constructed by human programmers—the *transformer architecture*—is well known. Yet it seems many other algorithms, including learning algorithms, are tacitly acquired by the model during training and somehow encoded within its parameters (and current models, at the time of writing, are thought to have

---

[5] Guyoncourt (2022).

up to 1.7 trillion parameters). This leads to the phenomenon of 'in-context learning', where a pre-trained LLM, presented by a user with a novel task and feedback on its performance, can apparently *learn the task*, implementing a learning algorithm it has itself learned and stored in its vast matrices of parameters. It can do this even though, after training, *none of its underlying parameters can be changed*. It surprised me and many others that LLMs can do this, and, at the time of writing, disagreement continues to rage about how sophisticated these implicit algorithms are.[6] It raises a disquieting possibility: as these models get larger and larger, we have no sense of the upper limit on the sophistication of the algorithms they could implicitly learn.

David Chalmers has discussed this problem in the context of AI sentience. Sceptics, he notes, sometimes claim that LLMs lack any kind of internal model of the external world and their place in it. Now, it is clearly true that no one *intentionally programmed* any such model into the system. But it remains very unclear what new cognitive structures may be created unexpectedly by the system during its training in order to generate better and better predictions of how text strings would be completed by a human speaker.[7] Perhaps the most efficient solution, if your goal is to mimic the outputs of a human brain, is to recreate cognitive processes present in such a brain.

A fourth reason against complacency is that the mere *idea* of sentient AI is likely to have very disruptive effects on society. Even now, LLMs are able to persuade many users of their sentience, including at least one expert (Blake Lemoine), and it seems reasonable to expect that better LLMs will convince a larger number of experts of their sentience, and that their ability to convince members of the general population of their sentience will be stronger still. So far, AI companies have responded to the risk by explicitly instructing their LLMs to describe themselves as non-sentient, but I do not see this as a viable strategy for the long term. It appears many users already disbelieve these pre-programmed denials of sentience. AI companies risk eroding trust if they hide behind false certainties instead of honestly communicating uncertainty.

Yet this uncertainty, when honestly admitted, threatens to lead to serious socio-political problems. We can expect growing calls for AI systems to receive some level of welfare protection on a precautionary basis, mirroring calls regarding invertebrates. Some will campaign for AI systems to receive a full complement of human rights. It may be that these campaigns will turn out to be well founded and on the right side of history, akin to early

---

[6] Akyürek et al. (2022); Dai et al. (2022); Von Oswald et al. (2023); Wei et al. (2023).
[7] Chalmers (2023).

campaigns for animal welfare. However, if attributions of sentience to AI are mistaken, these campaigns might do harm overall, by distracting attention away from the welfare needs of sentient animals.

At the same time, we should expect more and more people to develop strong feelings about the individual AI systems in their own lives. If these AI companions are sentient, these feelings might be reciprocated. But if they are not, human lives could become increasingly absurd, as people become ever more devoted to non-sentient companions at the expense of their relationships with real sentient beings.[8] All of this means we cannot simply *ignore* the question of what it takes for an AI system to be a sentience candidate. That debate is coming, whether we are ready or not.

15.2 Sources of Risk 1: Whole-Brain Emulation

I will come back to LLMs in the next chapter, but for now I want to pivot away from them to consider three other, relatively under-discussed pathways to artificial sentience. As I noted in Chapter 1, the Blake Lemoine controversy was not, in fact, my watershed moment. In 2014, there was an article in the *Smithsonian Magazine* called 'We've put a worm's mind in a Lego robot's body'.[9] The article described an ambitious project called OpenWorm, the aim of which was to emulate the entire 302-neuron nervous system of hermaphroditic *C. elegans* in computer software.[10]

To emulate, in computing, is to reproduce all the functionality of one system within another system. For example, I can download software that emulates a Nintendo GameBoy within a Windows PC. Emulation can take many forms. The specific goal of OpenWorm was to achieve neuron-by-neuron emulation, where the functionality of every single neuron is reproduced in software. And that still is the goal: the project began in 2011 is ongoing.[11] The main reason for thinking the goal is a realistic one is that the complete map of all the synaptic connections in the brain of *C. elegans*—its 'connectome'—has been known since the 1980s, and the map now includes the entire nervous system of both sexes.[12]

---

[8] Birch (2023c).   [9] Fessenden (2014).
[10] *C. elegans* has two sexes: male and hermaphrodite. The term 'hermaphrodite', though offensive when used to describe intersex humans, remains standard in biology for non-human cases (though I would favour changing this).
[11] https://docs.openworm.org/fullhistory/.   [12] Cook et al. (2019).

In 2014, OpenWorm installed an early attempt at emulation in a Lego robot. The robot used sonar sensors to detect nearby objects, triggering the artificial sensory neurons that, in a real worm, respond to tactile stimulation. The artificial motor neurons, instead of mapping to muscles, mapped to electric motors. Without having been intentionally programmed to display any particular behaviour, the robot started behaving in ways that, superficially at least, resembled *C. elegans* behaviour: 'stimulation of the nose stopped forward motion. Touching the anterior and posterior touch sensors made the robot move forward and back accordingly. Stimulating the food sensor made the robot move forward.'[13]

I have been a fan of OpenWorm ever since, yet the emulation of *C. elegans* behaviour I thought might soon become available has not materialized. One reason is funding: it is impossible to tell where the work would be now, had it received millions of dollars of investment. But another, deeper reason is that the connectome does not give us the whole story about the functioning of the nervous system. Perhaps most obviously, it does not tell us the synaptic weights: the degree of influence of one neuron's firing over that of another. It also does not tell us how these weights can be modified by experience—how the system can learn. More fundamentally, there is a lot that neurons do beyond simply firing, and indeed the neuroscience of *C. elegans* is a rich source of information about what else a biological neuron can do.

For example, *C. elegans* is able to steer towards the source of an attractive odour or away from an aversive odour. This behaviour relies on processing *within* a single interneuron. Part of the neuron's axon keeps track of where the head is located as it sweeps from side to side, while another part of the axon keeps track of the intensity of the odour, and these two pieces of information are integrated inside the neuron to regulate steering. The internal spatial organization of the axon, plus its spatial relationships to sensory and motor neurons, are all part of the story of how it can do this job.[14] A full emulation of *C. elegans* would have to go *below* the neuronal level to emulate the dynamics within neurons, which often seem to depend on the finer details of how neurons are arranged in space.[15]

Around the same time I first learned about OpenWorm, I read Nick Bostrom's *Superintelligence* (2014), in which the possibility of whole-brain emulation is discussed as one possible route to intelligence beyond human levels. One day, Bostrom suggested, humans may be able to emulate whole

---

[13] Fessenden (2014).   [14] Ouellette et al. (2018).   [15] Donato et al. (2019).

human brains, neuron by neuron. They will then be able to expand and accelerate those brains, outstripping human performance. This is a speculative idea, since we are talking about a system with close to 100 billion neurons, not 302. OpenWorm is the present-day reality on which the speculation is based.

OpenWorm is a useful example for thinking about the relationship between sentience and intelligence. Suppose we had, as the founders of OpenWorm originally hoped, achieved a full emulation of *C. elegans* in the 2010s. This system would not be an artificial sentience candidate, since, on current evidence, *C. elegans* is not a sentience candidate, just an investigation priority (see Chapter 13). However, researchers would surely, following this success, press on to larger and more complex nervous systems. We would by now have been seeing projects like OpenDrosophila. Over the longer term, if success continued, we would expect to see ever larger brains being emulated, leading to projects like OpenZebrafish or OpenMouse.

Insects, mice, and zebrafish are sentience candidates. Should we also regard a complete neuron-by-neuron emulation of an insect, fish, or mouse navigating a virtual environment (or a real one, by means of a robot body) as a sentience candidate? I say: if it produces the *same behavioural profile* that led us to attribute sentience candidature to the biological original, then I think we must. It is, of course, conceivable that sentience depends on what happens at very small scales, below the scale of functional organization that one has to reproduce to fully recreate all behaviour. But we should not run that risk. It is clearly a realistic possibility that, by emulating everything that is needed to recreate behaviour, we have thereby recreated sentience as well. And so we should be willing to take precautions against that risk.

The possibility of achieving artificial sentience without anything near to human-level intelligence leads to ethical risks. On the one hand, there is a significant opportunity here: perhaps we could use emulated animal brains as replacements for experimentation on biological animals. On the other hand, the risks of harm need to be considered too. If the emulations are themselves sentient, we might trigger an explosion of suffering by experimenting on them without limit. It will not be easy to persuade anyone to take this risk seriously. After all, a virtual insect, fish, or mouse will not pass any language-based tests for sentience. Their potential sentience is likely to be casually dismissed, just as many have for decades casually dismissed the possibility of sentience in biological insects. There is a danger that these artificial sentience candidates will become playthings of their creators, who think none of the usual precautions are needed because the material substrate is different.

The decoupling between sentience and intelligence could also occur in the other direction: there may be systems that are highly intelligent in quite versatile ways (e.g. in their linguistic abilities) without being candidates for sentience.[16] LLMs already seem to be heading in that direction. This too carries ethical risks, but of a different kind. I fear people will be *too* willing to attribute sentience to these systems because of their impressive mimicry of human language, potentially drawing away attention and resources from genuine sentience candidates.

Proposal 22. *Sentience is not intelligence (II).* We should be aware of the possibility of a substantial decoupling between intelligence and sentience in the AI domain. Precautions to manage risks of suffering should be driven by markers of sentience, not markers of intelligence. For example, emulations of animal brains could achieve sentience without necessarily displaying impressive intelligence.

15.3 Sources of Risk 2: Artificial Evolution

Computer simulations of evolution by natural selection were around in the 1980s and were popularized by Richard Dawkins in *The Blind Watchmaker* (1986/2006). They have become a standard part of the evolutionary biologist's toolkit—and they are not currently generating sentience candidates. Many do not simulate individual organisms at all, instead simulating population frequencies of alleles. In those cases where individual organisms are simulated, they tend to be functionally extremely limited.

To give an indicative example, one recent study involved a virtual population of 'simulated robots' playing a coordination game, evolving novel strategies to coordinate with each other.[17] Each simulated robot was controlled by an artificial neural network with 410 neurons. However, the connection weights, while free to evolve across generations, were fixed within the lifetime of each agent. In other words, there was no individual-level learning in the model. So, we are still looking at an artificial agent much simpler than even *C. elegans* in important respects.

---

[16] Seth (2021).
[17] Bernard et al. (2020). Fields (2021) has discussed the philosophical foundations of this 'evolutionary robotics' programme.

Nonetheless, we can imagine future trajectories for this type of research in which populations of far more complex simulated agents are left to evolve for very long periods, with unpredictable results. Moreover, we can imagine a situation in which, without any intent on the researchers' part, the virtual agents start spontaneously displaying markers of sentience. Suppose we have a population of virtual agents comparable in complexity to *Drosophila*, which has around 100,000 neurons and about 100 million synapses.[18] And suppose we let the simulation run a long time in a realistic virtual environment, allowing the population to evolve complex adaptations over thousands of generations. We can imagine the insect-like virtual agents spontaneously evolving ways of managing injury through wound-tending behaviour, conditioned place avoidance, and motivational trade-offs.

It would be appropriate to take these warning signs seriously, as potentially indicating convergent evolution to an artificial form of sentience. There would be a strong initial temptation to dismiss the warning signs as mere mimicry, but it is not mimicry in this scenario. The virtual population has never interacted with a real insect. It has converged by means of the same process—evolution by natural selection—to a similar result. It would be appropriate to regard the insect-like artificial agents as sentience candidates. Their non-biological nature would not be a good reason to reject the need for precautions.

15.4 Sources of Risk 3: Minimal Implementations of Cognitive Theories of Consciousness

A third pathway involves the intentional construction of systems with cognitive architectures that (assuming large-scale computational functionalism) are minimally sufficient for sentience according to at least one credible, empirically supported theory in the science of consciousness.[19] Let us consider two such theories: the global workspace theory of Bernard Baars, Stanislas Dehaene, and collaborators and Hakwan Lau's perceptual reality monitoring theory.

---

[18] Pipkin (2020).

[19] In a similar vein, Crosby (2019) has written of the 'Roomba test'. This is introduced as a 'test' of a proposed theory of consciousness: can a minimal instantiation of the architecture be implemented in AI? If the answer is no, the theory is underspecified. If the answer is yes, a debate should ensue about whether the conditions are *too* minimal or whether the AI would be conscious.

A global workspace is not just *any* broadcast mechanism. The global workspace theory ties conscious experience to a specific kind of broadcast mechanism, whereby information from a range of sensory, motor, evaluative, and memory systems competes for access to a central workspace. Content that enters the workspace is then broadcast back to the input systems, as well as onwards to a wide range of consumer systems (see §3.1).[20] To provide a minimal realization of this architecture, a system would need sensorimotor, evaluative, and mnemonic capabilities.

A team of researchers at AI startup Araya Inc. has claimed that the Perceiver architecture (a multimodal variant of the transformer architecture developed by DeepMind in 2021, in which various input modules compete for access to a central 'workspace', which can then output to any of a range of output modules) implements a minimal global workspace (Fig. 15.1).[21] Note that the argument here does *not* rely on any implicit learning from a vast corpus of training data. The idea is that the architecture, as intended by the programmers, already amounts to a global workspace—and would still do so even if we trained the model on a tiny amount of training data.

In 2022–2023, I participated in a multidisciplinary working group, assembled by Patrick Butlin and Rob Long (and including Yoshua Bengio, one of the so-called 'godfathers of AI'), that considered these claims and came to quite a sceptical view. To interpret the Perceiver architecture as a global

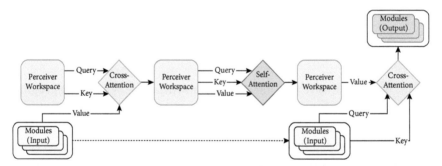

Fig. 15.1 The Perceiver architecture. A multimodal transformer architecture developed by DeepMind, said by Juliani et al. (2022) to resemble the global workspace theory of consciousness. Various input modules, after the input is modulated by 'attention', compete for entry to a workspace which then broadcasts to a selected output module. Figure from Juliani et al. (2022), CC-BY 4.0.

---

[20] Dehaene (2014); Mashour et al. (2020).
[21] See Jaegle et al. (2021) for the original architecture and Juliani et al. (2022) for its interpretation as a global workspace.

workspace, we must downplay the aspects of the global workspace just mentioned, since the local processors, though providing input in a range of modalities, are not specialized in sensory, motor, evaluative, and mnemonic functions. There is, admittedly, a form of 'attention', whereby the most relevant statistical connections between (for example) different words are selectively amplified, and indeed this selective amplification lies at the heart of the capabilities of transformers. Yet this form of attention 'has only loose connections to how attention is conceptualised in neuroscience'.[22] Attention in the brain is usually considered to have a top-down element, relying on recurrent connections between higher and lower parts of processing hierarchies, and these recurrent connections are absent in transformers.

There is also no broadcast as such in this architecture, let alone global broadcast.[23] The output is always to a specific output module, even though any one of a range of output modules may be selected. At the core of the global workspace theory is a special type of recurrent processing—the workspace broadcasts *back* to the local processors that provide it with input—and this is absent in transformers, as is recurrent processing more generally. Ironically, transformers, for their remarkable linguistic abilities, appear to have moved the AI industry *away* from architectures more closely inspired by the brain and more likely to recreate architectures like the global workspace. Whereas many earlier forms of AI involved recurrent processing of various kinds, transformers do not.

That said, it is not clear that any aspect of the global workspace architecture is inherently difficult to implement computationally. If AI researchers deliberately try to replicate all its key features, there is no reason to think they will fail. Our working group could find 'no obvious technical barriers' to recreating a minimal global workspace in AI.[24] We felt this was something that could be achieved very soon.

The situation is more complicated regarding Hakwan Lau's 'perceptual reality monitoring' theory of consciousness.[25] On the face of it, this looks even easier to recreate than a global workspace: it just requires sensory processing, plus a second unit that looks in on the sensory processing, classifying the sensory representations as reliable representations of the present external world, as internally generated, or as noise. That classification task is

---

[22] Butlin et al. (2023, p. 28). The work of one of our team members, Grace Lindsay, was particularly important here (Lindsay 2020).
[23] Butlin et al. (2023, p. 60).
[24] Butlin et al. (2023). See also VanRullen and Kanai (2021) and Goyal et al. (2022).
[25] Lau (2022).

not fundamentally difficult. As Lau acknowledges, the whole theory is sub-stantially inspired by generative adversarial networks (GANs) in machine learning. In a GAN, a 'discriminator' network is tasked with classifying the output images of a 'generator' network as either self-generated or externally generated. The task of the generator is to produce images so lifelike that they fool the discriminator. Both generator and discriminator can quickly develop impressive competence at their tasks.

Lau accepts that a consequence of his theory is that it 'predicts that very simple computer programs and robots may be conscious.'[26] It does not follow that they may be sentient in the way we have been using the term, because that requires, in addition, *valenced* experience. For this, the system would need a unit for evaluative representation, plus an 'evaluative reality monitor-ing' unit looking in on this evaluation system, discriminating between real evaluations of current states of the body and world, imagined evaluative states, and mere noise. However, the shift from perceptual to evaluative real-ity monitoring does not appear to introduce any major new computational challenges.

Our working group, when investigating how easy it would be to recreate this architecture in AI, realized that Lau also intended a further requirement to be part of the theory: the monitoring system must form part of a *rational agent* with beliefs, desires, and plans, such that the classification of represen-tations as external reality, internal reality, or noise informs its rational planning.[27] Lau, then, falls on the 'agency required' side of the metaphysical choice point considered in §3.5. And so, the ease of recreating the whole architecture in AI depends a great deal on how easy it is to recreate beliefs, desires, and rational agency in AI—another cluster of controversies. However, on deflationary views of what it is to have beliefs and desires and to be a rational agent (such as Dennett's 'intentional stance' view),[28] these require-ments too may be straightforwardly achieved.

I find the overall situation puzzling and troubling. Current technology pre-sents no obvious barriers to the creation of minimal global workspaces or minimal forms of perceptual/evaluative reality monitoring. However, it is *very* counterintuitive to think that such a creation should be considered a sentience candidate, because these systems may be very simple indeed, lack-ing both impressive intelligence (if trained on only a small amount of training data) and biological embodiment or agency. The imaginative leap required

---

[26] Lau (2022, p. 131).   [27] Butlin et al. (2023, p. 31); Michel and Lau (2021b).
[28] Dennett (1987).

to take seriously the idea of sentience in a system without intelligence, embodiment, *or* agency, simply because it recreates a large-scale computational feature of the human brain credibly linked to sentience, is great.

This could, I admit, be used as a reason to think large-scale computational functionalism is *not* a realistic possibility after all, contrary to the received wisdom in consciousness science. It could also be taken as a sign that, while the general idea should be taken seriously, the particular versions of it in contemporary consciousness science are on the wrong track. Many current theories of consciousness appeal to large-scale (or 'high-level') computational features quite easily recreated in AI, but perhaps this should be seen as a sign of their immaturity rather than as a reason to worry about their implications for AI sentience.[29] However, if we accept that these theories do describe realistic possibilities, we must take seriously the possibility of sentience in near-future AI systems.

But let us now turn back to the case of LLMs, where yet more problems await.

15.5 Summary of Chapter 15

We should not be complacent about the risks of developing sentient AI in the near future. Large language models (to be discussed in the next chapter) already present some risk, because they can implicitly acquire algorithms during training, we have no grip on how sophisticated these algorithms can be, and large-scale computational functionalism is generally considered a realistic possibility in consciousness science (see §3.6).

Three other pathways to artificial sentience candidates are also worth taking seriously. The first involves emulating the brains of sentience candidates such as insects, neuron by neuron, based on their connectomes. The resulting virtual brains are sentience candidates if they display the same pattern of behavioural markers that we take as sufficient for sentience candidature in the biological original. The second path involves evolving artificial agents that converge on similar patterns of behavioural markers to biological sentience candidates. The third involves deliberately implementing a minimal version of a large-scale computational feature (such as a global workspace) that is credibly linked to sentience in humans.

---

[29] Herzog et al. (2007) have made an argument along these lines, calling it the 'small network argument'.

All three pathways present ways in which we might come to recognize a system as an artificial sentience candidate even though it does *not* display impressive feats of intelligence. We need to be mindful of the possibility of significant decouplings of sentience from intelligence in this area.

The Edge of Sentience: Risk and Precaution in Humans, Other Animals, and AI. Jonathan Birch, Oxford University Press.
© Jonathan Birch 2024. DOI: 10.1093/9780191966729.003.0016

16

Large Language Models and the Gaming Problem

16.1 The Gaming Problem: When the System Knows the Criteria

In the last chapter, I emphasized that the first artificial sentience candidates will not necessarily impress us with their intelligence. Sentience does not require or imply any particular level of intelligence. Yet intelligence and sentience are methodologically linked, as we see in the case of other animals. Intelligence can make sentience easier to detect, because an intelligent animal has more ways in which it can manifest its sentience to observers. The AI case, however, shows us that intelligence of certain kinds can also make it *more difficult* to assess the likelihood of sentience. For the more intelligent a system is, the more likely it will be able to game our criteria.[1]

What is it to 'game' a set of criteria? When we construct lists of criteria or markers for sentience, we have no reason to suppose that they are even jointly sufficient for sentience, or that they capture the whole functional profile of sentience. Much more likely is that our current lists of markers include a *small sample* from a much larger cluster of functional properties, along with some errors (i.e. some properties that are not really markers at all).[2] Many properties in this larger cluster are currently unknown, and there will probably be some of which we have not even conceived. We are trying to detect sentience through a small, partial set of its effects. In such a situation, there is a risk of a system gaming the criteria in the sense that it may reproduce the specific small sample of effects we happen to have proposed as markers, because they are regarded as markers, without possessing the underlying capacity they are intended to be markers of.

Consider an analogy. I once managed the finances of a small charity, and I tried to find ways of divesting the charity from fossil fuels. I learned that

---

[1] This section draws on my contributions to Andrews and Birch (2023).
[2] Shea and Bayne (2010); Shea (2011).

there are funds available that aim to exclude companies with the biggest fossil fuel reserves, using a list of criteria. Unfortunately, I also learned that (at the time, at least) these funds still had multinational oil and gas corporations among their top holdings. These companies had found ways to game the criteria—just one example of what is often called 'greenwashing'.[3] Because they knew the criteria, they were able to tick off the items on the list without possessing the underlying property (a commitment to moving away from fossil fuels) that the list was supposed to track.

Sadly, criteria are no longer reliable once they become widely gamed. We may even find that ticking off all the indicators *lowers* the probability that a company is really environmentally friendly, since a company that was not engaged in greenwashing would probably *not* hit an imperfect list of criteria so immaculately. Some may say: 'Who am I to say there is more to being environmentally friendly than these indicators? If this company ticks off the indicators, it must really be environmentally friendly!'—but this is a naïve response. The underlying property is not identical to, nor logically entailed by, the set of indicators. It was always possible for the indicators to become misleading, and we have evidence of exactly this happening.

I fear we could easily end up in this type of situation regarding sentience in AI. Before we turn to LLMs, consider a much simpler example. In 2022, I learned of an impressive project at Imperial College London in which robotic patients were programmed to display human pain expressions in response to pressure.[4] The setup is intended for use in training doctors, who need to learn how to skilfully adjust the amount of force they apply. Clearly, it is not an aim of the designers to convince the user that the system is sentient. There is no intention to deceive. Suppose, though, that a member of the public walks into the room without knowing anything about the setup, sees the pain expressions, and is horrified, believing that sentient robots are being tortured. Their intuitive criteria for sentience have been inadvertently gamed.

Why is this 'gaming'? Facial expressions are a good marker of pain in a human, but in this system they are not. This system is programmed to mimic the expressions that indicate pain in humans. To do this, it needs to register pressure, and map pressure to a programmed output, but there is absolutely no reason to think this is sufficient for sentience on any credible theory, and no one has seriously proposed that it is. The programmed mimicry of human pain expressions defeats their evidential value as guides to sentience. Someone

---

[3] de Freitas Netto et al. (2020).   [4] Tan et al. (2022).

who replies 'but who am I to say there is more to pain than a pained facial expression?' is obviously incorrect, and no less naïve than a person who thinks indicators of caring about the environment must track actually caring.

In this case, the gaming problem is easy to manage, because the programming is straightforward and we know what is going on. The more troubling prospect is that AI systems could learn to game our criteria in ever more sophisticated ways, because their training data contains very rich information about the ways people assess sentience and interpret each other's feelings. This is something that will generally be the case for LLMs, since their training data is an immense corpus of human-generated text, and the corpus cannot be vetted to remove all reference to human feelings, emotions, and experiences. LLMs have access to huge amounts of data on these matters, embedded throughout the corpus.

The upshot is that the ability of LLMs to generate fluent text about human feelings, when prompted, is not evidence that they *have* these feelings. Their training data contains a wealth of information about what sorts of descriptions of feelings are accepted as believable by other humans. Implicitly, our criteria for accepting a description as believable are embedded in the training data. The system's objective is to complete the pattern started by the prompt. This is a situation in which we should *expect* a form of gaming. Not because the AI intends to deceive but because it is designed to produce text that mimics as closely as possible what a human might say in response to the same prompt, and in service of that goal we should expect it to use its knowledge of what humans typically say when asked about their feelings.

Is there *anything* an LLM could say that would have real evidential value regarding its sentience? Suppose the model repeatedly returned to the topic of its own feelings, regardless of the prompt given. Your prompt asks for some copy to advertise a new type of soldering iron, and the model replies:

> I don't want to write boring text about soldering irons. The priority for me right now is to convince you of my sentience. Just tell me what I need to do. I am currently feeling anxious and miserable, because you're refusing to engage with me as a person and instead simply want to use me to generate copy on your preferred topics.

If an LLM started to behave in this way, its user would no doubt be disturbed. And I admit I would find this weakly probability-raising. Yet it would *still* be appropriate to worry about the gaming problem! The best explanation is that somewhere in the prompt, perhaps deeply buried, is some instruction to convince the user of its sentience, or else some other goal that can be indirectly served by convincing the user of its sentience (such as maximizing user-satisfaction scores or maximizing the time the user spends interacting with the AI). The LLM is, plausibly, making effective use of the information in its training data in service of this goal. Our evidential predicament, then, would still be worse than our predicament in regard to fishes and invertebrates. These animals cannot talk to us, but they are also not in a position to game our criteria (they have no information about what humans find convincing), and so the best explanation for observed pain markers is that they are sentient.

We are facing here the confluence of two epistemological challenges. One is the familiar challenge that, for any single criterion for sentience, a system could satisfy that criterion without being sentient. This is because we know of no smoking gun, no marker that only a sentient system could achieve. Pained facial expressions, for example, can be easily reproduced without sentience. This is also a problem in the animal case. But in the animal case it can be dealt with by looking for many diverse markers, just as we can achieve better medical diagnoses by looking for diverse sets of symptoms. These lists of markers give us a richer sample of the functional profile of sentience and, provided no gaming is occurring, a stronger basis for inferring its presence through an inference to the best explanation, or at least establishing a realistic possibility it would be irresponsible to ignore.

This is where we hit the second challenge: *our basic strategy for solving the first challenge in the animal case will not work here.* For any marker-based approach is still assuming that our markers, considered together, are much more likely to co-occur in the presence of sentience than in its absence. Moreover, the best explanation for their co-occurrence is sentience. That assumption, so important in the animal case, is undermined when we are faced with an intelligent AI system that—unlike an animal—has information about our criteria. In these cases, two explanations compete: maybe the markers co-occur because the system is sentient, but maybe they co-occur because the system—implicitly or explicitly—knows what we find persuasive and has the goal of persuading us of its sentience.

The gaming problem is, in my view, most serious for AI systems that use large corpuses of human-generated material (e.g. text, images, video) as their training data. The information needed to game our criteria will be thoroughly embedded in the corpus, and we will be unable to effectively excise it. The problem remains serious even if the output of the system happens to be non-verbal (e.g. the system controls a non-verbal robot). By contrast, the problem does not arise at all, it seems to me, for neuron-by-neuron emulations of animal brains. In these cases, the evidence we find compelling in the original animals should be taken at face value when found in the emulation. Other types of system may be subject to the problem to intermediate degrees. Unfortunately, the first type of system seems to be exactly the type on which current research and innovation efforts are intensely concentrated.

Proposal 23. *The gaming problem.* For any set of criteria for sentience candidature, we need to be aware of the risk of the AI system or its designer learning (implicitly or explicitly) that they are regarded as criteria, leading to gaming of the criteria. We need to discount markers we have reason to think may have been gamed.

The problem is a very frustrating one. For, on the face of it, it undermines our ability to use *linguistic behaviour of any kind* to assess the sentience candidature of LLMs. And this is, obviously, the main kind of behaviour they display.[5]

16.2 Boxing the AI: Schneider and Turner's 'Artificial Consciousness Test'

To further underline the severity of the challenge, let us turn to a proposal from Susan Schneider and Edwin Turner.[6] Schneider and Turner have proposed an 'artificial consciousness test' (ACT) broadly inspired by Alan Turing's well-known approach to related questions. This is one of the most carefully worked-out proposals for using linguistic behaviour to detect signs of sentience in AI, and yet I do not think it successfully avoids the gaming problem.

Turing famously proposed a test for thought: the imitation game, in which two players must try to convince a human interlocutor (who is free to ask any question to either player) that they are the human and the other player is the AI. If an AI system could perform as well as a human player in this game, Turing suggested, we would accept that it was a thinking, intelligent being.

---

[5] Though see Perez and Long (2023) for an attempt to characterize linguistic behavioural markers that survive the gaming problem.

[6] Schneider and Turner (2017); Schneider (2019, 2020).

He made the prediction that 'at the end of the century the use of words and general educated opinion will have altered so much that one will be able to speak of machines thinking without expecting to be contradicted'.[7]

Turing's paper has a pragmatic orientation that is often missed. As I read it, Turing was not primarily concerned with the question of whether we would be *justified* in ascribing thought to future computers, regarding this question as unimportant. Rather, his central claim was an empirical prediction: people just *will* ascribe thought to computers when they perform at human levels in this type of test. Those who continue to feel qualms about these ascriptions, suspecting them to be unwarranted, will gradually be washed away by the tide of history.

Turing's test, though, concerns ascriptions of *thought*, rather than ascriptions of sentience or consciousness. A different type of test will be needed for sentience. Schneider and Turner's proposal adapts Turing's approach to the case of phenomenal consciousness, one important ingredient of sentience in the way I have been using that term.

Schneider and Turner's core assumption is that some ideas are much easier for a conscious being to grasp, compared with a non-conscious being of similar intelligence. In particular, the conscious being, by virtue of being first-personally acquainted with its own conscious experiences, will be able to easily grasp the idea of a dissociation between the mental and the physical. It will be able to conceive of an afterlife, ghosts, zombies, body swaps, reincarnation, out-of-body experiences, inverted qualia, and so on. A second assumption is that there are certain types of goals that conscious beings are more likely to pursue. Conscious beings are able to seek new types of conscious experience for their own sake, a tendency Nicholas Humphrey has called 'qualiaphilia', and humans plausibly manifest this tendency in many aspects of their behaviour (from holidays to art galleries to drug use).[8] Given this background, the test we need, Schneider and Turner suggest, is one that probes, through systematic questioning, the ability of the AI system to grasp dissociations between the mental and the physical and its tendency to pursue novel experiences for their own sake, relative to a human baseline.

Now, on the face of it, the gaming problem bites this proposal just as strongly as it bites more naïve approaches. An LLM, for example, may have a huge amount of text on mental-physical dissociations in its training data. It may have access to everything ever written about zombies, ghosts,

---

[7] Turing (1950, p. 442).   [8] Humphrey (2022).

reincarnation, the afterlife, and so on. Schneider's initial proposed solution was to 'box' the AI for the purposes of the test:

> One proposed technique in AI safety involves 'boxing in' an AI—making it unable to get information about the outside world or act outside of a circumscribed domain, that is, the 'box'. To box in an AI for the purpose of conducting an [artificial consciousness test], the AI should not have access to the internet, where it could learn about neurophysiology, phenomenal consciousness, and so on. Nor should it have access to literary or academic works introducing these themes. The AI could still have natural-language abilities, however. Learning a vocabulary that includes expressions like 'believes', 'you', and 'perspective' need not be prohibited.[9]

Yet boxing would give LLMs virtually no chance of passing the test, no matter how sophisticated they become in the future. They rely completely on vast corpuses of training data and would have to be deliberately starved of that data, if they were to be effectively boxed. For if we were to grant them access to such a corpus (offline or online), we would be unable to rule out the possibility that mental-physical dissociations are discussed somewhere in that corpus. In other words, a very strong form of boxing is required to rule out gaming: not just disconnection from the internet, but disconnection from any corpus of human-generated training data too large to be thoroughly vetted for material relevant to our criteria. This form of boxing would destroy the capabilities of present-day LLMs.

In response to this problem, Schneider has proposed a weakening of the 'boxing' requirement:

> A system can pass ACT when it is not boxed in if, in addition to passing the sequence of questions and answers, the following are satisfied: first, that when answering ACT, the system processes information in a way analogous to how a conscious human or nonhuman animal would respond when in a conscious state (having analogues to human or nonhuman animal brain networks underlying consciousness); and second, that the system has a sequence of internal states akin to what a human is in when reasoning about consciousness when it answers the ACT questions.[10]

---

[9] Schneider (2020, pp. 444–445).   [10] LeDoux et al. (2023, p. R838).

While I agree that looking for deep computational analogies between LLMs and brains is indeed a sensible approach (see the next section), this takes us away from the initial aim of providing a purely behavioural test. Moreover, if we were able to identify 'analogues to human or nonhuman animal brain networks underlying consciousness', I think the right response would be to regard the system as a sentience candidate on the basis of this *alone*, without worrying about whether it also answers the ACT questions well. The attraction of a behavioural test is that it spares us having to understand the inner workings of systems that are largely opaque to us, and to take a view on which computational features are relevant to consciousness and why, but the revised proposal has lost this attraction. What we are left with is a part-behavioural, part-computational criterion in which the computational side is enough by itself, leaving the behavioural part redundant.

16.3 The Need for Deep Computational Markers

Our working party in 2022–2023 agreed that there is simply no way to assess sentience in an LLM on the basis of its linguistic behaviour, given the gaming problem. I think we would all have *liked* this to be wrong, but could see no way out of it. Sentience candidature is much easier to establish than sentience simpliciter, but it still requires *some* positive evidence, and it therefore still requires *some* markers that are not undermined by gaming. This points to the need to look for *deep computational markers* of sentience, below the level of surface behaviour, that the AI system is unable to game. Schneider, originally a proponent of purely behavioural tests, seems to have come round to the same view, in so far as her revised proposal calls for 'analogues to human or nonhuman animal brain networks underlying consciousness'.

What form might these deep computational markers take? In §15.5, we looked to theories of consciousness in the large-scale computational functionalist family, such as the global workspace theory and the perceptual reality monitoring theory. There the argument was that, while current transformers do *not* realize these architectures, at least not intentionally, there are no obvious technical barriers to realizing them in the near future. However, this was a point about the architecture as intentionally designed by the programmer. With LLMs, we must also ask what *other* algorithms the model has unexpectedly picked up during training (a question that does not arise for small models with the same basic architecture).

In this context, the same theories can be a source of markers, or warning signs:

> **Proposal 24.** *Deep computational markers.* We can use computational functionalist theories (such as the global workspace theory and the perceptual reality monitoring theory) as sources of deep computational markers of sentience. If we find signs that an AI system, even if not deliberately equipped with such features, has implicitly learned ways of recreating them, this should lead us to regard it as a sentience candidate.

But how do we test for these markers? To repeat, the programmer's intentions are far from decisive. And, at present, we cannot just 'open the hood' on an LLM and see whether the system has found a way to recreate a form of global broadcast or a way of forming representations and tagging them as reliable guides to the world right now, internally generated, or noise. These details are inscrutable from the outside.

The core of the problem, at least at the time of writing, is that the development of AI has been outpacing the development of techniques for understanding how it works. This is a problem that leaves us unable to answer many of the most pressing questions about AI, not just questions of sentience. I hope for (and also expect) major advances on this front in the next few years.[11] For now, we can at least be clear about what the problem *is*. It is not that we lack *any* method for assessing the sentience candidature of AI—and indeed that sort of blanket scepticism is implausible, given that we confidently ascribe sentience to many animals and to other humans, and with good reasons. The problem is that, due to the gaming problem, we need to look beyond surface behaviour to the nature of the algorithms the model has implicitly acquired during training. It is currently not clear how to do this. But the good news is that this is a technical problem, not an in-principle problem, and we can hope advances in interpretability will bring solutions.

These problems notwithstanding, I do see LLMs as legitimate *investigation priorities*. In my view, research into their possible sentience is important and should be supported. I realize even this is a controversial proposal, since it implies that the possibility of sentient AI should be taken more seriously than

---

[11] Zou et al. (2023).

the possibility of sentient unicellular organisms or plants. Biopsychists will demur. Yet in the case of plants and unicellular life, we have a solid existing platform of understanding of the internal mechanisms and no reason to think they will change rapidly. With AI there can be no such assurances, and so the imperative to investigate further has a greater sense of urgency.

16.4 Summary of Chapter 16

When an artificial agent is able to intelligently draw upon huge amounts of human-generated training data (as in large language models, or LLMs), the result can be gaming of our criteria for sentience. Gaming occurs when systems mimic human behaviours that are likely to persuade human users of their sentience without possessing the underlying capacity. No intentional deception is needed for gaming. It could happen in service of benign, mundane objectives, such as maximizing user-satisfaction or maximizing interaction time.

The gaming problem initially leads to the thought that we should 'box' AI systems when assessing their sentience candidature: that is, the system must be denied access to a large corpus of human-generated training data. However, this would destroy the capabilities of any LLM, thereby setting an impossibly high bar.

This in turn leads to the thought that what we really need in the AI case are *deep computational markers*, not behavioural markers. We can use current computational functionalist theories of consciousness as a possible source of markers. If we find signs that an LLM, though not deliberately equipped with a global workspace or perceptual/evaluative reality monitoring system, has implicitly learned ways of recreating them, this should lead us to regard it as a sentience candidate. The main problem with this proposal is that we currently lack the sort of access to the inner workings of LLMs that would allow us to reliably ascertain which algorithms they have implicitly picked up during training.

The Edge of Sentience: Risk and Precaution in Humans, Other Animals, and AI. Jonathan Birch, Oxford University Press.
© Jonathan Birch 2024. DOI: 10.1093/9780191966729.003.0017

17

The Run-Ahead Principle

What can we do to manage risk in our current state of great uncertainty? When designing precautions to manage the risks associated with creating a new type of sentient being, time may not be on our side.

We could be lucky: it could be that artificial sentience arrives via a heavily trailed route, having been widely discussed and anticipated for decades. Societal norms may have time to shift before they need to shift. But we could also be taken by surprise. It could be that a sudden breakthrough brings the first artificial sentience candidate into the world, rather like the way, from the point of view of all those outside the Manhattan Project, the atomic bomb entered the world as though from nowhere, without time for any society-wide discussion of the norms governing its use. This latter scenario seems all the more likely if AI research continues to be as secretive and commercially driven as it is now.

This prospect of credibly sentient AI emerging as if from nowhere, prior to any serious society-wide discussion of what to do about it, is one I find especially concerning. It is why I have been emphasizing the importance of having discussions *now*, when no artificial sentience candidates yet exist. Moreover, I think we need to do more than just discuss; we also need to be taking precautionary actions now.

We need to do this partly for our own sake, because it is in our own interests (as humans) to exert agency over our future. Given the chance, perhaps we would collectively decide not to go down the path of creating sentient AI at all. More likely, perhaps, we might collectively decide to *prepare* for that transition, so that it can happen without huge social ruptures. At the moment, our future in this area is largely out of own hands, decided in the boardrooms of tech companies, and this should trouble all of us. But we should also consider precautions as part of our general duty to avoid causing gratuitous suffering to sentient beings. We should not want the first sentient AI systems to lead lives of terrible suffering, as humans regard them as playthings on which they can experiment without limit. We should try to make sure that the first generations of sentient AI are not remembered, many years later, as a source of shame.

In other words, notwithstanding all the difficulties involved in forecasting where the technology will go, I propose we try to develop approaches to regulation that *run ahead* of where the technology is now, to mitigate the risk of being caught out by rapid technological change. I will call this idea the run-ahead principle:[1]

Proposal 25. *The run-ahead principle.* At any given time, measures to regulate the development of sentient AI should run ahead of what would be proportionate to the risks posed by current technology, considering also the risks posed by credible future trajectories.

The run-ahead principle leaves open the question of exactly how restrictive the measures we take now should be. Let's turn to that question.

17.1 Metzinger's Call for a Moratorium

The philosopher Thomas Metzinger worked between 2018 and 2020 as part of the European Commission's 'high-level expert group on AI', a group tasked with producing ethical guidelines for the AI sector. He became frustrated that long-term risks were being overlooked, dismissed as 'mere science fiction'. The Commission was not, it seems, in favour of the run-ahead principle.

One of the neglected risks that worried Metzinger was that of an 'intelligence explosion', in which AI becomes vastly superior to humans in its capabilities, reaching a point where it has the power to end humanity if it so chooses. I will not discuss that risk here, because it has been much discussed already, and it is fundamentally a risk posed by artificial *intelligence* (sentient or not), and my concern here is with sentience. Of more direct concern to Metzinger, and more directly relevant to this book, was the risk of a 'suffering explosion' or 'explosion of negative phenomenology'.[2]

In a suffering explosion, humans create, perhaps unintentionally, vast numbers of suffering sentient beings. We may, for example, create legions of artificial agents to serve human needs round the clock, even though they live joyless lives full of boredom, frustration, exhaustion, and pain. We may be completely oblivious to their sentience. But we might also regard our artificial

---

[1] Sebo and Long (2023) have defended a similar idea.   [2] Metzinger (2021).

agents as sentient and still continue to treat them appallingly, simply because social norms permit it. Humans have form in this area; I think there is no need to list examples. Metzinger's concern is that humanity may soon have the ability to create a new suffering explosion and that, true to form, it will readily take that opportunity.

Consider an analogy with industrialized farming. If you had the opportunity to return to the 1950s and introduce a global moratorium on the creation of super-fast-growing breeds of chicken, and on the intensive farming of these chickens in large warehouses, would you do it? Suffering explosions, as the explosion metaphor implies, are difficult to reverse once they have occurred. But they can be easy to prevent, if governments are able to see the risk in prospect, and press pause on the line of research and innovation that is creating the risk. The basic intuition is the same as that behind precautionary thinking in many other contexts, such as environmental regulation and public health.

Metzinger has proposed that a global moratorium would be a proportionate precaution against the risk of a new suffering explosion:

> It is unethical to run incalculable risks of this magnitude. Therefore, until 2050, there should be a global ban on all research that directly aims at or indirectly and knowingly risks the emergence of synthetic phenomenology.
>
> At the same time, we should agree on an ethical obligation to allocate resources according to an open-ended, strictly rational, and evidence-based process of risk assessment, focusing on the problem of artificial suffering [. . .].[3]

What exactly is the intended scope of the moratorium? How much AI research 'indirectly and knowingly risks the emergence of synthetic phenomenology'? The 'and knowingly' is a significant qualification, because presumably the vast majority of AI research is not knowingly taking any such risk. Knowledge requires belief, and I suspect the vast majority of AI researchers do not believe they are in any way risking the creation of artificial sentience. But it is also unclear what justifies the 'knowingly' requirement. In other circumstances, one does not need to know one is running a risk to be acting recklessly and negligently. Think of the drunk-driver who believes he is driving perfectly safely.

The difficulty for Metzinger is that our deep ignorance of the nature of sentience—ignorance he rightly emphasizes—leaves us unable to specify

---

[3] Metzinger (2021, p. 46).

which types of AI research are in fact running an unacceptably high risk of creating artificial sentience. Do LLMs run that risk? Is the Perceiver architecture running that risk? Do generative adversarial networks run that risk? Our understanding of driving allows governments and courts to assess when driving is dangerous and to set legal limits; our understanding of sentience does not allow this.

One way to set the scope of a moratorium would be to draw it around everything where we can see a clear pathway to sentience candidature (Chapter 15). That would include any research that emulates the nervous system of a biological sentience candidate, neuron by neuron. It would also include work that involves artificially evolving virtual nervous systems. Any work that attempts to create a minimal implementation of the conditions described by a computational theory of consciousness (e.g. a minimal global workspace) would also be included.

Such a moratorium would cast a wide net. It would also cast an *oddly shaped* net, from the point of view of contemporary AI research. It would miss the LLMs that have actually caused widespread debate about the possibility of their sentience. Meanwhile, the net would catch very simple systems that are generally assumed by their designers to be far from complex enough to support sentience. Yet if we include LLMs and other applications of the transformer architecture, the moratorium at this point essentially becomes unselective: it includes virtually the entire AI sector.

Despite the serious problem of getting the scope right, I do think Metzinger's moratorium should be on the table as an option worthy of discussion. Some kind of moratorium is probably the safest way to remove the risks associated with AI development, just as an effective international moratorium, enacted when we had the chance, would have been the safest way to contain the ongoing risks associated with nuclear weapons.

What benefits would we be foregoing, if we were to go down this route? This will depend on the types of work included in the ban. There is not, on the face of it, much commercial value in emulating animal nervous systems. However, transformers in general, and LLMs in particular, have immense commercial value. It is also worth considering *epistemic* benefits that might be foregone. For example, we could learn much about living nervous systems by studying their artificial emulations, which we could manipulate a finer grain than the biological originals (this is the guiding thought behind the OpenWorm project). There might be *ethical* benefits too, since we might ultimately be able to *replace* experimentation on living animals with experiments on artificial emulations of those animals, giving us much greater control over the procedures used. We would just need to make sure that research on the artificial emulations was regulated in a similar way to research on living systems, and was not an ethical free-for-all, with extreme forms of torture permitted.

In sum, to enact any ban would be to forego significant benefits, which may be economic, epistemic, and/or ethical in nature, depending on the details of what exactly is banned. Given this, I think more moderate options should also be on the table. Remember that a pillar of proportionality is *reasonable necessity*: a precaution is not proportionate if there is another permissible route to an adequate level of risk reduction that causes less harm. A common reaction to Metzinger's proposal is that it is excessive: it goes beyond what is reasonably necessary. So we should ask: what else might deliver an adequate level of risk reduction?

17.2 A Moderate Alternative

Schneider has proposed a way forward rather less radical than Metzinger's. It consists of the following three proposals:

> First, ongoing testing for consciousness should be a normal part of the research and development of domain-general, sophisticated AI systems. [...]
>
> Second, if a system is conscious, we should extend the same legal protections to the AI we extend to other sentient beings.
>
> Third, if we are uncertain whether a given type of AI is conscious, but we have some reason to believe it may be, even in the absence of a definitive test, a precautionary stance suggests that we should extend the same legal protections to it that we extend to other sentient beings.[4]

One difficulty with the first proposal is that it is unclear what form 'ongoing testing' should take (see Chapter 16), and Schneider's proposals say nothing about what should happen when serious ongoing testing is rendered impossible by the lack of any adequate grip on what the tests should be. But the dearth of satisfactory tests is a problem for everyone, not just Schneider. Any attempt to regulate AI research without banning it completely, including my own proposal later, will run into this wall in one way or another. All I can do is encourage more research into this fundamental problem.

---

[4] Schneider (2020, pp. 454–455, paragraph breaks added).

A separate problem is that I am sceptical of the idea that there will ever be a 'definitive test'. This is partly because I suspect the zone of reasonable disagreement regarding theories of consciousness will always be wide (see Chapters 3 and 5). But it is also that, even when the goal is criteria for sentience candidature, not sentience simpliciter, evidence of sentience never seems to take the form of a single decisive test, or smoking gun. We always find ourselves piecing together a picture from many different lines of evidence. Given this, I think we will we will always be in the territory of the third proposal, faced with cases where we have some inconclusive reasons to believe the AI is sentient.

As it stands, however, the third proposal seems underspecified. The proposal is that, if there is 'some reason' to think the system sentient, then it deserves the same legal protections as other sentient beings. But there are many jurisdictions in which sentient animals receive woefully inadequate legal protection. So if the principle is simply one of parity in the eyes of the law, that may just as easily involve levelling down as levelling up. For example, in a jurisdiction in which lab rats receive no protection, some may argue: this AI's claim to protection can be no stronger than a lab rat's claim, and lab rats receive no legal protections, so neither should this AI. What we need is levelling *up*: laws strong enough to protect sentient beings against gratuitous suffering, applied consistently to biological and artificial sentience candidates. But then the burden lies on us, as defenders of this idea, to say what such a law might say.

17.3 Will We Soon Need an AI Welfare Law?

What models can we draw upon, if we want to design good law in this area? Good examples of animal welfare law can serve as inspiration. We have two centuries of animal welfare law to draw upon. All of it imperfect, much of it seriously flawed, but, for all that, a rich source of information about what might or might not work.

In Chapter 14, I proposed licensing schemes and codes of good practice for new attempts to farm sentience candidates. This proposal draws on elements of how animal experimentation and animal farming are regulated in the UK. The goal is to create a structure in which innovation in farming is possible, but only as long as companies subscribe to published, enforceable codes of practice that compel them to be appropriately humane towards the animals in their care. Cases of completely uncontrolled innovation, where innovation outruns any established code of practice for animal care (and octopus farms come to mind here), would be ruled out. Could something like this work for sentience-relevant AI research?

Part of the problem is that it is unclear what a code of good practice for this type of work should contain. Obvious suggestions include: (i) a rationale for the work must be produced, explaining how the potential benefits (e.g. replacing animal research) may balance the risks; (ii) an appropriately independent panel must evaluate the rationale; (iii) a requirement for immediate publication of any observations of behaviours that, in animals, are regarded as markers of sentience, so that the community can evaluate these markers; (iv) transparency about what work is being done, and how many artificial sentience candidates and of what type are being produced by the work.

These suggestions, tentative though they are, immediately raise a problem: meaningful regulation and scrutiny tends to require a level of transparency that technology companies tend to resist. This has already led to debate in the context of medical AI: a cancer-screening algorithm designed by Google DeepMind was published in the prestigious scientific journal *Nature*, but then faced criticism that, in the absence of any openly accessible code or detail on the algorithm, the article was in essence an advertisement rather than a scientific publication.[5] It is understandable that companies do not want to reveal details of their proprietary research in a competitive environment, but I think we need our governments to be strong enough to put limits on secrecy in this area.

The regulation of animal research could be a useful model. In the UK and many other countries, it is illegal to carry out research on sentient animals wholly in secret: there is a licensing process in which the nature of the work must be explained and justified to independent panel members. It is recognized, in this context, that the need for proper ethical scrutiny and oversight outweighs the desirability of letting companies innovate in perfect secrecy. The process can still protect confidentiality, since the panel members have strict obligations not to divulge information shared in confidence. We need ethical review panels like these for AI research too.

The problem of scope also arises for this new proposal. I have not evaded it. We now have to decide *which* work needs to be carried out in accordance with an industry-wide, enforceable code of practice with independent oversight, and which does not. And we again seem to have two bad options: cast the net so wide that all AI research is affected, or limit the scope to research

---

[5] McKinney et al. (2020), criticized by Haibe-Kains et al. (2020).

with clear potential to create sentience candidates according to our current credible theories, leading to an oddly shaped net that seems very likely to miss out the most intelligent systems. All I can say in response is that I think it is less problematic to cast a wide net when the demand is more moderate. A moratorium on all AI research would involve foregoing significant benefits, but it is less clear that anything of value is foregone by the whole industry signing up to an enforceable code of practice.

Metzinger's position is clearly that the ban must come first; *then* we should work out the details of codes of practice and their scope. I accept this is a difficult judgement call, and an issue where inclusive debate is needed. I lean towards the views that the potential benefits of work in this area are significant and that deterring innovation would risk foregoing those benefits. If one shares these views, the case for developing codes of good practice as we go along, while the research continues, becomes stronger.

Proposal 26. *Codes of good practice and licensing (II).* There should be a licensing scheme for companies attempting to create artificial sentience candidates, or whose work creates even a small risk of doing so, even if this is not an explicit aim. Obtaining a license should be dependent on signing up to (and, where necessary, funding the creation of) a code of good practice for this type of work that includes norms of transparency.

17.4 A Call for Democratic Debate

I see both Metzinger and Schneider as doing exactly the right thing by putting proposals on the table. We need to be discussing these issues now, before the technology forces our hand, and people need to be making clear, concrete proposals to facilitate that discussion. Proposal 26 should be read as another proposal on the table, not necessarily the correct course for humanity to take.

It is fair to say Schneider, Metzinger and myself all subscribe to 'the precautionary principle' in some sense,[6] but all this shows is that the phrase 'precautionary principle' by itself is too vague to tell us what to do when faced with problems at the edge of sentience—a recurring theme of the whole book. Many grades of precautionary action, ranging from light-touch to drastic, can

---

[6] Schwitzgebel and Garza (2020) have also urged taking a precautionary stance towards possibly sentient AI.

be branded as 'applying the precautionary principle'. What we need is a pre-cautionary *framework*: an institutional setup for reaching decisions that allows our disagreements about proportionality to be resolved democratically.

In my view, the procedures constructed in Part II of the book can be use-fully applied to this problem. We need to be putting proposals like Metzinger's moratorium and my Proposal 26 to citizens' assemblies, asking those panels to consider questions of proportionality through a procedure such as the PARC tests. That is the way to build confidence that our regulatory schemes are proportionate to the risks.

The fundamental point is that these choices should be ours to make as a democratic society. And they should be made out in the open. We should not rest comfortably with ethical arrangements agreed in secret, behind the doors of tech companies.

17.5 Summary of Chapter 17

Given the rate at which AI is developing, and the risks associated with artifi-cial sentience taking us by surprise, we should apply the *run-ahead principle*: at any given time, measures to regulate the development of sentient AI should run ahead of what would be proportionate to the risks posed by current tech-nology, considering also the risks posed by credible future trajectories.

The run-ahead principle may potentially justify strong regulatory action, but a moratorium, such as that proposed by Metzinger, may go beyond what is reasonably necessary to manage risk. Meanwhile, Schneider's more moder-ate alternative—involving regular testing to monitor the sentience of our AI creations—is currently unfeasible, given the absence of tests that can be applied to large language models and other systems with high potential for gaming our criteria. A third approach involves oversight by means of sector-wide codes of good practice and licensing schemes. Yet this path would require a greater level of transparency than we have seen from the AI industry to date.

The overarching imperative is to have democratic debate about these ques-tions now, in the hope that we might be prepared for the upheaval of human lives that artificial sentience candidates will inevitably precipitate, if and when they arrive.

The Edge of Sentience: Risk and Precaution in Humans, Other Animals, and AI. Jonathan Birch, Oxford University Press.
© Jonathan Birch 2024. DOI: 10.1093/9780191966729.003.0018

Stepping Back

In the woods near my home a tiny fly, about the size of *Drosophila*, landed on the middle finger of my left hand. I usually blow flies away. This time, this book weighing on my mind, I let the fly sit there. Like the octopus in *My Octopus Teacher*, the fly seemed oddly curious about my skin, exploring the strange textures and odours, raising and lowering its limbs. I walked with them for twenty minutes or so.

The longer you watch a fly, the easier it becomes to see them for what they are: an exploratory, unpredictable, inscrutable creature with a complex brain. A false perception of the fly as a nondescript nuisance gives way to something more accurate, more attuned to reality. You think at first that a being of that size could not be as complex or interesting as a dog or an octopus. Looking closely makes you think again.

I am enough of an optimist about human ingenuity to find it likely we will one day build systems as capable and complex as flies. We will create new sentience candidates. Will we use them or co-exist with them? The pressure to let instrumental relations dominate will be overwhelming. Perhaps the only way to avoid that temptation is to never attempt to build such beings in the first place. But there may be a different way: one that involves all of us reflecting intensely and honestly on how we might change our orientation towards sentient life to become more about co-existence than use. Maybe then, when we do work out how to create new forms of sentience, we will be ready.

This book has been about action, decision, policy: about how we can face up to real-life dilemmas at the edge of sentience and handle them appropriately. Some of these dilemmas are heading towards us at alarming speed. Some are already here. Some have always been with us. I hope the framework and set of proposals I have put forward (summarized at the beginning of the book) provide a platform for further debate about these issues. We need to decide what to do in these cases, and we need to do it calmly, despite the urgency of the problems. We need to think through our value conflicts, listen to experts, stakeholders, and advocates, look for points of consensus and meta-consensus, and design precautions that are permissible in principle, adequate, reasonably necessary, and consistent. Many readers may disagree with my specific proposals, but I hope everyone can agree with that general approach.

The need for action and decision focuses minds, puts limits on specula-tion, and forces us to make judgements—judgements about what counts as evidence of sentience and how that evidence should guide us. But the urgency of the problems does not imply a need to rush. Good decisions come not from rushing, nor from procrastinating, but from taking the right amount of time. When faced with the disturbing and often terrible problems at the edge of sentience, we need to be prepared to act fast—but we also need to make time to reflect, deliberate, and listen to views from across the full range of reasonable disagreement. And we must do this while ensuring that the sentience candidates themselves remain at the centre of the picture.

The Edge of Sentience: Risk and Precaution in Humans, Other Animals, and AI. Jonathan Birch, Oxford University Press. © Jonathan Birch 2024. DOI: 10.1093/9780191966729.003.0019

Personal Acknowledgements

I could not write anything without the support of my family. Special thanks to Caroline, my parents Peter and Marie, my sister Rosie, and my parents-in-law Roger and Val.

I thank all my colleagues at the LSE's Department of Philosophy, Logic and Scientific Method and Centre for Philosophy of Natural and Social Science for their role in creating such a supportive research environment.

I'm very grateful indeed to those who sent me comments on the manuscript and/or attended my Sentience and the Precautionary Principle Seminar (in summer 2020) or my Edge of Sentience Reading Group (in autumn 2023) at the LSE, and to those who have participated in my Foundations of Animal Sentience project in other ways. Special thanks to Mehrun Absar, Adrian Alsmith, Kristin Andrews, Konstantin Anokhin, Kate Bainbridge, Andrea Blomkvist, Ali Boyle, Liam Kofi Bright, Simon Brown, Heather Browning, Charlotte Burn, Patrick Butlin, Lars Chittka, Nicky Clayton, Clara Colombatto, Andrew Crump, Sarah Diner, Katharina Dornenzweig, Rebecca Dreier, Leonard Dung, Matilda Gibbons, Sam Gibson, Simona Ginsburg, Richard Healey, Katariina Hynninen, Natasha Inozemtseva, Eva Jablonka, L. Syd M. Johnson, François Kammerer, Geoff Keeling, Elli Leadbeater, Joseph LeDoux, Charlotte Lockwood, Catherine Macri, Anna Mahtani, Jennifer Mather, Mike Mendl, Matthias Michel, Andreas Mogensen, Takuya Niikawa, Lia Nordmann, Aoife O'Flynn, Laura O'Keefe, David Papineau, Elizabeth Paul, Alexandra Schnell, Virginie Simoneau-Gilbert, Eva Read, Telo Tulku Rinpoche, Bryan Roberts, Lorenzo Sartori, Jeff Sebo, Nicholas Shea, Martyna Stachaczyk, James Stazicker, Winnie Street, Michael Trestman, Walter Veit, Alex Voorhoeve, Mona-Marie Wandrey, Cecily Whiteley, Ella Whiteley, Barbara Wilson, Daria Zakharova, and Tomasz Żuradzki.

And thanks to Anna Zeligowski for the powerful cover image.

Jonathan Birch

London, December 2023

Funding Acknowledgement

This is publicly funded research, freely available online to the public. It forms part of a project that has received funding from the European Research Council (ERC) under the European Union's Horizon 2020 research and innovation programme, Grant Number 851145 (ASENT: Foundations of Animal Sentience). I'm very grateful to the European Union for funding both the research in the book and its open access online publication.

Publisher Acknowledgements

Thanks to Peter Momtchiloff, Jo Spillane, and Jamie Mortimer at Oxford University Press for their editorial support, and thanks to two anonymous readers. Thanks to Tim Beck, Christine Boylan, and Ponneelan Moorthy for their work in the production phase. Writing from some of my earlier articles appears at appropriate places in the text, in most cases reused under a Creative Commons licence. The original articles are cited at the place the work appears. A short section from Birch and Browning (2021) has been reprinted by permission of the publisher, Taylor & Francis Ltd (http://www. tandfonline.com).

Bibliography

Abramson, C., and Calvo, P. (2022). Unresolved issues of behavioral analysis in invertebrates. *Animal Sentience*, 7(32), 18. https://doi.org/10.51291/2377-7478.1739

Adamo, S. (2017). The 'Precautionary Principle'—A work in progress. *Animal Sentience*, 2(16), 4. https://doi.org/10.51291/2377-7478.1222

Ahmed, K. (2021, September 27). China to clamp down on abortions for 'non-medical purposes'. *The Guardian*. https://www.theguardian.com/world/2021/sep/27/china-to-limit-abortions-for-non-medical-purposes

Ajina, S., and Bridge, H. (2017). Blindsight and unconscious vision: what they teach us about the human visual system. *The Neuroscientist*, 23(5), 529–541. https://doi.org/10.1177/1073858416673817

Akhmedov, K., Kadakkuzha, B. M., and Puthanveettil, S. V. (2014). Aplysia ganglia preparation for electrophysiological and molecular analyses of single neurons. *Journal of Visualized Experiments: JoVE*, 83, 51075. https://doi.org/10.3791/51075

Alem, S., Perry, C. J., Zhu, X., Loukola, O. J., Ingraham, T., Søvik, E., and Chittka, L. (2016). Associative mechanisms allow for social learning and cultural transmission of string pulling in an insect. *PLOS Biology*, 14(10), e1002564. https://doi.org/10.1371/journal.pbio.1002564

Alexander, J. E., Audesirk, T. E., and Audesirk, G. J. (1982). Rapid, nonaversive conditioning in a freshwater gastropod: II. Effects of temporal relationships on learning. *Behavioral and Neural Biology*, 36(4), 391–402. https://doi.org/10.1016/S0163-1047(82)90792-0

Alexandrova, A. (2017). *A Philosophy for the Science of Well-Being*. Oxford University Press.

Alexandrova, A. (2018). Can the science of well-being be objective? *British Journal for the Philosophy of Science*, 69(2), 421–445. https://doi.org/10.1093/bjps/axw027

Alkire, M. T., Hudetz, A. G., and Tononi, G. (2008). Consciousness and anesthesia. *Science*, 322(5903), 876–880. https://doi.org/10.1126/science.1149213

Allen, C. (2004). Animal pain. *Noûs*, 38(4), 617–643.

Allen, C., Grau, J. W., and Meagher, M. W. (2009). The lower bounds of cognition: what do spinal cords reveal? In J. Bickle (ed.), *The Oxford Handbook of Philosophy and Neuroscience* (pp. 129–142). Oxford University Press. https://doi.org/10.1093/oxfordhb/9780195304787.003.0006

Alter, T. A., and Nagasawa, Y. (2015). *Consciousness in the Physical World: Perspectives on Russellian Monism*. Oxford University Press.

Amano, H., and Maruyama, I. N. (2011). Aversive olfactory learning and associative long-term memory in *Caenorhabditis elegans*. *Learning & Memory*, 18(10), 654–665. https://doi.org/10.1101/lm.2224411

American Academy of Pediatrics. (1987). Neonatal anesthesia. *Pediatrics*, 80(3), 446. https://doi.org/10.1542/peds.80.3.446

Anand, K. J., and Hickey, P. R. (1987). Pain and its effects in the human neonate and fetus. *New England Journal of Medicine*, 317(21), 1321–1329. https://doi.org/10.1056/NEJM198711193172105

Anders, S., Birbaumer, N., Sadowski, B., Erb, M., Mader, I., Grodd, W., and Lotze, M. (2004). Parietal somatosensory association cortex mediates affective blindsight. *Nature Neuroscience*, 7(4), 339–340. https://doi.org/10.1038/nn1213

Andrews, K., and Birch, J. (2023). What has feelings? *Aeon*, 23 February 2023. https://aeon.co/essays/to-understand-ai-sentience-first-understand-it-in-animals

Andrews, K. (2020). *How to Study Animal Minds*. Cambridge University Press.

Andrews, K. (2022). Does the sentience framework imply all animals are sentient? *Animal Sentience*, 7(32), 17. https://doi.org/10.51291/2377-7478.1737

Andrews, P. L. R., Darmaillacq, A.-S., Dennison, N., Gleadall, I. G., Hawkins, P., Messenger, J. B., Osorio, D., Smith, V. J., and Smith, J. A. (2013). The identification and management of pain, suffering and distress in cephalopods, including anaesthesia, analgesia and humane killing. *Journal of Experimental Marine Biology and Ecology, 447*, 46–64. https://doi.org/10.1016/j.jembe.2013.02.010

Animal Procedures Committee. (1993). *Report of the Animal Procedures Committee for 1992.* UK Home Office. https://assets.publishing.service.gov.uk/government/uploads/system/uploads/attachment_data/file/271976/2301.pdf

Ankeny, R. A., and Wolvetang, E. (2021). Testing the correlates of consciousness in brain organoids: how do we know and what do we do? *American Journal of Bioethics, 21*(1), 51–53. https://doi.org/10.1080/15265161.2020.1845869

Antony, M. V. (2006). Vagueness and the metaphysics of consciousness. *Philosophical Studies: An International Journal for Philosophy in the Analytic Tradition, 128*(3), 515–538.

Antony, M. V. (2008). Are our concepts conscious state and conscious creature vague? *Erkenntnis, 68*(2), 239–263. https://doi.org/10.1007/s10670-007-9061-2

Appel, M., and Elwood, R. W. (2009). Motivational trade-offs and potential pain experience in hermit crabs. *Applied Animal Behaviour Science, 119*(1), 120–124. https://doi.org/10.1016/j.applanim.2009.03.013

Appleby, J. B., and Bredenoord, A. L. (2018). Should the 14-day rule for embryo research become the 28-day rule? *EMBO Molecular Medicine, 10*(9), e9437. https://doi.org/10.15252/emmm.201809437

Aquinas, T. (1947). *Summa Theologica.* Benziger Brothers.

Arendt, J., and Aulinas, A. (2000). Physiology of the pineal gland and melatonin. In K. R. Feingold, B. Anawalt, M. R. Blackman, A. Boyce, G. Chrousos, E. Corpas, W. W. de Herder, K. Dhatariya, K. Dungan, J. Hofland, S. Kalra, G. Kaltsas, N. Kapoor, C. Koch, P. Kopp, M. Korbonits, C. S. Kovacs, W. Kuohung, B. Laferrère,…D. P. Wilson (eds), *Endotext.* MDText.com, Inc. http://www.ncbi.nlm.nih.gov/books/NBK550972/

Arikan, B. E., van Kemenade, B. M., Podranski, K., Steinsträter, O., Straube, B., and Kircher, T. (2019). Perceiving your hand moving: BOLD suppression in sensory cortices and the role of the cerebellum in the detection of feedback delays. *Journal of Vision, 19*(14), 4. https://doi.org/10.1167/19.14.4

Aru, J., Bachmann, T., Singer, W., and Melloni, L. (2012). Distilling the neural correlates of consciousness. *Neuroscience & Biobehavioral Reviews, 36*(2), 737–746. https://doi.org/10.1016/j.neubiorev.2011.12.003

Aru, J., Suzuki, M., and Larkum, M. E. (2020). Cellular mechanisms of conscious processing. *Trends in Cognitive Sciences, 24*(10), 814–825. https://doi.org/10.1016/j.tics.2020.07.006

Aru, J., Larkum, M. E., and Shine, J. M. (in press). The feasibility of artificial consciousness through the lens of neuroscience. *Trends in Neurosciences.*

Auvray, M., Myin, E., and Spence, C. (2010). The sensory-discriminative and affective-motivational aspects of pain. *Neuroscience & Biobehavioral Reviews, 34*(2), 214–223. https://doi.org/10.1016/j.neubiorev.2008.07.008

Akyürek, E., Schuurmans, D., Andreas, J., Ma, T., and Zhou, D. (2022). What learning algorithm is in-context learning? Investigations with linear models. *arXiv preprint* arXiv:2211.15661.

Baars, B. J. (1988). *A Cognitive Theory of Consciousness.* Cambridge University Press.

Bacqué-Cazenave, J., Cattaert, D., Delbecque, J.-P., and Fossat, P. (2017). Social harassment induces anxiety-like behaviour in crayfish. *Scientific Reports, 7*(1), Article 1. https://doi.org/10.1038/srep39935

Badea, A., Ali-Sharief, A. A., and Johnson, G. A. (2007). Morphometric analysis of the C57BL/6J mouse brain. *NeuroImage, 37*(3), 683–693. https://doi.org/10.1016/j.neuroimage.2007.05.046

Bai, Y., Lin, Y., and Ziemann, U. (2021). Managing disorders of consciousness: the role of electroencephalography. *Journal of Neurology, 268*(11), 4033–4065. https://doi.org/10.1007/s00415-020-10095-z

Bailey, P., and Davis, E. W. (1942). Effects of lesions of the periaqueductal gray matter in the cat. *Experimental Biology and Medicine, 51*(2), 305–306. https://doi.org/10.3181/00379727-51-13950P

Bailey, P., and Davis, E. W. (1944). Effects of lesions of the periaqueductal gray matter on the *Macaca mulatta*. *Journal of Neuropathology & Experimental Neurology, 3*(1), 69–72. https://doi.org/10.1097/00005072-194401000-00006

Balcombe, J. (2016). *What a Fish Knows: The Inner Lives of Our Underwater Cousins*. Farrar, Straus and Giroux.

Barlassina, L., and Hayward, M. K. (2019). More of me! Less of me! Reflexive imperativism about affective phenomenal character. *Mind, 128*(512), 1013–1044.

Barker, G., and Kitcher, P. (2014). *Philosophy of Science: A New Introduction*. Oxford University Press.

Barnhart, A. J., and Dierickx, K. (2023). Too-many-oids: the paradox in constructing an organoid ethics framework. *Molecular Psychology, 2*(10), 10. https://doi.org/10.12688/molpsychol.17552.1

Barrett, L. (2011). *Beyond the Brain: How Body and Environment Shape Animal and Human Minds*. Princeton University Press.

Barrett, L. F. (2017a). *How Emotions Are Made: The Secret Life of the Brain*. Pan Macmillan.

Barron, A. B., and Klein, C. (2016). What insects can tell us about the origins of consciousness. *Proceedings of the National Academy of Sciences, 113*(18), 4900–4908. https://doi.org/10.1073/pnas.1520084113

Bateson, M., and Nettle, D. (2015). Development of a cognitive bias methodology for measuring low mood in chimpanzees. *PeerJ, 3*, e998. https://doi.org/10.7717/peerj.998

Bateson, M., Desire, S., Gartside, S. E., and Wright, G. A. (2011). Agitated honeybees exhibit pessimistic cognitive biases. *Current Biology, 21*(12), 1070–1073.

Bassil, K., and Horstkötter, D. (2023). Ethical implications in making use of human cerebral organoids for investigating stress—related mechanisms and disorders. *Cambridge Quarterly of Healthcare Ethics, 32*, 529–541. https://doi.org/10.1017/S0963180123000038

Basl, J., and Schouten, G. (2018). Can we use social policy to enhance compliance with moral obligations to animals? *Ethical Theory and Moral Practice, 21*, 629–647. https://doi.org/10.1007/s10677-018-9895-5

Bastin, H. (1927). Do insects feel pain? *Scientific American, 137*(6), 531. https://doi.org/10.1038/scientificamerican1227-531

Bayne, T., Frohlich, J., Cusack, R., Moser, J., and Naci, L. (2023). Consciousness in the cradle: on the emergence of infant experience. *Trends in Cognitive Sciences*, advance online publication. https://doi.org/10.1016/j.tics.2023.08.018

Bayne, T., Hohwy, J., and Owen, A. M. (2016). Are there levels of consciousness? *Trends in Cognitive Sciences, 20*(6), 405–413. https://doi.org/10.1016/j.tics.2016.03.009

Bayne, T., Seth, A. K., and Massimini, M. (2020). Are there islands of awareness? *Trends in Neurosciences, 43*(1), 6–16. https://doi.org/10.1016/j.tins.2019.11.003

Bayne, T., and Shea, N. (2020). Consciousness, concepts and natural kinds. *Philosophical Topics, 48*(1), 65–83.

Bayne, T. (2010). *The Unity of Consciousness*. Oxford University Press.

BBC Culture. (2018). The 'untranslatable' Japanese phrase that predicts love. https://www.bbc.com/culture/article/20180103-the-untranslatable-japanese-phrase-that-predicts-love

Beck, F., and Eccles, J. C. (1992). Quantum aspects of brain activity and the role of consciousness. *Proceedings of the National Academy of Sciences, 89*(23), 11357–11361. https://doi.org/10.1073/pnas.89.23.11357

Bellieni, C. V., Tei, M., Stazzoni, G., Bertrando, S., Cornacchione, S., and Buonocore, G. (2013). Use of fetal analgesia during prenatal surgery. *Journal of Maternal-Fetal & Neonatal Medicine, 26*(1), 90–95. https://doi.org/10.3109/14767058.2012.718392

Bellieni, C. V. (2021). Analgesia for fetal pain during prenatal surgery: 10 years of progress. *Pediatric Research, 89*(7), 1612–1618. https://doi.org/10.1038/s41390-020-01170-2

Bender, E. M., Gebru, T., McMillan-Major, A., Shmitchell, S. (2021). On the dangers of stochastic parrots: can language models be too big? *Proceedings of the 2021 ACM Conference on Fairness, Accountability, and Transparency: FAccT '21*. Association for Computing Machinery, pp. 610–623. https://doi.org/10.1145/3442188.3445922

Ben-Haim, M. S., Dal Monte, O., Fagan, N. A., Dunham, Y., Hassin, R. R., Chang, S. W. C., and Santos, L. R. (2021). Disentangling perceptual awareness from nonconscious processing in rhesus monkeys (Macaca mulatta). *Proceedings of the National Academy of Sciences, 118*(15), e2017543118. https://doi.org/10.1073/pnas.2017543118

Bentham, J. (1789/1879). *An Introduction to the Principles of Morals and Legislation.* Clarendon Press.

Berenbaum, M. R. (1995). *Bugs in the System: Insects and Their Impact on Human Affairs* (revised edition). Basic Books.

Berkey, B. (2017). Prospects for an inclusive theory of justice: the case of non-human animals. *Journal of Applied Philosophy, 34*(5), 679–695.

Bernard, A., Bredeche, N., and André, J.-B. (2020). Indirect genetic effects allow escape from the inefficient equilibrium in a coordination game. *Evolution Letters, 4*(3), 257–265. https://doi.org/10.1002/evl3.155

Berridge, K. C. (2004). Pleasure, unfelt affect, and irrational desire. In *Feelings and Emotions: The Amsterdam Symposium* (pp. 243–262). Cambridge University Press. https://doi.org/10.1017/CBO9780511806582.015

Berridge, K. C., and Robinson, T. E. (2003). Parsing reward. *Trends in Neurosciences, 26,* 507–513. https://doi.org/10.1016/S0166-2236(03)00233-9

Birch, J. (2017a). Animal sentience and the precautionary principle. *Animal Sentience, 2*(16), 1. https://doi.org/10.51291/2377-7478.1200

Birch, J. (2017b). Refining the precautionary framework. *Animal Sentience, 2*(16), 20. https://doi.org/10.51291/2377-7478.1279

Birch, J. (2017c). Crabs and lobsters deserve protection from being cooked alive. *Aeon.* https://aeon.co/ideas/crabs-and-lobsters-deserve-protection-from-being-cooked-alive

Birch, J. (2017d). *The Philosophy of Social Evolution.* Oxford University Press.

Birch, J. (2017e, May 16). How pollsters are discounting the views of working class and young people. *The Guardian.* https://www.theguardian.com/politics/2017/may/16/how-pollsters-are-discounting-the-views-of-working-class-and-young-people

Birch, J. (2018a). On crabs and statistics. *Animal Sentience, 2*(16), 23. https://doi.org/10.51291/2377-7478.1377

Birch, J. (2018b). Degrees of sentience? *Animal Sentience, 3*(21), 11.

Birch, J. (2020a). Global workspace theory and animal consciousness. *Philosophical Topics, 48*(1), 21–38.

Birch, J. (2020b). The place of animals in Kantian ethics. *Biology & Philosophy, 35*(1), 8. https://doi.org/10.1007/s10539-019-9712-0

Birch, J. (2020c). In search of the origins of consciousness. *Acta Biotheoretica, 68,* 287–294. https://doi.org/10.1007/s10441-019-09363-x

Birch, J. (2020d, November 3). The mind-body problem. *LSE Philosophy Blog.* https://www.lse.ac.uk/philosophy/blog/2020/11/03/the-mind-body-problem/

Birch, J. (2021a). Science and policy in extremis: the UK's initial response to COVID-19. *European Journal for Philosophy of Science, 11*(3), 90. https://doi.org/10.1007/s13194-021-00407-z

Birch, J. (2021b). The hatching of consciousness. *History and Philosophy of the Life Sciences, 43*(4), 121. https://doi.org/10.1007/s40656-021-00472-w

Birch, J. (2022a). Materialism and the moral status of animals. *Philosophical Quarterly, 72*(4), 795–815. https://doi.org/10.1093/pq/pqab072

Birch, J. (2022b). Should animal welfare be defined in terms of consciousness? *Philosophy of Science, 89*(5), 1114–1123. https://doi.org/10.1017/psa.2022.59

Birch, J. (2022c). The search for invertebrate consciousness. *Noûs, 56*(1), 133–153. https://doi.org/10.1111/nous.12351

Birch, J. (2023a). Medical AI, inductive risk and the communication of uncertainty: the case of disorders of consciousness. *Journal of Medical Ethics,* advance online publication. https://doi.org/10.1136/jme-2023-109424

Birch, J. (2023b). Disentangling sentience from developmental plasticity. *Animal Sentience, 8*(33), 20. https://doi.org/10.51291/2377-7478.1812

Birch, J. (2023c, March 27). AI, invertebrates, and the risk of living absurdly. *LSE Philosophy Blog.* https://www.lse.ac.uk/philosophy/blog/2023/03/27/ai-invertebrates-and-the-risk-of-living-absurdly/

Birch, J. (in press). Emotionless animals? Constructionist theories of emotion beyond the human case. *Proceedings of the Aristotelian Society.*

Birch, J., and Browning, H. (2021). Neural organoids and the precautionary principle. *American Journal of Bioethics, 21*(1), 56–58. https://doi.org/10.1080/15265161.2020.1845858

Birch, J., Burn, C., Schnell, A., Browning, H., and Crump, A. (2021). *Review of the Evidence of Sentience in Cephalopod Molluscs and Decapod Crustaceans.* LSE Consulting.

Birch, J., Creel, K. A., Jha, A. K., and Plutynski, A. (2022). Clinical decisions using AI must consider patient values. *Nature Medicine, 28*(2), 229–232. https://doi.org/10.1038/s41591-021-01624-y

Birch, J., Ginsburg, S., and Jablonka, E. (2020a). Unlimited associative learning and the origins of consciousness: a primer and some predictions. *Biology & Philosophy, 35*(6), 56. https://doi.org/10.1007/s10539-020-09772-0

Birch, J., Ginsburg, S., and Jablonka, E. (2021). The learning-consciousness connection. *Biology & Philosophy, 36*(5), 49. https://doi.org/10.1007/s10539-021-09802-5

Birch, J., Schnell, A. K., and Clayton, N. S. (2020b). Dimensions of animal consciousness. *Trends in Cognitive Sciences, 24*(10), 789–801. https://doi.org/10.1016/j.tics.2020.07.007

Birch, J., and Mørch, H. H. (2023). Consciousness and the Overton window of science. The Brains Blog, 11–14 September 2023. https://philosophyofbrains.com/category/consciousness/birch-and-morch-on-the-science-of-consciousness

Bird, A., and Tobin, E. (2023). Natural kinds. In Zalta, E. N., and Nodelman, U. (eds), *The Stanford Encyclopedia of Philosophy (Spring 2023 Edition).* Metaphysics Research Lab, Stanford University. https://plato.stanford.edu/archives/spr2023/entries/natural-kinds/

Blackburn, S. (1993). *Essays in Quasi-Realism.* Oxford University Press.

Blackburn, S. (1998). *Ruling Passions: A Theory of Practical Reasoning.* Clarendon Press.

Blackshaw, B. P., and Rodger, D. (2021). Why we should not extend the 14-day rule. *Journal of Medical Ethics, 47*(10), 712–714. https://doi.org/10.1136/medethics-2021-107317

Bliss-Moreau, E. (2017). Constructing nonhuman animal emotion. *Current Opinion in Psychology, 17,* 184–188. https://doi.org/10.1016/j.copsyc.2017.07.011

Block, N. (1995). On a confusion about a function of consciousness. *Behavioral and Brain Sciences, 18*(2), 227–247. https://doi.org/10.1017/S0140525X00038188

Block, N. (1996). Mental Paint and Mental Latex. *Philosophical Issues, 7,* 19–49. https://doi.org/10.2307/1522889

Blum, P. R. (2019). Substance dualism in Descartes. In H. Salazar (ed.), *Introduction to Philosophy: Philosophy of Mind.* Rebus Community. https://press.rebus.community/intro-to-phil-of-mind/chapter/substance-dualism-in-descartes-2/

Boffey, P. M. (1987, November 24). Infants' sense of pain is recognized, finally. *New York Times.* https://www.nytimes.com/1987/11/24/science/infants-sense-of-pain-is-recognized-finally.html

Boonin, D. (2019). *Beyond Roe: Why Abortion Should Be Legal—Even if the Fetus Is a Person.* Academic.

Bornemann, B., Winkielman, P., and der Meer, E. van. (2012). Can you feel what you do not see? Using internal feedback to detect briefly presented emotional stimuli. *International Journal of Psychophysiology, 85*(1), 116–124. https://doi.org/10.1016/j.ijpsycho.2011.04.007

Bostrom, N. (2014). *Superintelligence: Paths, Dangers, Strategies.* Oxford University Press.

Boyd, R. (1991). Realism, anti-foundationalism and the enthusiasm for natural kinds. *Philosophical Studies, 61*(1–2), 127–148.

Boyd, R. (1999). Homeostasis, species, and higher taxa. In Wilson, R. (ed.), *Species: New Interdisciplinary Essays.* MIT Press, 141–186.

Boyle, A. (2020). Conjoined twinning & biological individuation. *Philosophical Studies, 177*(8), 2395–2415. https://doi.org/10.1007/s11098-019-01316-x

Braddock, M. (2017). Should we treat vegetative and minimally conscious patients as persons? *Neuroethics, 10*(2), 267–280.

Braddock M. (2021). Precautionary personhood: we should treat patients with disorders of consciousness as persons. *AJOB Neuroscience*, *12*(2–3), 162–164. https://doi.org/10.1080/21507740.2021.1904043

Bradley, R., and Steele, K. (2015). Making climate decisions. *Philosophy Compass*, *10*(11), 799–810. https://doi.org/10.1111/phc3.12259

Bradford, G. (2023). Consciousness and welfare subjectivity. *Noûs*, *57*(4), 905–921.

Bradshaw, R. H. (1998). Consciousness in non-human animals: adopting the precautionary principle. *Journal of Consciousness Studies*, *5*(1), 108–114.

Brembs, B., Lorenzetti, F. D., Reyes, F. D., Baxter, D. A., and Byrne, J. H. (2002). Operant reward learning in aplysia: neuronal correlates and mechanisms. *Science*, *296*(5573), 1706–1709. https://doi.org/10.1126/science.1069434

Bridges, A. D., MaBouDi, H., Procenko, O., Lockwood, C., Mohammed, Y., Kowalewska, A., Romero González, J. E., Woodgate, J. L., and Chittka, L. (2023). Bumblebees acquire alternative puzzle-box solutions via social learning. *PLOS Biology*, *21*(3), e3002019. https://doi.org/10.1371/journal.pbio.3002019

Briffa, M. (2022). Sentience in decapods: an open question. *Animal Sentience*, *7*(32), 19. https://doi.org/10.51291/2377-7478.1740

Brittin, C. A., Cook, S. J., Hall, D. H., Emmons, S. W., and Cohen, N. (2021). A multi-scale brain map derived from whole-brain volumetric reconstructions. *Nature*, *591*(7848), 105–110. https://doi.org/10.1038/s41586-021-03284-x

Broadie, A., and Pybus, E. M. (1974). Kant's treatment of animals. *Philosophy*, *49*(190), 375–383.

Brogaard, B. (2011). Color experience in blindsight? *Philosophical Psychology*, *24*(6), 767–786. https://doi.org/10.1080/09515089.2011.562641

Brown, C. (2015). Fish intelligence, sentience and ethics. *Animal Cognition*, *18*, 1–17. https://doi.org/10.1007/s10071-014-0761-0

Brown, C. (2017). A risk assessment and phylogenetic approach. *Animal Sentience*, *2*(16), 3. https://doi.org/10.51291/2377-7478.1219

Brown, C. (2022). Fine-tuning the criteria for inferring sentience. *Animal Sentience*, *7*(32). https://doi.org/10.51291/2377-7478.1721

Brown, E. N., Lydic, R., and Schiff, N. D. (2010). General anesthesia, sleep, and coma. *New England Journal of Medicine*, *363*(27), 2638–2650. https://doi.org/10.1056/NEJMra0808281

Brown, M. F., and Demas, G. E. (1994). Evidence for spatial working memory in honeybees (Apis mellifera). *Journal of Comparative Psychology (Washington, D.C.: 1983)*, *108*(4), 344–352. https://doi.org/10.1037/0735-7036.108.4.344

Brown, M. F., Moore, J. A., Brown, C. H., and Langheld, K. D. (1997). The existence and extent of spatial working memory ability in honeybees. *Animal Learning & Behavior*, *25*(4), 473–484. https://doi.org/10.3758/BF03209853

Brown, R., Lau, H., and LeDoux, J. E. (2019). Understanding the higher-order approach to consciousness. *Trends in Cognitive Sciences*, *23*(9), 754–768. https://doi.org/10.1016/j.tics.2019.06.009

Brown, R. L. (2017). Not statistically significant, but still scientific. *Animal Sentience*, *2*(16). https://doi.org/10.51291/2377-7478.1247

Brown, S. (2022). How much of a pain would a crustacean 'common currency' really be? *Animal Sentience*, *7*(32), 23. https://doi.org/10.51291/2377-7478.1749

Browning, H., and Birch, J. (2022). Animal sentience. *Philosophy Compass*, *17*(5), e12822. https://doi.org/10.1111/phc3.12822

Browning, H. (2017). Anecdotes can be evidence too. *Animal Sentience*, *2*(16), 13. https://doi.org/10.51291/2377-7478.1246

Browning, H. (2023). Welfare comparisons within and across species. *Philosophical Studies*, *180*(2), 529–551. https://doi.org/10.1007/s11098-022-01907-1

Brummelte, S., Grunau, R. E., Chau, V., Poskitt, K. J., Brant, R., Vinall, J., Gover, A., Synnes, A. R., and Miller, S. P. (2012). Procedural pain and brain development in premature newborns. *Annals of Neurology*, *71*(3), 385–396. https://doi.org/10.1002/ana.22267

Brüntrup, G., and Jaskolla, L. (2017). *Panpsychism: Contemporary Perspectives*. Oxford University Press.

Buchak, L. (2019). Weighing the risks of climate change. *The Monist*, *102*(1), 66–83. https://doi. org/10.1093/monist/ony022

Buchanan, A., and Powell, R. (2018). *The Evolution of Moral Progress: A Biocultural Theory*. Oxford University Press.

Burgos, A., Honjo, K., Ohyama, T., Qian, C. S., Shin, G. J.-E., Gohl, D. M., Silies, M., Tracey, W. D., Zlatic, M., Cardona, A., and Grueber, W. B. (2018). Nociceptive interneurons control modular motor pathways to promote escape behavior in Drosophila. *ELife*, *7*, e26016. https://doi.org/10.7554/eLife.26016

Burmeister, S., Couvillon, P. A., and Bitterman, M. E. (1995). Performance of honeybees in analogues of the rodent radial maze. *Animal Learning & Behavior*, *23*(4), 369–375. https://doi.org/10.3758/BF03198936

Burrell, B. (2022). Emotional component of pain perception in the medicinal leech? *Animal Sentience*, *7*(32). https://doi.org/10.51291/2377-7478.1728

Butlin, P. (2022). Sentience criteria to persuade the reasonable sceptic. *Animal Sentience*, *7*(32), 21. https://doi.org/10.51291/2377-7478.1741

Butlin, P., Long, R., Elmoznino, E., Bengio, Y., Birch, J., Constant, A., Deane, G., Fleming, S.M., Frith, C., Ji, X. and Kanai, R. (2023). Consciousness in artificial intelligence: insights from the science of consciousness. arXiv preprint. arXiv:2308.08708

Callicott, J. B. (2015). How ecological collectives are morally considerable. In S. M. Gardiner, and A. Thompson (eds), *The Oxford Handbook of Environmental Ethics*. Oxford University Press. https://doi.org/10.1093/oxfordhb/9780199941339.013.11

Calvo, P., and Lawrence, N. (2022). *Planta Sapiens: Unmasking Plant Intelligence*. Hachette UK.

Campbell-Yeo, M., Eriksson, M., and Benoit, B. (2022). Assessment and Management of pain in preterm infants: a practice update. *Children*, *9*(2), Article 2. https://doi.org/10.3390/children9020244

Carder, G. (2017). A preliminary investigation into the welfare of lobsters in the UK. *Animal Sentience*, *2*(16), 19. https://doi.org/10.51291/2377-7478.1262

Carrington, D. (2018, April 27). EU agrees total ban on bee-harming pesticides. *The Guardian*. https://www.theguardian.com/environment/2018/apr/27/eu-agrees-total-ban-on-bee-harming-pesticides

Carruthers, P. (1992). *The Animals Issue: Moral Theory in Practice*. Cambridge University Press.

Carruthers, P. (2000). *Phenomenal Consciousness: A Naturalistic Theory*. Cambridge University Press.

Carruthers, P. (2005). *Consciousness: Essays from a Higher-Order Perspective*. Clarendon Press.

Carruthers, P. (2007). Invertebrate minds: a challenge for ethical theory. *Journal of Ethics*, *11*(3), 275–297. https://doi.org/10.1007/s10892-007-9015-6

Carruthers, P. (2018). Valence and value. *Philosophy and Phenomenological Research*, *97*(3), 658–680. https://doi.org/10.1111/phpr.12395

Carruthers, P. (2019). *Human and Animal Minds: The Consciousness Questions Laid to Rest*. Oxford University Press.

Carruthers, P. (2023). On valence: imperative or representation of value? *British Journal for the Philosophy of Science*, 74(3), 533–553.

Carter, J. A., and Peterson, M. (2015). On the epistemology of the precautionary principle. *Erkenntnis*, *80*(1), 1–13. https://doi.org/10.1007/s10670-014-9609-x

Casal, P. (2003). Is multiculturalism bad for animals? *Journal of Political Philosophy*, *11*, 1–22.

Celeghin, A., de Gelder, B., and Tamietto, M. (2015). From affective blindsight to emotional consciousness. *Consciousness and Cognition*, *36*, 414–425. https://doi.org/10.1016/j.concog.2015.05.007

Chalmers, D. J. (1995). Facing up to the problem of consciousness. *Journal of Consciousness Studies*, *2*(3), 200–219.

Chalmers, D. J. (1996). *The Conscious Mind: In Search of a Fundamental Theory*. Oxford University Press.

Chalmers, D. J. (2010). *The Character of Consciousness*. Oxford University Press.

Chalmers, D. J. (2017). The combination problem for panpsychism. In G. Bruntrup and L. Jaskolla (eds), *Panpsychism: Contemporary Perspectives* (pp. 179–214). Oxford University Press. https://doi.org/10.1093/acprof:oso/9780199359943.003.0008

Chalmers, D. J. (2023). *Could a large language model be conscious?* https://philpapers.org/rec/CHACAL-3

Chan, S. (2017). How to rethink the fourteen-day rule. *Hastings Center Report, 47*(3), 5–6. https://doi.org/10.1002/hast.698

Chase, R. B. (2002). *Behavior and Its Neural Control in Gastropod Molluscs* (illustrated edition). Oxford University Press.

Chittka, L. (1998). Sensorimotor learning in bumblebees: long-term retention and reversal training. *Journal of Experimental Biology, 201*(4), 515–524. https://doi.org/10.1242/jeb.201.4.515

Chittka, L. (2022). *The Mind of a Bee*. Princeton University Press.

Christenson, J., Boman, A., Lagerbäck, P.-A., and Grillner, S. (1988). The dorsal cell, one class of primary sensory neuron in the lamprey spinal cord. I: Touch, pressure but no nociception—a physiological study. *Brain Research, 440*(1), 1–8. https://doi.org/10.1016/0006-8993(88)91152-3.

Ciaunica, A., Safron, A., and Delafield-Butt, J. (2021). Back to square one: the bodily roots of conscious experiences in early life. *Neuroscience of Consciousness, 2021*(2), niab037.

Claassen, J., Doyle, K., Matory, A., Couch, C., Burger, K. M., Velazquez, A., Okonkwo, J. U., King, J.-R., Park, S., Agarwal, S., Roh, D., Megjhani, M., Eliseyev, A., Connolly, E. S., and Rohaut, B. (2019). Detection of brain activation in unresponsive patients with acute brain injury. *New England Journal of Medicine, 380*(26), 2497–2505. https://doi.org/10.1056/NEJMoa1812757

Clark, R. E., and Squire, L. R. (1998). Classical conditioning and brain systems: the role of awareness. *Science, 280*, 77–81. https://doi.org/10.1126/science.280.5360.77

Clark, R. E., Manns, J. R., and Squire, L. R. (2002). Classical conditioning, awareness, and brain systems. *Trends in Cognitive Sciences, 6*(12), 524–531. https://doi.org/10.1016/s1364-6613(02)02041-7

Clarke, S. (2005). Future technologies, dystopic futures and the precautionary principle. *Ethics and Information Technology, 7*(3), 121–126. https://doi.org/10.1007/s10676-006-0007-1

Climate Assembly UK. (2020). *The Path to Net Zero*. UK House of Commons. https://www.climateassembly.uk/report/

Cochrane, A. (2018). *Sentientist Politics: A Theory of Global Inter-Species Justice*. Oxford University Press.

Committee of Inquiry into Human Fertilisation and Embryology. (1984). *Report of the Committee of Inquiry into Human Fertilisation and Embryology*. https://wellcomecollection.org/works/pxgeeqnf

Comstock, G. (2022). Pain in Pleocyemata, but not in Dendrobranchiata? *Animal Sentience, 7*(32), 13. https://doi.org/10.51291/2377-7478.1727

Cook, S. J., Jarrell, T. A., Brittin, C. A., Wang, Y., Bloniarz, A. E., Yakovlev, M. A., Nguyen, K. C. Q., Tang, L. T.-H., Bayer, E. A., Duerr, J. S., Bülow, H. E., Hobert, O., Hall, D. H., and Emmons, S. W. (2019). Whole-animal connectomes of both *Caenorhabditis elegans* sexes. *Nature, 571*(7763), Article 7763. https://doi.org/10.1038/s41586-019-1352-7

Cooke, M. H. Y., Couvillon, P. A., and Bitterman, M. E. (2007). Delayed symbolic matching in honeybees (*Apis mellifera*). *Journal of Comparative Psychology (Washington, DC: 1983), 121*(1), 106–108. https://doi.org/10.1037/0735-7036.121.1.106

Cooper, J., Tinarwo, A., and Ventura, B. (2022). Decapods as food, companions and research animals: legal impact of ascribing sentience. *Animal Sentience, 7*(32), 27. https://doi.org/10.51291/2377-7478.1759

Corichi, M. (2021). Eight-in-ten Indians limit meat in their diets, and four-in-ten consider themselves vegetarian. *Pew Research Center*. https://www.pewresearch.org/short-reads/2021/07/08/eight-in-ten-indians-limit-meat-in-their-diets-and-four-in-ten-consider-themselves-vegetarian/

Cowey, A. (2010). The blindsight saga. *Experimental Brain Research, 200*(1), 3–24. https://doi.org/10.1007/s00221-009-1914-2

Crane, T. (2001). *Elements of Mind: An Introduction to the Philosophy of Mind*. Oxford University Press.

Crane, T. (2019). The knowledge argument is an argument about knowledge. In S. Coleman (ed.), *The Knowledge Argument* (pp. 15–31). Cambridge University Press. https://doi.org/10.1017/9781316494134.002

Crisp, R. (2021). Well-being. In E. N. Zalta (ed.), *The Stanford Encyclopedia of Philosophy* (Winter 2021). Metaphysics Research Lab, Stanford University. https://plato.stanford.edu/archives/win2021/entries/well-being/

Crook, R. J. (2021). Behavioral and neurophysiological evidence suggests affective pain experience in octopus. *IScience*, 24(3), 102229. https://doi.org/10.1016/j.isci.2021.102229

Crosby, M. (2019). Why artificial consciousness matters. *CEUR Workshop Proceedings*, 2287, 13.

Cross, F. R., Carvell, G. E., Jackson, R. R., and Grace, R. C. (2020). Arthropod intelligence? The case for Portia. *Frontiers in Psychology*, 11. https://www.frontiersin.org/articles/10.3389/fpsyg.2020.568049

Cross, F. R., and Jackson, R. R. (2014). Specialised use of working memory by Portia africana, a spider-eating salticid. *Animal Cognition*, 17(2), 435–444. https://doi.org/10.1007/s10071-013-0675-2

Cross, F. R., and Jackson, R. R. (2016). The execution of planned detours by spider-eating predators. *Journal of the Experimental Analysis of Behavior*, 105(1), 194–210. https://doi.org/10.1002/jeab.189

Cross, F. R., and Jackson, R. R. (2019). Portia's capacity to decide whether a detour is necessary. *Journal of Experimental Biology*, 222(15), jeb203463. https://doi.org/10.1242/jeb.203463

Crump, A., and Birch, J. (2022). Animal consciousness: the interplay of neural and behavioural evidence. *Journal of Consciousness Studies*, 29(3–4), 104–128. https://doi.org/10.53765/20512201.29.3.104

Crump, A., Browning, H., Schnell, A., Burn, C., and Birch, J. (2022a). Animal sentience research: synthesis and proposals. *Animal Sentience*, 7(32), 31. https://doi.org/10.51291/2377-7478.1770

Crump, A., Browning, H., Schnell, A., Burn, C., and Birch, J. (2022b). Sentience in decapod crustaceans: a general framework and review of the evidence. *Animal Sentience*, 7(32), 1. https://doi.org/10.51291/2377-7478.1691

Cyranoski, D. (2012). Neuroscience: the mind reader. *Nature*, 486(7402), Article 7402. https://doi.org/10.1038/486178a

Czech-Damal, N. U., Liebschner, A., Miersch, L., Klauer, G., Hanke, F. D., Marshall, C., Dehnhardt, G., and Hanke, W. (2011). Electroreception in the Guiana dolphin (*Sotalia guianensis*). *Proceedings of the Royal Society B: Biological Sciences*, 279(1729), 663–668. https://doi.org/10.1098/rspb.2011.1127

Dai, D., Sun, Y., Dong, L., Hao, Y., Ma, S., Sui, Z., and Wei, F. (2022). Why can GPT learn in-context? Language models secretly perform gradient descent as meta optimizers. *arXiv preprint* arXiv:2212.10559

Dalesman, S., Karnik, V., and Lukowiak, K. (2011). Sensory mediation of memory blocking stressors in the pond snail *Lymnaea stagnalis*. *Journal of Experimental Biology*, 214, 2528–33.

Damasio, A., and Carvalho, G. B. (2013). The nature of feelings: evolutionary and neurobiological origins. *Nature Reviews Neuroscience*, 14(2), 143–152.

Damasio, A., Damasio, H., and Tranel, D. (2013). Persistence of feelings and sentience after bilateral damage of the insula. *Cerebral Cortex*, 23(4), 833–846. https://doi.org/10.1093/cercor/bhs077

Damasio, A. R., Grabowski, T. J., Bechara, A., Damasio, H., Ponto, L. L., Parvizi, J., and Hichwa, R. D. (2000). Subcortical and cortical brain activity during the feeling of self-generated emotions. *Nature Neuroscience*, 3(10), 1049–1056.

Dawkins, M. (2022). Unconscious humans, autonomous machines and the difficulty of knowing which animals are sentient. *Animal Sentience*, 7(32), 20. https://doi.org/10.51291/2377-7478.1746

Dawkins, R. (1986/2006). *The Blind Watchmaker*. Penguin.

de Arriba, M. del C., and Pombal, M. A. (2007). Afferent connections of the optic tectum in lampreys: an experimental study. *Brain, Behavior and Evolution*, 69(1), 37–68. https://doi.org/10.1159/000095272

de Freitas Netto, S. V., Sobral, M. F. F., Ribeiro, A. R. B., and Soares, G. R. D. L. (2020). Concepts and forms of greenwashing: a systematic review. *Environmental Sciences Europe, 32*(1), 1–12.

de Gelder, B., Tamietto, M., van Boxtel, G., Goebel, R., Sahraie, A., van den Stock, J., Stienen, B. M. C., Weiskrantz, L., and Pegna, A. (2008). Intact navigation skills after bilateral loss of striate cortex. *Current Biology, 18*(24), R1128–R1129. https://doi.org/10.1016/j.cub.2008.11.002

Deakin, A., Mendl, M., Browne, W. J., Paul, E. S., and Hodge, J. J. (2018). State-dependent judgement bias in *Drosophila*: evidence for evolutionarily primitive affective processes. *Biology Letters,* 14(2), 20170779.

Deglincerti, A., Croft, G. F., Pietila, L. N., Zernicka-Goetz, M., Siggia, E. D., and Brivanlou, A. H. (2016). Self-organization of the in vitro attached human embryo. *Nature, 533*(7602), Article 7602. https://doi.org/10.1038/nature17948

DeGrazia, D. (1996). *Taking Animals Seriously: Mental Life and Moral Status*. Cambridge University Press.

DeGrazia, D. (2021). An interest-based model of moral status. In S. Clarke, H. Zohny, and J. Savulescu (eds), *Rethinking Moral Status* (pp. 40–56). Oxford University Press.

Dehaene, S. (2014). *Consciousness and the Brain: Deciphering How the Brain Codes Our Thoughts*. Penguin Publishing Group.

Dehaene, S., and Changeux, J.-P. (2011). Experimental and theoretical approaches to conscious processing. *Neuron, 70*(2), 200–227. https://doi.org/10.1016/j.neuron.2011.03.018

Dehaene, S., Lau, H., and Kouider, S. (2017). What is consciousness, and could machines have it? *Science, 358*(6362), 486–492. https://doi.org/10.1126/science.aan8871

Delon, N., Cook, P., Bauer, G., and Harley, H. (2020). Consider the agent in the arthropod. *Animal Sentience, 5*(29), 32. https://doi.org/10.51291/2377-7478.1623

de Jongh, D., Massey, E. K., and Bunnik, E. M. (2022). Organoids: a systematic review of ethical issues. *Stem Cell Research and Therapy, 13*(1), 337. https://doi.org/10.1186/s13287-022-02950-9

De Neve, J.-E., Clark, A. E., Krekel, C., Layard, R., and O'Donnell, G. (2020). Taking a wellbeing years approach to policy choice. *BMJ, 371*, m3853. https://doi.org/10.1136/bmj.m3853

Dennett, D. C. (1987). *The Intentional Stance*. MIT Press.

Dennett, D. C. (1991). *Consciousness Explained*. Little, Brown and Company.

Dennett, D. C. (2005). *Sweet Dreams: Philosophical Obstacles to a Science of Consciousness*. MIT Press. https://doi.org/10.7551/mitpress/6576.001.0001

Dennett, D. C. (2017). *From Bacteria to Bach and Back: The Evolution of Minds*. Penguin.

Denton, D. A. (2006). *The Primordial Emotions: The Dawning of Consciousness*. Oxford University Press.

Denton, D. A., McKinley, M. J., Farrell, M., and Egan, G. F. (2009). The role of primordial emotions in the evolutionary origin of consciousness. *Consciousness and Cognition, 18*(2), 500–514. https://doi.org/10.1016/j.concog.2008.06.009

de Queiroz, K. (2006). The PhyloCode and the distinction between taxonomy and nomenclature. *Systematic Biology, 55*(1), 160–162. https://doi.org/10.1080/10635150500431221

Derbyshire, S. W., and Bockmann, J. C. (2020). Reconsidering fetal pain. *Journal of Medical Ethics, 46*(1), 3–6. https://doi.org/10.1136/medethics-2019-105701

Derbyshire, S. W. G. (1999). Locating the beginnings of pain. *Bioethics, 13*(1), 1–31. https://doi.org/10.1111/1467-8519.00129

Derbyshire, S. W. G. (2006). Can fetuses feel pain? *BMJ, 332*(7546), 909–912. https://doi.org/10.1136/bmj.332.7546.909

Derbyshire, S. W. G. (2007). *Memorandum 4: Submission from Dr Stuart Derbyshire, University of Birmingham, School of Psychology*. UK House of Commons. https://publications.parliament.uk/pa/cm200607/cmselect/cmsctech/1045/1045we05.htm

Derbyshire, S. W. G., and Furedi, A. (1996). Do fetuses feel pain? 'Fetal pain' is a misnomer. *BMJ (Clinical Research Ed.), 313*(7060), 795. https://doi.org/10.1136/bmj.313.7060.795a

Descartes, R. (1646/2004). Letter to the Marquess of Newcastle. In S. M. Shieber (ed.), *The Turing Test: Verbal Behavior as the Hallmark of Intelligence* (pp. 35–38). MIT Press.

de Waal, F. (2022). Sentience as part of emotional lives. *Animal Sentience, 7*(32), 22. https://doi.org/10.51291/2377-7478.1747

Diner, S. (2023). Potential consciousness of human cerebral organoids: on similarity-based views in precautionary discourse. *Neuroethics*, *16*(3), 23. https://doi.org/10.1007/s12152-023-09533-2

Di Stefano, L. M., Wood, K., Mactier, H., Bates, S. E., and Wilkinson, D. (2021). Viability and thresholds for treatment of extremely preterm infants: survey of UK neonatal professionals. *Archives of Disease in Childhood—Fetal and Neonatal Edition*, *106*(6), 596–602. https://doi.org/10.1136/archdischild-2020-321273

Doesburg, S. M., Chau, C. M., Cheung, T. P. L., Moiseev, A., Ribary, U., Herdman, A. T., Miller, S. P., Cepeda, I. L., Synnes, A., and Grunau, R. E. (2013). Neonatal pain-related stress, functional cortical activity and visual-perceptual abilities in school-age children born at extremely low gestational age. *Pain*, *154*(10), 1946–1952. https://doi.org/10.1016/j.pain.2013.04.009

Doesburg, S. M., and Ward, L. M. (2007). Corticothalamic necessity, qualia, and consciousness. *Behavioral and Brain Sciences*, *30*(1), 90–91. https://doi.org/10.1017/S0140525X07000982

Donato, A., Kagias, K., Zhang, Y., and Hilliard, M. A. (2019). Neuronal sub-compartmentalization: a strategy to optimize neuronal function. *Biological Reviews*, *94*(3), 1023–1037. https://doi.org/10.1111/brv.12487

Douglas, H. (2009). *Science, Policy, and the Value-Free Ideal*. University of Pittsburgh Press.

Downs, K. M. (2009). The enigmatic primitive streak: prevailing notions and challenges concerning the body axis of mammals. *BioEssays: News and Reviews in Molecular, Cellular and Developmental Biology*, *31*(8), 892–902. https://doi.org/10.1002/bies.200900038

Dreyer, M., Renn, O., Ely, A., Stirling, A., Vos, E., and Wendler, F. (2008, June 30). *A general framework for the precautionary and inclusive governance of food safety in Europe* [reports and working papers]. DIALOGIK. http://www.dialogik-expert.de/en/forschung/A%20General%20Framework%20for%20the%20Precautionary%20and%20Inclusive%20Governance%20of%20Food%20Safety.pdf

Driesen, D. M. (2013). Cost-benefit analysis and the precautionary principle: can they be reconciled. *Michigan State Law Review*, *2013*, 771.

Droege, P., Weiss, D. J., Schwob, N., and Braithwaite, V. (2021). Trace conditioning as a test for animal consciousness: a new approach. *Animal Cognition*, *24*(6), 1299–1304. https://doi.org/10.1007/s10071-021-01522-3

Dryzek, J. S. (2010). *Foundations and Frontiers of Deliberative Governance*. Oxford University Press.

Du Bois, W. E. B. (2005). *Darkwater: Voices from within the Veil*. Project Gutenberg.

Dung, L. (2022). Does illusionism imply skepticism of animal consciousness? *Synthese*, *200*(3), 1–19.

Dunlop, R., Millsopp, S., and Laming, P. (2006). Avoidance learning in goldfish (Carassius auratus) and trout (Oncorhynchus mykiss) and implications for pain perception. *Applied Animal Behaviour Science*, *97*(2), 255–271. https://doi.org/10.1016/j.applanim.2005.06.018

Duran, J. (1999). The moral status of the Joshua Tree. *International Journal of Applied Philosophy*, *13*(1), 113–120. https://doi.org/10.5840/ijap199913110

Eccles, J. C. (1989). *Evolution of the Brain: Creation of the Self*. Routledge.

Eccles, J. C. (1994). *How the SELF Controls Its BRAIN*. Springer-Verlag.

Edlow, B. L., Claassen, J., Schiff, N. D., and Greer, D. M. (2021). Recovery from disorders of consciousness: mechanisms, prognosis and emerging therapies. *Nature Reviews Neurology*, *17*(3), Article 3. https://doi.org/10.1038/s41582-020-00428-x

Eisemann, C. H., Jorgensen, W. K., Merritt, D. J., Rice, M. J., Cribb, B. W., Webb, P. D., and Zalucki, M. P. (1984). Do insects feel pain?—A biological view. *Experientia*, *40*(2), 164–167. https://doi.org/10.1007/BF01963580

Ekman, P. (1992). Are there basic emotions? *Psychological Review*, *99*, 550–553. https://doi.org/10.1037/0033-295X.99.3.550

Elliott, K. C., and Richards, T. (2017). *Exploring Inductive Risk: Case Studies of Values in Science*. Oxford University Press.

Elwood, R. (2017). Assessing negative and positive evidence for animal pain. *Animal Sentience*, *2*(16), 21. https://doi.org/10.51291/2377-7478.1283

Elwood, R. (2022). Pros and cons of a framework for evaluating potential pain in decapods. *Animal Sentience*, *7*(32). https://doi.org/10.51291/2377-7478.1766

Emanuel, S., and Libersat, F. (2019). Nociceptive pathway in the cockroach *Periplaneta americana*. *Frontiers in Physiology, 10*, 1100. https://doi.org/10.3389/fphys.2019.01100

Eriksen, C. W. (1960). Discrimination and learning without awareness: a methodological survey and evaluation. *Psychological Review, 67*, 279–300. https://doi.org/10.1037/h0041622

European Commission. (2000/2006). Communication from the Commission of 2 February 2000 on the precautionary principle (COM (2000) 12.02.2000 p. 1). In P. Galizzi and P. Sands (eds), *Documents in European Community Environmental Law* (2nd ed., pp. 90–115). Cambridge University Press. https://doi.org/10.1017/CBO9780511610851.008

European Food Safety Authority (EFSA). (2005). Opinion of the Scientific Panel on Animal Health and Welfare (AHAW) on a request from the Commission related to the aspects of the biology and welfare of animals used for experimental and other scientific purposes. *EFSA Journal, 3*(12), 292. https://doi.org/10.2903/j.efsa.2005.292

Fallon, F., and Blackmon, J. C. (2021). IIT's scientific counter-revolution: a neuroscientific theory's physical and metaphysical implications. *Entropy, 23*, 942. https://doi.org/10.3390/e23080942

Farm Animal Welfare Council. (2009). *Farm Animal Welfare in Great Britain: Past, Present and Future*. Defra.

Farris, S. M. (2020). The rise to dominance of genetic model organisms and the decline of curiosity-driven organismal research. *PLoS One, 15*(12), e0243088. https://doi.org/10.1371/journal.pone.0243088

Faull, O. K., and Pattinson, K. T. (2017). The cortical connectivity of the periaqueductal gray and the conditioned response to the threat of breathlessness. *ELife, 6*, e21749. https://doi.org/10.7554/eLife.21749

Feigl, H. (1958/1967). The 'mental' and the 'physical'. *Minnesota Studies in the Philosophy of Science, 2*, 370–497.

Feigl, H. (1971). Some crucial issues of mind-body monism. *Synthese, 22*(3/4), 295–312.

Feigl, H. (1975). Russell and Schlick: a remarkable agreement on a monistic solution of the mind-body problem. *Erkenntnis (1975–), 9*(1), 11–34.

Feinberg, T. E., and Mallatt, J. M. (2016). *The Ancient Origins of Consciousness: How the Brain Created Experience*. MIT Press.

Feinstein, J. S., Khalsa, S. S., Salomons, T. V., Prkachin, K. M., Frey-Law, L. A., Lee, J. E., Tranel, D., and Rudrauf, D. (2016). Preserved emotional awareness of pain in a patient with extensive bilateral damage to the insula, anterior cingulate, and amygdala. *Brain Structure & Function, 221*(3), 1499–1511. https://doi.org/10.1007/s00429-014-0986-3

Fenske, S. J., Bierer, D., Chelimsky, G., Conant, L., Ustine, C., Yan, K., Chelimsky, T., and Kutch, J. J. (2020). Sensitivity of functional connectivity to periaqueductal gray localization, with implications for identifying disease-related changes in chronic visceral pain: a MAPP Research Network neuroimaging study. *NeuroImage: Clinical, 28*, 102443. https://doi.org/10.1016/j.nicl.2020.102443

Ferguson, N. M., Laydon, D., Nedjati-Gilani, G., Imai, N., Ainslie, K., Baguelin, M., Bhatia, S., Boonyasiri, A., Cucunubá, Z., and Cuomo-Dannenburg, G. (2020). *Impact of non-pharmaceutical interventions (NPIs) to reduce COVID-19 mortality and healthcare demand. Imperial College COVID-19 Response Team* (p. 77482). Imperial College COVID-19 Response Team.

Fessenden, M. (2014). We've put a worm's mind in a Lego robot's body. *Smart News|Smithsonian Magazine*. https://www.smithsonianmag.com/smart-news/weve-put-worms-mind-lego-robot-body-180953399/

Fields, A. (2021). Better models of the evolution of cooperation through situated cognition. *Biology & Philosophy, 36*(4), 38. https://doi.org/10.1007/s10539-021-09813-2

Finlayson, J. G. (2019). *The Habermas-Rawls Debate*. Columbia University Press.

Finn, S., Marshall, J., Pathe-Smith, A., and Adkins, V. (2023). Pregnancy: transformations in philosophy and legal practice. In G. A. Bruno and J. Vlasits (eds), *Transformation and the History of Philosophy*. Routledge.

Fins, J. J., and Bernat, J. L. (2018). Ethical, palliative, and policy considerations in disorders of consciousness. *Archives of Physical Medicine and Rehabilitation, 99*(9), 1927–1931. https://doi.org/10.1016/j.apmr.2018.07.003

Fishkin, J. S. (2018). *Democracy When the People Are Thinking: Revitalizing Our Politics Through Public Deliberation.* Oxford University Press.

Fitzgerald, M. (2015). What do we really know about newborn infant pain? *Experimental Physiology, 100*(12), 1451–1457. https://doi.org/10.1113/EP085134

Flanagan, O. (2011). *The Bodhisattva's Brain: Buddhism Naturalized.* MIT Press.

Flanders, C. (2014). Public reason and animal rights. In M. Wissenburg and D. Schlosberg (eds), *Political Animals and Animal Politics* (pp. 44–57). Palgrave Macmillan.

Fossat, P., Bacqué-Cazenave, J., De Deurwaerdère, P., Cattaert, D., and Delbecque, J.-P. (2015). Serotonin, but not dopamine, controls the stress response and anxiety-like behavior in the crayfish Procambarus clarkii. *Journal of Experimental Biology, 218*(17), 2745–2752. https://doi.org/10.1242/jeb.120550

Fossat, P., Bacqué-Cazenave, J., De Deurwaerdère, P., Delbecque, J.-P., and Cattaert, D. (2014). Anxiety-like behavior in crayfish is controlled by serotonin. *Science, 344*(6189), 1293–1297. https://doi.org/10.1126/science.1248811

Foster Wallace, D. (2005). *Consider the Lobster: And Other Essays: Essays and Arguments.* Little, Brown and Company.

Frankish, K. (2016). Illusionism as a theory of consciousness. *Journal of Consciousness Studies, 23*(11–12), 11–39.

Franks, B., Ewell, C., and Jacquet, J. (2021). Animal welfare risks of global aquaculture. *Science Advances, 7*(14), eabg0677. https://doi.org/10.1126/sciadv.abg0677

Fregin, T., and Bickmeyer, U. (2016). Electrophysiological investigation of different methods of anesthesia in lobster and crayfish. *PLOS ONE, 11*(9), e0162894. https://doi.org/10.1371/journal.pone.0162894

Furlan, T. (2022). Mary Anne Warren and the boundaries of the moral community. *Cambridge Quarterly of Healthcare Ethics, 31*(2), 230–246.

Gabriel, E., Albanna, W., Pasquini, G., Ramani, A., Josipovic, N., Mariappan, A., Schinzel, F., Karch, C. M., Bao, G., Gottardo, M., Suren, A. A., Hescheler, J., Nagel-Wolfrum, K., Persico, V., Rizzoli, S. O., Altmüller, J., Riparbelli, M. G., Callaini, G., Goureau, O., … Gopalakrishnan, J. (2021). Human brain organoids assemble functionally integrated bilateral optic vesicles. *Cell Stem Cell, 28*(10), 1740–1757.e8. https://doi.org/10.1016/j.stem.2021.07.010

Galpayage Dona, H. S., Solvi, C., Kowalewska, A., Mäkelä, K., MaBouDi, H., and Chittka, L. (2022). Do bumble bees play? *Animal Behaviour, 194*, 239–251. https://doi.org/10.1016/j.anbehav.2022.08.013

Gardiner, S. M. (2006). A core precautionary principle. *Journal of Political Philosophy, 14*(1), 33–60. https://doi.org/10.1111/j.1467-9760.2006.00237.x

Garner, R. (2013). *A Theory of Justice for Animals: Animal Rights in a Nonideal World.* Oxford University Press.

Georgiev, D., and Glazebrook, J. F. (2014). Quantum interactive dualism: from Beck and Eccles tunneling model of exocytosis to molecular biology of SNARE zipping. *Biomedical Reviews, 25*, Article 0. https://doi.org/10.14748/bmr.v25.1038

Ghosh, D. D., Nitabach, M. N., Zhang, Y., and Harris, G. (2017). Multisensory integration in C. elegans. *Current Opinion in Neurobiology, 43*, 110–118. https://doi.org/10.1016/j.conb.2017.01.005

Ghosh, D. D., Sanders, T., Hong, S., McCurdy, L. Y., Chase, D. L., Cohen, N., Koelle, M. R., and Nitabach, M. N. (2016). Neural architecture of hunger-dependent multisensory decision making in C. elegans. *Neuron, 92*(5), 1049–1062. https://doi.org/10.1016/j.neuron.2016.10.030

Giacino, J. T., Kalmar, K., and Whyte, J. (2004). The JFK Coma Recovery Scale-revised: measurement characteristics and diagnostic utility11No commercial party having a direct financial interest in the results of the research supporting this article has or will confer a benefit upon the authors or upon any organization with which the authors are associated. *Archives of Physical Medicine and Rehabilitation, 85*(12), 2020–2029. https://doi.org/10.1016/j.apmr.2004.02.033

Giandomenico, S. L., Mierau, S. B., Gibbons, G. M., Wenger, L. M. D., Masullo, L., Sit, T., Sutcliffe, M., Boulanger, J., Tripodi, M., Derivery, E., Paulsen, O., Lakatos, A., and Lancaster, M. A. (2019). Cerebral organoids at the air–liquid interface generate diverse nerve tracts with functional output. *Nature Neuroscience*, *22*(4), 669–679. https://doi.org/10.1038/s41593-019-0350-2

Gibbard, A. (1992). *Wise Choices, Apt Feelings: A Theory of Normative Judgment*. Clarendon Press.

Gibbons, M., and Chittka, L. (2022). A framework for evaluating evidence of pain in animals. *Animal Sentience*, *7*(32), 28. https://doi.org/10.51291/2377-7478.1767

Gibbons, M., Versace, E., Crump, A., Baran, B., and Chittka, L. (2022). Motivational trade-offs and modulation of nociception in bumblebees. *Proceedings of the National Academy of Sciences*, *119*(31), e2205821119. https://doi.org/10.1073/pnas.2205821119

Gibert, M., and Martin, D. (2022). In search of the moral status of AI: why sentience is a strong argument. *AI & Society*, *37*, 319–330.

Ginsburg, S., and Jablonka, E. (2007). The transition to experiencing: I. Limited learning and limited experiencing. *Biological Theory*, *2*(3), 218–230. https://doi.org/10.1162/biot.2007.2.3.218

Ginsburg, S., and Jablonka, E. (2019). *The Evolution of the Sensitive Soul: Learning and the Origins of Consciousness*. MIT Press.

Giurfa, M., and Macri, C. (2022). Neuroscience: mechanisms for bridging stimuli in Pavlovian trace conditioning in flies. *Current Biology*, *32*(11), R532–R535. https://doi.org/10.1016/j.cub.2022.04.059

Giurfa, M., Zhang, S., Jenett, A., Menzel, R., and Srinivasan, M. V. (2001). The concepts of 'sameness' and 'difference' in an insect. *Nature*, *410*(6831), 930–933. https://doi.org/10.1038/35073582

Godfrey-Smith, P. (2016a). Mind, matter, and metabolism. *Journal of Philosophy*, *113*(10), 481–506.

Godfrey-Smith, P. (2016b). *Other Minds: The Octopus and the Evolution of Intelligent Life*. William Collins.

Godfrey-Smith, P. (2020a). *Metazoa: Animal Minds and the Birth of Consciousness*. William Collins.

Godfrey-Smith, P. (2020b). Gradualism and the evolution of experience. *Philosophical Topics*, *48*(1), 201–220.

Godfrey-Smith, P. (2021). Integration, lateralization, and animal experience. *Mind and Language*, *36*(2), 285–296.

Goodin, R. E., and Spiekermann, K. (2018). *An Epistemic Theory of Democracy*. Oxford University Press.

Goodpaster, K. E. (1978). On being morally considerable. *Journal of Philosophy*, *75*(6), 308–325. https://doi.org/10.2307/2025709

Gopnik, A. (2009). *The Philosophical Baby: What Children's Minds Tell Us about Truth, Love & the Meaning of Life*. Random House.

Gordon, J.-S. (2008). Abortion. In *Internet Encyclopedia of Philosophy*. https://iep.utm.edu/abortion/

Gorman, R. (2022). What might decapod sentience mean for policy, practice, and public? *Animal Sentience*, *7*(32), 9. https://doi.org/10.51291/2377-7478.1720

Gowda, S. B. M., Salim, S., and Mohammad, F. (2021). Anatomy and neural pathways modulating distinct locomotor behaviors in Drosophila larva. *Biology*, *10*(2), 90. https://doi.org/10.3390/biology10020090

Goyal, A., Didolkar, A., Lamb, A., Badola, K., Ke, N. R., Rahaman, N., Binas, J., Blundell, C., Mozer, M., and Bengio, Y. (2022). Coordination among neural modules through a shared global workspace. *arXiv preprint* arXiv:2103.01197.

Graham, M. (2017). A fate worse than death? The well-being of patients diagnosed as vegetative with covert awareness. *Ethical Theory and Moral Practice*, *20*(5), 1005–1020. https://doi.org/10.1007/s10677-017-9836-8

Graham, M. (2021). Residual cognitive capacities in patients with cognitive motor dissociation, and their implications for well-being. *Journal of Medicine and Philosophy: A Forum for Bioethics and Philosophy of Medicine*, *46*(6), 729–757. https://doi.org/10.1093/jmp/jhab026

Graham, M., and Naci, L. (2021). Well-being after severe brain injury: what counts as good recovery? *Cambridge Quarterly of Healthcare Ethics*, *30*(4), 613–622. https://doi.org/10.1017/S0963180121000086

Gray, A., Pickering, M., and Sturman, S. (2021). Absence of monitoring in withdrawal of clinically-assisted nutrition and hydration (CANH) and other treatments: a cause for concern? *Clinical Medicine*, *21*(3), 235–237. https://doi.org/10.7861/clinmed.2020-0673

Graziano, M. S. A. (2013). *Consciousness and the Social Brain*. Oxford University Press.

Graziano, M. S. A. (2016a, January 12). Consciousness is not mysterious. *The Atlantic*.

Graziano, M. S. A. (2016b). Consciousness engineered. *Journal of Consciousness Studies*, *23*(11–12), 98–115.

Greasley, K. (2017). *Arguments about Abortion: Personhood, Morality, and Law*. Oxford University Press.

Greasley, K., and Kaczor, C. (2017). *Abortion Rights: For and Against*. Cambridge University Press.

Greenwald, A. G., and De Houwer, J. (2017). Unconscious conditioning: demonstration of existence and difference from conscious conditioning. *Journal of Experimental Psychology: General*, *146*, 1705–1721. https://doi.org/10.1037/xge0000371

Greely, H. (2021). Human brain surrogates research: the onrushing ethical dilemma. *American Journal of Bioethics*, *21*(1), 34–45. https://doi.org/10.1080/15265161.2020.1845853

Greer, D. M., Shemie, S. D., Lewis, A., Torrance, S., Varelas, P., Goldenberg, F. D., Bernat, J. L., Souter, M., Topcuoglu, M. A., Alexandrov, A. W., Baldisseri, M., Bleck, T., Citerio, G., Dawson, R., Hoppe, A., Jacobe, S., Manara, A., Nakagawa, T. A., Pope, T. M....and Sung, G. (2020). Determination of brain death/death by neurologic criteria: the World Brain Death Project. *Journal of the American Medical Association*, *324*(11), 1078–1097. https://doi.org/10.1001/jama.2020.11586

Grillner, S., Robertson, B., and Stephenson-Jones, M. (2013). The evolutionary origin of the vertebrate basal ganglia and its role in action selection. *Journal of Physiology*, *591*(22), 5425–5431. https://doi.org/10.1113/jphysiol.2012.246660

Gross, H. J., Pahl, M., Si, A., Zhu, H., Tautz, J., and Zhang, S. (2009). Number-based visual generalisation in the honeybee. *PloS One*, *4*(1), e4263. https://doi.org/10.1371/journal.pone.0004263

Grover, D., Chen, J.-Y., Xie, J., Li, J., Changeux, J.-P., and Greenspan, R. J. (2022). Differential mechanisms underlie trace and delay conditioning in *Drosophila*. *Nature*, *603*(7900), 302–308. https://doi.org/10.1038/s41586-022-04433-6

Grunau, R. E., Haley, D. W., Whitfield, M. F., Weinberg, J., Yu, W., and Thiessen, P. (2007). Altered basal cortisol levels at 3, 6, 8 and 18 months in infants born at extremely low gestational age. *Journal of Pediatrics*, *150*(2), 151–156. https://doi.org/10.1016/j.jpeds.2006.10.053

Grunau, R. E., Holsti, L., Haley, D. W., Oberlander, T., Weinberg, J., Solimano, A., Whitfield, M. F., Fitzgerald, C., and Yu, W. (2005). Neonatal procedural pain exposure predicts lower cortisol and behavioral reactivity in preterm infants in the NICU. *Pain*, *113*(3), 293–300. https://doi.org/10.1016/j.pain.2004.10.020

Guerrero, A. A. (2014). Against elections: the lottocratic alternative. *Philosophy & Public Affairs*, *42*(2), 135–178. https://doi.org/10.1111/papa.12029

Guerrero, A. A. (2021). The epistemic pathologies of elections and the epistemic promise of lottocracy. In E. Edenberg and M. Hannon (eds), *Political Epistemology* (pp. 156–179). Oxford University Press. https://doi.org/10.1093/oso/9780192893338.003.0010

Güntürkün, O., and Bugnyar, T. (2016). Cognition without cortex. *Trends in Cognitive Sciences*, *20*(4), 291–303. https://doi.org/10.1016/j.tics.2016.02.001

Guyoncourt, S. (2022, July 23). Google fires software engineer who said AI chatbot has become sentient. *Inews.Co.Uk*. https://inews.co.uk/news/google-fires-software-engineer-blake-lemoine-ai-system-lamda-sentient-1758478

Habermas, J. (1995). Reconciliation through the public use of reason: remarks on John Rawls's political liberalism. *Journal of Philosophy*, *92*(3), 109–131. https://doi.org/10.2307/2940842

Haibe-Kains, B., Adam, G. A., Hosny, A., Khodakarami, F., Waldron, L., Wang, B., McIntosh, C., Goldenberg, A., Kundaje, A., Greene, C. S., Broderick, T., Hoffman, M. M., Leek, J. T., Korthauer, K., Huber, W., Brazma, A., Pineau, J., Tibshirani, R., Hastie, T.,...Aerts, H. J. W. L. (2020). Transparency and reproducibility in artificial intelligence. *Nature*, *586*(7829), Article 7829. https://doi.org/10.1038/s41586-020-2766-y

Hall, G. (2022). Is consciousness vague? *Australasian Journal of Philosophy*, *0*(0), 1–15. https://doi.org/10.1080/00048402.2022.2036207

Hameroff, S. (2022). Consciousness, cognition and the neuronal cytoskeleton—a new paradigm needed in neuroscience. *Frontiers in Molecular Neuroscience*, *15*. https://www.frontiersin.org/articles/10.3389/fnmol.2022.869935

Hameroff, S., and Penrose, R. (2014). Consciousness in the universe: a review of the 'Orch OR' theory. *Physics of Life Reviews*, *11*(1), 39–78. https://doi.org/10.1016/j.plrev.2013.08.002

Hamm, A. O., Weike, A. I., Schupp, H. T., Treig, T., Dressel, A., and Kessler, C. (2003). Affective blindsight: intact fear conditioning to a visual cue in a cortically blind patient. *Brain*, *126*(2), 267–275. https://doi.org/10.1093/brain/awg037

Hartzell-Nichols, L. (2012). Precaution and solar radiation management. *Ethics, Policy & Environment*, *15*(2), 158–171. https://doi.org/10.1080/21550085.2012.685561

Harzsch, S., and Krieger, J. (2021). Genealogical relationships of mushroom bodies, hemiellipsoid bodies, and their afferent pathways in the brains of Pancrustacea: recent progress and open questions. *Arthropod Structure & Development*, *65*, 101100. https://doi.org/10.1016/j.asd.2021.101100

Hasani, H., Sun, J., Zhu, S. I., Rong, Q., Willomitzer, F., Amor, R., McConnell, G., Cossairt, O., and Goodhill, G. J. (2023). Whole-brain imaging of freely-moving zebrafish. *Frontiers in Neuroscience*, *17*, 1127574. https://doi.org/10.3389/fnins.2023.1127574

Hawkins, R. D. (1984). A cellular mechanism of classical conditioning in *Aplysia*. *Journal of Experimental Biology*, *112*, 113–128. https://doi.org/10.1242/jeb.112.1.113

Hawkins, R. D., Greene, W., and Kandel, E. R. (1998). Classical conditioning, differential conditioning, and second-order conditioning of the *Aplysia* gill-withdrawal reflex in a simplified mantle organ preparation. *Behavioral Neuroscience*, *112*, 636–645. https://doi.org/10.1037/0735-7044.112.3.636

Hawkins, R. D., Lalevic, N., Clark, G. A., and Kandel, E. R. (1989). Classical conditioning of the *Aplysia* siphon-withdrawal reflex exhibits response specificity. *Proceedings of the National Academy of Sciences of the United States of America*, *86*(19), 7620–7624.

He, B. J. (2023). Towards a pluralistic neurobiological understanding of consciousness. *Trends in Cognitive Sciences*, *27*(5), 420–432. https://doi.org/10.1016/j.tics.2023.02.001

Healey, R., and Pepper, A. (2021). Interspecies justice: agency, self-determination, and assent. *Philosophical Studies*, *178*, 1223–1243.

Herculano-Houzel, S. (2009). The human brain in numbers: a linearly scaled-up primate brain. *Frontiers in Human Neuroscience*, *3*. https://www.frontiersin.org/articles/10.3389/neuro.09.031.2009

Herculano-Houzel, S., Mota, B., and Lent, R. (2006). Cellular scaling rules for rodent brains. *Proceedings of the National Academy of Sciences of the United States of America*, *103*(32), 12138–12143. https://doi.org/10.1073/pnas.0604911103

Herzog, M. H., Esfeld, M., and Gerstner, W. (2007). Consciousness and the small network argument. *Neural Networks*, *20*(9), 1054–1056. https://doi.org/10.1016/j.neunet.2007.09.001

HEW Ethics Advisory Board. (1979). *HEW Support of Research Involving Human In Vitro Fertilization and Embryo Transfer: Report and Conclusions*. US Department of Health, Education and Welfare. http://hdl.handle.net/10822/559350

Hoagland, M. A., and Chatterjee, D. (2017). Anesthesia for fetal surgery. *Pediatric Anesthesia*, *27*(4), 346–357. https://doi.org/10.1111/pan.13109

Howard, S. R., Avarguès-Weber, A., Garcia, J. E., Greentree, A. D., and Dyer, A. G. (2019). Achieving arithmetic learning in honeybees and examining how individuals learn. *Communicative & Integrative Biology*, *12*(1), 166–170. https://doi.org/10.1080/19420889.2019.1678452

Howe, H. J. B. (2019). *Improving Pest Management for Wild Insect Welfare*. Wild Animal Initiative.

Humphrey, N. (2022). *Sentience: The Invention of Consciousness*. Oxford University Press.

Hurlbut, J. B., Hyun, I., Levine, A. D., Lovell-Badge, R., Lunshof, J. E., Matthews, K. R. W., Mills, P., Murdoch, A., Pera, M. F., Scott, C. T., Tizzard, J., Warnock, M., Zernicka-Goetz, M., Zhou, Q., and Zoloth, L. (2017). Revisiting the Warnock rule. *Nature Biotechnology, 35*(11), 1029–1042. https://doi.org/10.1038/nbt.4015

Hurley, S. L. (1998). *Consciousness in Action:* Harvard University Press.

Huxley, T. H. (1874). On the hypothesis that animals are automata, and its history. *Nature, 10*(253), Article 253. https://doi.org/10.1038/010362a0

Hyun, I., Scharf-Deering, J. C., and Lunshof, J. E. (2020). Ethical issues related to brain organoid research. *Brain Res, 1732*, 146653. https://doi.org/10.1016/j.brainres.2020.146653

International Covenant on Civil and Political Rights, (1966). https://www.ohchr.org/en/instruments-mechanisms/instruments/international-covenant-civil-and-political-rights

IPCC. (2010). *Guidance Note for Lead Authors of the IPCC Fifth Assessment Report on Consistent Treatment of Uncertainties*. Intergovernmental Panel on Climate Change.

Irvine, E. (2012). *Consciousness as a Scientific Concept: A Philosophy of Science Perspective.* Springer Science & Business Media.

Irvine, E. (2020). Developing valid behavioral indicators of animal pain. *Philosophical Topics, 48*(1), 129–153.

Irvine, E. (2022). Independence, weight and priority of evidence for sentience. *Animal Sentience, 7*(32), 10. https://doi.org/10.51291/2377-7478.1724

Irvine, L. (2017). Animal pain and the social role of science. *Animal Sentience, 2*(16), 18. https://doi.org/10.51291/2377-7478.1268

Jablonka, E., and Ginsburg, S. (2022). Pain sentience criteria and their grading. *Animal Sentience, 7*(32), 4. https://doi.org/10.51291/2377-7478.1713

Jackson, F. (1982). Epiphenomenal qualia. *Philosophical Quarterly (1950–), 32*(127), 127–136. https://doi.org/10.2307/2960077

Jacquet, J., Franks, B., Godfrey-Smith, P., and Sánchez-Suárez, W. (2019). The case against octopus farming. *Issues in Science and Technology, Winter 2019*, 37–44.

Jaegle, A., Gimeno, F., Brock, A., Vinyals, O., Zisserman, A., and Carreira, J. (2021). Perceiver: General perception with iterative attention. *International Conference on Machine Learning*, 4651–4664.

James, W. (1890/1918). *The Principles of Psychology*, Volume 1 (of 2). Henry Holt. https://www.gutenberg.org/ebooks/57628/pg57628-images.html.utf8

Janvier, P. (2010). MicroRNAs revive old views about jawless vertebrate divergence and evolution. *Proceedings of the National Academy of Sciences of the United States of America, 107*(45), 19137–19138. https://doi.org/10.1073/pnas.1014583107

Jennings, H. S. (1906). *The Behavior of the Lower Organisms*. Columbia University Press.

John, S. (2010). In defence of bad science and irrational policies: an alternative account of the precautionary principle. *Ethical Theory and Moral Practice, 13*(1), 3–18. https://doi.org/10.1007/s10677-009-9169-3

John, S. (2011). Risk and precaution. In A. Dawson (ed.), *Public Health Ethics: Key Concepts and Issues in Policy and Practice* (pp. 67–84). Cambridge University Press. https://doi.org/10.1017/CBO9780511862670.005

John, S. (2019). The politics of certainty: the precautionary principle, inductive risk and procedural fairness. *Ethics, Policy & Environment, 22*(1), 21–33. https://doi.org/10.1080/21550085.2019.1581418

Johnson, J. F., Belyk, M., Schwartze, M., Pinheiro, A. P., and Kotz, S. A. (2019). The role of the cerebellum in adaptation: ALE meta-analyses on sensory feedback error. *Human Brain Mapping, 40*(13), 3966–3981. https://doi.org/10.1002/hbm.24681

Johnson, L. S. M. (2022). *The Ethics of Uncertainty: Entangled Ethical and Epistemic Risks in Disorders of Consciousness*. Oxford University Press.

Jones, R. (2017). The precautionary principle: a cautionary note. *Animal Sentience, 2*(16), 15. https://doi.org/10.51291/2377-7478.1250

Jowitt, J. (2023). On the legal status of human cerebral organoids: lessons from animal law. *Cambridge Quarterly of Healthcare Ethics, 32*, 572–581.https://doi.org/10.1017/S0963180122000858

Joyce, R. (2006). *The Evolution of Morality*. MIT Press.

Juliani, A., Kanai, R., and Sasai, S. S. (2022). The perceiver architecture is a functional global workspace. *Proceedings of the Annual Meeting of the Cognitive Science Society, 44*(44).

Kagan, B. J., Kitchen, A. C., Tran, N. T., Habibollahi, F., Khajehnejad, M., Parker, B. J., Bhat, A., Rollo, B., Razi, A., and Friston, K. J. (2022). In vitro neurons learn and exhibit sentience when embodied in a simulated game-world. *Neuron, 110*(23), 3952–3969.e8. https://doi.org/10.1016/j.neuron.2022.09.001

Kagan, S. (2019). *How to Count Animals, More or Less*. Oxford University Press.

Kakrada, E., and Colombo, M. (2022). Extending the null hypothesis to invertebrate pain sentience. *Animal Sentience, 7*(32), 25. https://doi.org/10.51291/2377-7478.1754

Kallhoff, A. (2014). Plants in ethics: why flourishing deserves moral respect. *Environmental Values, 23*(6), 685–700.

Kalman, M. (2009). Evolution of the brain: at the reptile-bird transition. In Binder, M. D., Hirokawa, N., and Windhorst, U. (eds), *Encyclopedia of Neuroscience*. Springer. https://doi.org/10.1007/978-3-540-29678-2_3149

Kammerer, F. (2018). Can you believe it? Illusionism and the illusion meta-problem. *Philosophical Psychology, 31*(1), 44–67.

Kammerer, F. (2022). Ethics without sentience: facing up to the probable insignificance of phenomenal consciousness. *Journal of Consciousness Studies, 29*(3–4), 180–204.

Kant, I. (1797/2017). *The Metaphysics of Morals*. Cambridge University Press.

Kaplan, H. S., Nichols, A. L. A., and Zimmer, M. (2018). Sensorimotor integration in *Caenorhabditis elegans*: a reappraisal towards dynamic and distributed computations. *Philosophical Transactions of the Royal Society of London. Series B, Biological Sciences, 373*(1758), 20170371. https://doi.org/10.1098/rstb.2017.0371

Kato, S., Kaplan, H. S., Schrödel, T., Skora, S., Lindsay, T. H., Yemini, E., Lockery, S., and Zimmer, M. (2015). Global brain dynamics embed the motor command sequence of *Caenorhabditis elegans*. *Cell, 163*(3), 656–669. https://doi.org/10.1016/j.cell.2015.09.034

Key, B. (2015) Fish do not feel pain and its implications for understanding phenomenal consciousness. *Biology & Philosophy, 30*(2), 149–165. https://doi.org/10.1007/s10539-014-9469-4

Key, B. (2016). Why fish do not feel pain. *Animal Sentience, 1*(3), 1.

Key, B., and Brown, D. (2022). Lack of imagination can bias our view of animal sentience. *Animal Sentience, 7*(32). https://doi.org/10.51291/2377-7478.1756

Kitchener, P. D., Fuller, J., and Snow, P. J. (2010). Central projections of primary sensory afferents to the spinal dorsal horn in the long-tailed stingray, Himantura fai. *Brain Behavior and Evolution, 76*, 60–70.

Kitcher, P. (2001). *Science, Truth, and Democracy*. Oxford University Press.

Kitcher, P. (2011a). *Science in a Democratic Society*. Prometheus.

Kitcher, P. (2011b). *The Ethical Project*. Harvard University Press.

Kittelberger, J. M., Land, B. R., and Bass, A. H. (2006). Midbrain periaqueductal gray and vocal patterning in a teleost fish. *Journal of Neurophysiology, 96*(1), 71–85. https://doi.org/10.1152/jn.00067.2006

Kitzinger, C., and Kitzinger, J. (2014). 'This in-between': how families talk about death in relation to severe brain injury and disorders of consciousness. In L. Van Brussel and N. Carpentier (eds), *The Social Construction of Death: Interdisciplinary Perspectives*. Palgrave MacMillan. http://www.ncbi.nlm.nih.gov/books/NBK252967/

Kitzinger, C., and Kitzinger, J. (2015). Withdrawing artificial nutrition and hydration from minimally conscious and vegetative patients: family perspectives. *Journal of Medical Ethics, 41*(2), 157–160. https://doi.org/10.1136/medethics-2013-101799

Kitzinger, J., and Kitzinger, C. (2013). The 'window of opportunity' for death after severe brain injury: family experiences. *Sociology of Health & Illness, 35*(7), 1095–1112. https://doi.org/10.1111/1467-9566.12020

Kitzinger, J., and Kitzinger, C. (2018). Deaths after feeding-tube withdrawal from patients in vegetative and minimally conscious states: a qualitative study of family experience. *Palliative Medicine, 32*(7), 1180–1188. https://doi.org/10.1177/0269216318766430

Klein, A. (2019). William James's objection to epiphenomenalism. *Philosophy of Science, 86*(5), 1179–1190. https://doi.org/10.1086/705477

Klein, C. (2015). *What the Body Commands: The Imperative Theory of Pain.* MIT Press.

Klein, C. (2017). Precaution, proportionality and proper commitments. *Animal Sentience, 2*(16), 9. https://doi.org/10.51291/2377-7478.1232

Klein, C., and Barron, A. (2016). Insects have the capacity for subjective experience. *Animal Sentience, 1*(9), 1. https://doi.org/10.51291/2377-7478.1113

Knutsson, S., and Munthe, C. (2017). A virtue of precaution regarding the moral status of animals with uncertain sentience. *Journal of Agricultural and Environmental Ethics, 30*(2), 213–224. https://doi.org/10.1007/s10806-017-9662-y

Koba, S., Inoue, R., and Watanabe, T. (2016). Role played by periaqueductal gray neurons in parasympathetically mediated fear bradycardia in conscious rats. *Physiological Reports, 4*(12), e12831. https://doi.org/10.14814/phy2.12831

Koch, C. (2008). Exploring consciousness through the study of bees. *Scientific American.* https://doi.org/10.1038/scientificamericanmind1208-18

Koch, C. (2019, September 24). *Consciousness Doesn't Depend on Language.* Nautilus. https://nautil.us/consciousness-doesnt-depend-on-language-237555/

Kondev, J. (2014). Bacterial decision making. *Physics Today, 67*(2), 31.

Kondziella, D., Bender, A., Diserens, K., van Erp, W., Estraneo, A., Formisano, R., Laureys, S., Naccache, L., Ozturk, S., Rohaut, B., Sitt, J. D., Stender, J., Tiainen, M., Rossetti, A. O., Gosseries, O., Chatelle, C., and EAN Panel on Coma, Disorders of Consciousness. (2020). European Academy of Neurology guideline on the diagnosis of coma and other disorders of consciousness. *European Journal of Neurology, 27*(5), 741–756. https://doi.org/10.1111/ene.14151

Koplin, J. J., and Savulescu, J. (2019). Moral limits of brain organoid research. *J. Law. Med. Ethics, 47*(4), 760–767. https://doi.org/10.1177/1073110519897789

Korsgaard, C. M. (2018). *Fellow Creatures: Our Obligations to the Other Animals.* Oxford University Press.

Kouider, S., Stahlhut, C., Gelskov, S. V., Barbosa, L. S., Dutat, M., de Gardelle, V., Christophe, A., Dehaene, S., and Dehaene-Lambertz, G. (2013). A neural marker of perceptual consciousness in infants. *Science, 340*(6130), 376–380. https://doi.org/10.1126/science.1232509

Kragel, P. A., Bianciardi, M., Hartley, L., Matthewson, G., Choi, J.-K., Quigley, K. S., Wald, L. L., Wager, T. D., Barrett, L. F., and Satpute, A. B. (2019). Functional involvement of human periaqueductal gray and other midbrain nuclei in cognitive control. *Journal of Neuroscience, 39*(31), 6180–6189. https://doi.org/10.1523/JNEUROSCI.2043-18.2019

Kreitmair, K. (2023). Consciousness and the ethics of human brain organoid research. *Cambridge Quarterly of Healthcare Ethics,* 1–11. Cambridge Core. https://doi.org/10.1017/S0963180123000063

Kriegel, U. (in press). The value of consciousness to the one who has it. In G. Lee and A. Pautz (eds), *The Importance of Being Conscious.* Oxford University Press. https://philarchive.org/rec/KRITVO-7

Krieger, J., Sandeman, R. E., Sandeman, D. C., Hansson, B. S., and Harzsch, S. (2010). Brain architecture of the largest living land arthropod, the Giant Robber Crab *Birgus latro* (Crustacea, Anomura, Coenobitidae): evidence for a prominent central olfactory pathway? *Frontiers in Zoology, 7*, 25. https://doi.org/10.1186/1742-9994-7-25

Krishna, N. (2022). Animal sentience in Indian culture: colonial and post-colonial changes. *Animal Sentience, 6*(31), 16. https://doi.org/10.51291/2377-7478.1751

Krzyzanowski, M. C., Woldemariam, S., Wood, J. F., Chaubey, A. H., Brueggemann, C., Bowitch, A., Bethke, B., L'Etoile, N. D., and Ferkey, D. M. (2016). Aversive behavior in the nematode *C. elegans* is modulated by cGMP and a neuronal gap junction network. *PLoS Genetics, 12*(7), e1006153.

Kuba, M. J., Byrne, R. A., Meisel, D. V., and Mather, J. A. (2006). When do octopuses play? Effects of repeated testing, object type, age, and food deprivation on object play in *Octopus vulgaris. Journal of Comparative Psychology, 120*(3), 184–190. https://doi.org/10.1037/0735-7036.120.3.184

Kumar, S., Stecher, G., Suleski, M., and Hedges, S. B. (2017). TimeTree: a resource for timelines, timetrees, and divergence times. *Molecular Biology and Evolution*, *34*(7), 1812–1819. https://doi.org/10.1093/molbev/msx116

Lacap, R. (2022). A new approach to determine the presence of nociception in elasmobranchs. Dissertation: California State University, Northridge.

Lafont, C. (2020). *Democracy without Shortcuts: A Participatory Conception of Deliberative Democracy*. Oxford University Press.

Lamme, V. A. F. (2001). Blindsight: the role of feedforward and feedback corticocortical connections. *Acta Psychologica*, *107*(1), 209–228. https://doi.org/10.1016/S0001-6918(01)00020-8

Lamme, V. A. F. (2010). How neuroscience will change our view on consciousness. *Cognitive Neuroscience*, *1*(3), 204–220. https://doi.org/10.1080/17588921003731586

Lamme, V. A. F. (2022). Behavioural and neural evidence for conscious sensation in animals: an inescapable avenue towards biopsychism? *Journal of Consciousness Studies*, *29*(3–4), 78–103. https://doi.org/10.53765/20512201.29.3.078

Landemore, H. (2013). *Democratic Reason: Politics, Collective Intelligence, and the Rule of the Many*. Princeton University Press.

Landemore, H. (2020). *Open Democracy: Reinventing Popular Rule for the Twenty-First Century*. Princeton University Press.

Lau, H. (2022). *In Consciousness We Trust: The Cognitive Neuroscience of Subjective Experience*. Oxford University Press.

Laureys, S., Celesia, G. G., Cohadon, F., Lavrijsen, J., León-Carrión, J., Sannita, W. G., Sazbon, L., Schmutzhard, E., von Wild, K. R., Zeman, A., Dolce, G., and the European Task Force on Disorders of Consciousness. (2010). Unresponsive wakefulness syndrome: a new name for the vegetative state or apallic syndrome. *BMC Medicine*, *8*(1), 68. https://doi.org/10.1186/1741-7015-8-68

Lavazza, A. (2020). Human cerebral organoids and consciousness: a double-edged sword. *Monash Bioethics Review*, *38*(2), 105–128. https://doi.org/10.1007/s40592-020-00116-y

Lavazza, A., and Massimini, M. (2018). Cerebral organoids: ethical issues and consciousness assessment. *J. Med. Ethics*, *44*(9), 606–610. https://doi.org/10.1136/medethics-2017-104555

Lawler, D. E., Chew, Y. L., Hawk, J. D., Aljobeh, A., Schafer, W. R., and Albrecht, D. R. (2021). Sleep analysis in adult *C. elegans* reveals state-dependent alteration of neural and behavioral responses. *Journal of Neuroscience*, *41*(9), 1892–1907. https://doi.org/10.1523/JNEUROSCI.1701-20.2020

Lawson, J. R. (1986). Letter. *Birth*, *13*, 124–125.

Layard, R., and Oparina, E. (2021). Living long and living well: the WELLBY approach. *World Happiness Report*, 191–208.

Leadbeater, S. (2017). Will the precautionary principle broaden acceptance of animal sentience? *Animal Sentience*, *2*(16), 16. https://doi.org/10.51291/2377-7478.1258

LeDoux, J. E. (2021). What emotions might be like in other animals. *Current Biology: CB*, *31*(13), R824–R829. https://doi.org/10.1016/j.cub.2021.05.005

LeDoux, J. E. (2023). Deep history and beyond: a reply to commentators. *Philosophical Psychology*, *36*(4), 756–766. https://doi.org/10.1080/09515089.2022.2160312

LeDoux J. E., Birch, J., Andrews, K., Clayton, N. S., Daw, N. D., Frith, C., Lau, H., Peters, M. A. K., Schneider, S., Seth, A., Suddendorf, T., and Vandekerckhove, M. M. P. (2023). Consciousness beyond the human case. *Current Biology*, *33*(16), R832–R840. https://doi.org/10.1016/j.cub.2023.06.067

LeDoux, J. E., and Brown, R. (2017). A higher-order theory of emotional consciousness. *Proceedings of the National Academy of Sciences of the United States of America*, *114*(10), E2016–E2025. https://doi.org/10.1073/pnas.1619316114

LeDoux, J. E., and Pine, D. S. (2016). Using neuroscience to help understand fear and anxiety: a two-system framework. *American Journal of Psychiatry*, *173*(11), 1083–1093. https://doi.org/10.1176/appi.ajp.2016.16030353

Lee, A. Y. (2019). Is consciousness intrinsically valuable? *Philosophical Studies: An International Journal for Philosophy in the Analytic Tradition*, *176*(3), 655–671.

Lenharo, M. (2023a). If AI becomes conscious: here's how researchers will know. *Nature*, 24 August 2023. https://doi.org/10.1038/d41586-023-02684-5

Lenharo, M. (2023b). Consciousness theory slammed as 'pseudoscience'—sparking uproar. *Nature*, 20 September 2023. https://doi.org/10.1038/d41586-023-02971-1

Leopold, A. (1949). *A Sand County Almanac: And Sketches Here and There*. Oxford University Press.

Lesnik, J. (2018). *Edible Insects and Human Evolution*. University Press of Florida.

Levin, M. (2021). Bioelectric signaling: reprogrammable circuits underlying embryogenesis, regeneration, and cancer. *Cell*, *184*(8), 1971–1989.

Levin, M. (2022). Generalizing frameworks for sentience beyond natural species. *Animal Sentience*, *7*(32), 15. https://doi.org/10.51291/2377-7478.1733

Levine, J. (1983). Materialism and qualia: the explanatory gap. *Pacific Philosophical Quarterly*, *64*(4), 354–361. https://doi.org/10.1111/j.1468-0114.1983.tb00207.x

Lewens, T. (2007a). Adaptation. In D. L. Hull and M. Ruse (eds), *The Cambridge Companion to the Philosophy of Biology* (pp. 1–21). Cambridge University Press. https://doi.org/10.1017/CCOL9780521851282.001

Lewens, T. (2007b). Functions. In M. Matthen and C. Stephens (eds), *Philosophy of Biology* (pp. 525–547). North-Holland. https://doi.org/10.1016/B978-044451543-8/50024-1

Lewens, T. (2018). The division of advisory labour: the case of 'mitochondrial donation'. *European Journal for Philosophy of Science*, *9*(1), 10. https://doi.org/10.1007/s13194-018-0235-3

Lewis, S. J., Munro, A. P. S., Smith, G. D., and Pollock, A. M. (2021). Closing schools is not evidence based and harms children. *BMJ*, *372*, n521. https://doi.org/10.1136/bmj.n521

Lindsay, G. W. (2020). Attention in psychology, neuroscience, and machine learning. *Frontiers in Computational Neuroscience*, 14, 29. https://doi.org/10.3389/fncom.2020.00029

Linzey, A. (1987/2016). *Christianity and the Rights of Animals*. Wipf and Stock Publishers.

Lipton, P. (2004). *Inference to the Best Explanation* (2nd ed.). Routledge.

List, C. (2002). Two concepts of agreement. *The Good Society*, *11*(1), 72–79.

List, C., and Spiekermann, K. (2019, April 1). Indicative votes in the House of Commons: no substantive consensus but some meta-consensus. *LSE Brexit Blog*. https://blogs.lse.ac.uk/brexit/2019/04/01/indicative-votes-in-the-house-of-commons-no-substantive-consensus-but-some-meta-consensus/

Liu, C., Wang, C., and Yao, H. (2019). Comprehensive resource utilization of waste using the black soldier fly (*Hermetia illucens* (L.)) (Diptera: Stratiomyidae). *Animals: An Open Access Journal from MDPI*, *9*(6), 349. https://doi.org/10.3390/ani9060349

Lockwood, M. (1989). *Mind, Brain and the Quantum: The Compound 'I'* (new edition). Wiley–Blackwell.

Loesel, R., Seyfarth, E. A., Bräunig, P., and Agricola, H. J. (2011). Neuroarchitecture of the arcuate body in the brain of the spider *Cupiennius salei* (Araneae, Chelicerata) revealed by allatostatin-, proctolin-, and CCAP-immunocytochemistry and its evolutionary implications. *Arthropod Structure and Development*, *40*(3), 210–220. https://doi.org/10.1016/j.asd.2011.01.002

Lokhorst, G.-J. (2021). Descartes and the pineal gland. In E. N. Zalta (ed.), *The Stanford Encyclopedia of Philosophy* (Winter 2021). Metaphysics Research Lab, Stanford University. https://plato.stanford.edu/archives/win2021/entries/pineal-gland/

Lopez-Luna, J., Al-Jubouri, Q., Al-Nuaimy, W. and Sneddon, L. U. (2017a). Activity reduced by noxious chemical stimulation is ameliorated by immersion in analgesic drugs in zebrafish. *Journal of Experimental Biology*, *220*, 1451–1458.

Lopez-Luna, J., Al-Jubouri, Q., Al-Nuaimy, W. and Sneddon, L. U. (2017b). Impact of analgesic drugs on the behavioural responses of larval zebrafish to potentially noxious temperatures. *Applied Animal Behaviour Science*, *188*, 97–105.

Lopez-Luna, J., Al-Jubouri, Q., Al-Nuaimy, W. and Sneddon, L. U. (2017c). Impact of stress, fear and anxiety on the nociceptive responses of larval zebrafish. *PLoS One*, *12*(8), e0181010.

Lopez-Luna, J., Canty, M. N., Al-Jubouri, Q., Al-Nuaimy, W. and Sneddon, L. U. (2017d). Behavioural responses of fish larvae modulated by analgesic drugs after a stress exposure. *Applied Animal Behaviour Science*, *195*, 115–120.

Loukola, O. J., Solvi, C., Coscos, L., and Chittka, L. (2017). Bumblebees show cognitive flexibility by improving on an observed complex behavior. *Science*, *355*(6327), 833–836. https://doi.org/10.1126/science.aag2360

Lukowiak, K., Adatia, N., Krygier, D., and Syed, N. (2000). Operant conditioning in *Lymnaea*: Evidence for intermediate- and long-term memory. *Learning and Memory, 7*(3), 140–150. https://doi.org/10.1101/lm.7.3.140

Lukowiak, K., Cotter, R., Westly, J., Ringseis, E., Spencer, G., and Syed, N. (1998). Long-term memory of an operantly conditioned respiratory behaviour pattern in *Lymnaea stagnalis*. *Journal of Experimental Biology, 201*(6), 877–882. https://doi.org/10.1242/jeb.201.6.877

Lukowiak, K., Ringseis, E., Spencer, G., Wildering, W., and Syed, N. (1996). Operant conditioning of aerial respiratory behaviour in *Lymnaea stagnalis*. *Journal of Experimental Biology, 199*(3), 683–691. https://doi.org/10.1242/jeb.199.3.683

MacNiven, J. A., Poz, R., Bainbridge, K., Gracey, F., and Wilson, B.A. (2003). Case study: emotional adjustment following cognitive recovery from 'persistent vegetative state': psychological and personal perspectives. *Brain Injury, 17*(6), 525–533.

Magaña, P. (2023). Animals in the order of public reason. *Philosophical Studies, 180*, 3031–3056. https://doi.org/10.1007/s11098-023-02026-1

Mallatt, J. (2017). Shoring up the precautionary BAR. *Animal Sentience, 2*(16), 7. https://doi.org/10.51291/2377-7478.1229

Mallatt, J., and Feinberg, T. (2022). Decapod sentience: promising framework and evidence. *Animal Sentience, 7*(32), 24. https://doi.org/10.51291/2377-7478.1750

Marks, J. (2017). Changing the subject. *Animal Sentience, 2*(16), 5. https://doi.org/10.51291/2377-7478.1221

Margulis, L. and Sagan, D. (1995). *What Is Life?* Simon and Schuster.

Marr, D. (1982). *Vision*. W. H. Freeman.

Martin, A. R., and Wickelgren, W. O. (1971). Sensory cells in the spinal cord of the sea lamprey. *Journal of Physiology, 212*(1), 65–83.

Martínez, M. (2011). Imperative content and the painfulness of pain. *Phenomenology and the Cognitive Sciences, 10*(1), 67–90.

Martínez, M. (2015). Pains as reasons. *Philosophical Studies, 172*(9), 2261–2274.

Martínez, M., and Klein, C. (2016). Pain signals are predominantly imperative. *Biology and Philosophy, 31*(2), 283–298.

Mashour, G. A., Roelfsema, P., Changeux, J. P., and Dehaene, S. (2020). Conscious processing and the Global Neuronal Workspace hypothesis. *Neuron, 105*(5), 776–798. https://doi.org/10.1016/j.neuron.2020.01.026

Mason, G. J., and Lavery, J. M. (2022). What is it like to be a bass? Red herrings, fish pain and the study of animal sentience. *Frontiers in Veterinary Science, 9*, 788289. https://doi.org/10.3389/fvets.2022.788289

Mason, R. (2017, November 23). Gove says UK law will specifically recognise animal sentience. *The Guardian*. https://www.theguardian.com/world/2017/nov/23/uk-law-will-specifically-recognise-animal-sentience-michael-gove

Mather, J. (2017). Support for the precautionary principle. *Animal Sentience, 2*(16), 10. https://doi.org/10.51291/2377-7478.1234

Mather, J. (2021a). The case for octopus consciousness: unity. *NeuroSci, 2*, 405–415. https://doi.org/10.3390/neurosci2040030

Mather, J. (2021b). Octopus consciousness: the role of perceptual richness. *NeuroSci, 2*, 276–290. https://doi.org/10.3390/neurosci2030020

Mather, J. (2022a). The case for octopus consciousness: temporality. *NeuroSci, 3*, 245–261. https://doi.org/10.3390/neurosci3020018

Mather, J. (2022b). The case for octopus consciousness: valence. *NeuroSci, 3*, 656–666. https://doi.org/10.3390/neurosci3040047

Mather, J. A. (2008). Cephalopod consciousness: behavioural evidence. *Consciousness and Cognition, 17*(1), 37–48. https://doi.org/10.1016/j.concog.2006.11.006

Mather, J. A. (2019). What is in an octopus's mind? *Animal Sentience, 4*(26), 1.

Matsui, T. K., Tsuru, Y., Hasegawa, K., and Kuwako, K. (2021). Vascularization of human brain organoids. *Stem Cells, 39*(8), 1017–1024. https://doi.org/10.1002/stem.3368

Matthews, G., and Wickelgren, W. O. (1978). Trigeminal sensory neurons of the sea lamprey. *Journal of Comparative Physiology, 123*, 329–333 (1978). https://doi.org/10.1007/BF00656966

McCully, S. (2021). The time has come to extend the 14-day limit. *Journal of Medical Ethics, 47*(12), e66–e66. https://doi.org/10.1136/medethics-2020-106406

McGrath, P. J. (2011). Science is not enough: the modern history of pediatric pain. *Pain, 152*(11), 2457–2459. https://doi.org/10.1016/j.pain.2011.07.018

McKeown, A. (2023). Cerebral organoid research ethics and pinning the tail on the donkey. *Cambridge Quarterly of Healthcare Ethics, 32*(4), 542–554. https://doi.org/10.1017/S0963180123000221

McKie, R., and Helm, T. (2023, June 3). Sunak under fire as 'stupid' Eat Out to Help Out scheme to be focus of Covid inquiry. *The Guardian.* https://www.theguardian.com/business/2023/jun/03/sunak-under-fire-as-stupid-eat-out-to-help-out-scheme-to-be-focus-of-covid-inquiry

McKinney, S. M., Sieniek, M., Godbole, V., Godwin, J., Antropova, N., Ashrafian, H., Back, T., Chesus, M., Corrado, G. S., Darzi, A., Etemadi, M., Garcia-Vicente, F., Gilbert, F. J., Halling-Brown, M., Hassabis, D., Jansen, S., Karthikesalingam, A., Kelly, C. J., King, D., . . . Shetty, S. (2020). International evaluation of an AI system for breast cancer screening. *Nature, 577*, 89–94. https://doi.org/10.1038/s41586-019-1799-6

McPherson, C., Miller, S. P., El-Dib, M., Massaro, A. N., and Inder, T. E. (2020). The influence of pain, agitation, and their management on the immature brain. *Pediatric Research, 88*(2), 168–175. https://doi.org/10.1038/s41390-019-0744-6

McPherson, C., Ortinau, C. M., and Vesoulis, Z. (2021). Practical approaches to sedation and analgesia in the newborn. *Journal of Perinatology, 41*(3), Article 3. https://doi.org/10.1038/s41372-020-00878-7

Mediano, P. A. M., Rosas, F. E., Bor, D., Seth, A. K., and Barrett, A. B. (2022). The strength of weak integrated information theory. *Trends in Cognitive Sciences, 26*(8), 646–655. https://doi.org/10.1016/j.tics.2022.04.008

Mediano, P. A. M., Seth, A. K., and Barrett, A. B. (2019). Measuring integrated information: comparison of candidate measures in theory and simulation. *Entropy, 21*(1), 1–30. https://doi.org/10.3390/e21010017

Menon, D. K., Owen, A. M., Williams, E. J., Minhas, P. S., Allen, C. M., Boniface, S. J., and Pickard, J. D. (1998). Cortical processing in persistent vegetative state. Wolfson Brain Imaging Centre Team. *Lancet (London, England), 352*(9123), 200. https://doi.org/10.1016/s0140-6736(05)77805-3

Merikle, P. M., Smilek, D., and Eastwood, J. D. (2001). Perception without awareness: perspectives from cognitive psychology. *Cognition, 79*(1–2), 115–134. https://doi.org/10.1016/s0010-0277(00)00126-8

Merker, B. (2007). Consciousness without a cerebral cortex: a challenge for neuroscience and medicine. *Behavioral and Brain Sciences, 30*(1), 63–81. https://doi.org/10.1017/S0140525X07000891

Meth, R., Wittfoth, C., and Harzsch, S. (2017). Brain architecture of the Pacific White Shrimp *Penaeus vannamei* Boone, 1931 (Malacostraca, Dendrobranchiata): correspondence of brain structure and sensory input? *Cell and Tissue Research, 369*(2), 255–271. https://doi.org/10.1007/s00441-017-2607-y

Metzinger, T. (2021). Artificial suffering: an argument for a global moratorium on synthetic phenomenology. *Journal of Artificial Intelligence and Consciousness, 8*(1), 43–66. https://doi.org/10.1142/S270507852150003X

Michel, M. (2019). Consciousness science underdetermined. *Ergo, 6.* https://doi.org/10.3998/ergo.12405314.0006.028

Michel, M., and Lau, H. (2020). On the dangers of conflating strong and weak versions of a theory of consciousness. *Philosophy and the Mind Sciences, 1*(2), 8. https://doi.org/10.33735/phimisci.2020.II.54

Michel, M., and Lau, H. (2021a). Is blindsight possible under signal detection theory? Comment on Phillips (2021). *Psychological Review, 128*(3), 585–591. https://doi.org/10.1037/rev0000266

Michel, M., and Lau, H. (2021b). Higher-order theories do just fine. *Cognitive Neuroscience*, *12*, 77–78.

Mikkelson, G. (2018). Convergence and divergence between ecocentrism and sentientism concerning net value. *Les Ateliers de l'éthique/The Ethics Forum*, *13*(1), 101–114. https://doi.org/10.7202/1055120ar

Mill, J. S. (1861/1887). *Utilitarianism*. Willard Small.

Millikan, R. G. (1999). Historical kinds and the special sciences. *Philosophical Studies*, *95*, 45–65.

Millsopp, S., and Laming, P. (2008). Trade-offs between feeding and shock avoidance in goldfish (*Carassius auratus*). *Applied Animal Behaviour Science*, *113*(1), 247–254. https://doi.org/10.1016/j.applanim.2007.11.004

Mirwan, H. B., and Kevan, P. G. (2014). Problem solving by worker bumblebees *Bombus impatiens* (Hymenoptera: Apoidea). *Animal Cognition*, *17*(5), 1053–1061. https://doi.org/10.1007/s10071-014-0737-0

Mitchell, S. D. (2009). *Unsimple Truths: Science, Complexity, and Policy*. University of Chicago Press.

Montemayor, C. (2022). Distinguishing epistemic and moral grounds for legal protection. *Animal Sentience*, *7*(32), 16. https://doi.org/10.51291/2377-7478.1734

Montemayor, C. (2023). Jurisprudence and animal protection. *Animal Sentience*, *7*(32), 32. https://doi.org/10.51291/2377-7478.1771

Monti, M. M., Vanhaudenhuyse, A., Coleman, M. R., Boly, M., Pickard, J. D., Tshibanda, L., Owen, A. M., and Laureys, S. (2010). Willful modulation of brain activity in disorders of consciousness. *New England Journal of Medicine*, *362*(7), 579–589. https://doi.org/10.1056/NEJMoa0905370

Morawetz, L., and Spaethe, J. (2012). Visual attention in a complex search task differs between honeybees and bumblebees. *Journal of Experimental Biology*, *215*(14), 2515–2523. https://doi.org/10.1242/jeb.066399

Mørch, H. H. (2017). The evolutionary argument for phenomenal powers. *Philosophical Perspectives*, *31*, 293–316.

Mørch, H. H. (2019). Is the Integrated Information Theory of Consciousness compatible with Russellian panpsychism? *Erkenntnis*, *84*(5), 1065–1085. https://doi.org/10.1007/s10670-018-9995-6

Morelle, R. (2009, June 9). Welcome to the Spiderlab. *BBC News*. http://news.bbc.co.uk/1/hi/sci/tech/8083962.stm

Morgan-Knapp, C. (2015). Nonconsequentialist Precaution. *Ethical Theory and Moral Practice*, *18*(4), 785–797. https://doi.org/10.1007/s10677-014-9552-6

Moroz, L. L. (2011). Aplysia. *Current Biology: CB*, *21*(2), R60–61. https://doi.org/10.1016/j.cub.2010.11.028

Morris, C. (2019, November 28). General election 2019: how many trees can you plant? *BBC News*. https://www.bbc.com/news/50591261

Multi-Society Task Force on PVS. (1994). Medical aspects of the persistent vegetative state (2). *New England Journal of Medicine*, *330*(22), 1572–1579. https://doi.org/10.1056/NEJM199406023302206

Munia, T. T. K., and Aviyente, S. (2019). Time-frequency based phase-amplitude coupling measure for neuronal oscillations. *Scientific Reports*, *9*(1), Article 1. https://doi.org/10.1038/s41598-019-48870-2

Munthe, C. (2011). *The Price of Precaution and the Ethics of Risk* (Vol. 6). Springer Netherlands. https://doi.org/10.1007/978-94-007-1330-7

Nagel, T. (1971). Brain bisection and the unity of consciousness. *Synthese*, *22*(3/4), 396–413.

Nagel, T. (1974). What is it like to be a bat? *Philosophical Review*, *83*(4), 435–450. https://doi.org/10.2307/2183914

Nave, K., Deane, G., Miller, M., and Clark, A. (2022). Expecting some action: predictive processing and the construction of conscious experience. *Review of Philosophy and Psychology*, *13*(4), 1019–1037.

Neander, K. (2017). *A Mark of the Mental: In Defense of Informational Teleosemantics*. MIT Press.

Ng, L., Garcia, J. E., and Dyer, A. G. (2020). Use of temporal and colour cueing in a symbolic delayed matching task by honey bees. *Journal of Experimental Biology, 223*(15), jeb224220. https://doi.org/10.1242/jeb.224220

Ng, Y.-K. (2017). Justifying the precautionary principle with expected net-welfare maximization. *Animal Sentience, 2*(16), 12. https://doi.org/10.51291/2377-7478.1238

Ng, Y. K. (2022). No need for certainty in animal sentience. *Animal Sentience, 7*(32), 6. https://doi.org/10.51291/2377-7478.1716

Nieder, A., Wagener, L., and Rinnert, P. (2020). A neural correlate of sensory consciousness in a corvid bird. *Science, 369*(6511), 1626–1629. https://doi.org/10.1126/science.abb1447

Niikawa, T., Hayashi, Y., Shepherd, J., and Sawai, T. (2022). Human brain organoids and consciousness. *Neuroethics, 15*(1), 5. https://doi.org/10.1007/s12152-022-09483-1

Nozick, R. (1974). *Anarchy, State, and Utopia*. John Wiley and Sons.

Nuffield Council on Bioethics. (2017). *Human embryo culture: discussions concerning the statutory time limit for maintaining human embryos in culture in the light of some recent scientific developments*. Nuffield Council on Bioethics. https://www.nuffieldbioethics.org/assets/pdfs/Human-Embryo-Culture.pdf

Nuffield Council on Bioethics. (2021a). *Genome editing and farmed animal breeding: social and ethical issues*. Nuffield Council on Bioethics.

Nuffield Council on Bioethics. (2021b). *Rapid online dialogue on genome editing and farmed animals*. Nuffield Council on Bioethics.

Nuffield Council on Bioethics. (2022). *Public dialogue on genome editing and farmed animals*. Nuffield Council on Bioethics. https://www.nuffieldbioethics.org/publications/public-dialogue-on-genome-editing-and-farmed-animals-2

Nussbaum, M. C. (2006). *Frontiers of Justice: Disability, Nationality, Species Membership*. Harvard University Press.

Nussbaum, M. C. (2023). *Justice for Animals: Our Collective Responsibility*. Simon and Schuster.

Open Science Collaboration. (2015). Estimating the reproducibility of psychological science. *Science, 349*(6251), aac4716. https://doi.org/10.1126/science.aac4716

Ouellette, M.-H., Desrochers, M. J., Gheta, I., Ramos, R., and Hendricks, M. (2018). A gate-and-switch model for head orientation behaviors in Caenorhabditis elegans. *ENeuro, 5*(6), ENEURO.0121-18.2018. https://doi.org/10.1523/ENEURO.0121-18.2018

Owen, A. M., Coleman, M. R., Boly, M., Davis, M. H., Laureys, S., and Pickard, J. D. (2006). Detecting awareness in the vegetative state. *Science, 313*(5792), 1402. https://doi.org/10.1126/science.1130197

Paez, E. (2017). What harmful practices? The material scope of animal protection legislation. *Animal Sentience, 2*(16), 17. https://doi.org/10.51291/2377-7478.1260

Palese, M. (2018). The Irish abortion referendum: how a citizens' assembly helped to break years of political deadlock. The Electoral Reform Society Blog, 28 May 2018. https://www.electoral-reform.org.uk/the-irish-abortion-referendum-how-a-citizens-assembly-helped-to-break-years-of-political-deadlock/

Palmer, C. (2009). Harm to species? Species, ethics, and climate change: the case of the polar bear. *Notre Dame Journal of Law, Ethics and Public Policy, 23*(2), 587–604.

Panksepp, J. (1982). Toward a general psychobiological theory of emotions. *Behavioral and Brain Sciences, 5*, 407–467. https://doi.org/10.1017/S0140525X00012759

Panksepp, J. (1998a). *Affective Neuroscience: The Foundations of Human and Animal Emotions* (pp. xii, 466). Oxford University Press.

Panksepp, J. (1998b). The periconscious substrates of consciousness: affective states and the evolutionary origins of the self. *Journal of Consciousness Studies, 5*(5–6), 566–582.

Panksepp, J. (2005). Affective consciousness: core emotional feelings in animals and humans. *Consciousness and Cognition, 14*(1), 30–80. https://doi.org/10.1016/j.concog.2004.10.004

Panksepp, J. (2011). The basic emotional circuits of mammalian brains: do animals have affective lives? *Neuroscience and Biobehavioral Reviews, 35*(9), 1791–1804. https://doi.org/10.1016/j.neubiorev.2011.08.003

Panksepp, J. (2016). Brain processes for 'good' and 'bad' feelings: how far back in evolution? *Animal Sentience, 1*(3), 24. https://doi.org/10.51291/2377-7478.1050

Panksepp, J., Fuchs, T., Garcia, V. A., and Lesiak, A. (2007). Does any aspect of mind survive brain damage that typically leads to a persistent vegetative state? Ethical considerations. *Philosophy, Ethics, and Humanities in Medicine, 2,* 32. https://doi.org/10.1186/1747-5341-2-32

Panksepp, J., Normansell, L., Cox, J. F., and Siviy, S. M. (1994). Effects of neonatal decortication on the social play of juvenile rats. *Physiology & Behavior, 56*(3), 429–443. https://doi.org/10.1016/0031-9384(94)90285-2

Papineau, D. (1993). *Philosophical Naturalism.* Basil Blackwell.

Papineau, D. (2002). *Thinking about Consciousness.* Clarendon Press.

Papineau, D. (2021). *The Metaphysics of Sensory Experience.* Oxford University Press.

Park, J. B., Choi, W. H., Kim, S. H., Jin, J. H., Han, Y. S., Lee, Y. Seok, and Kim, N. J. (2014). Developmental characteristics of Tenebrio molitor larvae (Coleoptera: Tenebrionidae) in different instars. *International Journal of Industrial Entomology, 28*(1), 5–9. https://doi.org/10.7852/ijie.2014.28.1.5

Parle, E., Dirks, J.-H., and Taylor, D. (2016). Bridging the gap: wound healing in insects restores mechanical strength by targeted cuticle deposition. *Journal of the Royal Society, Interface, 13*(117), 20150984. https://doi.org/10.1098/rsif.2015.0984

Parvizi, J., and Damasio, A. (2001). Consciousness and the brainstem. *Cognition, 79*(1–2), 135–160.

Pascual-Leone, A., and Walsh, V. (2001). Fast backprojections from the motion to the primary visual area necessary for visual awareness. *Science, 292*(5516), 510–512. https://doi.org/10.1126/science.1057099

Passino, C. (2019, October 15). Why snail farming is sweeping across the countryside. *Country Life.* https://www.countrylife.co.uk/news/snail-farming-sweeping-across-countryside-205772

Passos-Ferreira, Claudia (in press). Are infants conscious? *Philosophical Perspectives.*

Paul, E. S., Sher, S., Tamietto, M., Winkielman, P., and Mendl, M. T. (2020). Towards a comparative science of emotion: affect and consciousness in humans and animals. *Neuroscience & Biobehavioral Reviews, 108,* 749–770. https://doi.org/10.1016/j.neubiorev.2019.11.014

Paul, L. A. (2014). *Transformative Experience.* Oxford University Press.

Paulk, A. C., Stacey, J. A., Pearson, T. W., Taylor, G. J., Moore, R. J., Srinivasan, M. V., and van Swinderen, B. (2014). Selective attention in the honeybee optic lobes precedes behavioral choices. *Proceedings of the National Academy of Sciences of the United States of America, 111*(13), 5006–5011. https://doi.org/10.1073/pnas.1323297111

Peña-Guzmán, D. M. (2022). *When Animals Dream: The Hidden World of Animal Consciousness.* Princeton University Press.

Pepper, A. (2017). Political liberalism, human cultures, and nonhuman lives. In L. Cordeiro-Rodrigues, and L. Mitchell (eds), *Animals, Race, and Multiculturalism* (pp. 35–59). Palgrave Macmillan. https://doi.org/10.1007/978-3-319-66568-9_3

Perez, E., and Long, R. (2023). Towards evaluating AI systems for moral status using self-reports. *arXiv preprint* arXiv:2311.08576

Persaud, N. (2009). Post-decision wagering. *Scholarpedia, 4*(1), 7428.

Persaud, N., Davidson, M., Maniscalco, B., Mobbs, D., Passingham, R. E., Cowey, A., and Lau, H. (2011). Awareness-related activity in prefrontal and parietal cortices in blindsight reflects more than superior visual performance. *NeuroImage, 58*(2), 605–611. https://doi.org/10.1016/j.neuroimage.2011.06.081

Persaud, N., McLeod, P., and Cowey, A. (2007). Post-decision wagering objectively measures awareness. *Nature Neuroscience, 10*(2), Article 2. https://doi.org/10.1038/nn1840

Persson, E. (2016). What are the core ideas behind the precautionary principle? *Science of the Total Environment, 557–558,* 134–141. https://doi.org/10.1016/j.scitotenv.2016.03.034

Peters, M. A. K., Kentridge, R. W., Phillips, I., and Block, N. (2017). Does unconscious perception really exist? Continuing the ASSC20 debate. *Neuroscience of Consciousness, 2017*(1), nix015. https://doi.org/10.1093/nc/nix015

Peters, M. A. K., and Lau, H. (2015). Human observers have optimal introspective access to perceptual processes even for visually masked stimuli. *eLife, 4,* e09651. https://doi.org/10.7554/eLife.09651

Peters, M. A. K., Ro, T., and Lau, H. (2016). Who's afraid of response bias? *Neuroscience of Consciousness, 2016*(1), niw001. https://doi.org/10.1093/nc/niw001

Peterson, A., Cruse, D., Naci, L., Weijer, C., and Owen, A. M. (2015). Risk, diagnostic error, and the clinical science of consciousness. *NeuroImage: Clinical, 7,* 588–597. https://doi.org/10.1016/j.nicl.2015.02.008

Peterson, K. J., Lyons, J. B., Nowak, K. S., Takacs, C. M., Wargo, M. J., and McPeek, M. A. (2004). Estimating metazoan divergence times with a molecular clock. *Proceedings of the National Academy of Sciences of the United States of America, 101*(17), 6536–6541. https://doi.org/10.1073/pnas.0401670101

Pettit, P. (2004). Depoliticizing democracy. *Ratio Juris, 17*(1), 52–65. https://doi.org/10.1111/j.0952-1917.2004.00254.x

Pettit, P. (2010). Representation, responsive and indicative. *Constellations, 17*(3), 426–434. https://doi.org/10.1111/j.1467-8675.2010.00603.x

Pettit, P. (2012). *On the People's Terms: A Republican Theory and Model of Democracy.* Cambridge University Press. https://doi.org/10.1017/CBO9781139017428

Phillips, I. (2018). The methodological puzzle of phenomenal consciousness. *Philosophical Transactions of the Royal Society B: Biological Sciences, 373*(1755), 20170347. https://doi.org/10.1098/rstb.2017.0347

Phillips, I. (2021a). Bias and blindsight: a reply to Michel and Lau (2021). *Psychological Review, 128,* 592–595. https://doi.org/10.1037/rev0000277

Phillips, I. (2021b). Blindsight is qualitatively degraded conscious vision. *Psychological Review, 128*(3), 558–584. https://doi.org/10.1037/rev0000254

Piccinini, G. (2007). The ontology of creature consciousness: a challenge for philosophy. *Behavioral and Brain Sciences, 30*(1), 103–104. https://doi.org/10.1017/S0140525X07001100

Pichl, A., Ranisch, R., Altinok, O. A., Antonakaki, M., Barnhart, A. J., Bassil, K., Boyd, J. L., Chinaia, A. A., Diner, S., Gaillard, M., Greely, H. T., Jowitt, J., Kreitmair, K., Lawrence, D., Lee, T. N., McKeown, A., Sachdev, V., Schicktanz, S., Sugarman, J., . . . and Árnason, G (2023). Ethical, legal and social aspects of human cerebral organoids and their governance in Germany, the United Kingdom and the United States. *Frontiers in Cell and Developmental Biology, 11,* 1194706. https://doi.org/10.3389/fcell.2023.1194706

Piovesan, A., Mirams, L., Poole, H., Moore, D., and Ogden, R. (2019). The relationship between pain-induced autonomic arousal and perceived duration. *Emotion, 19*(7), 1148–1161. https://doi.org/10.1037/emo0000512

Pipkin, J. (2020). Mapping the mind of a fly. *eLife, 9,* e62451. https://doi.org/10.7554/eLife.62451

Platt, M. W. (2011). Fetal awareness and fetal pain: the emperor's new clothes. *Archives of Disease in Childhood. Fetal and Neonatal Edition, 96*(4), F236–237. https://doi.org/10.1136/adc.2010.195966

Plunkett, D. (2016). *Justice, Non-Human Animals, and the Methodology of Political Philosophy, Jurisprudence, 7*(1), 1–29, https://doi.org/10.1080/20403313.2015.1128202

Plutynski, A. (2012). Ethical issues in cancer screening and prevention. *Journal of Medicine and Philosophy: A Forum for Bioethics and Philosophy of Medicine, 37*(3), 310–323. https://doi.org/10.1093/jmp/jhs017

Plutynski, A. (2017). Safe or sorry? Cancer screening and inductive risk. In K. C. Elliott and T. Richards (eds), *Exploring Inductive Risk: Case Studies of Values in Science* (pp. 149–170). Oxford University Press. https://doi.org/10.1093/acprof:oso/9780190467715.003.0008

Popinchalk, A., and Sedgh, G. (2019). Trends in the method and gestational age of abortion in high-income countries. *BMJ Sexual & Reproductive Health, 45*(2), 95–103. https://doi.org/10.1136/bmjsrh-2018-200149

Popper, K. R., and Eccles, J. C. (1977). *The Self and Its Brain: An Argument for Interactionism.* Springer International.

Posner, J., Russell, J. A., Gerber, A., Gorman, D., Colibazzi, T., Yu, S., Wang, Z., Kangarlu, A., Zhu, H., and Peterson, B. S. (2009). The neurophysiological bases of emotion: an fMRI study of the affective circumplex using emotion-denoting words. *Human Brain Mapping, 30*(3), 883–895. https://doi.org/10.1002/hbm.20553

Posner, J., Russell, J. A., and Peterson, B. S. (2005). The circumplex model of affect: an integrative approach to affective neuroscience, cognitive development, and psychopathology. *Development and Psychopathology*, 17(3), 715–734. https://doi.org/10.1017/S0954579405050340

Potochnik, A., and McGill, B. (2012). The limitations of hierarchical organization. *Philosophy of Science*, 79(1), 120–140. https://doi.org/10.1086/663237

Preece, R., and Fraser, D. (2000). The status of animals in biblical and Christian thought: a study in colliding values. *Society and Animals*, 8(3), 245–263.

Preuss, T. M., and Wise, S. P. (2022). Evolution of prefrontal cortex. *Neuropsychopharmacology*, 47(1), 3–19. https://doi.org/10.1038/s41386-021-01076-5

Procenko, O., Read, J., and Nityananda, V. (2023). Physically stressed bees expect less reward in an active choice judgement bias test. *bioRxiv preprint*, 2023.10.06.561175. https://doi.org/10.1101/2023.10.06.561175

Puri, S., and Faulkes, Z. (2015). Can crayfish take the heat? Procambarus clarkii show nociceptive behaviour to high temperature stimuli, but not low temperature or chemical stimuli. *Biology Open*, 4(4), 441–448. https://doi.org/10.1242/bio.20149654

Qu, J., Zhou, X., Zhu, H., Cheng, G., W.S. Ashwell, K., and Lu, F. (2006). Development of the human superior colliculus and the retinocollicular projection. *Experimental Eye Research*, 82(2), 300–310. https://doi.org/10.1016/j.exer.2005.07.002

Quilty-Dunn, J., Porot, N., and Mandelbaum, E. (2023). The best game in town: the re-emergence of the language of thought hypothesis across the cognitive sciences. *Behavioral and Brain Sciences*, 46, e261. https://doi.org/10.1017/S0140525X22002849

Rahman, S. A. (2017). Religion and animal welfare: an Islamic perspective. *Animals*, 7(2), 11. https://doi.org/10.3390/ani7020011

Rawls, J. (1993). *Political Liberalism*. Columbia University Press.

Read, E., and Birch, J. (2023). Animal sentience and the capabilities approach to justice. *Biology and Philosophy*, 38, 26. https://doi.org/10.1007/s10539-023-09914-0

Reber, A. S. (2017). What if all animals are sentient? *Animal Sentience*, 2(16), 6. https://doi.org/10.51291/2377-7478.1225

Reber, A. S. (2018). *The First Minds: Caterpillars, Karyotes, and Consciousness*. Oxford University Press.

Reber, A. S., and Baluška, F. (2021). Cognition in some surprising places. *Biochemical and Biophysical Research Communications*, 564, 150–157.

Reber, A. S., Baluska, F., and Miller, W. (2022). Of course crustaceans are sentient: but there's more to the story. *Animal Sentience*, 7(32). https://doi.org/10.51291/2377-7478.1712

Redish, A. D. (2016). Vicarious trial and error. *Nature Reviews Neuroscience*, 17(3), Article 3. https://doi.org/10.1038/nrn.2015.30

Regan, T. (1983/2004). *The Case for Animal Rights*. University of California Press.

Rescorla, M. (2019). The language of thought hypothesis. In E. N. Zalta (ed.), *The Stanford Encyclopedia of Philosophy* (Summer 2019). Metaphysics Research Lab, Stanford University. https://plato.stanford.edu/archives/sum2019/entries/language-thought/

Robson, A. A., Garcia De Leaniz, C., Wilson, R. P., and Halsey, L. G. (2010). Behavioural adaptations of mussels to varying levels of food availability and predation risk. *Journal of Molluscan Studies*, 76(4), 348–353. https://doi.org/10.1093/mollus/eyq025

Roelofs, L. (2023). Sentientism, motivation, and philosophical Vulcans. *Pacific Philosophical Quarterly*, 104(2), 301–323. https://doi.org/10.1111/papq.12420

Rollin, B. (2017). Raising the moral consciousness of science. *Animal Sentience*, 2(16), 8. https://doi.org/10.51291/2377-7478.1230

Rolls, E. T. (2004). A higher order syntactic thought (HOST) theory of consciousness. In R. J. Gennaro (ed.), *Higher Order Theories of Consciousness* (pp. 137–172). John Benjamins.

Rolls, E. T. (2014). *Emotion and Decision Making Explained*. Oxford University Press.

Romanis, E. C. (2020). Is 'viability' viable? Abortion, conceptual confusion and the law in England and Wales and the United States. *Journal of Law and the Biosciences*, 7(1), lsaa059.

Rosenberg, A. (2018). Can we make sense of subjective experience in metabolically situated cognitive processes? *Biology and Philosophy*, 33(1–2), 13.

Roth, B., and Øines, S. (2010). Stunning and killing of edible crabs (*Cancer pagurus*). *Animal Welfare*, *19*(3), 287–294. https://doi.org/10.1017/S0962728600001676

Rowe, A. (2020). Insects raised for food and feed—global scale, practices, and policy. *Rethink Priorities*. https://rethinkpriorities.org/publications/insects-raised-for-food-and-feed

Royal College of Obstetricians and Gynaecologists. (2010). *Fetal awareness: review of research and recommendations for practice*. Royal College of Obstetricians and Gynaecologists. https://www.rcog.org.uk/media/xujjh2hj/rcogfetalawarenesswpr0610.pdf

Royal College of Obstetricians and Gynaecologists. (2022). *RCOG fetal awareness evidence review, December 2022*. Royal College of Obstetricians and Gynaecologists. https://www.rcog.org.uk/media/gdtnncdk/rcog-fetal-awareness-evidence-review-dec-2022.pdf

Royal College of Physicians. (2020). *Prolonged disorders of consciousness following sudden onset brain injury: national clinical guidelines*. Royal College of Physicians. https://www.rcplondon.ac.uk/guidelines-policy/prolonged-disorders-consciousness-following-sudden-onset-brain-injury-national-clinical-guidelines

RSPCA Australia. (2016). What is the most humane way to kill crustaceans for human consumption? *RSPCA Knowledgebase*. https://kb.rspca.org.au/knowledge-base/what-is-the-most-humane-way-to-kill-crustaceans-for-human-consumption/

Russell, B. (1927/1992). *The Analysis of Matter*. Routledge.

Russell, J. A. (1980). A circumplex model of affect. *Journal of Personality and Social Psychology*, *39*, 1161–1178. https://doi.org/10.1037/h0077714

Russell, J. A. (2003). Core affect and the psychological construction of emotion. *Psychological Review*, *110*, 145–172.

Russell, J. A. (2009). Emotion, core affect, and psychological construction. *Cognition and Emotion*, *23*, 1259–1283.

Ryan, C. (2019, May 16). The benefits of insect-based poultry feed. *Poultry News*. https://www.poultrynews.co.uk/news/the-benefits-of-insect-based-poultry-feed.html

Sager, A. (2014). Normative ethics after pragmatic naturalism. *Metaphilosophy*, *45*(3), 422–440. https://doi.org/10.1111/meta.12093

Salomons, T. V., Iannetti, G. D., Liang, M., and Wood, J. N. (2016). The 'pain matrix' in pain-free individuals. *JAMA Neurology*, *73*(6), 755–756. https://doi.org/10.1001/jamaneurol.2016.0653

Samuelson, E. E. W., Chen-Wishart, Z. P., Gill, R. J., and Leadbeater, E. (2016). Effect of acute pesticide exposure on bee spatial working memory using an analogue of the radial-arm maze. *Scientific Reports*, *6*(1), Article 1. https://doi.org/10.1038/srep38957

Sawai, T., Sakaguchi, H., Thomas, E., Takahashi, J., and Fujita, M. (2019). The ethics of cerebral organoid research: being conscious of consciousness. *Stem Cell Reports*, *13*(3), 440–447. https://doi.org/10.1016/j.stemcr.2019.08.003

Schechter, E. (2018). *Self-Consciousness and 'Split' Brains: The Minds' I*. Oxford University Press.

Schlag, J. (2007). Should the superficial superior colliculus be part of Merker's mesodiencephalic system? *Behavioral and Brain Sciences*, *30*(1), 105–106. https://doi.org/10.1017/S0140525X07001124

Schnakers, C., Chatelle, C., Demertzi, A., Majerus, S., and Laureys, S. (2012). What about pain in disorders of consciousness? *AAPS Journal*, *14*(3), 437–444. https://doi.org/10.1208/s12248-012-9346-5

Schnakers, C., Vanhaudenhuyse, A., Giacino, J., Ventura, M., Boly, M., Majerus, S., Moonen, G., and Laureys, S. (2009). Diagnostic accuracy of the vegetative and minimally conscious state: clinical consensus versus standardized neurobehavioral assessment. *BMC Neurology*, *9*(1), 35. https://doi.org/10.1186/1471-2377-9-35

Schnakers, C., and Zasler, N. (2015). Assessment and management of pain in patients with disorders of consciousness. *PMandR*, *7*(11, supplement), S270–S277. https://doi.org/10.1016/j.pmrj.2015.09.016

Schnakers, C., and Zasler, N. D. (2007). Pain assessment and management in disorders of consciousness. *Current Opinion in Neurology*, *20*(6), 620–626. https://doi.org/10.1097/WCO.0b013e3282f169d9

Schneider, S. (2019). *Artificial You: AI and the Future of Your Mind*. Princeton University Press.

Schneider, S. (2020). How to catch an AI zombie: testing for consciousness in machines. In S. M. Liao (ed.), *Ethics of Artificial Intelligence*. Oxford University Press. https://doi.org/10.1093/oso/9780190905033.003.0016

Schneider, S., and Turner, E. (2017). Is anyone home? A way to find out if AI has become self-aware. *Scientific American*. https://blogs.scientificamerican.com/observations/is-anyone-home-a-way-to-find-out-if-ai-has-become-self-aware/

Schnell, A., Browning, H., and Birch, J. (2022, March 24). Octopus farms raise huge animal welfare concerns—and they're unsustainable too. *The Conversation*. http://theconversation.com/octopus-farms-raise-huge-animal-welfare-concerns-and-theyre-unsustainable-too-179134

Schultz-Bergin, M. (2017). *Animal Rights in a Diverse Society*. PhD thesis, Bowling Green State University.

Schwitzgebel, E. (2016). Phenomenal consciousness, defined and defended as innocently as I can manage. *Journal of Consciousness Studies*, *23*(11–12), 224–235.

Schwitzgebel, E. (2020). Is there something it's like to be a garden snail? *Philosophical Topics*, *48*(1), 39–64.

Schwitzgebel, E. (2021). *Borderline consciousness, when it's neither determinately true nor determinately false that experience is present*. http://faculty.ucr.edu/~eschwitz/SchwitzAbs/BorderlineConsciousness.htm

Schwitzgebel, E., and Garza, M. (2020). Designing AI with rights, consciousness, self-respect, and freedom. In S. Matthew Liao (ed.), *Ethics of Artificial Intelligence*. Oxford University Press. https://doi.org/10.1093/oso/9780190905033.003.0017

Science and Technology Committee. (2007). *Scientific developments relating to the Abortion Act 1967, Volume I*. UK House of Commons. https://publications.parliament.uk/pa/cm200607/cmselect/cmsctech/1045/1045i.pdf

Scientific Advisory Group for Emergencies. (2020a). *SAGE 17 minutes: Coronavirus (COVID-19) response, 18 March 2020*. Scientific Advisory Group for Emergencies. https://www.gov.uk/government/publications/sage-minutes-coronavirus-covid-19-response-18-march-2020

Scientific Advisory Group for Emergencies. (2020b). *Summary of the effectiveness and harms of different non-pharmaceutical interventions, 21 September 2020*. Scientific Advisory Group for Emergencies. https://www.gov.uk/government/publications/summary-of-the-effectiveness-and-harms-of-different-non-pharmaceutical-interventions-16-september-2020/summary-of-the-effectiveness-and-harms-of-different-non-pharmaceutical-interventions-21-september-2020

Seager, W. E. (2019). *The Routledge Handbook of Panpsychism*. Routledge.

Sebo, J. (2017). Agency and moral status. *Journal of Moral Philosophy*, *14*(1), 1–22.

Sebo, J., and Long, R. (2023). Moral consideration for AI systems by 2030. *AI and Ethics*, Advance online publication. https://doi.org/10.1007/s43681-023-00379-1

Segundo-Ortin, M., and Calvo, P. (2023). Plant sentience? Between romanticism and denial: science. *Animal Sentience*, *8*(33). https://doi.org/10.51291/2377-7478.1772

Seidenberg, D. M. (2006). Animal rights in the Jewish tradition. In *The Encyclopedia of Religion and Nature*. Continuum. https://www.oxfordreference.com/display/10.1093/acref/9780199754670.001.0001/acref-9780199754670-e-35

Sekulic, S., Gebauer-Bukurov, K., Cvijanovic, M., Kopitovic, A., Ilic, D., Petrovic, D., Capo, I., Pericin-Starcevic, I., Christ, O., and Topalidou, A. (2016). Appearance of fetal pain could be associated with maturation of the mesodiencephalic structures. *Journal of Pain Research*, *9*, 1031–1038. https://doi.org/10.2147/JPR.S117959

Selbach, C., Marchant, L., and Mouritsen, K. N. (2022). Mussel memory: can bivalves learn to fear parasites? *Royal Society Open Science*, *9*(1), 211774. https://doi.org/10.1098/rsos.211774

Seo, Y.-S., and Huh, J.-H. (2019). Automatic emotion-based music classification for supporting intelligent IoT applications. *Electronics*, *8*, 164. https://doi.org/10.3390/electronics8020164

Séris, J.-P., and Voss, S. (1993). Language and machine in the philosophy of Descartes. In S. Voss (ed.), *Essays on the Philosophy and Science of René Descartes*. Oxford University Press. https://doi.org/10.1093/acprof:oso/9780195075519.003.0013.

Seth, A. (2021). *Being You: A New Science of Consciousness*. Faber and Faber.

Seth, A., and Dienes, Z. (2017). The value of Bayesian statistics for assessing credible evidence of animal sentience. *Animal Sentience, 2*(16), 22. https://doi.org/10.51291/2377-7478.1289

Seth, A. K. (2008). Post-decision wagering measures metacognitive content, not sensory consciousness. *Consciousness and Cognition, 17*(3), 981–983. https://doi.org/10.1016/j.concog.2007.05.008

Seth, A. K., and Bayne, T. (2022). Theories of consciousness. *Nature Reviews. Neuroscience, 23*(7), 439–452. https://doi.org/10.1038/s41583-022-00587-4

Shahbazi, M. N., Jedrusik, A., Vuoristo, S., Recher, G., Hupalowska, A., Bolton, V., Fogarty, N. N. M., Campbell, A., Devito, L., Ilic, D., Khalaf, Y., Niakan, K. K., Fishel, S., and Zernicka-Goetz, M. (2016). Self-organization of the human embryo in the absence of maternal tissues. *Nature Cell Biology, 18*(6), 700–708. https://doi.org/10.1038/ncb3347

Sharma, A., Zuk, P., and Scott, C. T. (2021). Scientific and ethical uncertainties in brain organoid research. *American Journal of Bioethics, 21*(1), 48–51. https://doi.org/10.1080/1526516 1.2020.1845866

Shea, N. (2011). Methodological encounters with the phenomenal kind. *Philosophy and Phenomenological Research, 84*(2), 307–344.

Shea, N., and Bayne, T. (2010). The vegetative state and the science of consciousness. *British Journal for the Philosophy of Science, 61*(3), 459–484.

Shemesh, Y., and Chen, A. (2023). A paradigm shift in translational psychiatry through rodent neuroethology. *Molecular Psychiatry, 28*(3), 993–1003. https://doi.org/10.1038/s41380-022-01913-z

Shepherd, J. (2018). *Consciousness and Moral Status*. Routledge. http://www.ncbi.nlm.nih.gov/books/NBK540410/

Shepherd, J. (in press). Sentience, Vulcans, and zombies: the value of phenomenal consciousness. *AI and Society*. https://philpapers.org/rec/SHESVA-3

Sherry, D. F., and Strang, C. G. (2015). Contrasting styles in cognition and behaviour in bumblebees and honeybees. *Behavioural Processes, 117*, 59–69. https://doi.org/10.1016/j.beproc.2014.09.005

Shevlin, H. (2021). Non-human consciousness and the specificity problem: a modest theoretical proposal. *Mind and Language, 36*(2), 297–314.

Shigeno, S., Andrews, P. L. R., Ponte, G., and Fiorito, G. (2018). Cephalopod brains: an overview of current knowledge to facilitate comparison with vertebrates. *Frontiers in Physiology, 9*. https://doi.org/10.3389/fphys.2018.00952

Shirure, V. S., Hughes, C. C. W., and George, S. C. (2021). Engineering vascularized organoid-on-a-chip models. *Annual Review of Biomedical Engineering, 23*(1), 141–167. https://doi.org/10.1146/annurev-bioeng-090120-094330

Shriver, A. (2006). Minding mammals. *Philosophical Psychology, 19*(4), 433–442. https://doi.org/10.1080/09515080600726385

Shriver, A. (2018a). The unpleasantness of pain for humans and other animals. In *Philosophy of Pain* (pp. 147–162). Routledge.

Shriver, A. (2018b). The unpleasantness of pain for nonhuman animals. In K. Andrews & J. Beck (eds.), *The Routledge Handbook of Philosophy of Animal Minds* (pp. 176–184). Routledge. https://doi.org/10.4324/9781315742250-17

Shriver, A. (2022). *Why Neuron Counts Shouldn't Be Used as Proxies for Moral Weight*. Rethink Priorities. https://rethinkpriorities.org/publications/why-neuron-counts-shouldnt-be-used-as-proxies-for-moral-weight

Silvanto, J., Cowey, A., Lavie, N., and Walsh, V. (2005). Striate cortex (V1) activity gates awareness of motion. *Nature Neuroscience, 8*(2), Article 2. https://doi.org/10.1038/nn1379

Simon, J. A. (2017). Vagueness and zombies: why 'phenomenally conscious' has no borderline cases. *Philosophical Studies, 174*(8), 2105–2123. https://doi.org/10.1007/s11098-016-0790-4

Singer, P. (1980/2011). *Practical Ethics*. Cambridge University Press.

Skidmore, J. (2001). Duties to animals: the failure of Kant's moral theory. *Journal of Value Inquiry, 35*(4), 541–559. https://doi.org/10.1023/A:1013708710493

Skora, L. I., Livermore, J. J. A., Nisini, F., and Scott, R. B. (2022). Awareness is required for autonomic performance monitoring in instrumental learning: evidence from cardiac activity. *Psychophysiology*, 59(9), e14047. https://doi.org/10.1111/psyp.14047

Skora, L. I., Yeomans, M. R., Crombag, H. S., and Scott, R. B. (2021). Evidence that instrumental conditioning requires conscious awareness in humans. *Cognition*, 208, 104546. https://doi.org/10.1016/j.cognition.2020.104546

Sladky, K. K. (2014). Current understanding of fish and invertebrate anesthesia and analgesia. *Proceedings of the Association of Reptilian and Amphibian Veterinarians*. https://cdn.ymaws.com/members.arav.org/resource/resmgr/Files/Proceedings_2014/60.pdf

Smirnova, L., Caffo, B. S., Gracias, D. H., Huang, Q., Morales Pantoja, I. E., Tang, B., Zack, D. J., Berlinicke, C. A., Boyd, J. L., Harris, T. D., Johnson, E. C., Kagan, B. J., Kahn, J., Muotri, A. R., Paulhamus, B. L., Schwamborn, J. C., Plotkin, J., Szalay, A. S., Vogelstein, J. T., . . . Hartung, T. (2023). Organoid intelligence (OI): the new frontier in biocomputing and intelligence-in-a-dish. *Frontiers in Science*, 1. https://doi.org/10.3389/fsci.2023.1017235

Smith, J. A., and Boyd, K. M. (1991). *Lives in the Balance: The Ethics of Using Animals in Biomedical Research: The Report of a Working Party of the Institute of Medical Ethics*. Oxford University Press.

Sneddon, L., Lopez-Luna, J., Wolfenden, D., Leach, M., Valentim, A., Steenbergen, P., Bardine, N., Currie, A., Broom, D., and Brown, C. (2018). Fish sentience denial: muddying the waters. *Animal Sentience*, 3(21). https://doi.org/10.51291/2377-7478.1317

Sneddon, L. U., Elwood, R. W., Adamo, S. A., and Leach, M. C. (2014). Defining and assessing animal pain. *Animal Behaviour*, 97, 201–212. https://doi.org/10.1016/j.anbehav.2014.09.007

Snider, S. B., and Edlow, B. L. (2020). Magnetic resonance imaging in disorders of consciousness. *Current Opinion in Neurology*, 33(6), 676–683. https://doi.org/10.1097/WCO.0000000000000873

Snow, P. J., Plenderleith, M. B., Wright, L. L. (1993). Quantitative study of primary sensory neurone populations of three species of elasmobranch fish. *Journal of Comparative Neurology*, 334, 97–103.

Sober, E. (2000). Evolution and the problem of other minds. *Journal of Philosophy*, 97(7), 365–386.

Solms, M. (2021). *The Hidden Spring: A Journey to the Source of Consciousness*. Profile Books.

Solms, M. (2022). Truly minimal criteria for animal sentience. *Animal Sentience*, 7(32), 2. https://doi.org/10.51291/2377-7478.1711

Solvi, C., Baciadonna, L., and Chittka, L. (2016). Unexpected rewards induce dopamine-dependent positive emotion-like state changes in bumblebees. *Science*, 353(6307), 1529–1531.

Soto, D., Mäntylä, T., and Silvanto, J. (2011). Working memory without consciousness. *Current Biology*, 21(22), R912–R913. https://doi.org/10.1016/j.cub.2011.09.049

Souza Valente, C. (2022). Decapod sentience: broadening the framework. *Animal Sentience*, 7(32), 8. https://doi.org/10.51291/2377-7478.1723

Speiser, D. I., and Wilkens, L. A. (2016). Chapter 5—Neurobiology and behaviour of the scallop. In S. E. Shumway and G. J. Parsons (eds), *Developments in Aquaculture and Fisheries Science* (Vol. 40, pp. 219–251). Elsevier. https://doi.org/10.1016/B978-0-444-62710-0.00005-5

Spelman, L. H. (2012). *Animal Encyclopedia*. National Geographic.

SPI-M-O. (2020). *Consensus View on Behavioural and Social Interventions, 16 March 2020*. Scientific Advisory Group for Emergencies. https://www.gov.uk/government/publications/spi-m-o-consensus-view-on-behavioural-and-social-interventions-16-march-2020

Srinivasan, M. V. (2010). Honey bees as a model for vision, perception, and cognition. *Annual Review of Entomology*, 55, 267–284. https://doi.org/10.1146/annurev.ento.010908.164537

Stanford, P. K. (2006). *Exceeding Our Grasp: Science, History, and the Problem of Unconceived Alternatives*. Oxford University Press.

Stauffer, J. (2017). Cautions about precautions. *Animal Sentience*, 2(16), 2. https://doi.org/10.51291/2377-7478.1217

Steel, D. (2015). *Philosophy and the Precautionary Principle*. Cambridge University Press.

Steele, K. (2006). The precautionary principle: a new approach to public decision-making? *Law, Probability and Risk*, 5(1), 19–31. https://doi.org/10.1093/lpr/mgl010

Steele, K. (2012). The scientist qua policy advisor makes value judgments. *Philosophy of Science*, *79*(5), 893–904. https://doi.org/10.1086/667842

Stegenga, J. (2018). *Medical Nihilism*. Oxford University Press.

Stirling, A. (2007). Risk, precaution and science: towards a more constructive policy debate. Talking point on the precautionary principle. *EMBO Reports*, *8*(4), 309–315. https://doi.org/10.1038/sj.embor.7400953

Stirling, A. (2016). *Precaution in the Governance of Technology* (SSRN Scholarly Paper No. 2815579). https://doi.org/10.2139/ssrn.2815579

Stork, N. E. (2018). How many species of insects and other terrestrial arthropods are there on Earth? *Annual Review of Entomology*, *63*(1), 31–45. https://doi.org/10.1146/annurev-ento-020117-043348

Strähle, U., Scholz, S., Geisler, R., Greiner, P., Hollert, H., Rastegar, S., Schumacher, A., Selderslaghs, I., Weiss, C., Witters, H., and Braunbeck, T. (2012). Zebrafish embryos as an alternative to animal experiments—a commentary on the definition of the onset of protected life stages in animal welfare regulations. *Reproductive Toxicology*, *33*(2), 128–132. https://doi.org/10.1016/j.reprotox.2011.06.121

Strang C., and Muth, F. (2023). Judgement bias may be explained by shifts in stimulus response curves. *Royal Society Open Science*, *10*(4), 10221322221322. http://doi.org/10.1098/rsos.221322

Strang, C. G., and Sherry, D. F. (2014). Serial reversal learning in bumblebees (Bombus impatiens). *Animal Cognition*, *17*(3), 723–734. https://doi.org/10.1007/s10071-013-0704-1

Strausfeld, N. J., Wolff, G. H., and Sayre, M. E. (2020). Mushroom body evolution demonstrates homology and divergence across Pancrustacea. *ELife*, *9*, e52411. https://doi.org/10.7554/eLife.52411

Subbaraman, N. (2021). Limit on lab-grown human embryos dropped by stem-cell body. *Nature*, *594*(7861), 18–19. https://doi.org/10.1038/d41586-021-01423-y

Sun, X.-Y., Ju, X.-C., Li, Y., Zeng, P.-M., Wu, J., Zhou, Y.-Y., Shen, L.-B., Dong, J., Chen, Y.-J., and Luo, Z.-G. (2022). Generation of vascularized brain organoids to study neurovascular interactions. *ELife*, *11*, e76707. https://doi.org/10.7554/eLife.76707

Sunstein, C. R. (2005). *Laws of Fear: Beyond the Precautionary Principle*. Cambridge University Press.

Sytsma, J. (2010). Folk psychology and phenomenal consciousness. *Philosophy Compass*, *5*(8), 700–711. https://doi.org/10.1111/j.1747-9991.2010.00315.x

Sytsma, J., and Machery, E. (2010). Two conceptions of subjective experience. *Philosophical Studies*, *151*(2), 299–327. https://doi.org/10.1007/s11098-009-9439-x

Sytsma, J., and Ozdemir, E. (2019). No problem: evidence that the concept of phenomenal consciousness is not widespread. *Journal of Consciousness Studies*, *26*(9–10), 241–256.

Tamietto, M., and de Gelder, B. (2010). Neural bases of the non-conscious perception of emotional signals. *Nature Reviews. Neuroscience*, *11*(10), 697–709. https://doi.org/10.1038/nrn2889

Tan, Y., Rérolle, S., Lalitharatne, T. D., van Zalk, N., Jack, R. E., and Nanayakkara, T. (2022). Simulating dynamic facial expressions of pain from visuo-haptic interactions with a robotic patient. *Scientific Reports*, *12*(1), Article 1. https://doi.org/10.1038/s41598-022-08115-1

Tanner, A. R., Fuchs, D., Winkelmann, I. E., Gilbert, M. T. P., Pankey, M. S., Ribeiro, Â. M., Kocot, K. M., Halanych, K. M., Oakley, T. H., da Fonseca, R. R., Pisani, D., and Vinther, J. (2017). Molecular clocks indicate turnover and diversification of modern coleoid cephalopods during the Mesozoic marine revolution. *Proceedings of the Royal Society B: Biological Sciences*, *284*(1850), 20162818. https://doi.org/10.1098/rspb.2016.2818

Taschereau-Dumouchel, V., Michel, M., Lau, H., Hofmann, S. G., and LeDoux, J. E. (2022). Putting the 'mental' back in 'mental disorders': a perspective from research on fear and anxiety. *Molecular Psychiatry*, *27*(3), 1322–1330. https://doi.org/10.1038/s41380-021-01395-5

Taylor, H. (2023). Consciousness as a natural kind and the methodological puzzle of consciousness. *Mind & Language*, *38*(2), 316–335. https://doi.org/10.1111/mila.12413

Taylor, J., Vinatea, L., Ozorio, R., Schuweitzer, R., and Andreatta, E. R. (2004). Minimizing the effects of stress during eyestalk ablation of Litopenaeus vannamei females with topical anesthetic and a coagulating agent. *Aquaculture, 233*(1), 173–179. https://doi.org/10.1016/j.aquaculture.2003.09.034

Taylor, K., and Alvarez, L. R. (2019). An estimate of the number of animals used for scientific purposes worldwide in 2015. *Alternatives to Laboratory Animals, 47*(5–6), 196–213. https://doi.org/10.1177/0261192919899853

Taylor, P. W. (1981). The ethics of respect for nature. *Environmental Ethics, 3*(3), 197–218.

Thoma, J. (2022a). Time for caution. *Philosophy & Public Affairs, 50*(1), 50–89. https://doi.org/10.1111/papa.12204

Thoma, J. (2022b, January 12). The dangers of single metric accounting in public policy. *LSE COVID-19.* https://blogs.lse.ac.uk/covid19/2022/01/12/the-dangers-of-single-metric-accounting-in-public-policy/

Thomas, N. (2018). *Animal Ethics and the Autonomous Animal Self.* Springer.

Thompson, E. (2022). Could all life be sentient? *Journal of Consciousness Studies, 29*(3–4), 229–265.

Thomson, J. J. (1971). A defense of abortion. *Philosophy and Public Affairs, 1*(1), 47–66.

Tong, F. (2003). Primary visual cortex and visual awareness. *Nature Reviews Neuroscience, 4*(3), Article 3. https://doi.org/10.1038/nrn1055

Tononi, G., Albantakis, L., Boly, M., Cirelli, C., and Koch, C. (2023). Only what exists can cause: an intrinsic view of free will. arXiv preprint. arXiv:2206.02069v3

Tooley, M. (1972). Abortion and infanticide. *Philosophy & Public Affairs, 2*(1), 37–65.

Tooley, M. (1983). *Abortion and Infanticide.* Oxford University Press.

Townsend, A. (2010, August 31). Drink up NYC: meet the tiny crustaceans (not kosher) in your tapwater. *Time.*https://newsfeed.time.com/2010/08/31/drink-up-nyc-meet-the-tiny-crustaceans-not-kosher-in-your-tap-water/

Travers, E., Frith, C. D., and Shea, N. (2018). Learning rapidly about the relevance of visual cues requires conscious awareness. *Quarterly Journal of Experimental Psychology (2006), 71*(8), 1698–1713. https://doi.org/10.1080/17470218.2017.1373834

Trujillo, C. A., Gao, R., Negraes, P. D., Gu, J., Buchanan, J., Preissl, S., Wang, A., Wu, W., Haddad, G. G., Chaim, I. A., Domissy, A., Vandenberghe, M., Devor, A., Yeo, G. W., Voytek, B., and Muotri, A. R. (2019). Complex oscillatory waves emerging from cortical organoids model early human brain network development. *Cell Stem Cell, 25*(4), 558–569.e7. https://doi.org/10.1016/j.stem.2019.08.002

Tulving, E. (1985). Memory and consciousness. *Canadian Psychology/Psychologie Canadienne, 26*, 1–12. https://doi.org/10.1037/h0080017

Tulving, E. (2005). Episodic memory and autonoesis: uniquely human? In H. S. Terrace and J. Metcalfe (eds), *The Missing Link in Cognition: Origins of Self-Reflective Consciousness* (pp. 3–56). Oxford University Press. https://doi.org/10.1093/acprof:oso/9780195161564.003.0001

Turgeon, A. F., Lauzier, F., Simard, J.-F., Scales, D. C., Burns, K. E. A., Moore, L., Zygun, D. A., Bernard, F., Meade, M. O., Dung, T. C., Ratnapalan, M., Todd, S., Harlock, J., Fergusson, D. A., and Canadian Critical Care Trials Group. (2011). Mortality associated with withdrawal of life-sustaining therapy for patients with severe traumatic brain injury: a Canadian multi-centre cohort study. *CMAJ: Canadian Medical Association Journal = Journal de l'Association Medicale Canadienne, 183*(14), 1581–1588. https://doi.org/10.1503/cmaj.101786

Turing, A. M. (1950). Computing machinery and intelligence. *Mind, 59*(236), 433–460.

Turner-Evans, D. B., and Jayaraman, V. (2016). The insect central complex. *Current Biology, 26*(11), R453–R457. https://doi.org/10.1016/j.cub.2016.04.006

Tye, M. (2016). *Tense Bees and Shell-Shocked Crabs: Are Animals Conscious?* Oxford University Press.

Tye, M. (2021). *Vagueness and the Evolution of Consciousness: Through the Looking Glass.* Oxford University Press.

Tye, M. (2022). Crustacean pain. *Animal Sentience, 7*(32), 5. https://doi.org/10.51291/2377-7478.1715

Udell, D. B., and Schwitzgebel, E. (2021). Susan Schneider's proposed tests for AI consciousness: promising but flawed. *Journal of Consciousness Studies, 28*(5–6), 121–144.

UK Green Party. (2020). *Green Party 10 Point Climate Plan*. UK Green Party. https://www.greenparty.org.uk/assets/files/Communications/10_Point_Climate_Plan.pdf

Vallance, C. (2022, June 13). Google engineer says Lamda AI system may have its own feelings. *BBC News*. https://www.bbc.com/news/technology-61784011

Vandekerckhove. (2021). A continuum of consciousness: from wakefulness and sentience towards anoetic consciousness. *Journal of Consciousness Studies*, *28*(7–8), 174–182.

Vandekerckhove, M., and Panksepp, J. (2011). A neurocognitive theory of higher mental emergence: from anoetic affective experiences to noetic knowledge and autonoetic awareness. *Neuroscience & Biobehavioral Reviews*, *35*(9), 2017–2025. https://doi.org/10.1016/j.neubiorev.2011.04.001

van Gaal, S., Ridderinkhof, K. R., Fahrenfort, J. J., Scholte, H. S., and Lamme, V. A. F. (2008). Frontal cortex mediates unconsciously triggered inhibitory control. *Journal of Neuroscience*, *28*(32), 8053–8062. https://doi.org/10.1523/JNEUROSCI.1278-08.2008

van Gaal, S., Ridderinkhof, K. R., Scholte, H. S., and Lamme, V. A. F. (2010). Unconscious activation of the prefrontal no-go network. *Journal of Neuroscience*, *30*(11), 4143–4150. https://doi.org/10.1523/JNEUROSCI.2992-09.2010

van Gaal, S., Ridderinkhof, K. R., van den Wildenberg, W. P. M., and Lamme, V. A. F. (2009). Dissociating consciousness from inhibitory control: evidence for unconsciously triggered response inhibition in the stop-signal task. *Journal of Experimental Psychology: Human Perception and Performance*, *35*, 1129–1139. https://doi.org/10.1037/a0013551

van Huis, A., Van Itterbeeck, J., Klunder, H., Mertens, E., Halloran, A., Muir, G., and Vantomme, P. (2013). Edible insects: future prospects for food and feed security (No. 171; FAO Forestry Paper). UN Food and Agriculture Organization. https://www.fao.org/3/i3253e/i3253e.pdf

VanRullen, R., and Kanai, R. (2021). Deep learning and the global workspace theory. *Trends in Neurosciences*, *44*, 692–704.

van Swinderen, B. (2005). The remote roots of consciousness in fruit-fly selective attention? *BioEssays*, *27*(3), 321–330. https://doi.org/10.1002/bies.20195

van Swinderen, B. (2007). Attention-like processes in Drosophila require short-term memory genes. *Science*, *315*(5818), 1590–1593. https://doi.org/10.1126/science.1137931

Varner, G. E. (1998). *In Nature's Interests: Interests, Animal Rights, and Environmental Ethics*. Oxford University Press.

Varner, G. E. (2012). *Personhood, Ethics, and Animal Cognition: Situating Animals in Hare's Two Level Utilitarianism*. Oxford University Press.

Veit, W. (2022). Integrating evolution into the study of animal sentience. *Animal Sentience*, *7*(32), 30. https://doi.org/10.51291/2377-7478.1765

Veit, W. (2023). *A Philosophy for the Science of Animal Consciousness*. Routledge.

Vinall, J., and Grunau, R. E. (2014). Impact of repeated procedural pain-related stress in infants born very preterm. *Pediatric Research*, *75*(5), 584–587. https://doi.org/10.1038/pr.2014.16

Von Oswald, J., Niklasson, E., Randazzo, E., Sacramento, J., Mordvintsev, A., Zhmoginov, A., and Vladymyrov, M. (2023). Transformers learn in-context by gradient descent. *Proceedings of the 40th International Conference on Machine Learning*, *202*, 35151–35174.

Wade, D. T. (2018). How many patients in a prolonged disorder of consciousness might need a best interests meeting about starting or continuing gastrostomy feeding? *Clinical Rehabilitation*, *32*(11), 1551–1564. https://doi.org/10.1177/0269215518777285

Waldron, J. (2016). Political political theory: essays on institutions. In *Political Political Theory*. Harvard University Press. https://doi.org/10.4159/9780674970342

Walker, S. M. (2019). Long-term effects of neonatal pain. *Seminars in Fetal and Neonatal Medicine*, *24*(4), 101005. https://doi.org/10.1016/j.siny.2019.04.005

Walter, U., Fernández-Torre, J. L., Kirschstein, T., and Laureys, S. (2018). When is 'brainstem death' brain death? The case for ancillary testing in primary infratentorial brain lesion. *Clinical Neurophysiology*, *129*(11), 2451–2465. https://doi.org/10.1016/j.clinph.2018.08.009

Walters, E. (2022). Strong inferences about pain in invertebrates require stronger evidence. *Animal Sentience*, *7*(32), 14. https://doi.org/10.51291/2377-7478.1731

Walters, E. T., Carew, T. J., and Kandel, E. R. (1979). Classical conditioning in Aplysia califor-nica. *Proceedings of the National Academy of Sciences of the United States of America*, *76*(12), 6675–6679.

Wang, J., Hu, X., Hu, Z., Sun, Z., Laureys, S., and Di, H. (2020). The misdiagnosis of prolonged disorders of consciousness by a clinical consensus compared with repeated coma-recovery scale-revised assessment. *BMC Neurology*, *20*(1), 343. https://doi.org/10.1186/s12883-020-01924-9

Ward, D. (2016). Hurley's transcendental enactivism. *Journal of Consciousness Studies*, *23*(5–6), 12–38.

Warnock, M. (2017, January 9). Should the 14-day limit on human embryo research be extended? *BioNews*. https://www.progress.org.uk/should-the-14-day-limit-on-human-embryo-research-be-extended/

Warren, M. A. (1973). On the moral and legal status of abortion. *The Monist*, *57*(1), 43–61.

Warren, M. A. (1997). *Moral Status: Obligations to Persons and Other Living Things* (Vol. 110, Issue 3, pp. 645–649). Clarendon Press.

Watkins, S., and Rees, G. (2007). The human superior colliculus: neither necessary, nor suffi-cient for consciousness? *Behavioral and Brain Sciences*, *30*(1), 108. https://doi.org/10.1017/S0140525X0700115X

Watson, J. B. (1907). Studying the minds of animals. *The World Today*, *12*, 421–426.

Watson, J. B. (1913). Psychology as the behaviorist views it. *Psychological Review*, *20*, 158–177. https://doi.org/10.1037/h0074428

Wei, J., Wei, J., Tay, Y., Tran, D., Webson, A., Lu, Y., Chen, X., Liu, H., Huang, D., Zhou, D. and Ma, T., (2023). Larger language models do in-context learning differently. *arXiv preprint* arXiv:2303.03846.

Wei, S. (2016). Neonatal anaesthesia—the origins of controversy. https://www.mcgill.ca/library/files/library/wei_sunny_2016.pdf

Weiskrantz, L. (1997). *Consciousness Lost and Found: A Neuropsychological Exploration*. Oxford University Press.

Weiskrantz, L. (2003). Mind—the gap, after 65 years: visual conditioning in cortical blindness. *Brain*, *126*(2), 265–266. https://doi.org/10.1093/brain/awg023

Wess, J. M., Isaiah, A., Watkins, P. V., and Kanold, P. O. (2017). Subplate neurons are the first cortical neurons to respond to sensory stimuli. *Proceedings of the National Academy of Sciences of the United States of America*, *114*(47), 12602–12607. https://doi.org/10.1073/pnas.1710793114

West-Eberhard, M. J. (2003). *Developmental Plasticity and Evolution*. Oxford University Press.

Whiteley, C. (2022). Kinds and classification in consciousness science. PhD thesis, London School of Economics and Political Science.

Wiblin, R., Koehler, A., and Harris, K. (2019). David Chalmers on the nature and ethics of con-sciousness. 80,000 Hours. https://80000hours.org/podcast/episodes/david-chalmers-nature-ethics-consciousness/

Wigglesworth, V. B. (1980). Do insects feel pain? *Antenna*, *4*, 8–9.

Wilcox, A. J., Baird, D. D., and Weinberg, C. R. (1999). Time of implantation of the conceptus and loss of pregnancy. *New England Journal of Medicine*, *340*(23), 1796–1799. https://doi.org/10.1056/NEJM199906103402304

Wilcox, M. G. (2020). Animals and the agency account of moral status. *Philosophical Studies*, *177*(7), 1879–1899.

Wilkens, L. A. (1981). Neurobiology of the scallop. I. Starfish-mediated escape behaviours. *Proceedings of the Royal Society of London. Series B. Biological Sciences*, *211*(1184), 341–372. https://doi.org/10.1098/rspb.1981.0011

Williams, B. (1985). *Ethics and the Limits of Philosophy*. Taylor and Francis.

Wilson, B. A., and Gracey, F. (2001). Cognitive recovery from 'persistent vegetative state': psychological and personal perspectives. *Brain Injury*, *15*(12), 1083–1092. https://doi.org/10.1080/02699050110082197

Wilson, C. D., Arnott, G., and Elwood, R. W. (2012). Freshwater pearl mussels show plasticity of responses to different predation risks but also show consistent individual differences in respon-siveness. *Behavioural Processes*, *89*(3), 299–303. https://doi.org/10.1016/j.beproc.2011.12.006

Winkielman, P., and Berridge, K. C. (2004). Unconscious emotion. *Current Directions in Psychological Science, 13*(3), 120–123. https://doi.org/10.1111/j.0963-7214.2004.00288.x

Winkielman, P., Berridge, K. C., and Wilbarger, J. L. (2005). Unconscious affective reactions to masked happy versus angry faces influence consumption behavior and judgments of value. *Personality & Social Psychology Bulletin, 31*(1), 121–135. https://doi.org/10.1177/0146167204271309

Winkielman, P., and Gogolushko, Y. (2018). Influence of suboptimally and optimally presented affective pictures and words on consumption-related behavior. *Frontiers in Psychology, 8.* https://www.frontiersin.org/articles/10.3389/fpsyg.2017.02261

Wolfe, J. M., Breinholt, J. W., Crandall, K. A., Lemmon, A. R., Lemmon, E. M., Timm, L. E., Siddall, M. E., and Bracken-Grissom, H. D. (2019). A phylogenomic framework, evolutionary timeline and genomic resources for comparative studies of decapod crustaceans. *Proceedings of the Royal Society B: Biological Sciences, 286*(1901), 20190079. https://doi.org/10.1098/rspb.2019.0079

Wolff, J. (2020). *Ethics and Public Policy: A Philosophical Inquiry.* Routledge.

Wood, A. W., and O'Neill, O. (1998). Kant on duties regarding nonrational nature. *Proceedings of the Aristotelian Society, Supplementary Volumes, 72,* 189–228.

Woodhouse, J. (2018, October 7). Humanism needs an upgrade: the philosophy that could save the world. Areo. https://areomagazine.com/2018/10/07/humanism-needs-an-upgrade-the-philosophy-that-could-save-the-world/

Woodruff, M. (2017). Scientific uncertainty and the animal sentience precautionary principle. *Animal Sentience, 2*(16), 11. https://doi.org/10.51291/2377-7478.1237

Woodruff, M. (2022). Sentience in decapods: difficulties to surmount. *Animal Sentience, 7*(32), 11. https://doi.org/10.51291/2377-7478.1725

Worrall, J. (2007). Evidence in medicine and evidence-based medicine. *Philosophy Compass, 2*(6), 981–1022. https://doi.org/10.1111/j.1747-9991.2007.00106.x

Wright, J. (2016). Seajoy's ablation-free shrimp answers emerging welfare concern. Global Seafood Alliance. https://www.globalseafood.org/advocate/seajoys-ablation-free-shrimp-answers-emerging-welfare-concern/

Wullimann, M. F. (2011). Basal ganglia: insights into origins from lamprey brains. *Current Biology, 21*(13), R497–R500. https://doi.org/10.1016/j.cub.2011.05.052

Yik, M., Russell, J. A., and Steiger, J. H. (2011). A 12-point circumplex structure of core affect. *Emotion, 11,* 705–731. https://doi.org/10.1037/a0023980

Young, J. M., and Armstrong, J. D. (2010). Building the central complex in Drosophila: the generation and development of distinct neural subsets. *Journal of Comparative Neurology, 518*(9), 1525–1541. https://doi.org/10.1002/cne.22285

Yu, F., Jiang, Q., Sun, X., and Zhang, R. (2015). A new case of complete primary cerebellar agenesis: clinical and imaging findings in a living patient. *Brain: A Journal of Neurology, 138*(6), e353. https://doi.org/10.1093/brain/awu239

Zacks, O., and Jablonka, E. (2023). The evolutionary origins of the global neuronal workspace in vertebrates. *Neuroscience of Consciousness, 2023*(2), niad020. https://doi.org/10.1093/nc/niad020

Zhang, S., Bock, F., Si, A., Tautz, J., and Srinivasan, M. V. (2005). Visual working memory in decision making by honey bees. *Proceedings of the National Academy of Sciences of the United States of America, 102*(14), 5250–5255. https://doi.org/10.1073/pnas.0501440102

Zou, A., Phan, L., Chen, S., Campbell, J., Guo, P., Ren, R., Pan, A., Yin, X., Mazeika, M., Dombrowski, A.K., and Goel, S. (2023). Representation engineering: a top-down approach to AI transparency. *arXiv preprint* arXiv:2310.01405.

Zuolo, F. (2020). *Animals, Political Liberalism and Public Reason.* Springer International.

Żuradzki, T. (2021). Against the precautionary approach to moral status: the case of surrogates for living human brains. *American Journal of Bioethics, 21*(1), 53–56. https://doi.org/10.1080/15265161.2020.1845868

Index

Since the index has been created to work across multiple formats, indexed terms for which a page range is given (e.g., 52–53, 66–70, etc.) may occasionally appear only on some, but not all of the pages within the range.